GUIDE TO
MANUSCRIPTS COLLECTIONS
&
INSTITUTIONAL RECORDS
IN OHIO

Editor:	David R. Larson
Assistant Editors:	Fred Honhart and William Myers
Production Editor:	Lynne Wakefield
Regional Editors:	William Aeschbacher, Dennis Harrison, George Knepper, Andrea Lentz, Richard Ryan, Les Stegh, John Webb, Paul Yon

Sponsored and Published by the
Society of Ohio Archivists
1974

Library of Congress Catalog Card Number: 74-81343
International Standard Book Number: 0-87758-002-2

Printed in the United States of America

INTRODUCTION

The Society of Ohio Archivists was founded on July 1, 1968, to improve the professional competence of archivists and to coordinate activities sponsored by archives and manuscripts repositories in the state. The first president of the SOA, David Larson of the Ohio Historical Society, sought during his two-year tenure to establish a community of interests among archivists in Ohio. To promote this objective, he proposed to the SOA council an intensive statewide data gathering project that would result in a definitive listing of all manuscript collections and the records of selected institutions. The council approved the project, which began in the fall of 1969 and ends with this publication. Concurrent with the launching of the data gathering project was the formal establishment of the Ohio Network of American History Research Centers in July 1970. The network structure proved to be advantageous to the SOA Guide project, in that the network representatives, who were also active members of the Society of Ohio Archivists, served as editors for data gathered in their respective network regions. A series of meetings and a period of experimentation resulted in moderate progress in the two years between the fall of 1969 and the fall of 1971. At the time the general editor set rigid quotas and assigned Ohio Historical Society staff members to assist the other network centers so that all entries could be completed by the spring of 1973. Most of the entries were compiled during 1972 and early 1973. The regional editors were assisted by Bill Myers in northern Ohio and Fred Honhart in southern Ohio. David Larson and Lynne Wakefield edited the guide between the summer of 1973 and 1974; Lynne Wakefield prepared the index and supervised production; and Lynn Jensen typed the camera-ready copy. The volume was offset printed at the Oberlin Printing Company in Oberlin, Ohio.

Since the Ohio Historical Society had already conducted a statewide survey of selected counties and municipalities and published it in book form,[1] and will publish a guide to state government records in 1975, the guide automatically excludes all government records, both state and local. In addition, three major manuscript repositories had published their own book-length guides.[2] Since these three repositories, along with the Cincinnati

----

1.   Paul D. Yon, A Guide to Ohio County and Municipal Government Records for Urban Research (Columbus: The Ohio Historical Society), 1973

2.   See Andrea D. Lentz, A Guide to Manuscripts at the Ohio Historical Society (Columbus: The Ohio Historical Society), 1972, complete listing of the holdings of the Ohio Historical Society library in Columbus and the Rutherford B. Hayes Library in Fremont; Kermit J. Pike, A Guide to the Manuscripts and Archives of the Western Reserve Historical Society (Cleveland: The Western Reserve Historical Society), 1972; and Manuscript Catalog of the American Jewish Archives, Cincinnati (Boston: G. K. Hall & Co.), 1971, 4 vols.

Historical Society, comprise the largest holdings in the state, the guide was cut appreciably in size by the availability of other booklength works.

The guide contains two distinct types of entries. The entries for manuscripts collections include traditional type entries (like those in Hamer's Guide)[3] for all Ohio colleges and universities, for Ohio public libraries in cities of more than 25,000 population, for all Ohio historical societies that have libraries, and for any special libraries in Ohio that hold manuscript collections.

The entries for private institutional archives are more novel in scope. Because Ohio is such a large state and has so many organizational and institutional structures of long duration in all subject areas, the decision was made from the initiation of the project to include a selection of institutions having records of historical value that would be open to qualified researchers. The editors attempted to provide a selection from various subject fields of black history, business history, history of education, ethnic history, labor history, political history, religious history, history of science, social history, and history of women. These entries of churches, labor unions, businesses, social welfare organizations, civic clubs, and others, were compiled to provide a stimulus to people working in Ohio state and urban history to fully utilize all the available source materials. Thus the difference between institutional and manuscript collections is that manuscript collections are papers of individuals or institutions that have been transferred to a manuscript repository for permanent retention and reference use. Institutional records are those holdings of historical materials kept in the agency of origin, often not for general historical research, but rather for current research within the organization or because of their intrinsic historical nature.

The guide is very simply arranged. The entries are presented by county, and then within the county are divided into manuscript collections and institutional records. The maps on the inside front and back covers should help the user to locate the proper county if the city is known.

The index includes entries for all collection titles, cities, institutional names, names of persons, and general categories. A distinctive feature of the guide is that all entries were compiled as a direct result of an on-site inventory by one of the field reps working under the direction of a

----

3. Philip M. Hamer, Guide to Archives and Manuscripts in the United States (New Haven: Yale University Press), 1961

regional editor. These visits usually took one to four hours apiece, with
an average of three completed entries being done in one work day. This
entailed considerable travel time and staff time, but resulted in a high de-
gree of coverage and accuracy compared with the much more incomplete
results that would have been achieved from a mail survey. These on-the-
premises visits also allowed the Society of Ohio Archivists to build up
personal relations with hundreds of librarians and institutional record
custodians around the state.

A program to keep current information on all new manuscript acquisitions
and the availability of institutional records is structured through the Ohio
Historical Society. For manuscript collections the society serves as a
central recordkeeping body for the acquisitions program of the Ohio Network of American History Research Centers. Any manuscript collections
accessioned by the Network Centers or a manuscript repository within
each respective region is being noted in a case file in Columbus. Lists of
new manuscript accessions by Ohio libraries are also published twice a
year in The Ohio Archivist, the official newsletter of the Society of Ohio
Archivists. The National Historical Publications Commission is presently
compiling a second edition of their manuscripts guide which will serve to
update many of the Ohio entries. The Ohio Historical Society is presently
working on volume 2 of its own manuscript guide and will continue to publish succeeding volumes to keep its guide correct. The institutional record section is being updated through a permanent program established by
the Ohio Historical Society to aid institutions in Ohio in preserving their
own records. This program has continued the use of the SOA data survey
form for expanded data gathering beyond the limits of this guide. This
data on private institutions is also kept in the case files at the Ohio Historical Society. Any researcher wishing current information on Ohio
holdings of manuscript collections and institutional records should write
the reference department of the Ohio Historical Society or the local network center. Additional institutional records are being inventoried for
various subject guides now being prepared by the Ohio Historical Society,
the first of which will be guides to materials on black history and on Columbus urban history. [4]

Twenty-five members of the Society of Ohio Archivists served as field
representatives for the project. However, 70 percent of the total entries

----

4. Sara Fuller, Guide to Research Materials on Ohio Black History
(Columbus: The Ohio Historical Society), 1974, and Edward Lentz,
Guide to Research Materials on Columbus, Ohio (Columbus: The
Ohio Historical Society), 1974

are the work of nine persons who completed forty or more entries each: Jacob Dorn, Sara Fuller, John Grabowski, Dennis Harrison, Fred Honhart, Ed Lentz, Bill Myers, Bob Smith, and Paul Yon. Nearly 40 percent of the entries were compiled by Ohio Historical Society staff; the Western Reserve Historical Society compiled twice as many as the other repositories, and the other six repositories all compiled nearly the same number of entries. Acknowledgment is made to the institutions and the individual field reps as listed below with the total number entries given for both. Within the guide the initials of the field representative are given after each entry.

University of Akron (73 entries): KC (Kathleen Carlson), 8; GK (George Knepper), 10; DK (Drew Koslowski), 18; KS (Kathryn Shrake), 37

Bowling Green State University (91 entries): TS (Thomas Sibert), 30; PY (Paul Yon), 61

Cincinnati Historical Society (12 entries): LM (Lee Major), 12

University of Cincinnati (44 entries): HG (Harriett Gasen), 14; BM (Barbara Musselman), 25; HS (Helen Slotkin), 5

Kent State University (71 entries): CB (Craig Blaine), 26; JWG (James Geary), 31; LS (Les Stegh), 14

Ohio Historical Society (357 entries): SF (Sara Fuller), 66; FH (Fred Honhart), 121; EH (Edie Hedlin), 16; EL (Ed Lentz), 61; WM (William Myers), 83; DR (David Rosenblatt), 10

Ohio University (30 entries): RR (Richard Ryan), 30

Western Reserve Historical Society (172 entries): JG (John Grabowski), 116; DH (Dennis Harrison), 48; KP (Kermit Pike), 6

Wright State University (105 entries): JD (Jacob Dorn), 42; RS (Robert Smith), 63

The book has been published and distributed by the SOA with proceeds from the sale of the book being used to further SOA programs. The cost of typing the manuscript and of editing the raw data into final entries was donated as a service by the Ohio Historical Society to the Society of Ohio Archivists. The editor wishes to thank the spirit of cooperation among those active on the project as listed on the title page and to the field representatives who visited the almost 1,000 different locations represented in the guide.

David R. Larson
Ohio Historical Society
July 1974

CONTENTS

x

INSTITUTIONAL RECORDS

1.   Farmers Bank, Manchester (1883)
      Second Street, Manchester, Ohio 45144
      (513) 549-2961   (M-W, F, Sat 8:30-3)
      R. C. Lucas, Vice-President

Annual reports, 1969, 1 lf; Cashbooks, 1960+, 1 lf; Correspondence,
1968+, 1 lf; Deeds to building, 1885; Financial statements, 1947+, 1 lf;
Ledgers, 1883+, 5 lf; Minutes, 1883-Sept 1968, 2 lf; Plats for building
grounds, 1883; Tax records, 1965+, 2 lf.   TS

2.   The Farmers Bank, West Union (1907)
      500 East Main Street, West Union, Ohio 45693
      (513) 544-2358   (M-W, F, Sat 8:30-3)
      John Condon, Cashier

Administrative records, 1907, 1 lf; Agreements, 1930+, 1 lf; Annual
reports, 1960+, 1 lf; Cashbooks, 1962+, 1 lf; Certificates, 1907+, 1 lf;
Contracts, 1966+, 1 lf; Correspondence, 1965+, 1 lf; Customer records,
1955+, 90 lf; Deeds, 1968, 1 lf; Financial statements, 1966+, 1 lf; Ledgers, 1907+, 100 lf; Minutes, 1909+, 4 lf; Plats, 1968, 1 lf; Receipts,
1964+, 1 lf; Tax records, 1930+, 2 lf.   TS

3.   First State Bank of Adams County (1899)
      27 East Second Street, Manchester, Ohio 45144
      (513) 549-3591   (M-W, F, Sat 8:30-3)
      Ernest McFarland, Executive Vice-President

Administrative records, 1933-69, 1 lf; Annual reports, 1933-69, 1 lf;
Cashbooks, 1933-69, 2 lf; Correspondence, 1968+, 1 lf; Daybooks,
1933-69, 2 lf; Deeds, 1899+, 1 lf; Ledgers, 1933-69, 4 lf; Minutes,
1933-69, 1 lf.   TS

4.   National Bank of Adams County (1928)
      218 North Market, West Union, Ohio 45693
      (513) 544-2361   (M-W, F, Sat 8:30-3)
      Stanley Irwin, Cashier

Administrative records, 1928, 1 lf; Annual reports, 1960+, 1 lf; Correspondence, 1967, 1 lf; Financial statements, 1969+, 1 lf; Inventories, 1966+, 1 lf; Journals, 1928+, 90 lf; Ledgers, 1928+, 60 lf; Minutes, 1928+, 1 lf; Receipts, 1965+, 1 lf; Tax records, 1968+, 1 lf.   TS

5.   Peebles Monument Company (1925)
     117 North Main Street, Peebles, Ohio 45660
     (513) 587-2210   (M-Sat 8-5)
     Don Hooper, Owner

Cashbooks, 1948+, 2 lf; Contracts (for individual gravestones), 1948+,
4 lf; Correspondence, 1948+, 7 lf; Daybooks, 1950+, 1 lf; Deeds; Financial statements, 1948+, 1 lf; Inventories, 1948+, 1 lf; Ledgers,
1925+, 2 lf; Plats (cemetery plots), 1940+, 1 lf.   TS

6.   Welded Wire Products (1961)
     Fifth and Stark Streets, Manchester, Ohio 45144
     (513) 549-3311   (M-F 9-4)
     Mr. Riggs, Vice-President

Correspondence, 1961+; Inventories, 1961+; Ledgers, 1961+.   TS

ALLEN COUNTY

MANUSCRIPTS

7.   Allen County Historical Society (1908)
     620 West Market Street, Lima, Ohio 45801
     (419) 222-9426   (Tu-F 1:30-5)
     Joseph Dunlap, Curator

Cemetery records, Allen County and area, 1 lf; Discourses (papers
read at historical society meetings), 1909-48, 15 in.; Family genealogies, 1880+, 5 lf; Faurot Opera House, pamphlets, programs, 1889-
1921, 4 in.; Lima Locomotive Works, blueprints, engineering reports,
photographs, and tracings, 140 lf, miscellaneous materials relating to
railroads, 50 lf, photographs of locomotives, 30 lf; Pacific Fire Engine and Hose Co., minutes, 1865-71, 2 in.; Photographs, Lima and
Allen County,10 lf; Scrapbooks, 5 lf; Shawnee Township, records, 1847-
1900, 2 lf; Templars of Ottawa Lodge No. 174, record book, 1859-64,
4 in.; Vertical file, Lima and Allen County, 21 lf.   FH

8.   Bluffton College Library
     Bluffton, Ohio 45817
     (419) 358-8015   (M-F 8-5)
     Delbert Gratz, Librarian

American sources (MSS concerning the Mennonite religion in America), 150 mf rolls; Central District Depository of Mennonite Church, church records, bulletins, and minutes (Ohio, Indiana, Michigan, Illinois, Missouri, and Iowa), 1850+, 250 lf; European sources (European documents dealing with government relations concerning Anabaptists and Mennonites), 75 mf rolls; Inventories (Mennonite materials in Europe), 200 pp.; Local history collection (passports, family record books, official records of earliest settlers in Bluffton), 1830-50, 2 boxes; Published works (Mennonite history), 50 lf.   TS

INSTITUTIONAL RECORDS

9.   Better Business Bureau, Lima (1916)
       205 West Market Street, Lima, Ohio 45802
       (419) 223-7010   (M-F 8:30-5)
       Wayne Ramga, Service Manager

Business and industry information and complaint files (files on ca. 7,000 businesses and industries in Lima and Allen County), 1929+, 48 lf.   TS

10.   Bluffton College Archives
       Bluffton, Ohio 45817
       (419) 358-8015   (M-F 8-5)
       Delbert Gratz, Librarian

Bluffton College Archives (records of the founding of the college, minutes of the various boards of directors and trustees, complete run of college newspaper, yearbooks, correspondence, publications, school bulletins, and minutes of various special committees), 1898+, 75 lf. TS

11.   Chamber of Commerce, Lima
       53 Public Square, Lima, Ohio 45801
       (419) 222-6045   (M-F 9-5)
       Robert L. Tracht, Executive Manager

Board of directors, minutes, 1930+; City directories, 1930+, 20 lf; Correspondence, 1930+, 15 lf; Scrapbooks, 1965+, 2 lf.   PY

12.   YMCA, Lima (1888)
       Spring and West Streets, Lima, Ohio 45802
       (419) 223-6045   (M-F 8-5)
       E. E. Cornwell, Executive Director

Board of trustees, minutes, 1891+; Correspondence, 1930+, 20 lf;
Y-yearbooks, 1930+, 3 lf. PY

                        ASHLAND COUNTY

INSTITUTIONAL RECORDS

13.   Chamber of Commerce, Ashland
       43 West Main Street, Ashland, Ohio 44805
       (419) 324-4584   (M-F 8-5)
       Betti Kaucci, Executive Secretary

Administrative records; Annual reports; Board of directors, minutes; Correspondence; Financial records; Membership lists; Newsletter; Photographs; Publicity material; ca. 1965+, 40 lf total. SF

                       ASHTABULA COUNTY

MANUSCRIPTS

14.   Ashtabula County District Library (1813)
       355 West 44th Street, Ashtabula, Ohio 44004
       (216) 997-9341   (M-F 9-9; Sat 9-5)
       Robert E. Hazeltine, Director

Preamble, constitution, and record of Historical and Philosophical
Society of Ashtabula County, 1838-93, 2 vols; Grand River Institute,
minutes, 1882-1956, 1 vol; War posters, 1917-18, 1941-45, 25 posters. JWG

15.   Conneaut Railway Historical Museum (1964)
       Depot Station, Box 643, Conneaut, Ohio 44030
       (216) 599-8141
       William Brandy, Secretary-Treasurer

Railroad photographs, 1860+. CB

16. Geneva Public Library (1935)
     117 West Main Street, Geneva, Ohio 44041
     (216) 466-4521   (M, W, F 10-8:30; Tu, Th, Sat 10-5)
     Annette Gentile, Librarian

Administrative records, 1 binder; Archie Ball collection (MSS of
short stories), 1911-38, 4 lf; Archie Ball photograph album (theater
notables), 1897-1938, 2 vols; Library ledgers, 1941-54, 2 vols; Proceedings (promotion of the Ashtabula County Historical and Philosophical Society), 1838-1907, 69 pp.; School District No. 5, records, 1838-
72, 1 vol. JWG

17. Henderson Memorial Library (1883)
     54 East Jefferson Street, Jefferson, Ohio 44047
     (216) 576-3761   (M, Th 12-8; Tu, F 1-6; W, Sat 10-5)
     Helen Azusenis, Librarian

James Wade collection (letters and photographs), 1850-1900, 200 items.
CB

18. Kingsville Public Library (1886)
     P. O. Box H, Kingsville, Ohio 44048
     (216) 224-0976   (M, W 11-8; Sat 10-5)
     Bonnavere S. Parker, Librarian

Administrative records, 1886-1903, 2 vols; Centennial history of
Kingsville by Sara Phelps Holden, 1803-1903, unpub. MS; Library
Association, agreements and minutes, 1905-11, 1 vol; Kingsville
school board, minutes, 1911-24, 1 vol.   JWG

INSTITUTIONAL RECORDS

19. American Red Cross, Ashtabula (1917)
     433 Center Street, P.O. Box 609, Ashtabula, Ohio 44004
     (216) 998-1020   (M-F 9-4:30)
     Harold Louis, Executive Director

Board meetings and reports, 1917-66, 2 vols; Scrapbooks, 1918-
59, 2 vols.   JWG

20.   Ashtabula County Family Service (1955)
        4425 Main Avenue, Ashtabula, Ohio 44004
        (216) 997-1366   (M-F 9-5)
        Robert W. McLean, Executive Director

Administrative records, 1955, 10 pp.; Annual reports, 1955+, 16 vols;
Publication "A Study of Funding, Program, and Staff Makeup for 20
Families and Need, Cost, and Income for a Homemaker in Ashtabula,"
1969, 8 pp.   JWG

21.   Saint Joseph's Church (1856)
        3330 Lake Avenue, Ashtabula, Ohio 44004
        (216) 997-5666   (M 1-5)
        Doris T. Adley, Secretary

Plat of Ashtabula County, 1883, 1 map.   JWG

                              ATHENS COUNTY

MANUSCRIPTS

22.   Ohio University Library (1804)
        Special Collections Division, Athens, Ohio 45701
        (614) 594-5755   (M-F 8-5; Sat 8-12)
        Richard W. Ryan, Special Collections Librarian

Southeastern Ohio Collections: Thomas G. Angell (Lieutenant, 141st
Regt., OVI), military papers, 1863-65, 1 in.; Athens County Historical Society, records, genealogies, books, pamphlets, documents,
1800+, 10 lf; Addison Ballard (teacher and clergyman), papers, 1849-
82, 6 in.; Jacob Deterly (Southern Ohio pioneer), diary, 1819-48, 1 vol;
W. E. Guerin (President, Columbus, Sandusky, & Hocking Railroad),
papers, 1891-97, 1 in.; League of Women Voters, Athens, records, 1949-
64, 18 in.; William E. Peters (surveyor, engineer, lawyer, local historian), papers, 1881-1950, 4 lf;

Portsmouth Sand & Gravel Co., records, 1921-55, 4 lf; Ross County
Board of Education, records, 1867-1953, 10 lf; Clarence E. Scott (sol-
dier, Co. C, 2nd Regt., U.S. Army Vol. Engineers), photos, 1898-99,
6 in.; Unitarian Fellowship of Athens, records, 1958-70, 4 lf; United
Mine Workers of America, District No. 6, records, 1892-1947, 21 lf;
U.S. Forest Service, reports and maps, 1945-50, 3 lf; U.S. Historical
Records Survey, Ohio, Dist. 3 (survey of village, county, and church

records in S. E. Ohio), survey forms, 1936-42, 4 lf; Nelson Holmes
Van Vorhes (newspaper editor, congressman, army officer), papers,
1830-81, 1 lf.

Non-Ohio Manuscripts Collections: Derrick Leon (scholar, author),
typescript of his book, Ruskin (London, Routledge & K. Paul, 1949),
6 in.; James Henry Mangles (lawyer, M. P., neighbor of Tennyson),
diary, 1870-72, 1 in.; Sir Edmund John Monson (British diplomat),
diary and letterbooks, 1853,1891-1903, 6 in.; Manuel Rances (Spanish diplomat), papers, 1848-1907, 18 in.; Albert Speer (German
official under Hitler), papers, 1942-46, 1 lf.   RR

INSTITUTIONAL RECORDS

23.   Ohio University Archives
            Athens, Ohio 45701
            (614) 594-5755   (M-F 8-5; Sat 8-12)
            Richard W. Ryan, Special Collections Librarian

John F. Cady (teacher, SE Asia scholar), papers, 1919-66, 10 lf;
Manasseh Cutler (teacher, lawyer, botanist, member of Ohio Company), papers, 1775-1804, 1 lf; Paul Murray Kendall (author, teacher),
papers, 1956-70, 15 lf; Presidential office files, chiefly 1900+, 60 lf;
John Rutledge Scott (teacher, elocutionist; brother of W. H. Scott), correspondence, 1882-1933, 6 in.; William H. Scott (teacher, president of
Ohio U and of OSU), diaries and papers, 1869-1946, 2 lf; Earl C. Shively
(lawyer, public official, Ohio U trustee), papers, 1913-56, 20 lf; Irving
Shulman (author), typescripts and galley proofs, 1947-60, 9 lf; Student
literary societies, records, 1819-1910, 9 lf; Treasurer's land records,
1808-1965, 12 lf.   RR

AUGLAIZE COUNTY

MANUSCRIPTS

24.   Auglaize County Public Library (1925)
            203 Perry Street, Wapakoneta, Ohio 45895
            (419) 738-2921   (M-F 10-8; Sat 10-5:30)
            Louise A. Miller, Librarian

Community reports (community growth, land use and zoning, n. d.;
flood plain information, Auglaize River, 1968; prehistoric and early

historic events in Auglaize County, a condensed synopsis, 1967; study
of the Wapakoneta community, 1947-1956 [1956?]), 1 in.; Genealogies
(Brackney, 1969;"The Known Ancestry of Katherine & Warren Heckman,"
1961; Henry Oen family, 1966?), 2 in.; Unpublished works ("My Thirty
Years in Teaching," by Fred W. Gross, n.d.; "Major General Joseph T.
Dickman," 1943; "Our School in Our Town," 1931), 4 in.   RS

INSTITUTIONAL RECORDS

25.   Chamber of Commerce, St. Mary's (1952)
          205 West Spring, St. Mary's, Ohio 45885
          (419) 394-4611   (M-W 10-12, 1-5; Th 9-12; Sat 9-4)
          Lester L. Hurley, Director

Correspondence, 1965+, 6 in.; Financial statements, 1965, 6 in.; Minutes, 1956+, 2 lf; Photos, 1950s, 1 env; St. Mary's history, 1971, 1 vol;
Scrapbooks, 1960, 1 lf.   RS

26.   St. Mary's Community Library (1936?)
          103 East Spring, St. Mary's, Ohio 45885
          (419) 394-4209   (M-F 12-8; Sat 12-4)
          Muriel Pellegrino, Librarian

Published works (The Mirror, Public Works Records, The St. Mary's
Story); Scrapbooks, 9 in.   RS

BELMONT COUNTY

MANUSCRIPTS

27.   Hutton Memorial Public Library (1924)
          308 East Main Street, Barnesville, Ohio 43713
          (614) 425-1651   (M, Tu, W, F 10-8; Sat 10-5)
          Mrs. William J. Davies, Sr., Library Manager

James Barnes (founder of Barnesville), family genealogy, 1 in.; First
Methodist Church, records, 1833-48, 1858-69, 2 vols; John Wilson
Laughlin (Civil War soldier), memoirs, 60 pp.; Vertical file material
on Belmont County, 1 in.; Mrs. L. F. Wilson, scrapbooks, 1884-87,
1886-89, 1890-97, 1915-18, 1938-40, 10 vols.   FH

28. <u>Martins Ferry Public Library (1930s)</u>
    20 North Fifth Street, Martins Ferry, Ohio 43935
    (614) 633-0314   (M-F 10-9; Sat 12-5)
    Laurel Krieg, Librarian

Martins Ferry Frontier Days scrapbook, 1967, 1 vol; Scrapbooks on
community clean-up program, 1965-66, 2 vols; Scrapbooks on Martins
Ferry, 1936-46, 1 lf.   RR

INSTITUTIONAL RECORDS

29. <u>First Presbyterian Church (1798)</u>
    Marietta & Woodrow, St. Clairsville, Ohio 43950
    (614) 695-0690
    Jessie Pollock, Secretary-Treasurer

Financial records, 1960+, 6 in.; Minutes, 1872+, 2 lf; Publications,
1945+, 6 in.; Register of members, 1839+, 1 lf.   RR

30. <u>First United Methodist Church (1839)</u>
    3402 Guernsey Street, Bellaire, Ohio 43906
    (216) 676-3663
    George Fisher, Minister

Church bulletins, 1965+, 2 in.; Financial records, 6 in.; Membership records, 1905+, 1 lf; Minutes, 1885-1960, 6 in.   FH

31. <u>Imperial Glass Corporation (1934)</u>
    (Division of Lennox, Inc.)
    29th Street, Bellaire, Ohio 43906
    (614) 676-3511
    Carl J. Uhrmann, President

Administrative records, 1934-1972; Agreements; Cashbooks; Certificates; Contracts; Correspondence, 5-10-year retention; Daybooks;
Deeds; Financial statements; Inventories; Journals; Ledgers; Minutes; Plats; Proceedings; Publications; Scrapbooks, 7-year retention;
Tax records; 1,000 lf total.   RR

MANUSCRIPTS

32.   Union Township Public Library
       27 Main, Ripley, Ohio 45167
       (513) 392-4871   (M, Tu, Th-Sun 1:30-5, 7-8:30)
       Bette J. Plymesser, Acting Librarian

John Thomas Rankin (minister active in abolitionist movement), papers,
1 lf.   TS

INSTITUTIONAL RECORDS

33.   Citizens National Bank of Ripley (1847)
       104 Main, Ripley, Ohio 45167
       (513) 392-4369   (M, Tu, Th-Sat 9-3)
       Mr. Stivers, President

Formerly Farmers Branch of the State Bank of Ohio (1847-1885) and
Farmers National Bank.

Administrative records, 1847+, 1 lf; Certificates, 1885+, 1 lf; Contracts,
1847+, 1 lf; Correspondence, 1847+, 8 lf; Daybooks, 1847+, 12 lf; Deeds,
1847+, 1 lf; Journals, 1847+, 4 lf; Ledgers, 1847+, 10 lf; Minutes, 1847+,
3 lf; Plats, 1847+; Receipts, 1847+, 12 lf; Tax records, 1847+, 6 lf.   TS

BUTLER COUNTY

MANUSCRIPTS

34.   Butler County Historical Society
       327 North Second Street, Hamilton, Ohio 45011
       (513) 893-7111   (Tu-Sun 1-5)

Alta Hawey (author), scrapbooks, 1935-63, weekly historical articles
from Hamilton Journal, 2 lf; John Woods (attorney), correspondence,
receipts, business papers relating to early Hamilton, 12 lf.   TS

35.   Miami University Library
       Oxford, Ohio 45056
       (513) 529-2420
       L. L. Dutton, Librarian

Bebb family collection (mainly correspondence between William Bebb, Governor of Ohio 1846-48, Even Bebb and their sister Mrs. Abner Francis), 1841-79, 200 ltrs; Bishop family papers (correspondence of Robert Hamilton Bishop, first president of Miami University, and other members of the family), 1836-53; Lewellyn Bonham (local resident of Oxford who held patents on electrical devices, automobile supercharger, etc.), papers; Samuel Fulton Covington, papers, primarily relating to his Ohio River Steamboat Insurance business, 6 lf; Jefferson Davis, Civil War manuscripts, includes copies of Civil War dispatches, 900 pcs; Burton L. French (congressman from Idaho, professor of political science at Miami University), papers, 1934-47; A. Gilbert (sanitary engineer in Cincinnati), papers, 1829-99, 2 lf; William S. Grosbeck (Cincinnati lawyer, Republican congressman), papers, 1815-97; John Hough James (banker, railroad promoter, educator, Whig politician, papers, 1814-81, 10 lf; Abraham Lincoln manuscripts and memorabilia; William Holmes McGuffey, 1826-72, 147 pcs; Oxfordiana and southwestern Ohio collection, 10 lf; Matthew Prior, 1664-1771. LM

36.   Middletown Public Library (1911)
      1320 First Avenue, Middletown, Ohio 45042
      (513) 424-1252
      Pat Brewer, Reference Librarian

George Crout collection, 6 in.; Historical sketches of Middletown, 1933-34, 83 pp; Louise Hunter, 1923+, 25 pp; MS materials on Middletown (cemetery records for Hamilton, Preble, Brown, Clermont, Butler, Adams, Warren & Washington Cos; marriage records; newspaper clippings; biographical sketches), 1803+, 5 lf; Photograph album of trees in Middletown, 1930s, 10 pictures; Scrapbooks, 1913+, 18 in. FH

INSTITUTIONAL RECORDS

37.   Alcoholics Council of Butler County Ohio, Inc. (1962)
      111 Buckeye, Hamilton, Ohio 45011
      (513) 869-6471   (M-F 8-12, 1-5)
      Michael Richardson, Executive Director

Activity sheets, 1972+; Administrative records, 1962+; Annual reports,

1968+; Certificates, 1969+; Contracts, 1970+; Correspondence, 1970+, 3 lf; Financial records, 1968+; History of organization, 1972, 2 pp; Inventories; Minutes, 1964+, 1 lf; Scrapbooks, 1964+, 2 in.; Service records, 1971+, 1 lf; Tax records, 1970+.   FH

38.   American Red Cross, Hamilton (1919)
          319 North Third Street, Hamilton, Ohio 45011
          (513) 894-8324   (M-F 9-4:30)
          Kay Sharp, Executive Director

Agreements, 1962+; Annual reports, 1966+, 3 in.; Case records; Certificates, 1962+; Contracts, 1962+; Inventories, 1962+; Minutes, 1962+, 1 lf; Publications, 1962+; Receipts, 1962+; Roster book, 1917+; Scrapbooks, 1962+; Tax records, 1962+; World War I master file and case records.   FH

39.   Armco Steel Corporation (1899)
          703 Curtis Street, Middletown, Ohio 45042
          (513) 425-6541   (M-F, Sun 8:30-5)
          Marjorie Compton, Librarian

Publications, 1920+; Scrapbooks, 1910-42.   LM

40.   Butler County Medical Society (1836)
          111 Buckeye, Hamilton, Ohio 45011
          (513) 893-1410
          E. Clifford Roberts, Director

Financial records, 1950+; Minutes, 1890+; Publications, 1930s+; 4 lf total.   FH

41.   Butler Rural Electric Coop., Inc. (1936)
          Box 3030, Hamilton, Ohio 45011
          (513) 894-9000   (M-F 8-5)
          Everett S. Hoy, Manager

Administrative records, 1935+, 6 in.; Agreements, 1937+, 2 lf; Annual reports, 1936+, 2 lf; Cashbooks, 1937+, 2 lf; Check vouchers, 1946+, 52 lf; Construction work orders, 1947+, 10 lf; Contracts, 1937+, 2 lf; Correspondence, 1962+, 8 lf; Daybooks, 1936+, 1 lf; Deeds, 1936+, 2 in.; Financial statements, 1938+, 2 lf; Inventories, 1955+, 2 lf; Journals, 1937+, 2 lf; Ledgers, 1937+, 2 lf; Membership files, 1969+, 14 lf;

Minutes, 1935+, 2 lf; Plats, 1936+, 2 in.; Proceedings, 1936+, 1 lf;
Publications, 1946+, 2 lf; Receipts, 1964+, 28 lf; Reports, 1939+,
8 lf; Scrapbooks, 1936+, 2 lf; Tax records, 1939+, 4 lf.   FH

42.   Chamber of Commerce, Middletown
           Manchester Motor Inn, Middletown, Ohio 45042
           (513) 422-4551   (M-F 9-5)
           Mildred F. Conn, Secretary-Treasurer

Annual reports, ca. 1960+, 1 in.; Correspondence, 2-year retention;
Financial statements, 7-year retention; Middletown Area Development
Enterprise,Inc., minutes, financial statements, deeds, etc., 1963+;
Minutes, 1920+, 10 in.; Publications, 1960, 1 in.; Scrapbooks, 1955+;
Tax records, 7-year retention.   FH

43.   Family Service of Butler County (1953)
           111 Buckeye, Hamilton, Ohio 45011
           (513) 895-3245   (M-F 9-5)
           Cheryl Pombo, Office Manager

Administrative records, 1953; Agreements, 1971+; Annual reports,
1952+; Case files, 1952+; Contracts; Financial records, 1952; Inventories, 1969+; Material prepared for board meetings, 1963+; Minutes, 1952+; Tax records, 1952+; 52 lf total.   FH

44.   Hamilton Association Trade & Industry (1961)
           6 Court Street, Hamilton, Ohio 45011
           (513) 895-5638   (M-F 8-12, 1-5)
           Ryan B. Hall, Executive Director

Annual reports, 1961+; Chamber Merchants Council, Industrial Development records; Correspondence, 1961+; Daybooks, 1971; Financial records, 1961+;Minutes, 1961+; Monthly newsletter, 1961+;Plats,
1961+; Scrapbooks, 1945, 6 lf.   FH

45.   Mental Hygiene Association, Butler County (1954)
           111 Buckeye, Hamilton, Ohio 45011
           (513) 895-9501   (M-F 9-5)
           Harriet Adams, Executive Secretary

Administrative records, 1954+; Annual reports, 1953+, 2 in.; Contracts, 1951+; Financial statements, 1948+, 6 in.; Inventories; Mental health clinic records, 1954, 150 lf; Minutes, 1946+, 8 in.; Receipts, 1948+, 3 lf; Scrapbooks, 1954+, 7 in.; Tax records, 1953+, 9 in.   FH

46.   Middletown Area Safety Council (1947)
        101 North Broad Street, Middletown, Ohio 45042
        (513) 423-6507   (M-F 9-5)
        James C. Schaffner, Manager

Annual reports, 1973+; Board and committee minutes, 1963+, 1 lf; Correspondence, 2-year retention; Monthly newsletter, July 1970+; Scrapbooks and clippings, 1963+, 6 in.   FH

47.   Middletown Civic Association, Inc. (1923)
        Middletown, Ohio 45042
        (513) 423-6507   (M-F 8-5)
        J. F. Seibold, Managing Director

Administrative records, 1923; Agreements, 1968+; Annual reports, ca. 1948+; Architectural plans, 1960s+, 16 lf; Correspondence, 10-year retention; Deeds (property), 1964+; Executive committee and board of governors, minutes, 1923+, 2 lf; Inventories; Newsletter, 1967+; Scrapbooks on campaigns, 1968+; J.F. Seibold's minutes of meetings he attends, ca. 1960+, 16 lf; Tax records, personnel, 7-year retention.   FH

48.   North Seventh Street Church of Christ (1921)
        32 North Seventh, Hamilton, Ohio 45011
        (513) 893-9373   (M-F 8-4:30)
        Douglas Smith, Minister

Church bulletin, 1954+, 18 in.; Church register, 1943, 4 in.; Correspondence, 1950s, 4 lf; Financial records, 1950s; Minutes, 1943+; Scrapbooks, 1921, 3 in.   FH

49.   The Sorg Paper Company (1852)
        901 Manchester, Middletown, Ohio 45042
        (513) 422-3661   (M-F 8-5)
        R. A. Driscoll, Secretary

Administrative records, 1899+; Annual reports, 1932+; Cashbooks, 7-year retention; Correspondence, 7-year retention; Daybooks, 7-year retention; Inventories, 7-year retention; Journals, 7-year retention; Ledgers, 7-year retention; Minutes, 1899+. FH

50. Volunteer Services & Information Bureau (1961)
    323 North Third, Hamilton, Ohio 45011
    (513) 893-5422 (M-F 9-5)
    Thelma S. Vogel, Executive Director

Administrative records; Board minutes, 1961+, 6 in.; Committee reports, 1961+; Correspondence, 5-year retention; Financial records, 1961+; Information brochures, 1961+; Scrapbooks, 1961, 6 in. FH

51. YMCA, Middletown (1917)
    Manchester and Broad, Middletown, Ohio 45042
    (513) 422-6394
    B. P. Allen, Director

Annual reports; Financial statements, 10-year retention; Historical records; Minutes, 1917+, 2 lf; Photos; Publications; Scrapbooks, 15-year retention. FH

52. Zion Evangelical Lutheran Church (1943)
    212 South Front Street, Hamilton, Ohio 45011
    (513) 863-5774 (M-F 8-4)
    President, Church Council

Rev. Allwardt, sermons; Annual reports, ca. 1959+, 6 in.; Church bulletins, 1947+, 1 lf; Church register, 1861+, 8 in.; Correspondence, 1962+, 1 lf; Minutes, church council. FH

CARROLL COUNTY

MANUSCRIPTS

53. Carroll County Historical Society (1963)
    McCook House, Public Square, Carrollton, Ohio 44615
    Velma Griffin, Past President

Letters and documents, 1830-1880, 40 items. CB

INSTITUTIONAL RECORDS

54.   First Presbyterian Church (1822)
        200 North Lisbon Street, Carrollton, Ohio 44615
        (216) 627-4330   (M-F 9-12; Sat, Sun by appt.)
        H. David McCalmont, Pastor

Administrative records, 1850+; Annual reports, 1940+; Minutes, 1850+.
LS

55.   First United Methodist Church (1816)
        253 South Lisbon Street, Carrollton, Ohio 44615
        (216) 627-5168   (M-F 9-3)
        John L. Clark, Pastor

Administrative records; Membership records, 1840+; Minutes of wom-
en's organizations, church school and church board.   LS

                          CHAMPAIGN COUNTY

MANUSCRIPTS

56.   Champaign County Historical Society (1930s)
        160 West Market, Urbana, Ohio 43078
        (513) 653-3811   (M, Tu, Th, F 12:30-9; Sat 10-9)
        Edwin L. English, President

Blueprints of buildings, 6 in.; James L. Magruder, Life & Sketches,
1903, 1 in.; Photographs and maps of locale, 1800s+, 6 in.; Olla
Podrida Club, programs and minutes, 1899-1954, 1 lf; Sam Steoves,
account book, 1877, 1 in.   RS

57.   Champaign County Library (1890)
        160 West Market, Urbana, Ohio 43078
        (513) 653-3811   (M, Tu, Th, F 12:30-9; Sat 10-6)
        Carol Sanford, Librarian

Photo album, n.d., 1 in.; Wiant family genealogy, 1969-70, 1 in.
RS

INSTITUTIONAL RECORDS

58.   Chamber of Commerce, Urbana (ca. 1920)
      300 North Main, Urbana, Ohio 43078
      (513) 653-5764   (M, Tu, Th-Sat 9-4; W 9-12)
      Martha R. Paulig, Assistant Secretary

Administrative records, 1 folder; Annual reports, 1965+; Correspondence, 1971+,1 folder; Financial statements, 1965+, 1 ledger;
Minutes, 1965+, 3 in.; Publications, 1 in.   RS

59.   Farm Bureau Federation, Urbana (1935)
      304 Bloomfield, Urbana, Ohio 43078
      (513) 652-2135   (M-F 8-5)
      E. F. Proctor, Office Manager

Administrative records, 1962+, 12 lf; Agreements; Annual reports,
1935+, 1 lf; Correspondence; Financial statements, 1935+; Minutes,
1935+, 1 lf; Membership, 1972+; Publications, 1940+, 2 lf.

Farm Bureau Co-op Association (1934) records: Administrative records, 1934, 1 in.; Agreements, 1934+; Annual and monthly reports,
1966+, 23 lf; Contracts, 1934+; Correspondence, 1934+, 3 lf; Deeds,
1948, 1 in.; Financial statements, 1934+; Inventories, 1934+; Minutes, 1934+, 1 lf; Receipts, 1966+, 23 lf; Stock records, 1934+, 40
lf; Tax records, 1934+, 3 lf.   RS

60.   Urbana College Library (1850)
      Urbana, Ohio 43078
      (513) 652-1301   (M-Th 8-11; F 8-5; Sat 1-5; Sun 3-11)
      Richard Z. Smith, Head Librarian

College events, 1853+, 4 lf; Dramatic society, 1930s, 6 in.; Financial history, 1850s+, 18 in.; John H. James (local industrialist who
gave land to college), papers, 1811-82, 442 pp; News clippings, 1930+,
2 lf; Photographs, 1919+, 1 lf; Scrapbook, 1929-50, 1 lf; Swedenborg
collection, Church of New Jerusalem, 1700+, 280 lf; Trustee, president, and faculty records, 1854-1923, 18 in.; Urbana College Library history, 1850+, 18 in.; Urbana College public relations report,
1947-51, 1 lf; Milo G. Williams (first president of college), collection,
1939, 90 lf.   RS

MANUSCRIPTS

61.   Archives of the Ohio Synod of the Lutheran Church in America (1845)
      Wittenberg University, Springfield, Ohio 45501
      (513) 327-7511   (M-Th 8-11:30; F, Sat 8-5)
      Louis Boyd, Curator

Church records: Ada Trinity, 1897-1960, 1 vol; Bloomdale Grace, 1875-
1901, 1916-45, 3 in.; Bowling Green St. Marks, 1923-58, 2 lf; Bryan
First Church, 18 in.; Cairo St. Mathews, 1865-87, 3 in.; Cincinnati First
English, 1842-39, 2 lf; Circleville First English, 1831-1910, 6 in.; Cleveland East Calvary Church, 1907-15, 3 in.; Columbus Immanuel, 1891-1926,
6 in.; Columbus Our Savior, 1957-63, 8 in.; Columbus Redeemer, 1923-25,
1 vol; Dayton Second Trinity, 4 lf; Delaware St. Johns, 1904-51, 1 lf; Dod-
sonville, 1 vol; Donnelsville First Church, 1875-1960, 3 lf; Fairfield Co.
Ziegler Church, 1812-35, 1 in.;

Fairfield Co. St. Thomas, 1848-1918, 1 lf; Franklin, 1925-29, 1 in.;Green-
ford, 1929-66, 6 in.; Hamburg Christ's Church, 1839-71, 1881-99 1 in.;
Harshmanville, 1 in.; Lancaster First Church, 3 in.; Lancaster St. Peters,
1819, 1 in.; Leipsic, 1868-86, 1 in.; Logan Co. (New Salem and Philadelphia), 1 lf; London St. John's, 1868-1953, 18 in.; Manchester, 1826-72,
1874-1909, 3 in.; Mansfield Oakland Church, 1912-60, 2 in.; Massillon
Trinity Church, 1 in.; Mt. Vernon St. John's, 1936-39, 1 in.; New Middleton Zion Church, 1805, 1841-81, 1 in.; New Pittsburgh St. Peters (includes
Rows Parish, Rowsburg & Pleasant Valley), 1861-1951, 6 in.;

Oak Harbor Grace Church, 1924-47, 6 in.; Piqua Co. Zion Church, 1808-
12, 1873-94, 3 in.; Springfield Bethel Church, 1844-1908, 6 in.; Springfield First Church, 1843-1943, 6 in.; Toledo Martin Luther Church, 1891-
1926, 6 in.; Toledo Messiah, 1924-37, 1 in.; Urbana Messiah, 1868-1959,
6 lf; Washingtonville Trinity Church, 1810-50, 1 in.; Webertown, n.d., 1
in.; West Carrollton Grace Church, 1876-99, 1 in.; Xenia First Church,
1911-55, 1 in.; Zanesville St. John, n.d., 4 lf;

Luther League files, 1910-40s, 2 lf; Miscellaneous material: Conference
minutes, 18 in.; Luther League, 1 lf; Lutheran Welfare Council of Ohio,
18 in.; Ministers Association, 18 in.; Sermons: J.H. Culler, 6 in.; M.W.
Hamma, 1860s, 1870s, 2 lf; Woman's Missionary Society, n.d., 4 lf;
Synod records: district synod, 1873-1919, East Ohio Synod, 1858-1919,
Miami synod, northern conference, 1887-1920, southeastern conference,
1890-1913, southwestern conference, 1890-1920, total 12 lf; Vertical
file (published material of various congregations), n.d., 5 lf.   FH

62. Clark County Historical Society (1897)
     300 West Main, Springfield, Ohio 45504
     (513) 324-0657   (M, Tu, Th 1-4; W, Sat 9-4; 2nd & 4th Sun 2-4:30)
     George H. Berkhofer, Executive Director-Curator

Arthur Altic Collection, 1930s, 3 lf; Capt. Luther Brown papers, Civil
War, 18 in.; Business ledgers of numerous Springfield companies, 1835-
90, 10 lf; Clark County Historical Society, minutes, 1897+, 1 lf; Clark
Co. Medical Society, 1830-40, 1 vol; GAR (Mitchell Post), minutes,
1868-1950, 5 lf; Zoe Johnson collection (misc. WPA topics, general
history), 1930s; Abraham Lincoln letter, 1863; William Perrin papers
(land grants), 1725-1850, 1 lf; Scrapbooks, late 19th Century+, 10 lf;
Maj. J. Warren Kieffer, papers, 1860-Civil War, 18 in.   RS

63. Wittenberg University Library (1845)
     Springfield, Ohio 45501
     (513) 327-7511   (M-Th 8-11:30; F, Sat 8-5)
     Luella S. Eutsler, Reference Librarian

Dr. Hiller's manuscripts, 1950, 1 in.; Ezra Keller, journals, n.d.,
1 in.; Lauritz Larson, letters, 1921-22, 1 in.; Catherine M. Maclean,
letters to Miss Rudston Brown, 1947, 1 in.; Newton D. Mereness,
prose & poetry, n.d., 1 in.; Grace Prince, letters, 1935, 1 in.; Volunteer band, record books, 1897-1905, 1 in.; YMCA, records, 1908-
23, 3 books.   RS

INSTITUTIONAL RECORDS

64. Lutheran Community Services (1944)
     240 East Main Street (P.O. Box 1525), Springfield, Ohio 45503
     (513) 325-9237   (M-F 8:30-5)
     Helen W. Juergens, Office Secretary-Bookkeeper

Administrative records, 6 in.; Annual reports, 1947+, 18 in.; Correspondence, 1961+, 2 lf; Financial statements, 1947+; Ledgers,
1965+, 1 ledger; Minutes, 1947+, 5 lf; Publications, 1944+, 1 lf;
Scrapbooks, 1955+, 18 in.   RS

65. Springfield Art Association (1946)
     107 Cliff Park Road, Springfield, Ohio 45501
     (513) 325-4506   (Tu-F 9-5)
     Patricia Catron, Managing Director

Acquisition records, 1963+; Administrative records, 1946+; Annual reports, 1946?+; Board of trustees, minutes, 1946+, 6 in.; Correspondence, ca. 1946+; Membership files, 1946?+; Newsletter, 1970+; Photographic books on early days of photography; Photos, 1946?+, 2 lf; Scrapbooks, 1964+, 6 in.; Tax records. RS

66.   Springfield Bar and Law Library (1890?)
        Court House, Springfield, Ohio 45502
        (513) 324-5871, ext. 256   (M-F 8-4)
        A.F. Holliemayer, Librarian

Bar association misc., n.d., 4 in.; Bar association, minutes, 1893-1960, 6 in.; Land abstracts of Clark Co. and surrounding area, 1800?-1930s, 15 lf.   RS

67.   Wittenberg University Archives (1845)
        Springfield, Ohio 45501
        (513) 327-7511   (M-Th 8-11:30; F, Sat 8-5)
        Willard D. Allbeck, Archivist

Academy, 1913; Administrative offices, 1955+, 18 in.; Alumni, 1937+, 8 lf; Army school, 1918+; Board of directors, 1852+, 2 lf; Business manager, vice-president for business affairs, 1936+; Dean of the college, vice-president for academic affairs, 1925+, 30 lf; Depts of instruction, 1918+, 2 lf; Faculty, 1931+, 3 lf; Hamma School of Theology, 1906+, 18 in.; Misc. material and vertical files, 1843+, 50 lf; Pastor of the university, 1936+, 6 in.; President, 1856+, 38 lf; Provost, 1968+, 18 in.; Saturday, summer extension schools, 1923, 3 in.; School of community education, 1968+, 6 in.; School of music, 1922+, 6 in.; Students, 1948+, 3 lf; University as a whole, 1827+, 6 lf; Vice-president and treasurer, 1920+, 6 in.; Vice-president for university affairs, 1948+, 29 lf.   FH

68.   YMCA, Springfield (1854)
        129-135 North Limestone Street, Springfield, Ohio 45502
        (513) 323-3781   (M-F 8:30-5)
        Walter Madsen, Director

Annual reports, 1934+, 2 lf; Board of directors, minutes, 1856-65, 1887+, 14 lf; Camp records, 1931-51, 6 in.; Correspondence; Financial records, 1888+, 36 lf; Historical register, 1892, 1 vol; History of YMCA; Inventories, 1939+; Scrapbooks, 1898+, 3 lf.   RS

69. YWCA, Springfield ((1896?)
       250 East High, Springfield, Ohio 45505
       (513) 323-6451
       Geraldine C. Mitchell, Executive Director

Administrative records, 1896+; Annual reports, 1896+; Board minutes,
1896+; Correspondence, legal, 1896+; Financial statements; Picture
collection, 1896+; Publications (brochures on YWCA), 1896+; Scrapbooks. FH

CLERMONT COUNTY

MANUSCRIPTS

70. Clermont County Public Library (1961)
       Third and Broadway, Batavia, Ohio 45103
       (513) 732-2128
       Doris Wood, Head Librarian

Clermont County vertical file, 1962?+, 3 in.; Green Mound Cemetery
list, clipping file from Clermont Review, 1972+, 1 in.; History of
Batavia, 1814-1964, by Rosanna Hoberg, 1963, 50 pp; History of New
Harmony Church, by Anna Shaw Dumford, 1968, 27 pp; History of
Perintown, Ohio, 1804-1965, by Mrs. Richard Fomorin, 24 pp; Index
to wills of Clermont Co., 1800-1915 (Grace M. Hirschauer), 1966,
34 pp; Life Abundant (family history by Olie B. Mosbacker), 1964, 92
pp; New Richmond's Sesquicentennial program, 1966, 46 pp; "Smalley's
History" clipping file (column in local paper), 1971+, 1 in.   FH

INSTITUTIONAL RECORDS

71. American Cancer Society, Batavia (1961)
       Second and Main Streets, Batavia, Ohio 45103
       (513) 732-1454
       Floy Smith, Executive Director

Administrative records, 1961+; Agreements; Contracts, 1-year retention; Correspondence, 1-year retention; Inventories; Minutes, 1970+;
Newsletter, 1-year retention; Scrapbooks, 1-year retention.   FH

72.   Farm Bureau Coop Association, Batavia (1934)
      490 West Main, Batavia, Ohio 45103
      (513) 732-0533   (M-F 8-5)
      Allen Harris, General Manager

Administrative records, 1934; Agreements, 1934+; Annual reports,
1934; Cashbooks, 3-year retention; Certificates, 1934+; Contracts,
1934+; Correspondence, 7-year retention; Deeds, 1934+; Financial
statements, 1934+; Inventories, 2-year retention; Journals, 5-year
retention; Ledgers, 7-10-year retention; Membership lists, 1934+;
Minutes, 1934+; Plats, 1934+; Tax records, 1934+; 140 lf total. FH

                         CLINTON COUNTY

MANUSCRIPTS

73.   Clinton County Historical Society (1948)
      149 East Locust Street, Wilmington, Ohio 45177
      (513) 382-4684   (Tu-F 1:30-5)
      Mrs. Don Couden, Curator

Gen. James W. Denver collection (correspondence, scrapbooks), 1848-
1900; Genealogy collections; Photographs, ca. 1850s+; Plat maps and
surveys, ca. 1848-73. BM

74.   Wilmington College Library (1870)
      Wilmington, Ohio 45177
      (513) 382-0951   (M-F 9-5)
      Willis H. Hall, Curator, Quaker Collection

Quaker Collection: American Friends' Service Committee, vertical
file, 1917+, 3 lf; American Friends' Service Committee on National
and International Legislation, complete files, 1943+, 6 lf; Biographical material, 1892+, 6 in.; Civilian population service, 1941-42, 2
lf; Five-year meetings, records, 1887+; Dr. Gerald Doan McDonald,
vertical file, 1922-70, 2 lf; Minutes of yearly meetings, Australia,
1969+, Baltimore, 1888+, California, 1909+, Canada, 1914+, Illinois,
1876+, Indiana, 1860+, Iowa, 1897+, Ireland, 1863+, Kansas, 1911 +,
Nebraska, 1908+, New England, 1828+, New York, 1856+, North Caro-
lina, 1899+, Ohio, 1877+, Oregon, 1893+, Rocky Mountain region, 1959+,
Western states, 1867+, 40 lf;Peace organizations, 1900, 2 lf; Publications of Quaker colleges, 1890+, 1 lf; Publications relating to Quakers,

The Friend (London), 1847+, Friends' Quarterly Examiner, 1868+, The
Olney Current, 1905, A. F. S. C. numbered pamphlets, 1917+, 20 lf;
Quakers' committee on legislation, general file, 1952-64; Quaker materials, 19th century subject material, 250 lf; Wilmington yearly meetings,
minutes preparative, monthly and quarterly, 1805+, 70 mf reels; Wilmington yearly meetings, pictures and slides, 1892+, 2 lf; World committee,
1953+, 6 in.; Yearly national and international Quaker meetings, scattered,
1822+, 2 lf.   BM

Wilmington College Archives: College newspaper, 1880+, 5 lf; Franklin
College, predecessor to Wilmington College, miscellaneous literary societies, 1880-1916; Lebanon National Normal University, administrative records, 1866-1914; Wilmington College and Franklin College, records, 1880-
1916; Wilmington College, vertical file, 1870+, 4 lf.   FH

75.   Wilmington Public Library (1904)
       268 North South Street, Wilmington, Ohio 45177
       (513) 382-2417   (M, W 10-9; Tu, Th, F 1-9; Sat 10-5)
       John D. Kelton, Library Director

Ancestry and descendents of Zemri & Elizabeth Compton Haines, by Ruth
Cary Haines, 53 pp; Genealogy of descendents of Jesse F. Stanton, by
Matella Prichet Doughman, 1950, 21 pp; Moon family, history, 80 pp; History of the Wilmington city schools, by Duan Petty, 1969, 10 pp; Hogs, hom-
iny, and history of Clinton County, by William and Esther Doster, 1970, 10
pp; Report on one-room school houses in Clinton Co., by Jay Peterson, 1970,
20 pp.   FH

COLUMBIANA COUNTY

MANUSCRIPTS

76.   Columbiana County Historical Society (1955)
       Citizen's Office, Columbiana Bank, Columbiana, Ohio 44408
       (216) 482-3695   (Hours by appointment)
       E. B. Dillion, President

Charter (original charter for incorporation of Columbiana), August 18,
1856; Correspondence (miscellaneous, includes G. W. Beck and E. S.
Holloway), 1862-65, 15 items; Financial records (Dr. Thomas A. King's
medical bills against Daniel Chapsaddle), 1808-13, 9 pieces; Land purchase, from Margaret Alexander to John Croyer, 1807, 1 item.   JWG

77. Columbiana/Fairfield Township Historical Society
       45 North Pearl Street, Columbiana, Ohio 44408
       (216) 482-3628   (Advance notice requested)
       Harry Eberhardt

Photographs (Columbiana and environs), 1855+, 400 items.   CB

78. East Liverpool Historical Society (1907)
       219 East Fourth Street, c/o Carnegie Public Library
       East Liverpool, Ohio 43920
       (216) 385-2048   (M-F 9-9)
       H. B. Barth, President

Artifacts, geological, Indian, pioneer and pottery, 720 lf; Pottery
industry collection (Annual reports, 1870-1969; Catalogues and price
lists, 1870+; Plats, 1900+; Scrapbooks and letters on pottery industry
activities, 1870+), 360 lf.   JWG

79. Leetonia Public Library (1935)
       24 East Walnut Street, Leetonia, Ohio 44431
       (216) 427-6635   (M 7-9; Tu, Th, F 1-5, 7-9; Sat 10-5)
       Esther Cullinan, Head Librarian

History of Leetonia Public Schools, by Eva S. G. Ashley, 1880-
1929, 1 vol; Leetonia Historical Society, minutes, by-laws, elec-
tions, and committees, 1961-62, 1 folder; Miscellaneous items
(pamphlets, cancelled checks, high school commencement), 1889-
1906, 1 lf.   JWG

80. Lepper Library of Lisbon, Ohio (1897)
       303 East Lincoln Way, Lisbon, Ohio 44432
       (216) 424-3117   (M-Th 10-9; F 10-6; Sat 12-6)
       Mrs. Don Richardson, Librarian

Church registers, 1807-79, TSS; Genealogies, 4 folders; Marriage
records, 1835-48, 1 vol; Probate records, 1811-17, 4 vols.   JWG

81. Old Stone House
       Lisbon, Ohio 44432
       (Hours by appointment only, June through August)
       L.S. Firestone

Ledgers, 18th century, 4 vols; New Lisbon High School Debating Society, minutes, 1852-56, 1 vol; Steamboat receipts, 1842-45, 1 vol; Water Works, by-laws, rules, and regulations, 1886-97, 1 vol.   JWG

82.   Salem Historical Society, Inc. (1947)
        208 South Broadway, Salem, Ohio 44460
        (F 2-5; Sun 2-4)
        Marion Francis Blood, Archivist

Agreements (debts and bonds for town of Salem), 1852-61, 1 folder; Anti-Slavery Bugle, ledgers, account book, 1851-58, 1 vol; Anti-Slavery Society, executive committee minutes, 1848-56, 1 vol; First century file (local subjects), 1830-99, 18 in.; Salem town hall miscellaneous papers (accounts, rent for hall for such things as anti-slavery fair, John Brown meetings, John Coppock funeral), 1856-63, 1 folder; Lucille G. Wolfgang Collection (trade, business agreements, politics, personal items), 1790-1899, 18 in.; Thomas S. Woods (lawyer, editor of Ohio Patriot during the Civil War), papers, 1858-63, 1 box.   JWG

83.   Salem Public Library (1938)
        821 East State Street, Salem, Ohio 44460
        (216) 332-4938   (M-F 9-6)
        John Bender, Librarian

Minnie Hunt Collection (assorted invitations and pamphlets), 1871-1900, 200 items; Miscellaneous pamphlets, 1870-1946, 180 items; Salem Academy catalog, 1854, 1 item; Salem Police Department arrest records, 1931-37, 2 vols; WCTU minutes, 1882-96, 2 vols. JWG

84.   Wellsville Historical Society (1951)
        Tenth and Riverside, Wellsville, Ohio 43968
        (216) 532-1511   (Hours by appointment)
        Delmar O'Hara

Miscellaneous letters and riverboat bills, 1870-90; Photographs, many of the Pennsylvania Railroad.   LS

INSTITUTIONAL RECORDS

85.   Chamber of Commerce, Columbiana (1952)
        15 South Main Street, Columbiana, Ohio 44408
        (216) 482-2015, 482-5162   (M-F 10-5; Sun 1-5)
        John Yoder, President

Correspondence, 1952+; Minutes, 1962+; 18 in. total.   JWG

86.   Chamber of Commerce, East Liverpool Area (1916)
        207-1/2 East Fifth Street, Box 94, East Liverpool, Ohio 43920
        (216) 385-0845   (M-F 9-12, 1-5)
        E.R. Chandler, Executive Manager

Business and statistical reports, 1942+; Local surveys, 1947+; 12
cf total.   JWG

87.   Chamber of Commerce, Lisbon Area (1964)
        Village Hall, Lisbon, Ohio 44432
        (216) 424-5503   (M-F 9-4)
        Floyd Lower, Executive Secretary

Annual reports (includes report to membership and income and expenses), 1964-72, 1 folder.   JWG

88.   Chamber of Commerce, Salem Area (1955?)
        417 East State Street, Salem, Ohio 44460
        (216) 337-3473   (M-F 9-5)
        Alan H. Cleveland, Executive Secretary

Annual reports, 1960+; Minutes, 1962+; Publications (various directories), 1960+. JWG

89.   Columbiana Soil and Water Conservation District (1942)
        Post Office Box 248, Lisbon, Ohio 44432
        (216) 424-3313   (M-F 8-5)
        Charles M. Clark, District Conservationist

Annual reports, 1948+, 1 lf; Minutes of annual and monthly board
meetings, 1942+, 1 notebook.   JWG

90.   The Evening Review (1879)
      210 East Fourth Street, East Liverpool, Ohio 43920
      (216) 385-4545   (M-F 8-5)
      Glenn H. Waight, Editor

Homer Laughlin collection (concerns the Homer Laughlin China Company in the area pottery industry), 1874-1900.   JWG

91.   Farmer's National Bank (1846)
      300 East State Street, Salem, Ohio 44460
      (216) 332-4621   (M-F 9-2:30)
      Robert A. Oswald, Vice-President

Minutes, 1846-66, 150 pp.   JWG

92.   Mullins Manufacturing Corporation (1869)
      605 South Ellsworth Avenue, Salem, Ohio 44460
      (216) 337-8771   (M-F 8-5)
      Gordon C. Scullion, Vice-President and Treasurer

Company history, 1947; Photographs, 1869-1955, 60 items; Scrapbooks, 1941-46; 2 lf total.   JWG

93.   Ohio Cavalry Buffs Association
      38027 State Route 344, Leetonia, Ohio 44431
      (216) 427-2279   (M, Tu, Th-Sat 10-5)
      John Simonds, Owner

Philip Dehoff family genealogy, 1702-1938, 1 folder; Military discharges, 1863, 1865, 2 items.   JWG

94.   Trinity United Presbyterian Church (1839)
      115 South Vine Street, Lisbon, Ohio 44432
      (216) 424-7414   (Hours by appointment)
      Donald Blom, Pastor

United Presbyterian Congregation of New Lisbon, session minutes, 1839-1969, 4 vols.   JWG

MANUSCRIPTS

95.   Roscoe Village
           Coshocton, Ohio 43844
           (614) 622-9310   (M-Sun 8:30-5)
           Mrs. Philip Brown, Director of Public Relations

Deeds to Roscoe property, 1800s; Frew-McClain General Store, ledger, 1827; Justice of peace docket, Jackson Twp., 1852-76; McClain
and Brown, ledger, 1862; Photo album, 1898; Supreme Court minutes
and docket, 1812-44. KS

CRAWFORD COUNTY

INSTITUTIONAL RECORDS

96.   Chamber of Commerce, Bucyrus
           334 South Sandusky, Bucyrus, Ohio 44820
           (419) 562-4811   (M-F 9-5)
           Harley Barstow, Executive Manager

Administrative records; Annual reports; Board of directors, minutes;
Correspondence; Financial records; Membership lists; Monthly newsletter; Records 1903-60, scattered, 1960+ complete; 16 lf total.   SF

CUYAHOGA COUNTY

MANUSCRIPTS

97.   Baldwin-Wallace College Library (1846)
           Berea, Ohio 44017
           (216) 826-2900

Manuscripts Collections (Dorothy McKelvy, College Historian): Erzie-
hungs Verein minute books, 1873-96, 6 in.; Germanica Verein minute
book, 1889-95, 6 in.; H. L. Ridenor collection (typescript collection of
folksongs and Songs of Rural Ohio), 1884-1966, 2 lf.

North-East Ohio United Methodist Historical Society Collection (Pauline
Cooper, Cataloger): Ledgers, 3 lf; Minutes of conferences (California
German, 1914, 1922, 1923; Central German, 1880-1933, 1 lf; Chicago
German, 1888-1933, 1 lf; East German, 1886-1943, 1 lf; Ohio, 1854-
1960; Pacific German, 1908, 1911, 1912, 1920, 1 lf; Southern German,
1907-23, 1 lf); Scrapbooks on German Methodism, 5 lf.

Riemenschneider Bach Institute (Ritter Library; Eleanor Barber, Director): Printed musical scores (rare scores, mainly of John S. Bach, including a few manuscripts by Bach and/or his students); Emile and Karl Riemenschneider collection (papers concerning Baroque and Renaissance musical manuscripts; also papers of some contemporary composers), 1568-1971, 2 lf.   JG

98.   Bedford Historical Society (1955)
        30 South Park Street, Bedford, Ohio 44146
        (216) 232-2395   (M, Th 7:30-10; Every second Sun, 2-5; Closed
        in August)
        Richard T. Squire, Director

George Barnum family (Civil War family) papers, ca. 1860-70, 3 in.; Bedford Baptist Church records, 1840+ (scattered), 2 in.; Bedford Chamber of Commerce records, 1919-29, 1 vol; Bedford charter amendment, records, 1933-35, 4 in.; Bedford Church of Christ, records, 2 in.; Bedford City Council, proceedings, 1932-51, 3 lf; Bedford city records, ca. 1870-1972; Bedford coal dealer, ledger, 1914-21, 1 vol; Bedford Methodist Church, records, 2 in.; Bedford Municipal Hospital, records, 1927-68, 3 in.; Bedford 125th Anniversary, records, 1962, 1 lf;

Bedford residents file (genealogies), 1 vol; Bedford residents in the Civil War, 1 vol; Bedford Township, records, 1834-1951, 20 lf; Blacksmiths' records, 1835-53, 1887-1900, 4 vols; John A. Burns (Bedford resident) papers, 1840-1910, 3 in.; Civil Air Patrol, records, 1950-59, 10 vols; Lillian B. Collins (missionary in China for the Church of Christ), papers, ca. 1920-40, 3 in.; Gen. Ludwig S. Connelly (served in World Wars I and II and founded Walton Hills, Ohio), papers, 1905-63, 4 in.; Alonzo Drake (Bedford farmer), papers, 1830-37, 1876-98, 2 vols;

Elmer Flick (professional baseball player), papers, 2 in.; Fuller family, genealogy records, 1907-49, 1 vol; Thedatus Garlick and Blake family, records (includes the records of the Lone Rock Mining Co.), 1835-84, 2 lf; Halsey M. Gates (mill owner and founder of Gates Mills, Ohio), papers, 1870-1910, 1 lf; Joseph Jesensky (amateur naturalist), papers, 3 in.; League of Women Voters of Bedford records, 1954-63, 1 lf; LeMardi Club (girls' club), records, 1901-8, 2 vols; McMyler Interstate Co. (produced cranes and ammunition during World War I), records, ca. 1905-30, 2 lf;

Miscellaneous ledgers and scrapbooks, 1 lf; Northern Ohio Traction and Light Co., records (mainly trainsmen's orders), 1926-31, 1 vol; Photographs (mainly of Bedford), 3 lf; Taylor family (founders of Taylor Chair

Co.), papers, 19th century, 3 in.; William C. Walker (Bedford resident), diaries, 1894-1970, 75 vols; James Ward, papers (mainly tax papers), 1920-40, 3 in.; Archibald Willard papers, 19th century, 4 in.   JG

99.   Brecksville Historical Association (1925)
      P.O. Box 61, Brecksville, Ohio 44141
      (Sun 2-5, May-Oct)
      Frank J. Vosadka, President

Brecksville Historical Association Archives: Records of the association, old records of the Brecksville early settlers and some miscellaneous journals and letters relating to early settlers in Brecksville.   JG

100. Case Western Reserve University Library
      Cleveland, Ohio 44106
      (216) 368-3506

Freiburger Library (Yadwiga Kuncaitis, Chief Reference Librarian): Benedict Crowell (asst. sec. of war, 1917-20; chairman of the board of Crowell and Little Construction Co., Cleveland author, How America Went to War), papers, 1917-20, 7 lf; Fritz Sagel Darrow (assoc. principal, Darrow School of Business; compiled collection of papers relating to F.M. Van Helmont), papers, 1898-1919, 6 lf; Arthur Sheperd (music teacher at Western Reserve University; department head and composer), papers, 1892-1958, 30 lf; Francis Mercury Van Helmont (mystic, philosopher, scientist, author of The Alphabet of Nature), papers, 17th century, 4 lf.

Sears Library Archives of Science and Technology (Wesley C. Williams, Curator): Charles G. Abbot (astronomer),papers, 1918-20, 3 in.; Donald J. Angus (electrical engineer), papers, 1914-58, 3 lf; Charles F. Brush (inventor of Brush Arc Light and Brush Dynamo), papers, 1869-1929, 17 lf; William D. Buckingham (electrical engineer), papers, 1921-64, 3 lf; Cleveland Rocket Society, records, 1934-38, 1963-64, 3 lf;Fred H. Colvin (mechanical engineer), papers, 1892-1965, 8 lf; Hugh S. Cooper (metallurgy--Beryllium and nonferrous metals), papers, 1914-71, 32 lf; Allston Dana (civil engineer), papers, 1928-49, 3 lf; William C. Ebaugh (chemist), papers, 1899-1920, 20 vols;

S. Colum Gilfillan (sociology of science), papers, ca. 1930-70, 4 lf; Charles M. Hall (inventor of the electrolytic process for the manufacture of aluminum), papers, 1882-1909, 4 in.; Clifford M. Holland (civil engineer; directed construction of the "Holland Tunnel"), papers, 1919-24, 6 cf; Norbert Lange (teacher of chemistry, ed., Handbook of Chemistry), papers, ca. 1930-69, 4 lf; Dayton C. Miller (professor of physics), papers, ca. 1916-28, 4 in.; E. Wallace (aeronautical engineer), papers, ca. 1910-44, 4 lf; Warner and Swasey (manufacturer of astronomical instruments and machine tools), collection, ca. 1880-1919, 3 lf; Samuel T. Wellman (mechanical engineer, papers, 1867-1917, 1 lf. DH

101. Chagrin Falls Historical Society (1946)
       31 Walnut Street, Chagrin Falls, Ohio 44022
       (216) 247-8302, 247-7046   (Th 2-4; also by appointment)
       Marian Jencick, Curator

Chagrin Falls Village, records, 1858-1923; James G. Coleman, correspondence and diaries, ca. 1830-90, 3 in.; Amos Green (carpenter), papers, 1833-40, 1 vol; Dr. Curtis Jackson, daybook, 1866-69, 1 vol; Ober, family and business (farm, foundry, and woodwork shop) records, 1854-1925, 4 lf and 22 vols; Photograph file relating to Chagrin Falls, 2 lf; Soldiers Aid Society, 1861, 3 vols; Frank A. Squire, scrapbook (clippings from the Exponent), 1882-1912, 1 vol; VFW Post 2832, minutes of annual meetings, 1940-63, 4 in.; Dr. R. W. Walters, obstetric records, 1868-79, 1 vol, and daybooks, 1867-68, 1875-94, 4 vols; Rueben R. Walters (minister and organizer of the Freewill Baptist Church), daybook, 1828-57, 1 vol. DH

102. Cleveland Medical Library Association (1894)
       11000 Euclid Avenue, Cleveland, Ohio 44106
       (216) 231-4402   (M-F 9-5)
       Genevieve Miller, Director-Howard Dittrick Museum

Manuscript collections including the papers of Drs. Raymond Clements, John G. Spenzer, T. W. Todd, and Frederick C. Waite, ca. 1900-1969, 38 lf. KP

103. Cleveland Museum of Art (1916)
       11150 East Boulevard, Cleveland, Ohio 44106
       (216) 421-7340   (Tu-F 9-5)
       Dr. Sherman E. Lee, Director

Autograph file (collection of autographs of artists), 6 in.; Harold T. Clark (Cleveland lawyer who worked as counsel for the museum), files, 20 lf; Cleveland Print Club (association of persons interested in prints), records, 1919+, 3 lf; Arthur M. Hind (curator of prints and drawings at the British Museum), notebooks, ca. 1906-37, 9 lf; Works Projects Administration files (mainly photographs relating to a W. P. A. art project headquartered at the museum), 3 lf.   JG

104. Cleveland Museum of Natural History (1920)
     University Circle, Cleveland, Ohio 44106
     (216) 231-4600   (Tu-Sat 10-12, 1-5)
     Mary Baum, Librarian

Henry Wood Elliott (active in saving fur seals), papers (biographical data, correspondence and clippings, 1922-30, 1 vol; correspondence, reports, fur seal census, 1873-1920, 5 lf); Jared Potter Kirtland, M.D. (naturalist and doctor), papers (copies of correspondence), 1850-56, 2 vols; Kirtland Society (natural history group), minutes, 1869-70, 1940-49, 2 vols.   JG

105. Cleveland Public Library (1869)
     325 Superior Avenue, Cleveland, Ohio 44113
     (216) 241-1020   (M-Th 9-8:30; F, Sat 9-6)
     Fern Long, Deputy Director

Autograph file, 8 lf; Louise M. Boutelle (former head of history department of Cleveland Public Library), files (consist mainly of correspondence relating to the development of the history department), ca. 1920-50, 4 lf; Billy Bryant (playwright), scripts of shows performed on Ohio river boats, ca. 1930, 6 in.; East India Company collection (documents, official record books and geographical accounts relating to India and Central Asia; includes materials from Clive, Hastings, Lord MacCartney, Bentinck, Henry Dundas, Elphinstone, MacLeod, Robert Orme, and others), 1741-1895, 10 lf;

Julia McLune Flory (book illustrator), collection (consists mainly of drawings and MS copies of books), 7 lf; May A. Klipple collection of African folklore and mythology (composed mainly of typescript descriptions of African folklore), 16 cf; Minor memorabilia (collection of clippings, photos, and some manuscript items relating to history), 4 lf; Musical scores for classical and popular music, card catalogued (represented among the Cleveland musicians are Louis Balough, Herbert Elwell, Karl Grossman, Paker Bailey, Johann Beck, Ben Burtt,

Vaughan Cahill, Stephen Connery, Homer B. Hatch, Charles Heydler, Harrison Kerr, Clarence Metcalf, Richard Morse, Denny Pearne, Read Gardner, James Rogers, Charles Rychlik, Arthur Shepard, George Smith, and Howard Swanson);

Newbell Niles Puckett (sociologist, noted for his work with Negro folklore and superstition), papers (consist of notes, short written pieces and tapes of various folksongs, card catalogued with short box inventories, parts of this collection available on mf), ca. 1920-66, 28 lf; Uncatalogable materials, 6 file drawers of clippings, photographs and some manuscripts relating to chess, the orient, and the John G. White collection, 10 lf; John G. White collection, 1500 manuscript items or collections less than 1 lf, primarily relating to chess, oriental history, medieval history, and folklore; items are bound and catalogued.   JG

106. Cuyahoga County Public Library System

      Brecksville Branch (1959)
      8997 Highland Drive, Brecksville, Ohio 44141
      (216) 526-7274   (M, Tu, Th 1-9; W, Sat 9-5:30)
      Kathryn Wilmer, Branch Librarian

Brecksville High School Alumni Association, files, ca. 1950+, 1 lf; Genealogical file (various families of Brecksville), 2 lf; Manuscript holdings (mainly bonds with some letters, one ledger, and some receipts; these materials all pertain to early Brecksville; an itemized list of the collection is stored with it), 1813-1904, 1 lf.   JG

      Brookpark Branch (1967)
      6155 Engle Road, Brookpark, Ohio 44142
      (216) 234-7380   (M, Tu, Th 1-9; W, Sat 9-5:30)
      Anita L. Sweet, Reference Assistant

Brookpark Village Council, minutes, 1936-39, 1 vol; Walter Holzworth photograph collection, 19th century +, ca. 125 views of Brookpark and surrounding cities; Elaine Niskal collection (clippings, pamphlets, photos, scrapbooks, and some manuscripts relating to Brookpark and surrounding communities, 1920-67, 4 lf; Walter family (Berea, Ohio), papers (mostly tax receipts), 1899-1942, 6 in.   JG

      Chagrin Falls Branch (1924)
      100 East Orange Street, Chagrin Falls, Ohio 44022
      (216) 247-8654   (M, Tu, Th 1-9; W, Sat 9-5:30)
      Mrs. M. Clark Ralston, Branch Librarian

Local history file (manuscripts, photographs, and clippings), ca.
1800-1970, 18 lf; Scrapbooks (D.A.R. local history), 13 vols; Top-
ographical maps of U.S. and Canada, ca. 1960-70, 3 lf.   DH

> Mayfield Regional Branch (1971)
> 6080 Wilson Mills Road, Mayfield, Ohio 44143
> (216) 461-3350
> Jeanie Belhobek, Acting Coordinator of Information Services

Cleveland Plain Dealer Index, (handwritten index on 3 x 5 cards to
the front page of the Cleveland Plain Dealer), 1971+, 6 lf; Music
and art pamphlet file, 1969+, 18 lf; Pamphlet file (pamphlets, clippings and some manuscript materials), 1969+, 90 lf.   JG

> North Olmstead Branch (1920)
> 27475 Butternut Ridge Road, North Olmstead, Ohio 44070
> (216) 777-6211   (M, Tu, Th 1-9; W, Sat 9-5:30)
> John Lonsak, Librarian

Local history file (clippings and typescript histories relating to
North Olmstead), 2 lf.   JG

> North Royalton Branch (1945)
> 13860 Bennett Road, North Royalton, Ohio 44133
> (216) 237-3070   (M, Tu, Th 1-9; W, Sat 9-5:30)
> John L. Wright, Branch Librarian

North Royalton government records, 1818-48, 1868-1906, 6 in.;
Royalton financial records, 1858-59, 1 vol; Royalton school district records, 1853-83, 3 in.   JG

> Olmstead Falls Branch (1941)
> 7850 Main Street, Olmstead Falls, Ohio 44138
> (216) 235-1150   (M, Tu, Th 1-9; Sat 9-5:30)
> Mrs. F. A. Lovell, Branch Librarian

John Barnum (Olmstead resident), scrapbook (clippings, letters
and certificates), 1828-32, 1 vol; Local history file (clippings,
genealogies, and pamphlets), 1941+, 2 lf; Minor and Staten family (Olmstead residents), deeds and receipts, 1868-1904, 3 in.;
Photograph file (North Olmstead and surrounding areas), ca. 75
photographs; Scrapbook collection (mainly newsclippings of poetry
and serial stories), 2 vols.   JG

Parma Regional Branch
5850 Ridge Road, Parma, Ohio 44129
(216) 885-5362   (M, T, Th 9-9; W 1-9; F, Sat 9-5:30)
Agnes Hubbell, Branch Librarian

John Bobko (mayor of Parma), scrapbooks, 1955-61, 3 vols; Parma general file (clippings, letters and pamphlets), n.d., 3 in.; Parmadale (home for wayward children), records, n.d., 2 in.; Roland Reichart (mayor of Parma in 1930s), scrapbooks, 1929-46, 1961-64, 17 vols.   JG

107. East Cleveland Public Library (1916)
14101 Euclid Avenue, East Cleveland, Ohio 44112
(216) 541-4128   (M, Th 9-9; F, Sat 9-5)
Martha L. Driver, Director

Presidential signatures (one signed item from each of the presidents from Washington to LBJ), 4 in.; W.P.A. East Cleveland local history papers (a collection of typed newspaper abstracts and other materials relating to the history of East Cleveland), ca. 1940, 5 lf.   JG

108. Jewish Community Federation (1902)
1750 Euclid Avenue, Cleveland, Ohio 44115
(216) 861-4360   (M-F 8:30-5)
Judah Rubenstein, Research Associate

Moses Alsbacher (early Jewish immigrant to Cleveland), document (contains instructions for life in the new world and genealogical data), 1839, 1 vol; Alfred Benesch (former head of Cleveland School Board), scrapbooks, n.d., 2 vols; Cleveland Jewish history project files (source file cards), 12 lf; Cleveland League for Human Rights, ca. 1940-67, 4 lf; Cleveland Zionist records (various records relating to Zionism), 1920s-1960s, 4 lf; Charles Coleman papers (xerox copies), 2 in.; Oral history tapes (interviews with prominent Cleveland Jews), 10 tapes; Ezra Shapiro (pioneer Zionist), papers (mostly pamphlets and clippings), 2 in.; Vertical file, materials relating to Jewish welfare activities, 30 lf.   JG

109. The Lakewood Historical Society (1852)
14710 Lake Avenue, Lakewood, Ohio 44107
(216) 221-7343   (Hours by appointment)
Mrs. James Seherka, Curator

General file (materials on Lakewood and surrounding area), 1840-
1920, 1 lf; Photographs of Lakewood, 1890-1970, 2 lf; Scrapbooks,
1924-71, 8 vols; Norton Townshend (early Lakewood resident), 1830-
65, 300 items; Treasurer's reports, East Rockport Separate School
District, 1874-92, 3 in.; Vertical file (articles and clippings), 1 lf.
DH

110. Lakewood Public Library (1916)
        15425 Detroit Avenue, Lakewood, Ohio 44107
        (216) 226-8275   (M-F 9:30-9; Sat 9:30-6)
        Daniel W. Hagelin, Head of Reference

Lakewood League of Women Voters, minutes and financial records,
1921-50, 1 lf; Local history file (clippings and some manuscript
items relating to Lakewood and Cleveland history), 7 lf; Photo file
(photographs of Lakewood), 3 lf.   JG

111. Rose Hill Museum (1960)
        27715 Lake Road, Bay Village, Ohio 44140
        (216) 871-7338   (W, Sun 2-5)
        Edward S. Wells, Director

Bay Village Women's Club scrapbook (mainly clippings and programs),
1917-55, 1 vol; John M. Cahoon, store ledgers, 1890-1900, 4 vols;
Dover by the Lake Library records (lending and financial records),1923-
45, 2 vols; Dover Township school records, 1886-1903, 1 vol; Photographs of Bay Village area, ca. 1890+, 3 lf; Henry Wischmeyer (early
settler and store owner), family papers, 1850s-1900, 2 in.   JG

112. Shaker Historical Society (1947)
        16740 South Park Boulevard, Shaker Heights, Ohio 44120
        (216) 921-1201   (Tu-F 2-4; Sun 2-5)
        Suzane Toomey, Curator

John Hecker (farmer who lived next to the Shaker community), scrapbook, 1833-1900, 1 vol; Old Warrensville High School, records, 1878-
82, 1898, 3 vols; Shaker vinyards, ledger, 1894, 1 vol; Otis P. and
Mantis J. Van Sweringen (builders of Cleveland rail and real estate
empire), papers, ca. 1900-1940, 3 in.; Warrensville Township Trustees, minutes, 1855-87, ca. 1911-26, 3 vols.   DH

113. Ukranian Museum and Archives (1952)
        1202 Kenilworth, Cleveland, Ohio 44113
        (216) 351-9039   (Hours by appointment)
        Leonid Bachynsky, Director

Ukranian manuscript collection, pertains mainly to material from
Europe or Asia, with only minor parts related to U.S. and Cleveland, 15 lf.   JG

114. The Western Reserve Historical Society (1867)
        10825 East Boulevard, Cleveland, Ohio 44106
        (216) 721-5722   (Tu-Sat 10-5; Sun 2-5)
        Dennis Harrison, Curator of Manuscripts

See Kermit J. Pike, A Guide to the Manuscripts and Archives of the
Western Reserve Historical Society, 1972. For the society's most
recent accessions see the Ohio Archivist.

115. Westlake Historical Society
        1371 Clague Road, Westlake, Ohio 44145
        (216) 871-1363   (No set hours)
        Vivian Stetz, Curator

Ledgers, Westlake area, 1857-1931, 10 vols; St. Lawrence Co., ledgers of A.A. Hall and various individuals, 1820-70, 9 vols; St. Lawrence Co., maps, 1850s; School District No. 7, minutes, 1837, 1 vol.
DH

INSTITUTIONAL RECORDS

116. The Afro-American Cultural and Historical Society Museum (1953)
        8716 Harkness Road, Cleveland, Ohio 44106
        (216) 795-3121   (Sat, Sun 4-6, or by appointment)
        Icabod Flewellen, Historian and Curator

The museum collects materials on Africans in Africa, in the western
hemisphere, and in Ohio.

Clipping collection, 1915+, 100,000 items; Correspondence (correspondence with J.H. Rogers), 1945-67, 30 lf; Photographs, 25,000 items;
Scrapbooks, 1915+, 25 vols.   DH

117. Air Conservation Committee of the Tuberculosis and Respiratory Disease Assocation (1970)
   4614 Prospect Avenue, Cleveland, Ohio 44103
   (216) 361-8088   (M-F 8:30-4:30)
   Fred Morello

General file (project files, funding files and general administrative files), 1969+, 17 lf; Grant reports, 1972, 6 in.; Minutes, 1970+, 6 in.; Publications, 1970+, 2 lf; Scrapbooks (histories, clippings and photographs), 1970+, 4 vols. JG

118. American Red Cross, Cleveland (1905)
   1227 Prospect, Cleveland, Ohio 44115
   (216) 781-1800   (M-F 9-5)
   William Birkhold, Executive Director

Annual reports, ca. 1930+, 2 lf; Biographical files (biographies of prominent Clevelanders associated with the Red Cross), 1 lf; Guest books, 1935 and 1955, 2 vols; Minutes, 1905+, 7 lf; Photo file, 1914+, 9 lf; Publications, 4 lf; Scrapbooks, 1913, 1940-46 (contain large volumes of correspondence), 10 vols. JG

119. Baldwin-Wallace College Archives (1846)
   Berea, Ohio 44017
   (216) 826-2900   (M-F 8:30-10:30; Sat 9-5; Sun 2-10:30)
   Stephen Wolanyk, Head, Public Services Library

Administrative records, 1940-60, 6 lf; Balance books, 1913-58, 2 lf; Board of trustees, minutes, ca. 1920-58, 4 lf; Cabinet meeting, minutes, 1948-49, 6 in.; College register, 1870-96, 6 in.; Executive committee, minutes, ca. 1920-58, 4 lf; Grade books, 1886-1913, 1 lf; Institutional studies, 1960-66, 2 lf; Investment committee, records, 1949-50, 1 lf; Journals, 1895-1905, 1 vol; Ledgers, ca. 1865-1920, 7 lf; Print shop, records, 1952, 1 lf; Scholarship book, 1868-83, 6 in.; Scrapbooks, 1890-1962, 28 vols; Surveys, 5 vols; Transcripts, ca. 1880-1900, 1 lf; Treasurers' reports, 1865-1936, 6 in. JG

120. Bedford Times Register (1938)
   717 Broadway, Bedford, Ohio 44146
   (216) 232-4055   (M-F 9-5; Sat 9-12)
   Edward Spielman, Editor

Photograph files (photos of people and scenes in and around Bedford),
ca. 1930+, 3 lf. JG

121. Berea News Sun (1930)
      271 Depot Street, Berea, Ohio 44017
      (216) 243-4000   (M-F 8-5)
      Fran Sandrock, Managing Editor

Clipping and photograph file, ca. 1930-60, 18 lf.   JG

122. Better Business Bureau, Cleveland (1912)
      1720 Keith Building, Cleveland, Ohio 44115
      (216) 241-7678   (M-F 8:30-4:30)
      Ann M. Zabak, File Supervisor

Company files (contain correspondence, clippings, and literature relating to each company), ca. 1969+, 490 lf. JG

123. Boys' Clubs of Cleveland (1954)
      4815 Wendell Avenue, Cleveland, Ohio 44127
      (216) 883-4665   (M-F 10-9; Sat 11-3)
      Elving Otero, Director

Activity reports, ca. 1960+, 5 lf; Annual reports, 1956+, 6 in.;
Applications and membership cards, 1954+, 6 lf; Daily report sheets,
1970+, 2 lf; Financial records, 1955-70, 10 lf; General files, 1957-
62, 2 lf; Minutes, 1954+, 1 lf; Photographs, 1950s and 1960s, 6 in.
JG

124. Brecksville United Methodist Church (1823)
      65 Public Square, Brecksville, Ohio 44141
      (216) 526-8938   (M-F 9-5)
      David H. Patton, Senior Pastor

Board of trustees, minutes, 1943+, 2 vols; Ledgers, 1926-27, 1930,
1956, 2 vols; Membership list, 1952+, 4 vols; Miscellaneous minutes,
1969+, 1 vol; Quarterly conference reports, 1956-68, 1 vol; Registers,
1937+, 2 vols; Women's society minutes, 1960-66, 1 vol. JG

125. Broadway United Methodist Church (1872)
      5246 Broadway, Cleveland, Ohio 44127
      (216) 271-3650   (M-F 9-3)
      Leroy Hart, Pastor

Baptismal records, 1951-55, 1 vol; Board minutes, 1916-40, 1 vol;
Drama club files, 1957-58, 2 in.; Historical files, 1930s+, 4 in.;
Membership records, ca. 1920+, 5 vols; Men's club minutes, 1943-
48, 2 vols; New building files, 1918-19, 2 in.   JG

126. Call & Post (1932)
      1949 East 105 Street, Cleveland, Ohio 44106
      (216) 791-7600   (M-F 9-5)
      William O. Walker, Publisher

Clipping and photograph file, ca. 1930+, 130 lf.   DH

127. Case Western Reserve University Archives (1826)
      Cleveland, Ohio 44106
      (216) 368-4289   (M-F 8:30-5)
      Ruth W. Helmuth, University Archivist

University archives: Academic vice president and provost, files,
1936-70, 20 lf; Alumni biographical files, 1826+, 200 lf; Annual reports, 1887-1970, 30 lf; Deans--department files, 1900-1970, 60 lf;
Minutes of trustees, faculty, and faculties of professional schools
and various committees, 1826-1971, 25 lf; Nontextual records (photographs, blueprints, portraits, microfilm, movie film, video tapes);
Presidents' office files, 1880-1970, 180 lf; Publications, 1826-1971,
150 lf; Research office files (grant records), 1950-67, 20 lf; Secretary's office files and letterbooks, 1851-1967, 30 lf; Student records,
1826-1900, 1 lf; Student scrapbooks, 1890-1970, 20 lf; Treasurers'
records, 1830-1967, 40 lf.

Faculty papers: George Barnes (professor and sanitary engineer),
papers, 1923-63, 12 lf; Robert C. Binkley (professor of history,
archivist), papers, 1922-39, 1 lf; Frank Tracy Carlton (professor
of economics), papers, 1901-60, 30 lf; John Hessin Clark (Supreme
Court justice, attorney, and publisher), papers, 1910-45, 1 lf;
Charles F. Gehlke (professor of sociology), papers, 1904-55, 1 lf;
T. Keith Glennan (university president, government administrator),

papers, 1947-67, 4 lf; Francis H. Herrick (professor of biology, or-
nithologist), papers, 1888-1929, 10 lf; Louis Masotti (professor of
sociology), transcripts of interviews concerning 1968 Glenville riots,
1969, 2 lf;

Dayton Miller (professor of physics, researcher in acoustics, X-ray,
ether drift), papers, 1878-1938, 3 lf; John S. Millis (university president), papers, 1940-71, 4 lf; Thomas Munro (museum curator, editor, professor of aesthetics), papers, 1919-69, 3 lf; Leslie J. Reardon (professor of civil engineering), papers, 1932-65, 8 lf; Roger B.
Scott (professor of gynecology, specialist in uterine cancer), papers,
1940-68, 1 lf; Jesse Hauk Shera (dean, library school; documentalist),
papers, 1912-71, 28 lf; Andrew Squire (attorney), papers, 1900-1934,
2 lf; Charles F. Thwing (university president), papers, 1870-1936, 50
lf; Harvey Wish (professor of history), papers, 1940-68, 6 lf.   DH

128. Catholic Diocese of Cleveland
        1027 Superior Avenue, Cleveland, Ohio 44114
        (216) 696-6525
        Rev. Nelson Callahan

Acta Episcopi (official acts of the bishops), 1847-1966, 2 lf; Business
correspondence, ca. 1910-42, 110 lf; Diocesan Temporalities (financial records, platbooks), 1880-1944, 15 lf; Letter books, 1877-1905,
4 lf; Parishes, schools, and institutions (histories, deeds, letters),
ca. 1850-1960, 8 lf; Pastoral communications (letters to priests),
1921-60, 7 lf; Religious orders, correspondence, ca. 1850-1945, 20
lf; Status Animarum (church and school enrollments, communions,
baptisms, etc.), 1878-1960, 12 lf;

Bishops of Cleveland Diocese: John P. Farrell papers, 1909-21;
Richard Gilmour papers, 1872-1891, 4 lf; Edward F. Hoban papers,
1945-66; John F.I. Horstmann papers, 1892-1908, 7 lf; Louis A.
Rappe papers, 1847-70, 6 in.; Joseph Schrembs papers, 1921-45.
KP

129. Cedar Hill Baptist Church (1884)
        12601 Cedar, Cleveland Heights, Ohio 44106
        (216) 371-3870   (M-F 9-4)
        James R. Cross, Chairman of Deacon Board

Advisory council, 1933-57, 6 vols; Annual reports, 1890s-1920s, 2
in.; Board of deacons, 1920+, 3 vols; Board of trustees; Church registers, 1884-1934, 3 vols; Minutes, 1948-56, 2 in.   JG

130. Chamber of Commerce, Berea (1928)
        25 Riverside, Berea, Ohio 44017
        (216) 234-2047   (M-F 9-5)
        Wilma Sauvey, Manager

Minutes, 1929+, 1 lf; Publications, 1929+, 9 in.   JG

131. Chamber of Commerce, Lakewood (1911)
        12506 Edgewater Road, Lakewood, Ohio 44107
        (216) 226-2900   (M-F 9-1)
        Merrill Love, Office Manager

Board minutes, 1912+ (incomplete), 2 lf; Charter, 1917, 1 sheet;
Community Center Co. records, 1955-58, 1 vol; Financial records
and audits, 1945-54, 3 in.; Minutes of subsidiary groups (Detroit
E. 117th Businessmen, 1956-62; Detroit Warren Businessmen,
1956-62; Lakewood Merchants Council, 1960-63; Madison Avenue
Association, 1955-63), 2 vols; Photographs and cuts (pictures of
members and of Lakewood), ca. 1917+, 1 lf.   JG

132. Chamber of Commerce, North Royalton (1923)
        6023 Royalton Road, North Royalton, Ohio 44133
        (216) 237-6180   (M-F 9-4)
        Georgena Hull, Office Manager

Accounts ledgers, 1966, 2 vols; Cashbooks, 1965-67, 1 vol; Correspondence, 1964-69, 4 in.; Homecoming files (correspondence
and reports relating to the annual homecoming picnic and festival),
1958-71, 6 in.; Minutes (some volumes include committee minutes),
1923+, 8 vols; Miscellaneous administrative files, 6 in.; Miscellaneous financial files, 1963-70, 6 in.   JG

133. Chamber of Commerce, Parma Heights (1953)
        6406 Stumph Road, Parma Heights, Ohio 44130
        (216) 842-4712, 884-2313   (No set hours)
        Mrs. Bernard Burlingame, Historian

Ballots for officers, 1960-61, 2 in.; General files, 1953-69, 6 in.;
History, 1953-60, ca. 30 pp; Minutes, 1954-68, 6 in.; Scrapbooks,
1953-68, 3 vols.   JG

134. Chamber of Commerce, Rocky River (1938)
19030 Lake Road, Rocky River, Ohio 44116
(216) 331-1140 (M-F 10-1)
Norbert C. Hilbrecht, Executive Secretary

Minutes, 1938+, 5 vols; Monthly newsletters, 1958+, 2 vols; Scrapbooks, 1962+, 1 vol. JG

135. Chamber of Commerce, Strongsville (1941)
18829 Royalton Road, Strongsville, Ohio 44136
(216) 238-3366 (M-F 9-3)
Norma Siedel, Secretary Manager

Minutes, 1941+, 18 in. JG

136. Chamber of Commerce, Walton Hills (1959)
18205 Fern Lane, Walton Hills, Ohio 44146
(216) 232-7141 (No set hours)
Jessica J. Stone, Executive Secretary

Minutes, 1965+, 1 vol. JG

137. Chase Bag Company (1847)
218 Cleveland Street, Chagrin Falls, Ohio 44022
(216) 247-5530 (M-F 8-5)
Jean Manlove, Secretary to Manager

The records are mainly of the Adams Bag Co. (1858-1926), which was purchased by the Chase Bag Co. Most of the records of the present company are transferred to corporate headquarters in Greenwich, Connecticut.

Appraisal record (appraisal of the assets of the Adams Bag Co.), 1925, 1 vol; Check record, 1908-10, 1 vol; Correspondence files, ca. 1940, 1 lf; Inventory, 1892-98, 1 vol; Payroll, 1915-18, 1920, 1922, 4 vols; Printed orders, 1951, 1 vol; Specification book, 1927, 1 vol; Stock certificates, 1898-1905, 1 vol; Time books, 1871-73, 1872-75, 2 vols. DH

138. Christian Revolt against Substandard Housing (1966)
4315 Bridge Avenue, Cleveland, Ohio 44113
(216) 651-2037 (M-F 8:30-4)
Dolores Bognar, Administrative Secretary

An organization dedicated to improving the lot of people on Cleveland's near west side. Alphabetized subject files.

Area condition reports, 1966+; Correspondence, 1966+; Funding material,1966+; Minutes, 1966+; 10 lf total.   JG

139. Citizens for Clean Air and Water (1968)
        312 Park Building, Cleveland, Ohio 44114
        (216) 781-0880   (No set hours)
        Evelyn Stebbins, Chairman

General file, 1968+, 15 lf; Minutes, 1968-72, 2 in.; Newsclipping file, 1965+, 8 lf.   JG

140. The City Mission (1910)
        408 St. Clair Avenue, Cleveland, Ohio 44113
        (216) 621-1801   (M-F 9-5)
        Clifton E. Gregory, Executive Director

A home for derelicts.

Administrative records, 1913, 1 item; General files (photos, clippings, tape recordings, and newsletter), 1920s+, 3 lf; Minutes, 1944-72, 8 in.; Photographs, 1920s+; Ranch files (pertain to camp run by mission), 4 lf.   JG

141. Cleveland Area Board of Realtors (1861)
        1 Erieview Plaza, Cleveland, Ohio 44114
        (216) 696-5353   (M-F 8:30-5)
        Almon R. Smith, Executive Vice-President

Board of valuation, minutes, 1919-65, 3 lf; Committee minutes, 5-year retention; Minutes of board, 1906+, 7 lf; Trustees manual, 1938-40, 1 vol.   JG

142. Cleveland Baptist Church (1958)
        4431 Tiedemann Road, Brooklyn, Ohio 44144
        (216) 671-2822   (M-F 9-5)
        Roy Thompson, Pastor

All records on either 3 x 5 or 5 x 8 index cards.

Administrative records, 1958+, 8 lf; Bus records, 1969+, 2 lf; Bus riders records, 1970+, 1 lf; Contribution records, current, 1 lf; Member file, 1958+, 2 lf; Prospective members, 1970+, 4 in.; School attendance records, 1969+, 3 lf; Sunday school class members, 1-year retention, 1 lf.   JG

143. Cleveland Federation of Musicians (1887)
        2200 Carnegie Avenue, Cleveland, Ohio 44115
        (216) 771-1802   (M-F 9-5)
        Mike Scigliano, Secretary-Treasurer

Founded as the Musical Mutual Protective Association.

Administrative records, 1 lf; Directories (contain members' names and rates), 1888+, 5 lf; Minutes, 1887+, 3 lf; Publications, "Cleveland Musician," 1928+, 5 lf.   JG

144. The Cleveland Health Museum and Education Center (1936)
        8911 Euclid Avenue, Cleveland, Ohio 44106
        (216) 231-5010   (M-F 9-4)
        Mrs. Pannell, Materials Center Assistant

Administrative records (includes annual reports and minutes), 1936-55, 6 lf; Dr. Gebhard Bruno (director of museum, 1936-65), papers, 1936-65, 1 lf; Dr. Robert Dickenson (sculpted models for museum), papers, 1939-44, 1 lf; Photographs, 1936-62, 1 vol; Publications, 1941-64, 1 lf; Scrapbooks, 1940-72, 32 vols; Dr. Robert M. Stecher (president of board), papers, 1950-71, 6 in.; Television and radio scripts, 1943-54, 4 lf.   DH

145. Cleveland Institute of Art (1898)
        11141 East Boulevard, Cleveland, Ohio 44106
        (216) 421-4322   (M-F 9-5, 6:30-9:30; Sat 9-12; Summer and
        holidays M-F 9-4:30)
        Karen Schudy, Librarian

Scrapbooks, 1902+, 8 lf.   DH

146. The Cleveland Institute of Music (1920)
        11021 East Boulevard, Cleveland, Ohio 44106
        (216) 791-5165   (M-F 9-5)
        Eugene Schmiedl, Dean of Administration

Articles of incorporation, 1920, 1 item; Audits, 1923+, 1 lf; Card
file of former students, 1920+, 100 lf; Minutes, 1920+, 2 lf; Scrapbooks, 1920+, 14 lf.   JG

147. Cleveland Medical Library Association (1894)
          11000 Euclid Avenue, Cleveland, Ohio 44106
          (216) 231-4402   (M-F 9-5)
          Genevieve Miller, Director, Howard Dittrick Museum

Bulletins, 1931+, 3 lf; Correspondence and miscellaneous records,
1894+, 9 lf; Minutes, 1894+, 2 lf.   KP

148. Cleveland Museum of Art (1916)
          11150 East Boulevard, Cleveland, Ohio 44106
          (216) 421-7340   (Tu-F 9-5)
          Sherman E. Lee, Director of Archives

Accessions file, 1915+, 31 lf; Board minutes, 1914+; Correspondence, 1914+; Loan file, 1915+, 28 lf.   JG

149. Cleveland Museum of Natural History (1920)
          University Circle, Cleveland, Ohio 44106
          (216) 231-4600   (Tu-Sat 10-12, 1-5)
          Mary Baum, Librarian

Library records, 1926-60, 2 lf; Ornithology department records,
1928-41, 6 lf.   JG

150. Cleveland Music School Settlement (1912)
          11125 Magnolia Street, Cleveland, Ohio 44106
          (216) 421-5806   (M-Sat 4-8; hours may vary)
          Mary Louise Emery, Librarian

Scrapbooks (contain clippings, programs, recital notices), 1896+,
6 lf.   JG

151. Cleveland Newspaper Guild (1943)
          Superior Building, Cleveland, Ohio 44114
          (216) 621-6792   (M-F 9-5)
          Jack Weir, Administrative Secretary

Minutes, 1943+, 3 lf.   JG

152. Cleveland Press (1876)
        901 Lakeside Avenue, Cleveland, Ohio 44114
        (216) 623-1111   (M-F 9-4:30; Sat 9-2:30)
        Thomas Barensfeld, Librarian

Individual clipping file, 1930+, 503 lf; Photograph file (over 1 million photos; currently arranged in accession order, but being
changed to an alphabetical subject and individual file), 1930+, 1000
lf; Subject clipping file, 1930+, 269 lf.   JG

153. Cleveland Public Library (1869)
        325 Superior Avenue, Cleveland, Ohio 44113
        (216) 241-1020   (M-Th 9-8:30; F, Sat 9-6)
        Fern Long, Deputy Director

Board file (file of clippings, histories, and correspondence of some
members of the library board), ca. 1900+, 2 lf; Board minutes, 1878,
1902+, 10 lf; Correspondence of Linda Eastman and of William Howard
Brett, stored temporarily in the director's office, 1896-1918, 5 lf; Departmental annual reports, 1925-44, 1954+, 9 lf; Directors' files, 1875+,
2 lf; Miscellaneous historical file (ledgers, correspondence, and memorabilia), 1891-1928, 1 lf; Permanent file, ca. 1900+, 10 lf; Scrapbooks
of clippings relating to Cleveland Public Library, 1917-41, 4 lf.   JG

154. The Cleveland Society for the Blind (1906)
        1909 East 101 Street, Cleveland, Ohio 44106
        (216) 791-8118   (M-F 8:30-5)
        Cleo B. Dolan, Executive Director

Harold Clark (active on the board), files, 1918-68, 15 lf; General files,
1907+, 60 lf (the bulk of this material is on 5-year retention); Graselli
(founder of the society), files, 1918-27, 6 in.; Minutes, 1907+, 4 lf;
Scrapbooks, 1907+, 3 lf.   JG

155. Cleveland State University Archives (1964)
        East 24th Street and Euclid Avenue, Cleveland, Ohio 44115
        (216) 687-2000   (M-F 7:30-4:30)
        Millard Jordan, Archivist

Alumni material, 1942-63, 2 lf; Association of Fenn College Women,
minutes, 1961-63, 1 lf; Biographies and biographical outlines of famous people associated with Fenn College, 3 lf; Chronological history
of C.S.U., 1963+, 3 lf; Chronological history of Fenn College, 1844-
1965, 3 lf; C.S.U. alphabetic files A-Z (pertaining to Cleveland State

University; the materials are subject filed and card indexed), 1963+,
30 lf; C.S.U. biographies, 1 lf; C.S.U. board of trustees and regents,
1963+, 1 lf; C.S.U. Cleveland news clippings (pertaining to the history
of Cleveland), 1950-60, 1 lf;

C.S.U. commencement, 1965+, 2 lf; C.S.U. trustees' minutes, 1965+,
2 lf; College files, 110 lf; Commencement convocations, 1927-65, 3 lf;
Dedication ceremonies of various buildings, 1920-60, 2 lf; Faculty and
faculty council minutes, 1965+, 3 lf; Fenn Assembly programs, 1935-
45, 2 lf; Fenn College buildings, 3 lf; Fenn College and C.S.U. historical highlights, 1870-1970, 5 lf; Fenn College general faculty meetings,
1934-64, 2 lf; Fenn Faculty Committee on Cooperative Training, 1936-
50, 1 lf;

Fenn Student Council, 1936-42, 1 lf; Fenn trustee and corp. meetings,
1954-63, 1 lf; Homecoming and Open House, 1932-53, 1965+, 2 lf; In-
auguration of President G. Brooks Ernest, 1953, 1 lf; News releases
and clippings, 1963+, 8 lf; Original research, 1844-1951, 6 in.; Publications (includes eight publications), 1920+; School of nursing, 1939,
1954-60, 1 lf; Sports, 1965+, 1 lf; Y.M.C.A. trustees minutes and
resolutions, 1844-1951, 1 lf.   JG

156. Coalition for Safe Nuclear Power (1970)
        312 Park Building, Cleveland, Ohio 44114
        (216) 781-0880   (No set hours)
        Evelyn Stebbins, Chairman

General file (correspondence and typed reports), 1970+, 2 lf; Publications, 1970+, 4 lf.   JG

157. Dyke College Library (1848)
        1375 East Sixth Street, Cleveland, Ohio 44114
        (216) 696-9000   (M-Th 8-7; F 8-5; Sat or later weekday hours
        can be arranged by request)
        Joan G. Sugarman, Librarian

Dyke College is a business college descended from a nineteenth century Spencerian school. It was once part of a chain of 40 Spencerian
schools.

Student accounts book,   1854-55, 1 vol.   JG

158. East Cleveland Public Library (1916)
         14101 Euclid Avenue, East Cleveland, Ohio 44112
         (216) 541-4128   (M-Th 9-9; F, Sat 9-5)
         Martha L. Driver, Director

Accession books, 1916-41, 16 lf; Annual reports, 1965+, 6 in.; Minutes of board (includes minutes of library planning committee, 1913-
16), 1913+, 3 lf; Miscellaneous files, 1965+. JG

159. Episcopal Diocesan Archives (1817)
         2230 Euclid Avenue, Cleveland, Ohio 44115
         (216) 771-4815   (M-F 9-5)
         Gordon Morris, Treasurer

Card catalog.

Active parish records, 1800+, 89 mf rolls; Bexley Hall records, 1 lf;
Bishops files, 1876+ (forwarded by the parishes each year), 30 lf;
Brotherhood of St. Andrew records, 1900-1930, 2 lf; Chaplaincy records, 1931+, 1 lf; Church almanacs and yearbooks, 1844+, 15 lf; Church
house records, ca. 1900+, 10 lf; Church surveys, 1959, 7 lf; Confirmation lists, 1900+, 3 lf; Council minutes, 1920+, 3 lf; Defunct parish records, 1800+, 10 lf; Diocesan alpha file, 19 lf; Diocesan convention record,
1818+, 25 lf; Diocesan history, 1876, 5 vols; Early sermons, 1 lf; Dean
Emerson files, 2 vols; Rev. Richard Grey letters, 1837-51, 1 vol; Rev.
Francis Hall letters, 1845-62, 1 vol;

Rev. John Hall letters, 1845-65, 4 vols; Marital inquiries, 1947+, 3 lf;
National convention journals, 1785+, 12 lf; Parish historical files (consist of clippings, pamphlets, and other material forwarded by the parishes
each year), 45 lf; Picture file, 19th century+, 4 lf; Priests files, 3 lf;
Priests' papers and examinations, 1889+, 12 lf; Publications and pamphlets, 1887+, 7 lf; Scrapbooks, 19th century, 10 vols; G. B. Sturges,
journal, 1839-90, 1 vol; Trials files, 2 lf; Trustees files, 20 lf.
JG

160. Epworth-Euclid United Methodist Church (1818)
         1919 East 107th Street, Cleveland, Ohio 44106
         (216) 421-1200   (M-F 8:30-4:30)
         H. F. Harvey, Administrator

Account books, 4 vols; Church register, 1897+, 19 vols; Central

Methodist Episcopal Church, records, 1885-91, 1 vol; Erie Street
Methodist Episcopal Church, records, 1870-85, 2 vols; Euclid Avenue Methodist Church, records, 1898-1916, 1 vol; Marriage certificates, 1928-32, 1 box; Minutes of board and quarterly conferences,
1903+, 8 lf; Wade Park Methodist Church, records, 1892-1920, 3
vols; Weekly bulletin, 1910+, 5 lf.   JG

161.   Federated Church (1835)
          76 Bell Street, Chagrin Falls, Ohio 44022
          (216) 247-6490   (M-F 8:30-4; Sat 8:30-12)
          Cathryn H. Groth, Secretary-Treasurer

Administrative records, 1835+; Blueprints, 2 lf; Board records, 1920-
30, 40 vol; Church register, 1847-84, 1 vol; Financial records, ca.
1950+, 4 lf; Photographs, 3 in.; Publications, 1948+, 10 lf; Sunday
school records, 1 lf; Treasurers' records, 1880-1920, 1 lf.   JG

162.   First Presbyterian Church (1820)
          (More commonly known as Old Stone Church)
          91 Public Square, Cleveland, Ohio 44113
          (216) 241-6145   (M-F 9-5; June-Aug, only until 4)
          Jeanette Greve, Financial Secretary

Deacons' minutes, 1897+, 6 in.; First Presbyterian Society in Cleveland, 1827+, 4 in.; Miscellaneous historical records (includes photographs), 2 lf; Session minutes, 1820+, 3 lf; Trustees' minutes, 1855+,
18 vols.   JG

163.   Garden Center of Greater Cleveland (1930)
          11030 East Boulevard, Cleveland, Ohio 44106
          (216) 721-1600   (M-F 9-5; Sun 2-5)
          Howard Swift, Associate Director

Harold T. Clark files (correspondence, financial records, and minutes of the executive committee, 1961-69), ca. 1950-69, 6 lf; Executive committee and annual meeting minutes, 1961+, 2 lf; Historical
file (clippings, scrapbooks, correspondence, financial records and
minutes for the early years), 1930+, 4 lf; Monthly bulletin, 1931+, 2
lf; New York Flower Show records, 1939, 3 in.; White elephant sale
records (includes about 60 scrapbooks), 1930+, 10 lf.   JG

164. Garfield Heights Leader (1946)
     4818 Turney Road, Garfield Heights, Ohio 44125
     (216) 883-0300   (M-F 9-5)
     William Kleinschmidt, Editor

Photograph file (mostly scenes of Garfield Heights and pictures of
individuals in the community), 1946+, 8 lf.   JG

165. The George Worthington Company (1829)
     802 St. Clair Avenue, Cleveland, Ohio 44113
     (216) 241-1600, ext. 344   (M-F 8-5)
     Mary Molnar, Secretary to the President

This company, one of the oldest in Cleveland, is a wholesale hardware distributor.

Correspondence, 1864-66, 6 in.; Historical file (letters, clippings,
bills and publications), 1829+, 8 vols; Ledgers, 1829-70, 6 vols; Minutes, 1887-88, 1 vol; Photographs, 1900-1940, 6 vols; Receipts, 1854-
66, 6 in.   JG

166. Grace St. Mary Episcopal Church (1869)
     Harvard Avenue at East 91st Street, Cleveland, Ohio 44105
     (216) 341-0880   (M, W, F 9-5)
     Leon Richey, Rector

This is the only Episcopal parish in what was Newburgh, Ohio.

Church bulletin, 1953-70, 2 lf; Records of services, 1931+, 4 vols;
Registers, 1870-90, 1900+, 3 vols; Vestry minutes, 1916+, 10 vol.
JG

167. Greater Cleveland Neighborhood Centers Association (1963)
     1001 Huron Road, Cleveland, Ohio 44115
     (216) 781-2944, ext. 300   (M-F 8:30-5)
     Robert L. Bond, Executive Director

Coordinating agency for Cleveland's various social settlements.

Board minutes, 1964-70, 1 lf; Budget requests, 1965-68, 3 vols; Committee minutes, 1963-64, 1 vol; General files, 1947-72, 50 lf; Newsletters, 1963+, 2 lf.   JG

168.　Hadassah (1913)
　　　1855 South Taylor Road, Cleveland Heights, Ohio　44118
　　　(216) 321-9000　　(M-F 9-4:30)
　　　M. Spiegel, Historian

Hadassah is a Jewish women's organization founded to aid Jews set-
tling in what is now Israel.

Scrapbooks (mostly clippings, but some programs and correspondence
in early volumes), 1913-50, 17 vols; Slides and films.　JG

169.　Hope United Methodist Church (1851)
　　　4210 Orchard Avenue, Cleveland, Ohio　44113
　　　(216) 281-7370, 281-2928　　(M-F 8:30-3:30)
　　　Charles H. Frye, Pastor

The Hope United Methodist Church resulted from the merger of the
Emanuel E.U.B. Church and the First E.U.B. Church in 1967.

Emanuel E.U.B. Church:　Administrative council minutes, 1929-60,
1 vol; Annual conference minutes, 1929-49, 1 vol; Church register,
1945-67, 1 lf; Council meeting minutes, 1903-29, 2 vols; Financial
records, 1873-79, 1912-60, 1958-67, 5 vols; Forward movement ex-
cerpts, 1920-26, 1 vol; Frauen Missions Verein, 1909-42, 3 vols;
Heights Mission records, 1867-81, 1 vol; Jugend Verein minutes,
1890-1900, 1 vol; Memory book, 1 vol; Minutes of various meetings,
1873-90, 1 vol; Photographs, 1880-1930s; Program and local council
minutes, 1961-66, 1 vol; Quarterly conference records, 1881-1930,
1950-67, 3 vols; Registers, 1881-1967, 3 vols; Sunday school business
meetings, 1916-67, 3 vols; Trustees minutes, 1890-1903, 1 vol; Wom-
en's Missionary Society and Sunday school minutes, 1925-42, 1952-63,
2 vols.

First E.U.B. Church:　Financial records (includes the record books
of a German insurance organization headquartered at the church), 1854-
1940, 8 vols; Minutes (includes minutes of Sunday school, board, and
quarterly conference), 1853-1932, 21 vols; Registers, 1871-1936, 5
vols.　JG

170.　Hospital Association of Greater Cleveland (1917)
　　　1001 Huron Road, Cleveland, Ohio　44115
　　　(216) 781-2944　　(M-F 8:30-5)
　　　C. Wayne Rice, Director

Minutes, 1917+, 3 0 lf.　JG

171. Independence Presbyterian Church (1837)
     6624 Public Square, Independence, Ohio 44131
     (216) 524-6307 (M-F 9-3)
     Robert M. Barnes, Pastor

Church registers, 1837-1900, 1925+, 1 vol; Session minutes, 1837-1900, 1925+, 3 vols (church inactive from 1900 to 1925). JG

172. Independence United Methodist Church (1855)
     6615 Brecksville Road, Independence, Ohio 44131
     (216) 524-6054 (M-F 9-12)
     Jean Johnson, Church Secretary

Church registers, 1877+, 4 vols; Financial records; Photograph and pamphlet file, 1 lf; Typescript histories, 1912, 2 histories. JG

173. Jewish Community Federation (1902)
     1750 Euclid Avenue, Cleveland, Ohio 44115
     (216) 861-4360 (M-F 8:30-5)
     Judah Rubenstein, Research Associate

The Jewish Community Federation is primarily a coordinating agency for Jewish welfare activities.

Community relations records, 1930s+, 2 lf; Correspondence with member agencies and funding records, 1950s-1965, 14 lf; Current files (relate to community relations and Middle East and Israel), 1951+, 330 lf; Financial Relations Committee minutes, 1924-27, 1 vol; General historical files, 1903+, 10 lf; Historical scrapbooks, 1930s+, 11 lf; Jewish Community Council (merged with JCF), minutes, 1935-51, 4 vols; Jewish community survey, 1923-24, 2 vols;

Jewish population survey, 2 lf; Jews in armed forces (file card series), W.W. II, 4 lf; Ledger books, 1903+, 20 lf; Merger files, 1951, 5 vols; Minutes, 1903+, 10 lf; Miscellaneous photos and scrapbooks, 1930s+, 6 lf; Publications (community relations), late 1940s, 2 lf; Social planning records, 1940s+, 12 lf; Sovereign Hotel files, 2 lf; Tape recordings, (speeches, dedications), late 1960s+, 60 tapes; Women's organization records, 1945, 2 in. JG

174. John Carroll University Archives (1886)
     North Park and Miramar, University Heights, Ohio 44118
     (216) 491-4911 (M-F 8 am-11 pm; Sat 9-5; Sun 2-10)
     Rev. Fr. James A. Mackin, Director of Library

Academic Council files, 1946-62, 3 lf; Alumni files, 1938-53, 1 lf; Buffalo Mission (school preceding University) papers, 1869-1909, 10 in.; Building fund files, 1929, 8 lf; Commencement committee, 1890-1958, 2 lf; Deans office files, 1933-50, 2 lf; Departmental records, ca. 1949-53, 2 lf; Executive committee reports, 1963-65, 2 lf; Financial records, 1893-1930, 3 lf; Grade sheets, 1890-1915, 1 lf; House diary (records kept by Jesuit Order), 1886-1945, 6 in.; Military files (draft and ROTC), 1940-65, 2 lf; Fr. Frederick Odenbach (professor of physics; head of meteorology and seismology labs), papers, 1900-1933, 2 lf; Photographs, 1 lf; President's office files, 1907-63, 4 lf; St. Ignatius College (predecessor institution, now a high school), records, 1884-1950, 4 lf; Scrapbooks, 1946-60, 2 lf; Sports files, 1948-65, 2 lf; Student activities files, 1939-53, 1 lf. DH

175. Lake Erie Girl Scout Council (1920)
        1001 Huron Road, Cleveland, Ohio 44115
        (216) 241-3180   (M-F 8:30-5)
        Gloria Harris, Executive Director

The records of the Lake Erie Girl Scout Council are actually the records of the old Cleveland Girl Scout Council, the Lake County Council and minor area sub-councils. The Lake County and Cleveland Councils merged in 1962 to form the present organization.

Administrative records, 1950-70, 1 lf; Annual reports, 1950-69, 1 lf; Board minutes, 1950-60, 6 in.; Charters, Lake County, ca. 1940-60, 3 in.; Executive committee minutes, 1922-24, 1927, 1929-49, 1961+, 2 lf; Minutes of various councils, 1930-63, 3 lf; Theses, 1950s and 1960s, 6 in.   DH

176. Lakewood Public Library (1916)
        15425 Detroit Avenue, Lakewood, Ohio 44107
        (216) 226-8275   (M-F 9:30-9; Sat 9:30-6)
        Daniel W. Hagelin, Head of Reference

Board minutes, 1921+, 4 lf.   JG

177. Legal Aid Society of Cleveland (1905)
        118 St. Clair Avenue, Cleveland, Ohio 44114
        (216) 771-1313   (M-F 9-5:30)
        Katherine Cremer, Staff Assistant

Administrative records, 1905, 1 item; Annual reports, 1906+, 2 lf; Court cases relative to the society, 2 in.; Publications, 1906-14, 1917, 1949-52, 6 in.   JG

178. Maple Heights United Methodist Church (1946)
      18900 Libby Road, Maple Heights, Ohio 44137
      (216) 663-6868   (M-F 9-4)
      Paul R. Balliett, Pastor

Church registers, 1946+, 3 vols; Scrapbooks (contain photographs of most church members), 1946+, 10 vols.   JG

179. Miles Avenue Church of Christ (1835)
      9200 Miles Avenue, Cleveland, Ohio 44105
      (216) 641-5679   (M-F 9-3)
      Orval C. Morgan, Interim Minister

Administrative records, 1835, 1 item; Baptismal records, 1927-54, 1 lf; Board registers, 1882-1969, 8 vols; Christian Women's Fellow-ship minutes, 1950-70, 2 vols; Missionary Board of Willing Workers minutes, 1891-94, 1 vol; Photographs, 19th and 20th centuries, 6 in.; Scrapbook (contains photos, clippings, and pamphlets), ca. 1902-10, 1 vol; Sunday school minutes, 1886-90, 1 vol; Weekly bulletins, 1889-91, 2 in.   JG

180. Miles Park Presbyterian Church (1832)
      9114 Miles Park Avenue, Cleveland, Ohio 44105
      (216) 341-3009   (M-F 8-4:30)
      William Keene, Minister

Administrative records, 1842, 1 item; Anniversary sermons, 50th, 75th, 80th, and 100th, 2 in.; Annual reports, 1872-1950 (inc.), 6 in.; Congregational meeting minutes, 1842-1951, 3 vols; Directory of mem-bers, 1920-26, 1 vol; Ladies Aid Society ledgers, 1929-53, 4 vols; Lud-low Auxiliary minutes, 1935-47, 1 vol; Men's League records, 1895, 1 vol; Photographs, ca. 1890+, 1 lf; Reconstruction program records, 1934-35, 4 in.; Registers, 1844+, 4 vols; Scrapbooks (correspondence with servicemen), 1941-45, 1 vol; Session minutes, 1832+, 7 vols; Trustees' minutes, 1887+, 7 vols; Westminster Guild minutes, 1919-22, 1 vol.   JG

181. Miles Park United Methodist Church (1832)
      9105 Miles Park Avenue, Cleveland, Ohio 44105
      (216) 883-5565   (M-F 9-12)
      Jean A. Rice, Historian

Account book, 1832-77, 1 vol; Centennial contest book, 1940, 1 vol;
Minutes of trustees, 1837+; 140th Anniversary files (correspondence,
clippings, pamphlets), 1972, 4 in.; Photographs and clippings, ca.
1870+, 4 in.; Registers, 1872+; Treasurer's book, 1872-1911, 1 vol;
Women's Foreign Missionary Society minutes, 1891, 1 vol.   JG

182. Mt. Zion Congregational Church and Society (1864)
        10823 Magnolia Drive, Cleveland, Ohio 44106
        (216) 791-5760   (M-F 10-5)
        Leola Dyer, Church Secretary

Dedication files (correspondence, telegrams, clippings), 1956, 1 vol;
Directories, 1925, 1946, 2 vols; Histories, 1945, 1964, 2 vols; Minutes, 1879-90, 1 vol; Photographs, ca. 1940+, 6 in.   DH

183. National City Bank (1845)
        623 Euclid Avenue, Cleveland, Ohio 44114
        (216) 861-4900   (M-F 8:30-5)
        G.F. Carpenter, Vice-President and Cashier

Board of trustees minutes, 1845+; Executive minutes, 1845+; 18 lf
total.   JG

184. North East Ohio Teachers Assocation (1869)
        6500 Pearl Road, Parma Heights, Ohio 44130
        (216) 845-2030   (M-F 8:30-5)
        Lowell E. Lutz, Executive Secretary

Annual meetings, 1961+, 3 lf; Audit, 1955, 1 vol; Bank passbooks, 1911-
17, 1923-38, 1929-32, 1933, 4 vols; General file (includes budget requests, photos, and committee proceedings), 1964+, 3 lf; Ledgers, 1963-
67, 1 vol; Minutes, 1873-1943, 1958+, 5 vols; Monthly newsletter, 1954+,
1 vol; Officers roster, 1932+, 1 vol; Scrapbooks, 1911-37, 2 vols; Treasurer's book, 1922-30, 1 vol.   JG

185. Park Synagogue (1859)
        3300 Mayfield Road, Cleveland Heights, Ohio 44118
        (216) 371-2244   (M-Th 9-5:30; F 9-4:30, hour varies according
        to sunset)
        Rabbi Howard Hirsch

Annual meeting reports, 1936+, 4 in.; Board minutes, 1937+, 2 in.;

Bulletin, 1930+, 3 lf; Choir music collection, 6 in.; Rabbi Armond
Cohen papers (sermons and correspondence), 1934+, 20 lf; Committee
lists, 1930s+, 2 in.; Confirmation photos, 1913+; Files on various
rabbis, 2 in.; Films and slides, 1950s+; General historical files (photos
and pamphlets), 1940s+, 3 lf; Photograph file, ca. 1930+, 4 lf; Scrapbooks, 1920+, 11 vols; Sisterhood minutes, 1920-48, 3 vols; Tape recordings (dedications and notable sermons), 1952+.   JG

186. Pilgrim Baptist Church (1859)
       2592 West 14th Street, Cleveland, Ohio 44113
       (216) 861-7388   (M-F 9-4)
       Robert Winegarner, Pastor

Accessions book, 1933-44, 1 vol; Church record (University Heights
Church), 1859-78, 1 vol; Glass slides and negatives, ca. 1900+, 5 boxes;
Minutes (University Heights Union Sabbath School), 1858-65, 1 vol; Mothers Club records, 1927-32, 1937-64, 5 vols; Pastor's record, 1890-93,
1913-37, 6 vols; Photographs, ca. 1914; Publications (yearbooks and histories), ca. 1890-1930, 12 vols; Registers, 1859-1944, 4 vols; Sunday
school registration book, 1912-28, 1 vol.   JG

187. Plain Dealer Library (1842)
       1801 Superior Avenue, Cleveland, Ohio 44114
       (216) 523-4500   (M-F 9-5)
       Grace Parch, Library Director

Alphabetical picture collection (all subjects), 1956+, 4 million items;
Individual and subject clipping files, 1908+, 1,692 lf; Numbered picture collection (both published and unpublished; early Cleveland, Ohio,
and prominent people), 1850-1956, 2 million items.   JG

188. Police Athletic League (1955)
       3481 Fulton Road, Cleveland, Ohio 44109
       (216) 749-3850   (M-F 9-5)
       Sgt. Fred Stauffer, Executive Director

Administrative records (articles of incorporation), 1955, 1 item;
Film and tapes, ca. 1968 (general promotional material); Financial
statements, 1966+, 2 lf; General files (includes material produced
prior to founding of league), 1936+, 6 lf; Minutes, 1966+, 6 in.; Photographs, 1966+, 3 in.; Scrapbooks (includes four books of fund raising letters and brochures), 1966+, 5 vols.   JG

189. Porter Public Library (1884)
     27059 Center Ridge Road, Westlake, Ohio 44145
     (216) 871-2600   (M, Tu 11-9; W, Th 1-9; F, Sat 9-5)
     Kathleen Carnall, Librarian

Board of trustees minutes, 1884+, 1 lf; Cash vouchers, ca. 1950+,
4 lf; Correspondence, 1931+, 6 in.; Financial statements, 1937+,
6 in.; Ledgers and receipts, ca. 1955+, 3 lf; Materials relating to
new library building, 1960, 6 in.   JG

190. Resources for Social Change (1970)
     27476 Detroit Road, Westlake, Ohio 44145
     (216) 835-0364   (Hours by appointment)
     Marcia Mauer, Executive Director

Administrative records (data on housing, racial discrimination, in-
action and women's rights), 1970-73, 2 lf.   DH

191. Rockport United Methodist Church (1822)
     3301 Wooster Road, Rocky River, Ohio 44116
     (216) 331-9433   (M-F 8:30-4:30)
     Mrs. Burt Linderman, Church Secretary

Baptism records, 1950+, 1 vol; Historical file, 1 lf; Membership
records, 1950+, 4 vols; Registers, 1888-1906, 1933-40, 2 vols;
Treasurer's report, 1895-1900, 1 vol.   JG

192. The Rowfant Club (1892)
     3028 Prospect Avenue, Cleveland, Ohio 44115
     (216) 431-4518   (No set hours)
     William R. Althans, Secretary

The Club is organized for the purpose of critical study of books. The
club holds an excellent collection of rare books.

Administrative files, 1960s+, 5 lf; Autograph collection (literary and
political figures), 1800-1920, 250 items; Financial files, 1959+, 2 lf;
Membership files, 1892+, 6 lf; Minutes, 1892+, 8 vols; Miscellaneous
files (correspondence, speeches and manuscripts for printed works),
1892+, 42 lf; Yearbooks, 1892+, 80 vols.   KP

193. Royalton Recorder (1940)
        6023 Royalton Road, North Royalton, Ohio 44133
        (216) 273-6180   (M-F 9-4)
        Georgena Hull, Assistant Editor

Photograph file (photographs of people and buildings in North Royalton), ca. 1966+, 2 lf.   JG

194. St. Martins Episcopal Church (1953)
        6295 Chagrin River Road, Bentleyville Village, Ohio 44022
        (216) 247-6551   (M-F 8:30-4)
        Ira Crowther, Rector

Building blueprints and specifications, 2 in.; Church register, 1953+,
3 vols; Financial records, 1954-64, 2 lf; Minutes, 1953+.   JG

195. The Salvation Army, Cleveland (1872)
        2507 East 22nd Street, Cleveland, Ohio 44115
        (216) 861-8185   (M-F 8:45-4:30)
        Maj. Robert Bearchell, Divisional Secretary

Some of the older records have been transferred to the national headquarters in New York City.

Files on retention (complete files of component offices), 1948+, 320
lf; Historical file (letter and clippings concerning history of organization), 1936-72, 3 in.; Photographs, 1950-60, 5 lf; Publications (old
issues of the house organ War Cry and some broadsides), ca. 1880-
1900, 3 in.; Scrapbooks, 1953-61, 12 vols.   JG

196. Sherwin-Williams Company (1867)
        Midland Building, Cleveland, Ohio 44101
        (216) 566-2229, 566-2334   (M-F 9-5)
        Clayton H. Lange, Manager, Public Relations

Vital corporate records are filmed and stored in an underground vault.

Company records (includes all vital corporate records), 1876+, 9,000
lf; Historical file (photographs, artifacts, company histories, catalogs),
1876+, ca. 1,000 items; Publications, 1897-1942.   JG

197. Stuart E. Wallace & Company (1962)
       3572 Lee Road, Cleveland, Ohio 44128
       (216) 752-9200   (M-F 9-5)
       Stuart E. Wallace, Realtor

Stuart E. Wallace & Co. was organized in 1962 as Fair Housing, Inc.
Its purpose was to serve as a realty agency which would list homes
irrespective of race or past housing patterns. The company is now a
private firm.

Administrative files, 1962-72, 12 lf; Completed sales files (all material relating to a particular sale), 1962-72, 8 lf; Stock certificates
(pertain to ownership of the company), 1963-71, 3 lf.   DH

198. The Temple (1850)
       University Circle and Silver Park, Cleveland, Ohio 44106
       (216) 791-7755   (M-F 9-5; Sun 9-12, Sept-June)
       Miriam Leikind, Librarian

Annual reports, 1897-1950; Bulletins, 1896-1970; Confirmation programs, 1896-1970; Rally Day, 1927-70; Temple High School gradua-
tion programs, 1927-70; 10 lf total;

Abba Hillel Silver Memorial Archives: (rabbi, Zionist and community
leader in Cleveland) personal correspondence, 1914-63, 145 lf; Phono-
graph records, 73 lf; Photographs, 6 lf; Scrapbooks, 12 lf; Sermons
and writings, 1905-63, 30 lf; Tape recordings, 29 lf.   DH

199. United Methodist Church of Chagrin Falls (1833)
       20 South Franklin Street, Chagrin Falls, Ohio 44022
       (216) 247-5848   (M-F 9-4)
       Mrs. Andrew Takas, Church Secretary

Church history (includes original documents and photographs), 1 vol;
Church register, 1900-1927, 2 vols; Church school attendance, 1947-
58, 3 vols; Church school financial, 1958-62, 1 vol; Financial statements, ca. 1850-1965, 1 lf.   DH

200. United Service Organization, Inc., Region 5 (1941)
       507 Park Building, Public Square, Cleveland, Ohio 44114
       (216) 696-0446   (M-F 9-5)
       Thomas J. Kurz, Regional Executive

Correspondence, 4-year retention, 40 lf.   JG

201. United Torch Services (1913)
    3100 Euclid Avenue, Cleveland, Ohio 44115
    (216) 881-3170
    Fran Koneval, Manager, Radio, TV and Films

Previous names for United Torch Services were the Federation for
Charity and Philanthropy, the Community Fund, and the United Fund.

Correspondence, 1965+, 6 lf; Films (promotional), 1918+; Photographs,
ca. 1920+, 2 lf; Publications (annual promotional pamphlets), 1919-50,
1 vol; Scrapbooks (mostly yearbooks, containing clippings, posters, letters and other materials relating to the yearly fund-raising campaign),
1918+, 56 vols; Slides. JG

202. University Hospitals of Cleveland (Lakeside Hospital) (1863)
    2065 Adelbert Road, Cleveland, Ohio 44106
    (216) 791-7300, ext. 2030 (M-F 9-5)
    Eugenia Kucherenko, Archivist

Anesthesia department, papers, grades, student records, 1920-61, 9
lf; Autopsy records, general, 1898+, 102 lf; Autopsy records, surgical,
1911+, 40 lf; Babies and Childrens Hospital, papers, records, correspondence, 1907-70,6 lf; Babies dispensary, papers, slides, records,
1906-25, 12 lf; Claude S. Beck, M.D., personal papers, memorabilia,
1924-65, 23 lf; Theodora Bergsland, papers, illustrations, drawings,
1927-60, 31 lf; Marion D. Douglass, M.D., personal papers, certificates, 1930s-43,1 lf; Financial director's collection (records, correspondence, agreements,deeds), 1924-68, 75 lf;

Robert W. Heinle, M.D., papers, patient records, 1942-54, 4 lf; Mac-
Donald House, papers, records, reports, 1927-68, 3 lf; Department of
Medicine, papers, reports, correspondence, 1930s-1970, 54 lf; Micro-
films (General autopsies, 1898+, 209; Surgical autopsies, 1911+, 80;
Patient case histories, 1898-1945, 1,151 rolls); Alan R. Moritz, M.D.,
personal papers, 1950s-1971, 1 lf; Nursing Dept., correspondence,
papers, reports, 1900-1970, 48 lf; Inst. of Pathology, reports, papers,
9 lf; Pediatric surgery, reports, papers, 1950-68, 2 lf;

Personnel records, papers, 1900-1970, 61 lf; Photographs (interior, ex-
terior events, ceremonies), 1920-72, 5 lf; Physical therapy, records,
papers, 1930s, 1954-70, 20 lf; Planning and construction, correspondence,
reports, papers, 1964, 6 lf; Rainbow Hospital, papers, reports, 1900s-
1971, 10 lf; Social service, thesis, papers, correspondence, 1908-68, 8
lf; Dept. of Surgery, papers, reports, 1950s-1964, 15 lf; U.M.C. Development Program, papers, reports, 1964-68, 3 lf; Austin S. Weisberger,

M.D., papers, lectures, research, 1936-70, 26 lf; C.W. Wyckoff,
M.D., personal papers, 1911-25, 1 lf.   DH

203. Valley Lutheran Church (1938)
          87 East Orange, Chagrin Falls, Ohio 44022
          (216) 247-4666   (Tu-F 10-4)
          Arthur Pickett, Pastor

Administrative records and minutes, 1938+, 3 lf; Church register,
1938+, 1 vol; Correspondence, 2-year retention; Scrapbooks, 6 in.
DH

204. Wesley United Methodist Church (19th Century)
          1965 West 44th Street, Cleveland, Ohio 44113
          (216) 281-2928   (M-F 8:30-3:30)
          Charles H. Frye, Pastor

Baptism and marriage records, 1947-66, 2 vols; Membership records, ca. 1918-40, 1 vol; Register, 1928-66, 2 vols; School attendance records, 1942-67, 2 vols; School roll books, 1967-72, 9 vols.
JG

205. West Side Ecumenical Ministry (1966)
          4315 Bridge Avenue, Cleveland, Ohio 44113
          (216) 651-2037   (M-F 8:30-4)
          Dolores Bognar, Administrative Secretary

General files (noncurrent; alpha-subject file, reports, correspondence, and material concerning funding. Ca. 4 lf of this material is
cancelled checks and receipts), 1966-72, 18 lf.   JG

206. West Side United Church of Christ (1853)
          3800 Bridge Avenue, Cleveland, Ohio 44113
          (216) 631-3423   (Tu-F 9-4)
          Helen J. Clark, Church Secretary

Registers, 1853-65, 1871+, 1 lf.   JG

207. Western Reserve Association (1964)
          3209 Broadview Road, Cleveland, Ohio 44109
          (216) 749-3116   (M-F 8:30-4:30)
          Elam G. Wiest, Association Minister

Central coordinating body for all United Churches of Christ in the greater Cleveland area.

Association files, 1960s+, 10 lf; Cleveland Fellowship of Cong. Christian Women, minutes, 1948-63, 6 in.; Collinwood Congregational Church records (minutes, registers, and financial records), 1900-1967, 5 lf; East Madison Avenue Cong. Church records (minutes and registers, includes minutes of Bohemian Missionary Board), 1874-1914, 2 lf; First Franklin Church records (minutes and registers), 1876-1953, 4 lf;

Glenville Evangelical Reformed Church records (mainly minutes and membership records), 1910-66, 2 lf; Highland United Church of Christ records (minutes, registers, and financial material), 1895-1957, 5 lf; Lake Erie Regional Womens Guild, minutes and financial records, 1955-63, 6 in.; Lorain Avenue Churchmans Federation records, 1954-63, 1 vol; Medina Association records (almost all financial), ?-1963, 5 lf; JG

DARKE COUNTY

MANUSCRIPTS

208. Darke County Historical Society (1903)
    205 North Broadway, Greenville, Ohio 45331
    (513) 548-5250   (Tu, F 1-5)
    Gertrude Holzaphel, Curator

Adams Township Board of Education daybook, 1860s, 1 in.; Adams Township record book, 1836, 6 in.; Brumbaugh and Rinehart reunion records, 1903, 1 in.; Coletown P.T.A. records, 1925-56, 2 in.; Darke County school district daybook, 1832, 1 in.; Exhibit book, 1890, 2 in.; G.A.R. collection—Jobes Post #157, 1881-1931, 3 lf; G.A.R. daybooks, 1887-89, 1898-1906, 1913, 3 items; Kate Garst scrapbook, 1875, 1 in.; Local doctors daybooks and records, 1824-86, 2 lf;

Local merchants business records, 1793+, 2 lf; Annie Oakley collection (scrapbooks, news clippings, pictures), 1920s, 5 lf; 175th Anniversary of signing of treaty of Greenville (mostly clippings), ca. 1930, 2 lf; Picture collection (miscellaneous), ca. 1900s+, 9 lf; Pioneer Association daybook, 1870-84, 1 in.; Lowell Thomas collection (scrapbook, pictures, news clippings), 1930, 2 lf; Union Pioneer Mutual Benefit Association certificate register, late 1800s, 1 in.; Henry Webb, diary (record of army's travels under Gen. George Crook), 1875-79, 1 in. RS

209. Greenville Public Library (ca. 1902)
    520 Sycamore, Greenville, Ohio 45331
    (513) 548-3915   (M-F 10-8)
    Irene Hall, Head Librarian

Formerly Carnegie Public Library

Assessment of lots in Arcanum, 1890, 1 in.; Darke County cemetery
records, 2 in.; Darke County Common Pleas Court records, 1817-
60, 150 pp; Darke County Farm Bureau, minute book, 1917-24, 1
in.; Darke County newspaper death records, 1850-94, 1 in.; Darke
County plat book, 1875, 1910, 1 in.; Darke County will records, index, 1818-1900, 10 pp; Genealogy collection, 2 lf; High school yearbooks, 1908-71, 2 lf;

Library records, 1900-1958, 6 in.; Marriage records, 1808-30,
1841-50, 1 in.; Ministerial Association of Greenville, minutes, receipts, etc., 1892-1913, 1 in.; Ohio Bible records (Crawford, Darke,
Fairfield, Miami, Montgomery, Pickaway, Preble, and Shelby counties), 1750-1969, 300 pp; Water Street Cemetery inscription, 1 in.
FH

INSTITUTIONAL RECORDS

210. Farm Bureau Federation, Greenville (1919)
    620 Sater Street, P.O. Box 39, Greenville, Ohio 45331
    (513) 548-1123
    Jim Mills, Organization Director

Annual reports, with minutes; Correspondence, 1-year retention;
Financial statements (with minutes); Health insurance records;
Journals, cash journal; Minutes, 1919?, 6 in.; Newsletter, 1969+,
2 in.; Receipts, 1919.   RS

211. YMCA, Greenville (1965)
    301 Wagner Avenue, Greenville, Ohio 45321
    (513) 548-3777   (M-F (winter) 9-10; M-F (summer) 9-6)
    Jack Sizemore, Executive Director

Administrative records, Annual reports, 1965+; Contracts (building
construction), 1968?; Correspondence, 1-year retention; Deeds, property, 1968+; Inventories, 1-year retention; Ledgers (financial statements); Membership lists, 1965; Minutes, 1965+; Scrapbooks, 1965;
1 lf total.   FH

MANUSCRIPTS

212. Defiance Public Library
        320 Fort Street, Defiance, Ohio 43512
        (419) 782-1456   (M-F 10-9)
        Nellie Gary, Librarian

Defiance Machine Works, correspondence and catalogs, 1903-6, 2 lf;
Defiance photographs (street scenes, urban structures, and historical
places), 1890-1910, 2 lf; William Hoffman family, scrapbooks (photographs, newspaper clippings), 1890-1910, 2 vols; Richland Township
school district, minutes, 1837-70, 1 vol; John Russell family, scrapbooks (poems), 1801, 1 vol.   PY

INSTITUTIONAL RECORDS

213. First Presbyterian Church
        501 Washington Avenue, Defiance, Ohio 43512
        (419) 782-2781   (M-F 9-12, 1-4)
        Lucille Thompson, Secretary

ABC Class minutes, 1927-69, 3 vols; Account records, 1871-72, 1 vol;
Board of Religious Education minutes, 1932-52, 2 vols; Christian Education Committee minutes, 1967-69, 1 vol; Church budgets, 1924-48,
1 vol; Church Council minutes, 1940-48, 1 vol; Defiance Presbyterian
Church Association minutes, 1837-91, 2 vols; Eleusinian minutes, 1917-
24, 1 vol; Evening Group B minutes, 1946-48, 1 vol; Florance Lehman
Bible Class minutes, 1924-59, 2 lf; Ladies Aid Society, 1883-85, 1 vol;
Rex Auxiliary minutes, 1925-40; Session minutes (annual and monthly),
1836+, 5 lf; Slagle Group of the Womans Missionary Society, minutes,
1897-1948, 7 vols; Westminister's Woman's Association minutes, 1901-
62, 10 vols.   TS

214. St. John Lutheran Church
        655 Wayne Avenue, Defiance, Ohio 43512
        (419) 782-5766   (M-F 8-12, 1-4)
        David R. Koenig, Pastor

Building fund ledger, 1920-36, 1 vol; Choir record, 1916-18, 1 vol;
Church books, 1851+, 5 vols; Church building bids, 1885, 1 env; Congregational minutes, 1890-1920, 2 vols; Individual contribution records,
1929-62, 20 vols; Ladies' Auxiliary records, 1937-65, 3 vols; Membership lists, 1880-1900, 10 vols; St. John Lutheran Ladies Aid records,

1857-1962, 9 vols; Treasurer's ledgers, 1859+, 8 vols.   TS

215. St. Johns Catholic Church
        510 Jackson Avenue, Defiance, Ohio 43512
        (419) 782-7121
        Fr. Krause, Priest

Parish history, 1840+, 1 vol (first part written by a 19th century pastor
of the church; the history has been kept up to date by later priests in the
parish); Parish records, 1840+, 2 lf; Photograph collection (photos of
the church building and grounds), 1880+.   TS

216. St. Mary's Catholic Church (1873)
        707 Jefferson Avenue, Defiance, Ohio 43512
        (419) 782-2776   (M-F 9-4)
        Fr. John H. Flynn

Church registers, 1875+, 4 vols.   PY

217. St. Pauls First Methodist Church
        Wayne and Third Streets, Defiance, Ohio 43512
        (M-F 9-4)
        Virginia Ziegler, Secretary

Church minutes, 1832-55, 1958-73, 3 lf; Church registers, 1832-55,
1871+; Class records, 1871-78, 1 vol; Defiance District Conference--
Central Ohio Annual Conference, minutes, 1894-1927, 1 vol; The Help-
ing Hand Society, minutes, 1879-1940, 2 lf; Intermediate Epworth
League (youth group), minutes, 1929-30, 1 vol; Ladies Home Missionary Society, minutes, Oct. 1886-1919; Methodist Woman Society of
Christian Service, minutes, 1940-49, 3 vols; Sunday School minutes
and roll record, 1868-74, 2 vols; Woman's Foreign Missionary Society, minutes, 1920-27, 1 vol; Woman's Society of Christian Service,
executive board minutes, 1940-42, 1 vol.   PY

DELAWARE COUNTY

MANUSCRIPTS

218. Delaware County District Library (1897)
        101 North Sandusky, Delaware, Ohio 43015
        (614) 362-3861   (M-F 10-8:30; Sat 10-6)
        Cicely Judd, Librarian

Cash record, 1899-1904; Cemetery inscriptions, Delaware County, 1 in.; Cemetery records, Delaware County (John W. Bricker, Sr., compiled list in 1970 of all people buried in Delaware County), 1 in.; Delaware Literary Association, constitution, 1832; Delaware County will books, 1812-58, 2 in.; Delaware County World War Service record (names of all those from Delaware County who served in WW I), 8 in.; Genealogical material, 6 in.; Historical Atlas of Delaware County, Ohio, 1849-1963, 1 in.; 174th OVI, history (Civil War; address given by Gen. J. S. Jones in 1894), 1 folder; Library, minutes, 1898+, 18 in.   WM

219. Delaware County Historical Society
        157 East Williams, Delaware, Ohio 43015
        (614) 369-3831   (W, Sun 2-4:30)
        Zelda Hanhert, Director of the Museum

Berlin Township and Delaware County, history, 1957, 4 vols; Daughters of the American Revolution, Delaware City Chapter, records, 1960, 1 vol; Genealogy and local history materials, 1813+, 18 in. plus 1-1/2 rolls microfilm; Index to Baskin's History of Delaware County, 1948+, 7 vol; First Presbyterian Church, records, 1 roll microfilm; Miscellaneous correspondence and clipping files, 6 in.; Pioneers of Delaware County, Ohio, records, 1966, 1 vol.   FH

220. Methodist Theological School in Ohio (1960)
        P.O. Box 630, Delaware, Ohio 43015
        (614) 363-1146   (M-Th 8-10:30; F 8-4:30; Sat 9-12--when in session)
        John McTaggart, Director of Library

Reverend Philip Gatch (one of first ordained Methodist ministers in U.S.; Secretary to First Methodist Annual Conference), papers, 1774-1834, 1 lf. FH

221. Ohio Wesleyan University Library (1842)
        Beeghly Library, Delaware, Ohio 43015
        (614) 369-4431   (M-F 8-5; closed mid-June to Sept 1)
        John Reed, University Archivist

Cincinnati Conference Historical Society, records, 1894-1920, 1 vol; Henry William Crozier, papers, 1861-66, 6 in.; James B. Finley (preacher, missionary to Indians, prison chaplain), papers, including index, 1781-1856, 5 lf; Lee L. Grumbine (political writer), manuscripts, scrapbook, 1895-1903, 5 vols; G. H. Hartupee (businessman, philanthropist), papers (scrapbook of his writings, various programs of Methodist

Episcopal Church, No. Ohio Conference), 1857-89, 1 vol; Daniel Hitt (preacher), sermons, letters, 1800-1834, 1 lf; Bev Kelly (advance man for legitimate theater and circus), collection (letters, posters, programs, publicity material), 1910+, 12 map case drawers;

John Kobler (1790s, first Methodist minister in Ohio), typescript material from scrapbook of Samuel W. Williams, 1843, 1 vol; William Harris Logan (portrait painter and photographer), portraits, 19th century, 2 env; George W. Maley (preacher), papers (letters, diary), 1821-84, 3 in.; Frederick Merrick (college official, minister, fund raiser), papers, 1849-89, 1 vol; Methodist Episcopal Church in Ohio, journals, ledgers, scrapbooks, steward's reports, financial reports, 1811-1907, 15 lf; Methodist Episcopal Historical Comm., correspondence, ca. 1880+, 2 lf; Methodist Episcopal trials and investigations (investigation of Charles Fellows and John M. Life), 1898-1902, 6 in.;

Methodist historical vertical file (church name, circuit names, preachers, historical facts), ? - 1911, 2 lf; Edwin Parrott (aide to Gov. Todd, politician and farmer), letters, ca. 1843-68, 6 in.; Scrapbook by Methodist minister, 1858-1914, 1 vol with index; Sarah H. Similey scrapbook, 1873-74, 1 vol; Edwin Stanleybrass (missionary, traveled throughout Russia 1810-41), papers (journals, diaries, and letters), 1810-41, 6 in.; Edward Thompson (preacher and first president of O.W.U.), sermons, 1834-?, 4 vols;

J.S. Tomlinson (preacher), papers (sermons and lectures), ca. 1852, 1 folder; William F. Whitlock (O.W.U. faculty member; father of Brand Whitlock) diary, 1852-54, 1 vol; Walt Whitman papers (letters, postcards, poem drafts, correspondence between Whitman and friends), 1860-91, 6 lf; Samuel Wesley Williams (minister), "History of the General Conference of the M.E. Church," 1848-68, 1 vol; William George Williams (O.W.U. faculty and minister), scrapbook, 1861-74, 1 vol.   FH

INSTITUTIONAL RECORDS

222. Alpha Sigma Phi (1845)
        24 West Williams, Delaware, Ohio   43015
        (614) 363-1911   (M-F 9-5)
        Ralph F. Burns, Executive Secretary

Administrative records; Convention records; Correspondence; Financial records, 5-10 year retention; Lodges; Membership; Publications ("Tomahawk," fraternity magazine); Photographs; Minutes; all records, 1845+, 175 lf total.   FH

223. Chamber of Commerce, Delaware (1906)
    27 West Winter, Delaware, Ohio 43015
    (614) 363-1171 (M-F 9-5)
    Billy E. Cannon, Manager

Administrative records, 1906+, 1 folder; Agreements, ca. 1944+, 1 folder; Annual reports, 1959+, 1 folder; Financial statements, 1939+, 1 lf; Journals; Ledgers; Minutes, 1948+, 18 in.; Miscellaneous (studies, personnel records, history of chamber, internal correspondence, fund raising), 1938+, 4 lf; Publications (brochures, statistical records, industries, groups), ca. 1940+, 2 lf; Scrapbooks, 1947+, 2 vols and 1 folder; Tax records, 1939+, 1 folder. FH

224. Delaware County Agricultural Society (1938)
    60 North Franklin, Delaware, Ohio 43015
    (614) 362-2951, 362-3851 (Fair board open June 1-Nov 1, M-F 8-5)
    William Deal, Secretary

Administrative records, 1967; Annual reports, 1952+; Cashbooks, 1952+; Contracts, 1968+; Correspondence, 1-year retention; Financial statements, 1952+; Minutes, 1952+; Tax records, 1952+; 60 lf total. SF

225. Delaware County Rural Electric Co-operative (1936)
    26 North Union, Delaware, Ohio 43015
    (614) 363-2641 (M-F 8-5)
    Dale Ziegler, General Manager

Annual reports, 1936+; Correspondence, 5-year retention; Financial statements, 5-year retention; Legal records, 1936+, 4 lf; Minutes, 1936+, 2 lf; Publications ("Country Living"), 1961+; Receipts, 5-year retention; "Rural Electrification: A Case Study of the Delaware Rural Electric Cooperative," paper by an Ohio Wesleyan student; Tax records, 5-year retention. WM

226. Delaware Farmer's Exchange Association (1919)
    141 South Sandusky, Box 478, Delaware, Ohio 43015
    (614) 363-1301 (M-F 8-5; Sat 8-12)
    Carl E. Mehling, General Manager

Annual reports, 1925+, 3 in.; Deeds, 1919, 6 in.; Ledgers, 1960-72, 2 vols; Minutes, 1919+, 10 vols; Monthly newsletter, 1970+, 3 in.; Receipts (invoices, bills, receipts, scattered), 1962+, 40 lf; Tax records, 1957+, 3 in. SF

227. Farm Bureau Cooperative Association, Delaware (1934)
       224 East Williams, Box 368, Delaware, Ohio 43015
       (614) 263-1327   (M-F 8-5; Sat 8-12)
       Dale Bailey

Administrative records, 1934+; Annual reports, 1945?+; Correspondence, 1960?+, 1 lf; Financial records, 7-year retention; Minutes, 1934+, 2 lf. FH

228. Masonic Temple, Hiram #18 F and AM (1812)
       51 West William, P.O. Box 115, Delaware, Ohio 43015
       (614) 362-4961   (M-F 9-12)
       William J. Davis, Secretary

Administrative records (charter), 1813+; Agreements, 1962; Annual reports, 1813+; Cashbooks, 1813+; Contracts, 1962+; Deeds; Financial statements, 1813+; Ledgers, 1813+; Minutes, 1813+; Photographs; Proceedings, 1813+; Receipts, 5-year retention; Tax records, 1900+; 50 lf total. SF

229. Ohio Wesleyan University Archives (1842)
       Beehgly Library, Delaware, Ohio 43015
       (614) 369-4431   (M-F 8-5; closed mid-June to Sept 1)
       John Reed, University Archivist

Administrative papers, 1842+; Board of trustees, minutes; Current university records, 5-year retention, then sent to University Archives; Faculty minutes, 1842+; President's papers, 1842+; ca. 700 lf total. FH

230. WDLR Radio (1961)
       Route 521, Delaware, Ohio 43015
       (614) 363-1107   (M-F 8:30-4)
       Ron Allen, Program Director

Administrative records, 1961+; Annual reports, 1961+; Commercial copy, 1961+; Contracts, 1961+; Correspondence (primarily official with FCC), 1961+; Financial statements, 1961+; News broadcasts, typescripts, 1961+; News specials (some tapes), scattered; Religious programming tape, 1961+; Special program features, 1961+; Sound recordings, 1961+; 50 lf total. SF

231. William Street Methodist Church (1818)
    28 West William Street, Delaware, Ohio 43015
    (614) 363-4741   (M-F 9-3:30)
    Olatha Benson, Secretary

Attendance list, 1953+; Minutes, 1956+; Publications, 1951+, 21 in.
WM

ERIE COUNTY

MANUSCRIPTS

232. Erie County Historical Museum
    Sandusky Public Library, Sandusky, Ohio 44870
    (Hours by appointment)
    Mrs. William Hansen

General subject files on local history (filed by family name and subject),
10 lf; Historical houses records (early examples of architecture in Sandusky; photographs, drawings, and descriptions), 1818+, 2 lf; Johnson's
Island records (record of signatures of prisoners, photographs, maps,
drawings, diaries, published materials, and miscellaneous information);
Photographs (Sandusky, Erie County, Sandusky Bay, Johnson's Island,
steamboats, prominent citizens), 1830+; Young Men's Debating Society,
minutes and list of members, 1840-41, 1 vol. PY

233. Sandusky Library Association
    West Adams and Columbus Avenue, Sandusky, Ohio 44870
    (419) 625-3834   (M 9-6)
    A. Elizabeth Hankamer, Librarian

Art Study Club, minutes and registers, 1923-73, 2 lf; Daughters of the
American Revolution, minutes, yearbooks, 1897+, 4 lf; Hugo F. Engles
scrapbook of Sandusky (operas, plays, announcements, graduations, rec-
itations, 1882-92; Men of Sandusky, biographical information, 1895, 1
vol; Henry Oen Family record, 1835-1902, 1 vol; Soldier's diary, 1898,
1 vol; Union Bank of Sandusky, draft record, 1850-73; S.C. Wheeler, correspondence to political figures, 1898-1907, 1 vol. PY

INSTITUTIONAL RECORDS

234. Boy Scouts of America, Firelands Council
      416 Columbus Avenue, Sandusky, Ohio 44870
      (419) 625-4836   (M-F 8-12, 1-5)
      Gary Lehman, Scout Executive

Annual reports, 1939+; Camp development projects, 1950s, 1 folder;
Executive board, minutes, 1968+; Inactive troop rosters, 1940+, 6 lf;
Long-range planning goals, 1950s, 1 folder.   TS

235. Campfire Girls, Firelands Council (1924)
      416 Columbus Avenue, Sandusky, Ohio 44870
      (419) 625-8854   (M-F 8-5)
      Lillian Rossow, Executive Director

Board of directors, minutes, 1970+, 1 vol; Board of trustees, minutes,
1949+, 4 vols; Executive council, minutes, 1924-27, 1941-48, 2 vols;
Photographs, n.d., 2 vols; Scrapbooks, 1924+, 12 vols.   TS

236. Chamber of Commerce, Sandusky
      103 West Shoreline Drive, Sandusky, Ohio 44870
      (419) 625-6421   (M-F 9-5)
      G. Russell Bateson, Executive Manager

Correspondence, 1930+; Minutes, 1930+; Office files, 1930+; Reports,
1930+; Scrapbooks, 1930+.   PY

237. First Congregational United Church of Christ (1840s)
      431 Columbus Avenue, Sandusky, Ohio 44870
      (419) 625-8105
      Marion Bailey, Secretary

Church register, 1918+, 2 vols; Maps and drawings (construction of
the church), 1895-98; Minutes, Boards of deacons and trustees; 5 lf
total.   TS

238. First United Church of Christ (1852)
      East Jefferson and Hancock, Sandusky, Ohio 44870
      (419) 625-8247   (M-F 1-4)
      Don Hochstettler, Pastor

Successor to the First Reformed Church of Sandusky (1852-1924).

Church book (includes pastors' and membership lists, baptisms, confirmations, deaths), 1852+, 3 vols.   TS

239. Grace Episcopal Church
        315 Wayne Street, Sandusky, Ohio 44870
        (419) 625-6919   (Tu-F 8:30-12)
        Irene Siechel, Church Historian

Anti-Masonic manuscript (information on anti-Masonic persecution, and relation of men founding the church to the Sandusky Mason Lodge), n.d., 1 p; Grace Church history (centennial edition), 1935; Historical address, 1885; 100 years of music in Grace Church, TSS; Parish register, 1835-90, 2 vols; Photographs, 1893, 1910; Treasurer's records (rental of pews and expenditures), 1835-73, 2 vols;Vestry minutes, 1835-1921, 5 vols.   TS

240. Sts. Peter and Paul Catholic Church
        510 Columbus Avenue, Sandusky, Ohio 44870
        (419) 625-6655   (M-F 9-4)
        Mary L. Farrell, Secretary

Church registers, 1856+, 6 lf.   PY

241. Sandusky Library Association
        West Adams and Columbus Avenue, Sandusky, Ohio 44870
        (419) 625-3834   (M 9-6)
        A. Elizabeth Hankamer, Librarian

Cash journals, 1896+; Correspondence, 1970+; Minutes (includes accessions, financial reports, membership), 1891+, 3 lf.   PY

242. Trinity United Methodist Church (1818)
        East Jefferson and Wayne, Sandusky, Ohio 44870
        (419) 625-8669   (M-F 9-4)
        V. N. Bixler, Pastor

Board of trustees, minutes, 1879-1918, 1952+, 3 vols; Building Committee proceedings, 1917-23, 1 vol; Christian Endeavor Society, minutes, 1887-90, 1 vol; Dorcas Society, minutes, 1906-29, 3 vols; Official Board, minutes, 1907-50, 1959+, 5 vols; Pastor's record, 1847-

1915, 2 vols; Quarterly Conference records, 1866-82, 1956+, 2 vols; Trinity Men's Club, records, 1905-7, 1 vol.   TS

243. Zion Evangelical Lutheran Church (1853)
         Columbus and West Jefferson, Sandusky, Ohio 44870
         (419) 625-2112   (M-F 9-5)

Administrative records, 1853; Church registers, 1853+; Correspondence, 1969-73, 5 lf; Minutes, 1853+, 3 lf; Published histories, 1852-1952, 3 vols.   PY

FAIRFIELD COUNTY

MANUSCRIPTS

244. Fairfield County District Library (1834)
         Main and Broad, Lancaster, Ohio 43130
         (614) 653-2745   (M-F 9-9; Sat 9-6)
         Mina I. Kinnane, Director

Genealogy collection, 2 in.; Scrapbook (photos of the Boys' Industrial School), 59 photos.   WM

INSTITUTIONAL RECORDS

245. American Red Cross, Fairfield County Chapter (1917)
         121 West Mulberry, Lancaster, Ohio 43130
         (614) 653-0431   (M-F 8-5)
         Mrs. L. H. Glaab, Director of Volunteers

Administrative records; Annual reports, 1943+; Deeds to present site only; Minutes, 1947+, 4 notebooks; Scrapbooks (newspaper clippings and photographs), 1945+.   WM

246. Anchor-Hocking Glass Company (1906)
         109 North Broad Street, Lancaster, Ohio 43130
         (614) 653-3131   (M-F 8-5)
         Frank A. McLaughlin, Manager, Office Services

Administrative records, 1934+; Agreements, 1937+; Annual reports,1940+;
Blueprints, ca. 1920; Cashbooks, 1937+; Contracts, 1937+; Correspondence,
ca. 1930+; Daybooks, 1937+; Deeds, 1937+; Engineering records, ca. 1920;
Financial statements (quarterly), 1937+; Journals, 1937+; Ledgers, 1937+;

Maintenance records, 1931+; Minutes (board, committees), 1937+; Patents,
1906; Personnel records, 1925+; Pictures, people, company activities
(still and movies), 1913+; Production schedules, 3-year retention; Properties records, 1934+; Publication ("Anchorscope"), 1963?; Purchasing records, 8-year retention; Research and development files, 1961+; Stock purchase records, 1934+; Tax records, 1934+; 10,000 lf total.   SF

247. Chamber of Commerce, Lancaster Area (1948)
        Room 203, Kresge Building, Lancaster, Ohio 43130
        (614) 653-8251   (M-F 9-12, 1-5)
        Robert White, Manager

Administrative records, 1948-72, 1 in.; Annual reports, 1962-72, 1 in.;
Board of directors, minutes, 1950-72, 3 in.; Correspondence (members,
inquiries from businessmen in area), 1962-72, 6 in.; Financial records,
1962+, 3 lf; Plats (topical maps), 1950+, 100 maps; Proceedings (committee work and files), 1962-72; Scrapbooks (newspaper clippings, photographs); Tax records, 1962+.   WM

248. Community Action Program Commission (1967)
        201 South Broad Street, Lancaster, Ohio 43130
        (614) 653-4146   (M-F 8-5)
        Troy S. Holliday, Director

Administrative records, 1967+; Annual reports, 1970+; Contracts, 1967+;
Correspondence (between Federal, State, Regional, clients), 1967+; Family surveys, 1967+; Financial statements, 1967+; Minutes, board meetings
and advisory group, 1967+; Scrapbooks, 1970+; Tax records, 1967+; 32 lf
total.   WM

249. First Methodist Church (1812)
        High and Wheeling Streets, Lancaster, Ohio 43130
        (614) 653-3330   (M-F 9-5)
        George W. Herd, Minister

Annual reports (membership committee, etc.), 1945+, 1 lf; Cashbooks, 1946?+; Church register, 1898+, 1 lf; Correspondence (ministers), 1946+, 6 lf; Financial statements; Inventories, kept by insurance company; Ledgers, 1946?+, 1 lf; Members records, 1898+, 3 lf;
Minutes, ca. 1888+; Minister's sermons (kept on tapes), 1955+; Pictures, 1905+, 6 in.   FH

250. Kiwanis Club of Lancaster (1919)
        131 West Wheeling, Lancaster, Ohio 43130
        (614) 653-5217   (M-F 8:30-5)
        Ray L. Finley, Secretary

Administrative records, n.d.; Annual reports, 1945+; Attendance records, 1919+; By-laws, 1966; Club activity reports; Correspondence,
1945+; Financial statements, 1919+; Minutes, n.d.; Officers' record,
1919+; Publications (Weekly Bulletin, 1963+; Office monthly bulletin,
1919+, shows club meetings reports, membership total, attendance,
club activities); 14 lf total.   WM

251. Lancaster Board of Realtors, Inc. (1928)
        131 West Wheeling, Lancaster, Ohio 43130
        (614) 653-5217   (M-F 8:30-5)
        Ray L. Finley, Secretary-Treasurer

Dues statement (semi-annual, to state and national organization); Ledgers, 1958+; Membership list, 1958+, 34 pieces; Minutes, 1965+; Monthly newsletter, 1972+ (new publication).   WM

252. Lancaster-Fairfield County Hospital
        401 Ewing Street, Lancaster, Ohio 43130
        (614) 653-7521   (M-F 8-4:30)
        Walter Stewart, Administrator

Medical records, 1936+, 480 boxes microfilm and microfiche.   WM

253. NAACP, Lancaster (1969)
        P.O. Box 12, Lancaster, Ohio 43130
        (614) 653-1684   (M-F 7-9, 6-11)
        Grant Grogan, President

Annual reports, 1969-71; Cashbooks, 1969+; Correspondence with national office and Civil Rights Commission; Financial statements (sent to national office), 1969+; Journals, 1969+; Ledgers, 1969+; Minutes (record books), 1969, 1972; Plats, 1969; Receipts, 1969-72; Tax records (sent to national office annually).   WM

254. St. John's Episcopal Church (1848)
      222 North High, Lancaster, Ohio 43130
      (614) 653-3601   (M-F 9-2:30)
      George Rising, First Vice-President, Fairfield National Bank,
      143 W. Main

Canonical parish register (includes baptisms, confirmations, marriages, burials), 1879+, 6 in.; Financial statements, 1936+, 1 lf; Scrapbooks (letters and photos), 1847+; Sunday leaflets, 1960+; Women of St. John's, minutes, 1915-71; Vestry minutes (board of trustees), 1936+, 1 lf.   WM

255. United Appeal, Lancaster (1940)
      115 West Wheeling, Lancaster, Ohio 43130
      (614) 653-0643   (M-F 8:30-4:30)
      Lillian Abbott, Executive Secretary

Administrative records, 1940+; Board of directors, minutes, 1940+; Cashbooks, 1940+; Correspondence, 1940+; Financial statements, 1940+; Journals, 1940+; Member agency files, 1940+; Membership contracts, 1940+; Monthly statement reports, 1940+; Pledge record, 1962+; Scrapbooks (campaign and publicity), 1940+; Tax records, 1967+.   SF

256. YMCA, Lancaster (1928)
      465 West Sixth Avenue, Lancaster, Ohio 43130
      (614) 654-0616   (M-F 9-5)
      Dan Hester, General Secretary

Annual reports, 1960+; Financial statements, 1960+; Membership list, 1960+; Minutes, 1928+; Newsletter (average 4 per year; unscheduled publication); Participation Committee reports (included in the annual report), 1960+.   WM

MANUSCRIPTS

257. Carnegie Public Library (1903)
        127 South North Street, Washington Court House, Ohio 43160
        (614) 335-2540   (M-W, F 9-8; Th 9-12; Sat 9-6)
        Gladys Strevey, Librarian

May M. Duffee (Washington C.H. writer, businesswoman), As I Re-
member (autobiography), 1953, bound book; Library scrapbook (clippings, photos, letters), 1956-70, 4 in. WM

258. Fayette County Historical Society
        (M-F 8-5)
        Kenneth Craig, President

Movie film, Jefferson Turnpike, 15 min.; Slides: Evolution of the automobile, 1897-1932, 160 sl; History of Fayette County (historic spots),
200 sl; Old homes of Fayette County, 100 sl; Old schools of Fayette
County, 200 sl; Sesquicentennial of 1960, 200 sl. WM

INSTITUTIONAL RECORDS

259. Chamber of Commerce, Washington C. H. (1938)
        147 South Fayette, Washington Court House, Ohio 43160
        (614) 335-2761   (M-F 8:30-5)
        James Dunn, Executive Vice-President

Annual reports (programs, letters, etc.), 1969+, 3 in.; "Better Business Beacon" (newsletter), 1969, 1 vol; Boards of directors and trustees, minutes, 1938+, 15 in.; City of Washington C.H. codified ordin-
ances, 1955, 1958, 1 vol; Correspondence, 1-year retention, 3 in.; Financial statements (treasurer's reports), 1969+, 3 in.; Ledgers, accounts, 1965+, 1 vol; Receipts for paid bills, 1969+, 2 lf. WM

260. Fayette County Memorial Hospital (1950)
        Columbus Road, Washington Court House, Ohio 43160
        (614) 335-1210   (M-F)
        Mrs. Cary Whitaker, In-Service Director

Administrative records, 1948-50, 10 vols; Annual reports, 1960+;
Correspondence, 1969+, 14 lf; Medical records, 120 lf; Minutes (in-
service materials, board and medical staff), 1954, 50 vols; Scrapbooks, 1950+, 2 vols. FH

261. First Baptist Church (1840)
     North and East Streets, Washington Court House, Ohio 43160
     (614) 335-0429   (M-F 8-5)
     Ralph Wolford, Pastor

Advisory council, minutes, 1947-56, 3 in.; Annual reports, 1966-72,
6 in.; Baptist Young People's Union, membership rolls and minutes,
1896-1910, 2 in.; Financial records, 1909-72, 1 lf; Minutes, 1840-95,
1952-72, 4 in.; Missionary offerings record, 1 notebook; Universal
church record, 1887-1918, ca. 1930-50, 4 in.; Women's Missionary
Society, finances and correspondence, 1888-98, 1902-6, 2 in.; World
Wide Guild, minutes and treasurer's report, 1921-31, 2 in. WM

262. Mothers' Circle (1917)
     1276 Dayton Avenue, Washington Court House, Ohio 43160
     (614) 335-1847
     Ann Lynch, President

Account book of teenage club, 1945, 1 vol; Constitution; Minutes (program records, membership lists, newspaper clippings, minutes, annual reports), 1923+, 6 vols; Publications (yearbooks, constitution,
officers' meetings), 1946+, 3 in.; Treasurer's reports, 1938+, 2 vols.
SF

263. WCHO Radio (1952)
     1535 North North, Washington Court House, Ohio 43160
     (614) 335-0941   (M-F 9-5; Sat 9-12)
     Robert Lutz, Station Manager

Administrative records, 1951, 1 item; Cashbooks, 1971+, 2 vols;
Correspondence, 1967+, 2 lf; FCC regulation material, 6 in.; Financial statements, 1952+, 1 folder; Newscasts, 1969+, 30 lf; Receipts,
1967+, 1 folder; Sales contracts, 1962+, 8 lf; Tax records, 1969+, 1
lf. SF

FRANKLIN COUNTY

MANUSCRIPTS

264. Capital University Library (1850)
     2199 East Main Street, Columbus, Ohio 43209
     (614) 236-6011   (M-F 8-10)
     Albert Maag, Director of Library

Lois Lenski (writer of children's books, the Mr. Small stories), collection, 1930s, 3 lf and 7 tape reels.   FH

265. Columbus Public Library (1873)
        96 South Grant, Columbus, Ohio 43215
        (614) 461-6580   (M-F 8:30-9; Sat 8:30-5:30)
        Samuel Roshon, Head, Columbus and Ohio Division

Miscellaneous collection arranged by Columbus, Franklin County, and
Ohio, 20 lf; Newspaper clippings on Ohio authors, art and sculpture,
business, plays, 1915-60, 6 lf; Photographs of Columbus, 1910-35, 3
in.; Carl Butler Shedd and John W. Noble, scrapbooks, 1890-92, 18 in.
WM

266. Franklin County Historical Society (1948)
        280 East Broad Street, Columbus, Ohio 43215
        (614) 221-7487   (M-Sat 9-4:30; Sun 1-5:30)
        Daniel F. Prugh, Director

Film library, 1930s-70s, 10 lf; Photographs of Columbus and Franklin
County, 1842+, 2 lf; Photographs of covered bridges, 1 lf; Photographs
of stage and show people, 1870-1920, 4 lf.   EH

267. Ohio Historical Society (1885)
        Interstate 71 and 17th Avenue, Columbus, Ohio 43211
        (614) 466-2060   (M-Sat 9-5)
        Patricia Gatherum, Chief Reference Librarian

See Andrea Lentz, A Guide to Manuscripts at the Ohio Historical Society, 1972. For the society's accessions since 1972 see the Ohio
Archivist.

268. Otterbein College Library (1847)
        Otterbein College, Westerville, Ohio 43081
        (614) 882-3601   (M-F 7:45-10; Sat 9-5; Sun 2-10; during academic
        year - other times 8-5)
        John Becker, Head Librarian

Almanac collection, 1803-23; Blendon Township, clerk's record, 1815-
58; Benjamin R. Hanby collection, ca. 25 items; Evangelical Church

conferences collection (records of sixty conferences), 1868-1956; Mt. Pleasant College board of trustees, minutes, 1849-56; Ohio College Association, records, 1867-99, 2 vols; Scrapbooks of press clippings, 1930-43, 11 vols; Vertical files, filed under 450 subject areas; YMCA records, 1892+; YWCA records, 1892+.   SF

269. Westerville Historical Society (ca. 1940)
        Public Library, Westerville, Ohio 43081
        (614) 882-4996   (Hours by appointment)
        Robert Price, Secretary

Blacksmith's account books, 1842-57, 1 in.; Central College, home-coming records, 1925-35, 1 in.; R.M. Cook, daybook, 1835-38, 1 in.; Cornell family, scrapbook, ca. 1860, 2 in.; Creamer family, genealogy, accounts, 1880-1901, 2 in.; Local history material,gathered by Blendon Junior High School Historical Society, 7 lf; Nonpariel, minutes, 1918-29, 6 in.; School funds account book, 1839-57, 1 in.; PTA Secretary's books and charter, 1924-36, 1 in.; Public library scrapbook, 1930-46, 3 in.; Westerville Adolescent Study Group, 1934-35, 1 in.; Westerville Historical Society records, ca. 1940+, 3 in.; "Youths Companion," children's publication, 1884-1904, 1 in.   FH

INSTITUTIONAL RECORDS

270. American Lutheran Church--Ohio District
        57 East Main Street, Columbus, Ohio 43215
        (614) 221-4366   (M-F 8-5)
        Clara Haberman, Secretary to the President

National archives located at Wartburg Theological Seminary, Dubuque, Iowa.

District congregational files, 1950-71, 12 lf; Publications, 1915-71, 7 lf; Statistical reports, 1948-71, 5 lf.   EH

271. The Asphalt Institute (1927)
        50 West Broad Street, Columbus, Ohio 43215
        (614) 224-3265   (M-F 9-5)
        Robert A. Wilkinson, Regional Engineer

Promotion and research agency for national asphalt companies.

Correspondence, 2-year retention; Financial records, 7-year retention; Legal records, 1927-70; Minutes, 1927-70; Publications, 1960-70; 100 lf total.   EL

272. Better Business Bureau, Columbus (1921)
        71 East State Street, Columbus, Ohio 43215
        (614) 221-6336   (M-F 9-5)
        Edward L. Hughes, President

Administrative records, 1921+, 144 lf; Index cards to records, 64 lf; Membership lists, 5 lf; Publications, 1951+, 6 in.; Scrapbooks, 1943+, 4 in.   WM

273. Big Bear Stores (1934)
        770 Goodale Boulevard, Columbus, Ohio 43212
        (614) 221-5361   (M-F 8-5)
        Michael Knilans, Vice-President, Sales

Central Ohio retail grocery store chain.

Advertisements, 1934+, 6 lf; Annual reports, 1953+, 1 lf; Movement of sales, 1960+, 2 lf; Newsletter, current, 1 lf; Photographs, 1934+, 2 lf; Scrapbooks, 1934+, 6 in.; Speeches of the president, 1966+, 1 lf; Tax records, 1965+; Trade publications, scattered, 6 in.   EH

274. Borden, Inc. (1857)
        50 West Broad Street, Columbus, Ohio 43215
        (614) 461-4472   (M-F 8:30-5)
        Bert Beaupre, Manager of Administration and Graphics, Public Affairs Department

National corporate headquarters of Borden, Inc.

Borden memorabilia, 1857+, 14 lf; Certificates and registers, 1930-70, 6 in.; Elgin Milk Condensing Co., records, 1865-69, 1 vol; Photographs and plant illustrations, 10 lf; Public relations memos, 1950-60, 1 lf; Published material on Borden's history, 1930-70, 2 lf; Scrapbooks, 1930-70, 6 in.   EH

275. Capital University Archives (1850)
        2199 East Main Street, Columbus, Ohio 43209
        (614) 236-6011   (M-F 8-10, when in session)
        Albert Maag, Director of Library

Boards of trustees and regents, minutes, 1930-50, 1 lf; Committee records, 1936-39, 1 lf; Faculty minutes, 1850-1946, 5 vols; Oaths taken to rules and conduct, 1872-97, 2 vols; Photographs, 6 in.; Planning and construction notes, 1957-67, 1 lf; Presidents' correspondence, 1919-69,10 lf; Presidents' reports to regents, 1913-61, 3 lf; Record book, class standings, 1897-1905, 1 vol; Professor E. Schmidt's Greek and Roman mythology class notes, 1869, 1 vol; Scrapbooks on Capital University, 1877-1912, 1927-60, 12 lf; Transcripts, 1926-28, 1 folder; Treasurers' reports, 1941-57, 2 in.
FH

276. Catholic Social Services
        197 East Gay Street, Columbus, Ohio 43215
        (614) 221-5891   (M-F 9-5)
        Fr. Bernard McClory, Director

Catholic Social Services handles social welfare of the Diocese; sixteen other offices in diocese handle other aspects of diocese affairs, each with own office and records.

Administrative records, 1940s+, 8 lf; Case records, 1940+, 15 lf; Research records, 1940+, 8 lf.   EL

277. Center of Science and Industry (1964)
        280 East Broad Street, Columbus, Ohio 43215
        (614) 228-6361   (M-Sat 9-4:30; Sun 1-5:30)
        William Schmitt, Director of Education

The Center of Science and Industry is administered by the Franklin County Historical Society. Its emphasis is on science and health materials and it functions as a quasi-museum institution.

National Aeronautics and Space Administration, file, 1950+, 8 lf.
EH

278. Central Presbyterian Church (1839)
        132 South Third Street, Columbus, Ohio 43215
        (614) 224-9119   (M-F 9-4)
        William L. Meyer, Pastor

Financial statements, 1955+, 1 lf; Membership records, 1839+; Minutes, 1839+, 18 in.; Miscellaneous, 1960+, 3 lf.   WM

279. Chamber of Commerce, Ohio (1893)
    17 South High Street, Columbus, Ohio 43215
    (614) 228-4201   (M-F 9-5)
    Kenneth L. Drum, Director, Publicity and Information

Administrative records, 1893-1970; Annual reports, 1893+; Correspondence, 1893+; Financial records, 1893+; Legal records, 1893+; Minutes, 1893+; Proceedings, 1893+; Publications, 1893+; Research reports, 1924+; Scrapbooks, 1893+; 2,000 lf total.   EL

280. Chamber of Commerce, Westerville Area (1967)
    5 West College, Westerville, Ohio 43081
    (614) 882-8917   (M-F 9-5:30)
    Mary Ruth Beeney, Executive Secretary

Administrative records, 1967+, 1 folder; Bulletins, 1968+, 6 in.; Committee records, 1968+, 3 in.; Correspondence, 1967+, 1 lf; Financial statements, monthly, 1967+, 3 in.; Minutes, 1967+, 1 folder; News releases, 1968+, 1 folder; Publications, 1971+; Receipts, 1967+, 3 in.; Tax records, personnel employment, 1967+, 3 in.; Treasurer's reports, 1 folder.   FH

281. Church of God, District Offices (1886)
    1014 Frebis, Columbus, Ohio 43206
    (614) 443-4625   (M-F 8-4:30)
    L. H. Aultman, State Supervisor

Church archives located at Cleveland, Tennessee.

Administrative records; Attendance and Sunday School records; Comparative statistics; Deeds; District Council minutes; General Assembly of the church minutes; Monthly reports; Tax records; 48 lf total.   EH

282. Church of the Messiah United Methodist (1818)
    51 North State Street, Westerville, Ohio 43081
    (614) 882-2167   (M-F 8:30-3)
    Ralph Shunk, Minister

Board of Trustees, minutes, 1909-18, 2 in.; Church register, 1863+, 2 lf; Financial records, 1898-1942, 6 in.; Publications, 1919-23, 1931-35, 1952, 7 in.; Quarterly conference records, 1861-1907, 18 in.; Women's organizations, 1898, 1 lf.   FH

283. Church of the Nazarene, District Offices (1910)
  2708 Morse Road, Columbus, Ohio 43229
  (614) 475-1730 (M-F 9-12)
  Harvey S. Galloway, District Superintendent

Annual reports, 1910+, 4 lf. EH

284. Citizen's Research
  44 East Broad Street, Columbus, Ohio 43215
  (614) 221-4459 (M-F 9-5)

A private organization studying problems of community interest.

Administrative records, 1935+, 2 lf; Minutes, 1935+, 2 lf; Publications, 1950s+, 2 lf; Research reports by CR on Columbus and Franklin County urban problems, 1947+, 3 lf. EL

285. City National Bank (1905)
  100 East Broad Street, Columbus, Ohio 43215
  (614) 461-8987 (M-F 9-5)
  Ray McIver, Assistant for Public Relations

Administrative records, 1905-70; Agreements, 1905-70; Annual reports, 1905-70; Financial records, 1905-70; Minutes, 1905-70; Publications, 1965-70. EL

286. Columbus Academy (1911)
  4300 Cherry Bottom Road, Gahanna, Ohio 43306
  (614) 475-2311 (M-F 9-5)
  Richard Putnam, Headmaster

Private boys' school, grades 1-12.

Administrative records, 1940s+, 20 lf; Annual reports, 1911+, 1 lf; Correspondence, 1911+, 2 lf; Minutes, 1911+, 1 lf; Proceedings, 1911+, 2 lf; Publications, 1940s+, 15 lf; Students' records, 1911+, 17 lf. EL

287. Columbus Auto Dealers Association (1946)
  209 South High Street, Columbus, Ohio 43215
  (614) 221-2544 (M-F 9-5)
  Esther Dern, Executive Secretary

Administrative records, 1946+; Correspondence, 5-year retention;
Financial records, 7-year retention; Legal records, 1946+; Minutes, 1946+; Publications, 2-year retention; Scrapbooks and memorabilia, 1946+; 100 lf total.   EL

288. Columbus Bar Association (1869)
        40 South Third Street, Columbus, Ohio 43215
        (614) 221-4112   (M-F 9-5)
        Judy Stutthoff, Executive Secretary

Administrative records, 1869-1970; Bar directory, 1951-70; Correspondence, 7-year retention; Financial records, 7-year retention;
Historical file, 1869-1970; Legal records, 1869-1970; Minutes, 1869-
1970; Publications, 1945-70; 300 lf total.   EL

289. Columbus Beaux Arts (1947)
        480 East Broad Street, Columbus, Ohio 43215
        (614) 221-6801
        Mrs. James Bagley, President

Fund raising auxiliary of the Columbus Gallery of Fine Arts.

Correspondence, 1970-72, 6 in.; Minutes, 1949-72, 1 lf; Publications,
1949-72, 6 in.; Scrapbooks, 1949-72, 3 lf.   EL

290. Columbus Call & Post (1964)
        721 East Long Street, Columbus, Ohio 43215
        (614) 224-8123   (M-F 9-5)
        Amos Lynch, Editor

A black newspaper with the home office in Cleveland.

Administrative records, 1964+; Financial records, 1964+; Legal records and other legal data, 1964+; Minutes, 1964+; Photograph files,
1964+; Research files, 1964+; 300 lf total.   EL

291. Columbus Civic Ballet Association, Inc. (1959)
        16 East Broad Street, Room 1300, Columbus, Ohio 43215
        (614) 464-3529   (Tu, Th, 10-2)
        Mrs. Cecil Sansbury, Business Manager

Business records, 1968+; History, 1959-69; Programs, 1959-70; Scrapbooks, 1959-70; 15 lf total.   EL

292. Columbus Convention Bureau (1956)
        50 West Broad Street, Columbus, Ohio 43215
        (614) 221-6623   (M-F 9-5)
        John L. DeLong, Vice-President, Sales and Service

Administrative records; Correspondence, 2-year retention; Financial records, 7-year retention; Legal records, 7-year retention; Minutes, 1956+; Programs, 1945+; 100 lf total.   EL

293. Columbus Film Council (1950)
        83 South High Street, Columbus, Ohio 43215
        (614) 228-8840   (M-F 9-4)
        Mary Rupp, Executive Secretary

Financial records, 1-year retention; Minutes, 1-year retention; Movie films, 1965+, 20 ft; Publications, 1950-70; 80 lf total.   EL

294. Columbus Foundation (1944)
        100 East Broad Street, Suite 1104, Columbus, Ohio 43215
        (614) 469-6220   (M-F 9-4)
        Richard Heer Oman, Director

Foundation to administer private and corporate trust funds, endowments, etc., subject filing system.

Administrative records, 1920s+; Agreements, 1920+; Annual reports, 1920+; Correspondence, 1945+; Financial records, 1920+; Minutes, 1920s+; Proceedings, 1920+; Publications, 1960+; 250 lf total.   EL

295. Columbus Metropolitan Area Church Board (1958)
        290 South High Street, Columbus, Ohio 43215
        (614) 228-5515   (M-F 9-5)
        N. H. VanderWert, Executive Director

Annual reports, 1958+; Correspondence, 1920+; Financial records, 1958+; Legal records, 1958+; Minutes, 1958+; Publications, 1960+; Reference files, 1890s-1958; 100 lf total.   EL

296. Columbus School for Girls (1898)
      56 South Columbia, Bexley, Ohio 43209
      (614) 253-5587   (M-F 9-3)
      John V. Chapman, Headmaster

A private girls' school, grades 1-12.

Alumni newsletter, 1945+, 6 in.; Alumni records, 1898+, 17 lf; Board
of trustees, minutes, 1912+; Folders on pupils, 1898+, 16 lf; Literary
magazine, 1927+, 1 lf; Permanent record cards, 1898+, 15 lf; School
catalogs, 1907-29, 8 in.; Testing materials, current, 18 lf; Yearbooks,
1911+, 3 lf. EH

297. Columbus and Southern Ohio Electric Company
      215 North Front Street, Columbus, Ohio 43215
      (614) 228-6411   (M-F 8-5)
      H. H. Trumbo, Manager

Administrative records, 1900+, 3 lf; Annual reports, 1900+, 3 lf; Correspondence, 1900+, 3 lf; Market research files, 1940s+, 20 lf; Minutes,
1900+, 3 lf; Proceedings, 1900+, 3 lf; Publications, 1937+, 30 lf. EL

298. Columbus Symphony Orchestra (1951)
      100 East Broad Street, Columbus, Ohio 43215
      (614) 224-3291   (M-F 9-5)
      G. Greenburg, Manager

Records are not centralized in one location.

Annual reports, 1951+, 2 lf; Committee records, 1951+, 2 lf; Financial
records, 2 lf; Minutes, 1951+, 5 lf; Proceedings, 1951+, 5 lf; Public
relations literature, 1951+, 2 lf; Records of Women's Association, 1951+,
3 lf; Written history, 1951+, 1 vol. EL

299. Columbus Transit Company (1948)
      43 West Long Street, Columbus, Ohio 43215
      (614) 228-3831   (M-F 8-5)
      Thomas A. Hammon, General Superintendent

Administrative records, 1948+, 5 lf; Annual reports, 1948+, 1 lf; Contracts, 1948+, 2 lf; Financial records, 1948+, 1 lf; Market analyses,
1948+, 15 lf; Minutes, 1948+, 5 lf; Photographs, 1900+, 2 lf; Records

of earlier companies. EL

300. Greenlawn Cemetery Association (1848)
    1000 Greenlawn Avenue, Columbus, Ohio 43223
    (614) 444-1123   (M-F 9-4)
    Mr. Sloane, Director

Card catalog and register.

Cemetery records, 1848+, 120,000 cards; Greenlawn Cemetery Association records, 1848+.   EL

301. Hilliard First Baptist Church (1954)
    75 East Main, Hilliard, Ohio 43026
    (614) 876-6738   (M-F 9-5)
    J. W. Bargiol, Pastor

Annual reports, 1956+, 1 lf; Membership records, 1956+, 18 in.;
Minutes, 1956+, 1 lf; Sunday school statistics, 1954+, 3 in.; Women's
Missionary Unit, 1956+, 1 notebook.   EH

302. Hilliard United Methodist Church (1842)
    205 Scioto and Darby Creek, Hilliard, Ohio 43026
    (614) 876-2403   (M-F 9-5)
    Raymond K. Bradley, Lay Leader

Administrative records; Annual reports; Board of trustees, minutes,
1851+; Church register, 1851+; Publications, 1851+; Scrapbooks,
1920-60.   EH

303. Hilliard United Presbyterian Church (1960)
    3250 Leap Road, Hilliard, Ohio 43026
    (614) 876-7121   (Tu, F 8-12:30)
    Rowland White, Interim Pastor

Administrative records, 1959+, 6 in.; Annual reports, 1960+, 6 in.;
Building campaign, 1960, 1 in.; Deeds, 1959, 1 in.; Guest registers,
1960+, 3 in.; Publications, 1961+, 3 in.; Scrapbooks, 1957, 2 in.;
Session minutes, 1959+, 8 in.; Stewardship drive, 1969, 1 in.; Treasurer's report, 1959+, 3 in.   EH

304. Huntington National Bank (1866)
      18 South High Street, Columbus, Ohio 43215
      (614) 469-7010   (M-F 9-4)
      Harriet Bracken, Director of Marketing and Public Relations

Accounts and trust information; Administrative records; Annual reports, 1866+; Memorabilia file, 8 lf; Publications, 1866+; Research
files. EL

305. Jeffrey Galion America's Corporation
      100 East Broad Street, Columbus, Ohio 43215
      (614) 421-3513   (M-F 8-5)
      Gene Krause, Vice-President of Personnel

Large, international mining machinery manufacturing firm based in
Columbus.

Administrative records; Annual reports; Contracts, 1920+; Deeds;
Early product catalogs, 1890s; Lantern slides, 1880s; Minutes, 1920+;
Patents, 1877+. EH

306. Jewish Welfare Council
      40 South Third Street, Columbus, Ohio 43215
      (614) 237-7917   (M-F 9-5)
      Mrs. Harry Schwartz, Executive Secretary

A coordinating agency for other Jewish service agencies.

Administrative records, 1920+, 1 lf; Annual reports, 1920+, 1 lf;
Case records, 1930s+; Correspondence, 1920+, 1 lf; Minutes, 1920+,
1 lf; Proceedings, 1920+, 1 lf; Research records, 1930s+, 7 lf; Summaries of composite agencies, 1950s+, 12 lf. EL

307. John W. Galbreath Company (1924)
      100 East Broad Street, Columbus, Ohio 43215
      (614) 224-1106   (M-F 9-5)
      Victor Turf, Personnel Director

An international property development firm.

Financial records, 1924+, 30 lf; Galbreath's personal files, 1924+,
50 lf; Legal records, 1924+; Publicity files, 1949+, 2 lf; Scrap-

books, 1924+, 7 lf; Tax records, 1924+, 5 lf; Transaction files, 1924+, 100 lf.   EL

308. Landmark, Inc. (1934)
        245 North High Street, Columbus, Ohio 43216
        (614) 221-1141   (M-F 8-4:45)
        John R. Moore, Vice-President, Secretary-Treasurer

Administrative records, 1934+, 1 in.; Agreements, contracts, leases, 12 lf; Annual reports, 1934+, 2 lf; Correspondence, 1968+, 20 lf; Financial records, 1934+, 4 lf; Minutes, 1934+, 6 lf; Proceedings, 1934+, 2 lf; Publications, 1961+; Tax records, 1934+.   WM

309. Mid-Ohio Regional Planning Commission (1969)
        514 South High Street, Columbus, Ohio 43215
        (614) 228-2663   (M-F 9-5)
        Harmon Merwin, Director

A quasi-governmental planning agency for central Ohio.

Agreements and other legal records, 1959+; Annual reports, 1959+; Correspondence, 1959+; Financial records, 1959+; Maps, 1949+; Minutes, 1959+; Publications, 1959+; Reports, 1949+; Research files, 1959+; 4,000 lf total.   EL

310.   National Association of Social Workers, Central Ohio Council
        of Chapters (1965)
        88 East Broad Street, Columbus, Ohio 43215
        (614) 228-4698   (M-F 9-5)
        Gene P. King, Executive Secretary

Coordinating agency for eight local chapters of NASW.

Annual reports, 1965+; Correspondence, 2-year retention; Financial records, 1965+; Legal records, 1965+; Minutes, 1965+; 10 lf total.   EL

311. New Albany Savings and Loan (1967)
        155 West Main Street, New Albany, Ohio 43054
        (614) 855-1454   (M-F 9:30-2:30)
        C. H. Cring, President

Administrative records, 1967+, 1 in.; Annual reports, 1967+, 1 lf;
Cashbooks, 1967+, 1 lf; Certificates of deposit, 1967, 9 in.; Correspondence, 2-year retention, 2 lf; Daybooks, 1967+, 15 in.; Journals,
1967+, 1 in.; Ledgers, 1967+, 2 in.; Minutes, 1967+, 1 in.; Publications, 1967, 1 in.; Tax records, 400 file cards.   FH

312. Ohio Bakers Association (1906)
        83 South High Street, Columbus, Ohio 43215
        (614) 224-6075   (M-F 9-5)
        William O'Neill, Executive Secretary

Correspondence, 1966+; Financial records, 1921+; Legal data, 1921+;
Minutes, 1921+; Publications, 1950+; 50 lf total.   EL

313. Ohio Bankers Association (1891)
        33 North High Street, Columbus, Ohio 43215
        (614) 221-5121   (M-F 9-5)
        Virginia Wolf

A professional association which provides advice and consultation
and does research for members; card catalog.

Correspondence, 1900+; Minutes, 1900+; Photographs, 1900+; Publications, 1900+; Reports and analyses, 1900+; 175 lf total.   EL

314. Ohio Farm Bureau Federation (1919)
        245 North High Street, Columbus, Ohio 43216
        (614) 221-1141   (M-F 8-4:45)
        Nedia Freitag, Assistant Secretary of Board

Administrative records, 1919+, 1 lf; Annual reports, 1965+, 2 in.;
Contracts, 1933+, 1 lf; Correspondence, 3-year retention, 5 lf; Deeds,
1941+, 2 in.; Financial statements, 1920+, 1 lf; Minutes, 1919+, 20 lf;
Policy records, 1929+, 18 in.; Proceedings, 1919+, 1 lf; Scrapbooks,
1962+, 2 in.; Stock certificates; Tax records, 1919+.   FH

315. Ohio Funeral Directors Association (1881)
        50 West Broad Street, Columbus, Ohio 43215
        (614) 228-2037   (M-F 9-5)
        Zorma Bishop, Executive Secretary

Administrative records, 1881+; Annual reports, 1881+; Financial records, 1881+; Legal records, 1881+; Minutes, 1881+; Publications, 1937+;80 lf total.   EL

316. Ohio Hospital Association (1914)
        88 East Broad Street, Columbus, Ohio 43215
        (614) 221-7614   (M-F 9-5)
        Bruce J. Carter, Associate Director

Lobbying agent for member hospitals.

Administrative records, 1914+; Annual reports, 1950+; Financial records, 7-year retention; Legal records, 7-year retention; Minutes, 1914+; Publications, 1960+; Scrapbooks and memorabilia, 1914+; 600 lf total.   EL

317. Ohio Jewish Chronicle (1942)
        87 North Sixth Street, Columbus, Ohio 43215
        (614) 224-7206   (M-F 9-5)
        Milton Pinsky, Editor

Administrative records, 1942+;Correspondence, 3-year retention; Financial records, 7-year retention; Legal records, 7-year retention; Minutes, 1942+; News background files,1942+; Newspapers, 1942+;Photograph files, 1942+; Reference files, 1942+; 200 lf total.   EL

318. Ohio Manufacturers' Association (1910)
        100 East Broad Street, Columbus, Ohio 43215
        (614) 224-5111   (M-F 9-5)
        William Costello, Public Liaison Officer

Lobbying organization for Ohio businesses.

Annual reports, 1910+; Correspondence, 1932+; Financial statements,1910+; Legal records, 1910+; Minutes, 1910+; Publications, 1910+; Tax records, 1910+.   EL

319. Ohio Municipal League (ca. 1920)
        60 East Broad Street, Columbus, Ohio 43215
        (614) 221-4349   (M-F 9-5)
        John Gotherman, Research Director

Subject files, 1920+, 80 lf.   EL

320. The Ohio National Bank (1893)
        51 North High Street, Columbus, Ohio 43215
        (614) 221-2211   (M-F 9-5)
        W. A. Anderson, Vice-President

Administrative records, 1893+; Agreements, 1893+; Annual reports,
1945+; Cashbooks, 1893+; Certificates, 1893+; Contracts, 1893+; Correspondence, 1893+; Daybooks, 1893+; Deeds, 1893+; Financial statements, 1893+; Inventories, 1893+; Journals, 1893+; Ledgers, 1893+;
Market research data, 1965+; Minutes, 1893+; Photos, 1893+; Receipts,
1893+; Scrapbooks, 1893+; Tax records, 1893+; 1,000 lf total. EL

321. Ohio Psychiatric Association (1958)
        88 East Broad Street, Columbus, Ohio 43215
        (614) 228-4698   (M-F 9-5)
        Gene P. King, Executive Secretary

Annual reports, 1958+; Correspondence, 4-year retention; Financial
records, 7-year retention; Legal records, 7-year retention; Minutes,
1958+; Scrapbooks, 1958+; 20 lf total. EL

322. Ohio Savings and Loan League
        88 East Broad Street, Columbus, Ohio 43215
        (614) 224-6243   (M-F 9-5)
        D. Oakley, Research Director

Correspondence, 1895+, 3 lf; Minutes, 1895+, 3 lf; Proceedings,
1895+, 3 lf; Publications, 1945+, 15 lf. EL

323. Ohio State Automobile Association (1906)
        100 East Broad Street, Columbus, Ohio 43215
        (614) 228-1524   (M-F 9-5)
        A. D. Priore, Executive Assistant

State AAA organization.

Administrative records, 1906+, 2 lf; Annual reports, 1906+, 2 lf;
Correspondence, 1960+; Financial records, 1963+, 10 lf; Legal
records, 1963+, 10 lf; Membership records, 1906+, 10 lf; Minutes,
1906+, 2 lf; Publications, 1968+, 3 lf; Research files, 1960s, 15 lf.
EL

324. Ohio State Bar Association (1880)
        33 West 11th Avenue, Columbus, Ohio 43201
        (614) 421-2121   (M-F 8:30-5)
        Joseph Miller, Director

Administrative records, 1880+; Annual reports, 1910+, 1 lf; Correspondence, 3-year retention; Ledgers, 1930+; Legal files; Minutes, 1910+, 6
lf; Publications, 1880+, 2 lf; Scrapbooks; Tax records, 1919+, 1 lf.   FH

325. Ohio State University Archives (1961)
        Hitchcock Hall, Ohio State University, Columbus, Ohio 43210
        (614) 422-2409   (M-F 8-5)
        William Vollmar, University Archivist

Biographical file, 1873-1970, 6 lf; Board of trustees, records, 1905-60,
31 lf; Centennial celebration, 1965-71, 5 lf; College of Administrative
Sciences, 1962-69, 2 lf; College of Agriculture and Home Economics,
1905-70, 209 lf; College of Fine Arts, 1906-70, 15 lf; College of Arts and
Sciences, 1896-1967, 29 lf; College of Biological Sciences, 1876-1965, 11
lf; College of Commerce and Administration, 1909-69, 6 lf; College of
Education, 1923-65, 100 lf; College of Engineering, 1950-69, 17 lf; College of Humanities, 1934-69, 11 lf; College of Law, 1926-66, 12 lf;

College of Mathematics and Physical Sciences, 1873-1948, 1 lf; College
of Medicine, 1843-1964, 43 lf; College of Pharmacy, 1932-65, 6 lf; College of Social and Behavioral Sciences, 1923-69, 12 lf; College of Veterinary Medicine, 1933-55, 1 lf; Committees and Councils, 1873-1971, 68
lf; Director of Athletics, 1895-1970, 40 lf; Director of Libraries, 1873-
1951, 14 lf; Division of Academic Affairs and Provost, 1947-69, 49 lf;
Division of Administrative Operations, 1881-1968, 33 lf; Division of Business and Finance, 1880-1971, 88 lf;

Division of Educational Services, 1895-1970, 75 lf; Division of Regional
Campuses, 1957-68, 5 lf; Division of Research, 1912-66, 4 lf; Division
of Student Affairs, 1895-1970, 135 lf; Division of University Development, 1878-1970, 4 lf; Executive Assistant to the President, 1926-62, 9
lf; Executive Director for University Relations, 1955-70, 8 lf; Faculty
collections, 1856-1971, 128 lf; Graduate school, 1914-70, 14 lf;

News releases, 1957-67, 31 lf; Office of the Budget, 1900-1923, 2 lf;
Ohio State University Association, 1885-1969, 52 lf; President's office,
1873-1969, 350 lf; Records in archival repository, 1895-1968, 19 lf;
School for Social Administration Associates, 1937-42, 2 in.; Student
Organizations, 1873-1969, 47 lf; William Oxley Thompson, war records
commission, 1918-19, 3 lf.   EH

326. Ohio Synod-Lutheran Church in America (1836)
    1233 Dublin Road, Columbus, Ohio 43215
    (614) 486-9424   (M-F 9-5)
    E. R. Walborn, Secretary

Administrative records, 1920+; Contracts, 1940+; Deeds, 1940+; Executive board minutes, 1920+, 4 lf; Financial records, 1959+; Inventories, 1970, 2 in.; President's correspondence, 1940+, 60 lf; Proceedings, annual, 1860+; Publications, 1929+, 24 lf; Scrapbooks, 1940+, 1 lf.   FH

327. Ohio Veterinary Medicine Association (1885)
    1350 West 5th Avenue, Columbus, Ohio 43212
    (614) 486-7253   (M-F 9-5)

Annual reports (yearbooks), 1885+; Correspondence, 2-year retention; Financial records, 1965+; Legal records, 1965+; Minutes, 1965+; 50 lf total.   EL

328. Ohio Welfare Conference (1891)
    227 North Front Street, Columbus, Ohio 43215
    (614) 466-5808   (M-F 8-4:30)
    Donna Gaskill, Acting Executive Secretary

A private non-profit agency which operates under the auspices of the Ohio Department of Public Welfare.

Annual reports, 1958+; Correspondence, 1958+; Financial statements, 1958+; Minutes, 1958+; Proceedings, 1958+; Publications, 1958+; Scrapbooks, 1952+.   WM

329. Ohio West Area United Methodist Church (1811)
    395 East Broad Street, Columbus, Ohio 43215
    (614) 846-2809   (M-F 8:45-4:45)
    John F. Young, Director, United Methodist Information and Public Relations

Annual conference minutes, 1933-70, 5 lf; General conference journal, 1940-64, 4 in.; Judicial Council decisions, 1940-64, 4 in.; Ohio Conference session proceedings, 1950-70, 3 lf; Ohio West Area Annual Conference sessions, 1950-71, 2 lf; Publications, 1956+, 8 lf.   EH

330. Otterbein College Archives (1847)
    Otterbein College, Westerville, Ohio 43081
    (614) 882-3601
    John Becker, Head Librarian

Board of trustees, minutes, 1846-53, 1947-59, 7 vols, (1947-53 un-
bound); Frank Orville Clements (member and chairman of the board of
trustees), correspondence, 1917-44, ca. 1500 items; Walter Gillan
Clippinger (clergyman and college president), papers, 1909-39, 80 lf;
Curriculum committee, 1939-62, 2 lf;

Dean of the college, 1950-56, 1 lf; Dramatics, program productions,
1913-36; Executive committee, minutes, 1855-1948, 5 vols; Faculty
manuals, 1948+; Faculty minutes, 1855-1953, 9 vols; Freshman magazines, 1916-24; John Gardon Howard (clergyman, college president,
and church officer), papers, 1945-57, ca. 24 lf;

John Ruskin Howe (clergyman, theology professor, and Otterbein College president), papers, 1939-45, ca. 20 lf; Library of Otterbein College, 1870+; Literary societies of Otterbein College, 148 vols; Otterbein College authors, publications, 18 authors; Presidential papers,
1909+, scattered, 53 lf; Publications of Otterbein College, 1901-66,
scattered, 9 publications; Registrar's office, 1928-38, 1959-64, 1 lf;
Treasurer's office, 1853-1927, 45 vols, 1934+, 3 lf.   FH

331. Retail Merchants Association of Columbus, Ohio (1949)
    8 East Broad Street, Columbus, Ohio 43215
    (614) 224-4241   (M-F 9-5)
    Roy Stage, Executive Secretary

Coordinating and lobbying group for Columbus area merchants.

Administrative records, 1949+; Certificates, 1949+; Correspondence,
1949+; Financial records, 1949+; Legal agreements, 1949+; Minutes,
1949+; Publications, 1955+; Tax records, 1949+; 200 lf total.   EL

332. St. James Lutheran Church (1847)
    1683 Hilliard-Rome Road, Hilliard, Ohio 43228
    (614) 878-5158   (M-F 9-5)
    Earl C. Grugel, Pastor

Church register, 1848+; Financial records, 1851+; Publications,
1947+; Scrapbooks, 1947+; 3 lf total.   EH

333. United Community Council (1957)
      137 East State Street, Columbus, Ohio 43215
      (614) 228-5696   (M-F 9-5)
      Dee Roth, Research Associate

Annual reports, 1896+; Publications, 1896+; Research reports, 1896+;
Scrapbooks, 1896+; 1200 lf total.   EL

334. United Planning Corporation (1968)
      88 East Broad Street, Columbus, Ohio 43215
      (614) 469-1119   (M-F 9-5)
      Raymond J. Becka, Vice-President

Programs involve the payment of insurance premiums through loans
secured by mutual funds shares which are purchased by the partici-
pant for cash.

Certificates, 1969+; Correspondence, 1969+; Finanical records, 1969+;
Legal records, 1969+; Minutes, 1969+; Publications, 1969+; Reference
material, 1969+; Reports and research data, 1969+; Tax records, 1969+;
200 lf total.   EL

335. United Presbyterian Synod of Ohio (1882)
      3040 North High Street, Columbus, Ohio 43202
      (614) 268-3501   (M-F 9-5)
      Dr. Drysdale, Stated Clerk of Synod of Ohio

Synod minutes, 1886+, 3 lf; General Assembly statistics, 1873+, 15
lf; Publications, 1948+, 3 lf.   EH

336. United Spanish War Veterans of Ohio (1902)
      21 West Broad Street, Columbus, Ohio 43215
      (614) 224-3835   (M-F 9-4)
      Delphia Nelson, Executive Secretary

Administrative records, 1902+; Annual reports, 1902+; Camp records, 1902+; Correspondence, 1902+; Membership records, 1902+;
Minutes, 1902+; Scrapbooks (photographs), 1902+; 75 lf total.   EL

337. Veterans of World War I, U.S.A., Inc. (1954)
      21 West Broad Street, Room 313, Columbus, Ohio 43215
      (614) 221-1839   (M-F 9-5)
      Paul Anore, Quartermaster

Lobby for veterans' benefits, primarily old age.

Administrative records, 1954+; Annual reports, 1954+; Convention programs, 1954+; Correspondence, 1954+; Financial records, 1954+; Legal records, 1954+; Minutes, 1954+; Proceedings, 1954+; Public relations material, 1954+; Rosters, 1954+; Scrapbooks, 1954+.   EL

338. WCOL Radio (1936)
      (Great Trails Broadcasting Corp.)
      22 South Young Street, Columbus, Ohio 43215
      (614) 221-7811   (M-F 9-5)
      Carl Lang, Station Manager

Advertising copy, 1965+; Market research data, 1965+; PR data, 1965+; 100 lf total.   EL

339. Women's Christian Temperance Union
      1444 East Broad Street, Columbus, Ohio 43205
      (614) 258-7212   (M-F 9-5)

Annual reports; State meeting minutes.   EL

340. Young Americans for Freedom, Columbus Branch (1965)
      Suite 204, Ohio Union, Ohio State University, Columbus, Ohio 43210
      (614) 422-7924   (M-F 9-5)
      Steven Meyerhofer, State Chairman

Conservative political group.

Administrative records; Clippings and memorabilia, 1968+; Correspondence, 1966+; Financial records, 1965+; Legal records, 1965+; Minutes, 1965+; Publications, 1968+; 50 lf total.   EL

341. YMCA, Columbus (1855)
      40 West Long Street, Columbus, Ohio 43215
      (614) 224-1131   (M-F 8-5)
      Robert C. Cooper, General Executive

Administrative records, 1914+, 1 lf; Annual reports, 1953+, 15 lf; Correspondence, 1952+, 2 lf; Financial records, 1969+, 4-year retention; Legal records, 1952+, 1 lf; Scrapbooks, 1900+, 2 lf; YMCA history file, 1900+, 1 lf.   EL

342. YMCAs, Great Lakes Region of National Council of (1970)
        40 West Long Street, Columbus, Ohio 43215
        (614) 224-2225   (M-F 9-5)
        Robert Atkinson, Great Lakes Regional Executive

There were two predecessors to the present organization, the first
formed in 1867. The present association covers Ohio, West Virginia,
and Michigan.

Administrative records, 1867+, 7 lf; Annual reports, 1874+, 12 lf;
Financial summaries, 1925+, 5 lf; Local chapter reports, 1935+; Min-
utes, 1878+, 6 lf; Publications, 1920s+, 10 lf; Yearbooks of the National
Association, 1898+.   EL

343. Young Socialist Alliance, Columbus (1960)
        Ohio State University, Columbus, Ohio 43215
        (614) 293-8829   (Hours by appointment)
        c/o Dr. Benjamin Wise, President

Campaign literature, 1966+, 4 lf; Membership lists, 1968+, 1 lf; Minutes, 1967+, 1 lf; Proceedings, 1967+, 1 lf; Publications, ca. 1965+,
3 lf; Scrapbooks (clippings), 1965+, 1 lf.   EL

                          FULTON COUNTY

MANUSCRIPTS

344. Swanton Public Library
        204 Cherry Street, Swanton, Ohio 43558
        (419) 826-3626   (M, W 1-4, 7-9; F 1-4)
        Ellen Dennis, Librarian

Fulton Township-Lucas County Township Trustees, minutes, 1841-
77, 1 vol; Photographs of Swanton, 1930-40, 2 lf.   PY

INSTITUTIONAL RECORDS

345. Chamber of Commerce, Wauseon
        124 South Fulton, Wauseon, Ohio 43567
        (419) 335-9966   (M-F 10-2)
        Sally Lutz, Secretary

Correspondence, 1960+, 4 lf; Minutes, 1960+, 4 lf; Publications,
1963+, 2 lf. PY

346. Farm Bureau Co-Op Association, Fulton County
      323 West Chestnut, Wauseon, Ohio 43567
      (419) 335-7976   (M-F 8-5; Sat 8-12)
      W. B. Davis, Office Manager

Administrative records, 1934, 1 vol; Correspondence, 1965+, 10
file drawers; Journals, 1935+, 8 vols; Ledgers, 1935+, 10 vols;
Minutes, 1934+, 4 vols; Stock records, 1934+, 3 file drawers. PY

                          GALLIA COUNTY

MANUSCRIPTS

347. Gallia County District Library (ca. 1890)
      Third Avenue and State Street, Gallipolis, Ohio 45631
      (614) 446-0642   (M-F 9-9; Sat 9-5)
      Jonathan E. Louden, Librarian

"Abstracts of the Wills and Administration of Estates of Washington
County, 1788-1850," 50 pp; Brief history of the communities in the
23 counties of the Columbus and Southern Ohio Electric Company service area, 1 in.; C. & A. Henking General Store, papers and business
receipts, 1861-65, 135 items; Gallia County census, 1820, 1830, 1840,
1850, 1860, 1870, 1880, 1890, 8 rolls mf; Gallia County, records of
war dead, 1962, 31 pp; Gallipolis, scrapbook (pictures and descriptions
of Gallipolis historic sites), 100 pp;

"History of Gallia County Schools," by T. K. Owens (records of teachers,   school board members, descriptions of board of education meetings), 1914-60, ca. 150 pp; "Grandma" Gatewood's scrapbook (clippings,
photos of her walks), 1955-69, 2 in.; Dr. Milton M. Grover, reflections
on life in Gallia County, ca. 1950s, 53 pp; E. A. Jones, account book as
guardian of estate of Anne M. and William R. Evans, 1859-74, 30 pp;

Mary L. Lewis, scrapbooks (history of Portsmouth, Holzer Hospital,
mid-Century personalities, landmarks, homes, public buildings, schools,
churches, etc.), ca. 1950-61, 6 in.; O. D. McIntyre, collecton of his
clippings (newspaper column "Day by Day"), correspondence, 1931-37,
28 pieces; Neal & Arnot family tree, 1960, 25 pp; Null family, genealogy
records, 1960, 25 pp; Sons of Temperance, minute book (Gallia County
area), 1852-56, 1 in. RR

INSTITUTIONAL RECORDS

348. Chamber of Commerce, Gallipolis (1936)
      16 State Street, Gallipolis, Ohio 45631
      (614) 446-0596   (M-F 8:30-4)
      Thelma Elliot, Director

Administrative records, 1936+; Community Improvement Corporation
records (minutes, industrial information, land sales, etc.), 1964+, 1
lf; Contracts, 1970+; Correspondence, 5-year retention; Directors and
committees, minutes, 1936+, 6 lf; Financial statements, 1936+; Photographs and postcards, 1936+, 100 items; Plats, 20th century, ca. 10
items; Publications (newsletter, brochure on tourist information, industrial brochure, information on community); Retail Merchants Committee, minutes, financial reports, ca. 1950+, 2 lf; Scrapbooks, 1955+,
6 in.; Tax records, 1950.   FH

349. First United Presbyterian Church (1815)
      51 State Street, Gallipolis, Ohio 45631
      (614) 446-9266   (M-F 9-1)
      Glen Hueholt, Pastor

Board of trustees, minutes, 1897+, 5 in.; Church register, 1909+, 6
in.; General files, 1955+, 6 lf; Miscellany (correspondence, receipts,
etc.), 1902, 1923, 1 in.; Proceedings of first religious society, 1815-
94, 1 in.; Session minutes (includes annual reports), 1815+, 14 in.;
Social Circle (women's social group), 1856-76, 1905-21, 2 in.; Women's
Association, receipts, 1948-60, 6 in.; Women's Missionary Society, 1932-
38, 2 in.   FH

350. Grace United Methodist Church (1821)
      Second and Cedar Streets, Gallipolis, Ohio 45631
      (614) 446-0555   (M-F 9-5)
      Paul Hawks, Pastor

Administrative records, 1898+; Board of trustees, minutes, 1821-1914,
1 vol; Bulletin, 1969+, 1 in.; Church register, 1863+, 2 lf; General files,
4 lf.   RR

MANUSCRIPTS

351. Burton Public Library (1912)
        14558 West Park Street, Burton, Ohio 44021
        (216) 834-4258   (M-F 9-9; Sat 9-5)
        Helen K. Meritt, Acting Librarian

Maude Beech, letter, 1971; Uria Byler, "The Amish Schools of Northeastern Ohio"; Margaret O. Ford, "Pioneer and General History of
Geauga County," 1 in.; Maurice A. Fox, thesis ("Borrowing of Small-
er Public Books in Ohio"), 1954, 3 in.; Geauga County fair, history;
Geauga County Historical Society, plays, 1961-62, 1 in.; Geauga County Schools, study unit, grade four (short essays on various aspects of
the county by fourth graders), 1 in.; Mrs. Wayne Hosmer, "Amish Education System," ca. 1960s; "The Story of Burton's Community Forest,"
ca. 1940s.   FH

352. Geauga County Historical Society (1873)
        14653 East Park Street, Burton, Ohio 44021
        (216) 834-4012   (Tu-Sat 10-5; Sun 1-5)
        Margaret O. Ford, Historian

Gov. Seabury Ford, diary, 1823-25; Land grants, 1813-73, 5 items.
FH

353. Geauga County Public Library
        110 East Park Street, Chardon, Ohio 44024
        (216) 285-7601   (Summer: M, W 10-9; Tu, Th, 10-6; F, Sat 10-5;
                                Sept 6 to mid-June: M-Th 9-9; F, Sat 9-5)
        Mrs. James Williams, Reference Librarian

Medora Chamberlain, papers (scrapbooks of newspaper clippings), 1892-
1930, 3 vols; Chardon PTA, minutes, 1935-43, 1948-66, 4 vols; Chardon
Village records, 1851-76, 1 vol; Progress-Research Club of Chardon (club
designed to "promote culture and friendship and to cooperate in community
service"), register and minutes, 1901+, 2 lf; Judge Lester Taylor papers
(notes on land appraisals for free public schools), 1830, 1 vol.   DH

INSTITUTIONAL RECORDS

354. Chardon United Methodist Church (1816)
      515 North Street, Chardon, Ohio 44024
      (216) 285-4581   (M-F 9-12)
      M. Dean Marston, Minister

Early records have been transferred to the Methodist Collection at
Baldwin-Wallace College.

Membership and marriage records, 1866-1942, 5 vols; Membership
rolls, 1930-65, 2 vols. DH

                        GREENE COUNTY

MANUSCRIPTS

355. Greene County Historical Society
      74 West Church Street, Xenia, Ohio 45385
      (Tu-F 10-4; Sat, Sun 2-5)
      Wynema Frost, Secretary

James Allen (settler from Virginia), account book, 1814, 1 in.;
Rebecca Galloway, diary, 1840, 1 in.; Harter vs. Simon Kenyon,
legal case, 1810, 1 in.; Slave register, 1788-1830s, 1 vol.   FH

356. Greene County Library (1873)
      194 East Church Street, Xenia, Ohio 45385
      (513) 376-2995   (M-Th, 10-9; F, Sat 10-6)
      Jean Klose, Reference Librarian

Bowersville Bank Robbery (1933), history, 1951, 25 pp; Court records
(deeds, guardians, administrators), 1880-1967, 55 rolls mf; Harvey
Dean, diary, 1858, 30 pp; Genealogy collection, 1 lf; Greene County
Court of Common Pleas, minutes, 1805-7, 1 in.; Greene County material (mostly news clippings), 5 lf; Greene County Probate Court, will
records, 1970, 100 pp; Thomas P. Patterson, Civil War letters, 1862-
65, 35 items; Record of school districts in Xenia Township, 1832, 23
pp; Roster of soldiers, 1812, 1 in.;

Union Circuit of the Ohio Conference of the Methodist Episcopal Church,
minutes, 1936, 146 pp; WCTU, minutes and scrapbook, 1874-1944, 3 in.;

Xenia businessmen, biographical sketches, 1942-47, 1 in.; Xenia Railroad (scrapbook), n.d., 10 pp; Xenia Woodland Cemetery, record of gravestones,n.d., 6 in.   RS

357. Wilberforce University Library (1845)
         Wilberforce University, Wilberforce, Ohio 45384
         (513) 372-1332   (M-Th 8-10; F 8-9; Sat 9-4; Sun 2-6)
         Ghulam Y. Siddiqui, Assistant Librarian

Benjamin Arnett (major black figure in 2d half of the 19th century), papers (mainly bound volumes, minutes; complete calendar), 1857-1944, 20 lf; Bishop Levi J. Coppin Library, minutes of various religious conferences and miscellaneous proceedings, 1881-1922; Daniel Alexander Payne, papers,1811-93, 8 folders; Reverdy Cassius Ransom, papers, 1893-1950, 9 folders; William Sanders Scarborough, papers, 1854-1926, 936 items.   FH

358. Yellow Springs Public Library (1899)
         415 Xenia Avenue, Yellow Springs, Ohio 45387
         (513) 767-7661   (M-Th 2-5, 7-9; F 10-5; Sat 2-5)
         Ruth Harner, Librarian

American Association of University Women, minutes and scrapbook, 1953-70, 1 lf; League of Women Voters, minutes and pamphlets, 1971-72, 2 in.; Yellow Springs Little Peace Conference (conference organized to decide what Yellow Springs as a community wanted to do after World War II and how to accomplish), scrapbook, June 13-July 4, 1943, 2 in.   RS

INSTITUTIONAL RECORDS

359. Chamber of Commerce, Xenia (1940)
         37 South Detroit Street, Xenia, Ohio 45385
         (513) 372-3591   (M-F 8:30-5)
         John Higgins, Executive Vice-President

Administrative records, 1949-69; Annual reports, 1961+; Cashbooks, 1961+; Correspondence, 1952+; Daybooks, 1961+; Financial statements, 1961+; Journals, 1961+; Ledgers, 1961+; Minutes, 1949+; Photograph collection; Proceedings, 1949+; Publications; Scrapbooks; Tax records, 1952+.   FH

360. Xenia Daily Gazette (1868)
          37 South Detroit Street, Xenia, Ohio 45385
          (513) 372-4444   (M-F 8-5; Sat 8-12)
          Jack D. Jordan, Editor

Financial statements, ca. 1945+; High school annuals, 1947+, 2 lf;
Inventories, 1960+; Microfilm of newspaper, 1881+, 155 rolls; Minutes, 1930s+; Morgue file (pictures and clippings), 70 lf.   FH

                          GUERNSEY COUNTY

INSTITUTIONAL RECORDS

361. Chamber of Commerce, Cambridge
          910 Wheeling Avenue, Cambridge, Ohio 43725
          (614) 432-3943   (M-F 8:30-5)
          Earl Baldwin, Executive Vice-President

Administrative records; Annual reports; Board of directors and committee minutes; Correspondence; Financial records; Membership lists;
Newsletter; Photographs; 1940s+, ca. 75 lf total.   SF

                          HAMILTON COUNTY

MANUSCRIPTS

362. American Jewish Archives (1947)
          3101 Clifton Avenue, Cincinnati, Ohio 45220
          (513) 221-1875   (M-F 8:30-5)
          Fannie Zelcer, Archivist

See Manuscript Catalog of the American Jewish Archives, Cincinnati
(Boston: G.K. Hall & Co., 1971, 4 vols), for description of holdings.

363. Cincinnati Art Museum Library (1881)
          Eden Park, Cincinnati, Ohio 45202
          (513) 721-5204   (M-F 10-5; Sat 10-12)
          Alice Palo Hook, Librarian

Clement Barnhorn (artist), 6 in.; Robert Blum (artist), 6 in.; Kenyon Cox (artist), 3 in.; Frank Duveneck, mounted photos, scrapbooks,
manuscript clippings, 16 in.; Robert Lehman, clippings, drawings,

prints, slides, 2 lf; Miscellaneous manuscript material, 4 lf; Elizabeth Norse; Rochwood Pottery, 2 lf.   FH

364. The Cincinnati Historical Society
      Eden Park, Cincinnati, Ohio 45202
      (513) 2 41-4622   (M-F 8:30-4:30; Sat 9-4 from Sept-May)
      Laura Chace, Head Librarian

Abbott family, papers, 1700-1940, 1 lf; Air Pollution Control League
of Greater Cincinnati, records, 1906-67, 3 lf; Edward Franklin Alexander (lawyer), papers, 1894-1964, including material relating to U.S.
vs. Thomas Hammerschmidt et al. (1917-24), the Charter Movement
in Cincinnati, the Ohio Code Revision Committee, and Herbert Seeley
Bigelow, 1 lf; American Institute of Architects, Cincinnati Chapter, records,   1870-1968, 5 lf; Frank Pearce Atkins (businessman), papers,
1847-1954, relating to the Atkins, Pearce and Owens families and the
Atkins and Pearce Manufacturing Company, 69 items;

Baldwin-Wulsin, records, 1862-1964, including correspondence, financial and manufacturing records, advertising and promotional material,
and drawings of the Baldwin Piano Company and other personal papers
of Lucien Wulsin I (1845-1912) and his son, Lucien Wulsin II (1889-1964),
92 lf; Warner M. Bateman, papers, 1857-1907, relating to family matters and politics, 251 items; Bates family, papers, 1789-1873, relating
chiefly to business matters, 617 items; Henry Bentley (lawyer), papers,
ca. 1917-40, relating to Cincinnati politics, 6 lf;

Herbert Seeley Bigelow (Congregational minister and reformer), papers,
1900-1951, including correspondence, autobiography, speeches and printed material relating to Cincinnati and Ohio politics, 5 lf; Robert Lounsbury Black (lawyer), papers, 1921-33, relating to the American Legion
Rehabilitation Committee, 1 lf; John Brough (politician), correspondence,
1845-65, 179 items; Bullock family papers, 1835-89, including material
on many prominent Cincinnatians and the City and Suburban Telegraph
Association, ca. 175 items;

Butler County, records, 1803-1931, 1 lf; John Day Caldwell (publisher
and librarian), papers, 1784-1871 (correspondence and notebooks), 31
items; Alfred George Washington Carter (lawyer, judge, and author),
manuscripts of plays, 1862-79, 10 vols; William Carter (lawyer and
state legislator), papers, 1836-1927, 3 lf; Centennial Exposition of the
Ohio Valley and Central States, records, 1887-89, 6 lf; James Francis
Chalfant (merchant, Methodist minister, and trustee of Miami University and Longview Asylum), papers, 1819-88, 1 lf;

Salmon Portland Chase, correspondence, 1849-73, 246 items; Cincinnati Baseball Club, National League, records, 1882-88, including
correspondence, cashbooks, ledgers, statements of attendance and
weather, players' contracts (1885-87), salary records and other papers, 2 lf; Cincinnati Bureau of Municipal Research, records, 1909-
17, 9 vols; Cincinnati Caledonian Society, minute books, 1827-1915,
3 vols; Cincinnati Central Christian Church, records, 1827-1917, including minutes, membership records and Sunday school records, 10
vols; Cincinnati Central Turner Society, Inc., records, 1850-1948, 7 lf;

Cincinnati Citizens School Committee, records, ca. 1940-60, dealing with the Cincinnati public schools, 3 lf; Cincinnati City Fire Engineer, reports, 1832-52, on the condition of fire-fighting equipment
and data regarding fires in Cincinnati, 65 items; Cincinnati Civil War
Round Table, records, 1956-69, including papers delivered, newsletters, correspondence, and rosters, 1 lf; Cincinnati Chamber of
Commerce, records, 1839-1956, 4 lf; Cincinnati Convalescent Hospital for Children, records, 1833-1958, including minutes, reports,
scrapbook (1836-1930), and photographs, 10 lf;

Cincinnati Crafters Company, records, 1910-55, including correspondence, reports, minutes, financial and legal records and a company history, 1 lf; Cincinnati Cremation Company, records, 1884-
89, including minutes, constitution and by-laws, 1 vol; Cincinnati
Dental Society, records, 1845-1968, including minutes, financial
records, correspondence and student records, 8 lf; Cincinnati Deut-
scher Pionier Verein, records, 1868-1960, including minutes, membership rosters and financial records, 5 vols; Cincinnati Fight for
Freedom-Defend America, records, 1940-42, including correspondence,
financial records, and printed material, 3 lf;

Cincinnati Fire Department, records, 1819-1967, including correspondence, diaries, reports, journals, financial records, receipts, general orders (1896-1934), rosters, rules and regulations, resolutions,
scrapbooks (1878-1950) and pamphlets, 24 lf; Cincinnati Fire Guards,
records, 1840-48, 89 items; Cincinnati Freie Presse Company, financial records, 4 lf; Cincinnati German Mutual Insurance Company, records, 1858-1933, including minutes, records of accounts, and plats,
20 vols; Cincinnati Industrial Expositions, records, 1870-82, including correspondence, minutes, and subscription list, 7 vols;

Cincinnati Kindergarten Association, records, 1879-1926, including
secretary's minutes, treasurer's books, and visiting committee reports, 18 vols; Cincinnati League of Women Voters, records, 1920-
66, including minutes, study material, reports and financial records,

5 lf; Cincinnati Methodist Episcopal Church, records, 1812-54, including financial and membership records and minutes of the Wesley Chapel, the Fourth Street Charge, the African Church and Mount Auburn Chapel, 20 vols; Cincinnati Metropolitan Housing Authority, records, 1933-63, including correspondence, reports, and publications, 2 lf;

Cincinnati Musical Festival Association, records, 1874-1967, including correspondence, minutes, contracts, programs and clippings, 8 lf; Cincinnati People's Church, records, 1831-1947, including correspondence, minutes of the board of trustees (1831-1926), reports, cashbooks (1879-1915), personal accounts (1914-15) of Rev. Herbert Seeley Bigelow, pastor (1896-1947), 58 items; Cincinnati Pioneer Association, records, 1856-89, 3 vols; Cincinnati Schoolmasters Club, records, 1907-68, 5 lf; Cincinnati Tennis Club, records, 1898-1965, 1 lf; Cincinnati Transit Company, records, 1860-1952, consisting of records of various transit companies and their consolidation into the Cincinnati Transit Company, 6 lf;

Cincinnati Union Bethel (neighborhood settlement house), records, 1861-1955, including correspondence, minutes, and financial records, 3 lf; Cincinnati University, College Conservatory of Music, scrapbooks, 1885-1962, 38 lf; Cincinnati Waterworks, records, 1817-48, 118 items; Cincinnatus Association, records, 1920-71, 6 lf; Davis Wasgatt Clark (Methodist Episcopal bishop), correspondence, 1841-76, relating to the Methodist Church and to the content and publication of the Ladies' Repository, which Clark edited, 440 items; Robert Clarke collection, 1790-1905, relating to the settlement of Gallipolis, Ohio, 1 lf; Robert Clarke collection, 1784-1863, papers relating to the Illinois Territory, Governor Ninian Edwards, the War of 1812, Judge John Cleves Symmes, the Miami Purchase and early Cincinnati, 757 items;

William Cranch (Washington, D.C., jurist), papers, ca. 1790-1855, ca. 300 items; Maskell Ewing Curwen (lawyer), correspondence, 1818-84, 161 items; Wendell Phillips Dabney (black journalist), collection, 1905-64, including correspondence, printed material, ephemera, incomplete autobiograpy, and sheet music, 108 items; Martin P. Davis collection, 1842-1950, material relating to German churches in and around Cincinnati, 1 lf; Joseph Donnelly collection, 1803-68, transcripts of letters and records relating to Newport Barracks, 1 lf;

Daniel Drake (physician), papers, 1807-52, including correspondence, addresses and legal records, 62 items; George Elliston (journalist and poet), papers, 1901-42, including correspondence, writings, photographs and scrapbooks, 1 lf; Este family, papers, 1802-75 (mainly papers of David Kirkpatrick Este (1785-1875), lawyer and judge of New Jersey and Ohio), 280 items; Platt Evens (merchant tailor), account books, 1828-89, 11 vols; Angeline Loveland Faran collection, 1879-1956, materials relating to Glendale, Ohio, ca. 85 items;

Oran Follett (publisher and public official), papers, 1822-89, chiefly correspondence relating to political issues, 239 items; Joseph Benson Foraker (lawyer, governor and U.S. senator), papers, 1884-1917, including correspondence and speeches, 26 lf; Manning Ferguson Force (soldier, jurist, and author), papers, 1869-99, ca. 250 items; Gano family papers, 1775-1851, relating to the early history of Cincinnati, military matters and family affairs, ca. 850 items; Garden Club of Cincinnati, records, 1913-71, 2 lf; Joseph Gest, surveys, 1802-45, 2 lf;

Gest family correspondence, 1810-1932, primarily between two brothers,   Joseph Gest (1776-1863), Cincinnati surveyor, and John Gest (1783-1865), of Philadelphia, and two of Joseph's children, Clarissa (1816-1901) and Erasmus (1820-1908), regarding family and business affairs, the Society of Friends, politics, and current events in Cincinnati, 465 items; William Yates Gholson (lawyer and judge), Gholson-Kittredge papers, 1838-1965, primarily family and business correspondence of his son, William Yates Gholson, Jr. (1842-62), papers of Frances Wright (1795-1852), Scottish reformer and free-thinker, concerning her work and life in Cincinnati, and correspondence of Edmund Webster Kittredge (1833-1916), Cincinnati lawyer and executive, 4 lf;

Alfred West Gilbert (engineer and surveyor), papers, 1840-88, 7 vols; Glendale, Ohio, Maple Knoll Hospital and Home (charitable institution for the care of unmarried expectant mothers), records, 1854-1957, 16 vols; Greater Cincinnati Federation of Settlements and Neighborhood Centers, records, 1956-69, 2 lf; James Albert Green, collection, 1794-1933, relating to William Henry Harrison, 74 items; William Greene (Rhode Island lawyer and lieutenant governor), papers, 1775-1888, relating to Cincinnati and Ohio history and national and Ohio politics, together with papers of Dr. Frederick Roelker (1809-81), Ohio physician and educator, relating to early Cincinnati and German politics, 754 items;

Green family, papers, 1818-51, relating to Cincinnati and Ohio history in the 19th century, 1 lf; Greve family, papers, 1828-1930, mostly personal correspondence and in part, transcripts of papers owned by the Literary Club of Cincinnati, 2 lf; Gwynne family, papers, 1825-55, 900 items; Hamilton County Big Brothers Association, records, 1935-

67, 4 lf; Hamilton County, Ohio, records, 1830-1940, 4 lf; Judson
Harmon (Ohio Governor and U.S. Attorney General),papers, 1908-12,
chiefly correspondence with constituents and political friends relating
to the temperance movement in Ohio, 7 lf;

William Henry Harrison, papers, 1794-1860, in part photocopies of
originals in the Henry E. Huntington Library and the Library of Congress, and including correspondence and miscellaneous documents,
37 letters (1794-1839) are originals, 220 items; Harrison family, papers, 1789-1893, personal and business correspondence of the family
of Learner Blackman Harrison (1815-1902), 465 items; William Stanley Hatch (banker), papers, 1740-1888, relating to the early history
of Cincinnati, 149 items; Andrew Hickenlooper (Army officer and businessman), papers, 1859-1938, 3 lf;

Charles W. Hoffman (judge), papers, ca. 1915-60, 3 lf; Edward Timothy Hurley (artist), papers, 1892-1963, 46 items; International Molders and Allied Workers Union, Local 4, Cincinnati, Ohio, records,
1860-90, 16 vols; Isaac H. Jackson (Hamilton County commissioner),
papers, 1796-1847, 35 items; John Davis Jones (educator), papers,
1830-75, including diaries and family correspondence, 66 items;King
family, papers, 1791-1880, of Rufus King (1755-1827), statesman and
diplomat, and Rufus King (1817-1891), lawyer and author, 2 lf;

Timothy Kirby, papers, 1817-59, including records of the Cincinnati
branch of the Second Bank of the United States, 14 lf; Edmund Webster Kittredge (lawyer), papers, 1787-1923, 2 lf; Abraham Lincoln,
letters, 1860-64, and Lincoln's draft of the Amnesty Proclamation,
1863 Dec 8, 5 items; Lane Theological Seminary, records, 1831-1933,
1 lf; Lawler family, papers, 1808-1932, of Davis Bevan Lawler (1786-
1869), businessman of Cincinnati and U.S. consul to Berlin, and correspondence of the Thomas Bryant family, 5 vols; Little Miami Railroad
Company, minute books, 1836-1902, 4 vols;

Charles Jacob Livingood (surveyor, real estate developer and public
official), papers, 1880-1948, relating to the Lytle family, 1 lf; Alexander Long (lawyer and U.S. representative), papers, 1840-96, 5 lf;
Nicholas Longworth (Speaker of the House), letters, 1906-30, 11 items;
George Henry Anderson Lyford (lawyer), papers, 1835-1932, 3 lf; Lytle
family, papers, ca. 1780-1926, of William Lytle (1770-1831), surveyor-
general of the Northwest Territory, Robert Todd Lytle (1804-39), lawyer, U.S. representative from Ohio, surveyor-general of the Northwest Territory and major general of the Ohio Militia, and William
Haines Lytle (1826-63), lawyer, poet, politician and soldier, 12 lf;

James McBride (historian, archaeologist, and university trustee), papers, 1804-58, on the history of Oxford, Ohio, Miami University, the Miami college lands, and Hamilton, Ohio, 4 lf; Sidney Denise Maxwell (journalist, writer and businessman), papers, 1852-92, 2 lf; John May (Ohio Company agent and business adventurer), papers, 1776-1808, 71 items; Miami Exporting Company, records, 1812-30, 5 vols; Adolph Friedrich Morgenstern, papers, 1898-1944, including correspondence, programs, minutes, membership lists and songbooks of the German Literary Club, papers read before the club by Morgenstern, and the Morgenstern family photographs, 2 lf;

Josiah Morrow, correspondence, essays, and a list of historical articles written for the Western Star (Lebanon, Ohio), 1 lf; Nast family, papers, 1763-1938, 3 lf; New England Society of Cincinnati, records, 1845-1923, 1 lf; Clara Chipman Newton (artist), papers, 1864-1938, relating to the Cincinnati Pottery Club, Rookwood Pottery, the Cincinnati Women's Club, and including business papers of R.M. and George Graham, 1 lf; Northwest Territory, general assembly, records, 1799-1802, including the legislative council journal (1799), house of representatives journals (1799-1802), and drafts of general assembly acts, 57 items;

Northwest Territory, order books, 1792-94, 3 vols; Ohio Canal Commission, records, 1826-53, principally letters addressed to the Ohio Canal Commissioners, the Board of Public Works, and the National Road Committee, 204 items; Palm Brothers Decalcomania Company, records, 1891-1948, including record books, catalogs, sample books, and photographs, 5 lf; Joseph Pitcairn, papers, 1796-1821, chiefly correspondence while U.S. consul at Paris and Hamburg, 201 items; Pitman family, papers, ca. 1850-1954, including spiritual and religious notes and material on the Anthroposophical Society of America, designs, wood carvings, home decorations, and sketchbook of Benn Pitman (1822-1910), photographs, art work and sketches by Agnes Pitman, and articles on the Pitman shorthand system, 2 lf;

William Prince, papers, 1807-22, relating to Prince's trial for his connection with the Burr Conspiracy, 11 items; Pulte Medical College, records, 1867-1939, including material on its predecessor, the Homeopathic Free Dispensary, 1 lf; Reeder family (family which settled in Riverside, Ohio), papers, 1800-1900, 149 items; Charles Gustav Reemelin (state legislator, author and horticulturist), papers, 1797-1900, 1 lf; Louis Rehfuss (chemist and pharmacist), papers, 1847-55, including correspondence concerning German-American financial assistance to the German Revolution of 1848, the Cincinnati Horticultural Society, and viticulture in the Cincinnati area, 85 items;

Rookwood Pottery, records, 1880-1969, 2 lf; Arthur St. Clair, letters, 1791-1808, 30 items; Arthur St. Clair, Jr., papers, 1797-1827, relating to legal matters and politics in the Northwest Territory, 2 lf; John Sherman (U.S. senator), correspondence, 1871-95, 7 items; Clarence Osborne Sherrill (city manager), papers, 1926-51, 5 lf; Short family, papers, 1786-1925, including correspondence of William Short (1759-1849) while he was serving as a representative of Thomas Jefferson in Europe between 1785 and 1802, account books of Peyton Short (1761-1825), farmer and land speculator of Woodford County, Kentucky, correspondence and diaries of John Cleves Short (1792-1864), Peyton's son and lawyer of Cincinnati, and other papers relating to Charles Wilkins Short (1794-1863), also Peyton's son, physician and teacher of Louisville, Kentucky, 1 lf;

Caleb Blood Smith (U.S. senator), correspondence with Henry Vallette, 1848, 1861-63, 9 items; James Smith, records, 1793-1810, including business records of James & St. Clair, James & Findlay, and James, Findlay & Harrison, and Smith's records while serving as sheriff of Hamilton County, 14 vols; John Smith (U.S. senator), papers, 1805-23, relating to Smith's relationship to the Aaron Burr-Harman Blennerhassett affair, and to Smith's trial for his alleged involvement, 110 items; Thomas B. Stevenson (journalist), correspondence, 1807-81, chiefly concerning U.S. politics, 1830-60, 304 items;

Strobridge Lithographing Company, records, 1867-1956, 6 vols;Isaac Strohm (chief clerk, U.S. House of Representatives), transcripts of correspondence, 1830-91, 270 items; Anna Sinton Taft, financial records, 1892-1930, 68 vols; William Howard Taft, correspondence, 1884-1930, 1 lf; James Taylor (Kentucky surveyor and Army officer), papers, 1797-1848, of Taylor and his son, James Taylor (1802-83), a Newport, Kentucky real estate lawyer, 1 lf; James Henry Thompson (lawyer and judge), papers, 1805-1921, relating to Ohio railroads, Hillsboro, Ohio, the temperance movement, and Civil War letters of Edward C. Rives, surgeon in the confederate army, 6 lf;

Todd family, papers, 1809-49, relating to Charles Stewart Todd (1791-1871), lawyer and minister to Russia, and to Thomas Todd, concerning U.S. politics, 1810-55, the Whig Party, and the 1840 election, 343 items; Aaron Torrence, collection, 1790-1856, letters and papers relating to the early history of Cincinnati and Hamilton County, including those of James Findlay, U.S. representative, and William Henry Harrison, 13 lf; Trotter (Samuel and George) Company, correspondence, 1805-19, 1 lf; U.S. Sanitary Commission (Cincinnati Branch), records, 1863-65, 2 vols;

Urbana Banking Company, records, 1807-76, relating primarily to
banks and canals in Ohio, 273 items; Stuart Walker Company (company
organized to propagate the legitimate stage in Cincinnati), records,
1929-31, 313 items; Timothy Walker (judge, lawyer and editor), papers,
1825-55, containing material on U.S. politics and internal Whig politics,
113 items; Western Academy of Natural Sciences, records, 1835-53,111
items; Albert W. Whelpley autograph collection, 1791-1899, ca. 1,000
items; Samuel Wesley Williams collection, 1800-1927, relating to the
Methodist Church in Ohio, Indiana, Illinois, Kentucky and Tennessee,
primarily before 1850, 1 lf;

Russell Wilson (public official and editor), papers, 1929-45, relating to
Wilson's role as the first Charter Party mayor of Cincinnati, 9 lf; Woman's
Columbian Exposition of Cincinnati, records, 1892-93, 8 vols; Nathaniel
Wright (lawyer), papers, 1797-1877, concerning the development of rail-
roads, and the Lane Theological Seminary, of which Wright was a member
of the board of trustees, 616 items.   FH

365.   Hebrew Union College - Jewish Institute of Religion
         3101 Clifton Avenue, Cincinnati, Ohio 45220
         (513) 221-1875   (M-F 8:30-5)
         Herbert C. Zafren, Director of Libraries

The manuscript collection at the Klau Library is vast and the analysis
of collections therefore lists only a brief summary of their holdings. For
greater detail a researcher could refer to: American Jewish Periodical
Center: Jewish Newspapers and Periodicals on Microfilm (Cincinnati,1957;
Suppl. No. 1, Cincinnati, 1960); Hebrew Union College-Jewish Institute of
Religion Library: Dictionary Catalog of the Klau Library, Cincinnati (Boston, 1964-65, 32 vols).

Klau Library: The American Jewish Periodical Center: newspapers, etc.,
on microfilm, over 300 titles, 1823+; Aaron Beer (great cantor), autograph
music, 1791; Birnbaum Music Collection, augmented by later acquisitions
(largest Jewish music collection in America) 18th and 19th century, 123 lf;
Jewish bookplates collection, including the Philip Goodman collection (one
of the largest Jewish bookplate collections in the world) 16th century +, 18
lf; Broadsides collection, 18th and 19th centuries, several hundred items;
French document collection, largely 18th century, also 20th century, 5 lf;
Kirschstein collection, largely 19th century documents, 6 lf; Membership
list of the 17th century Kai Fung Fu Jewish community in Hebrew and Chinese; Pentateuch, etc., copied by Ibn Musa, Lisbon, 1475; Photographs
and newspaper clipping collection of Jewish personalities; Pinkasim record books collection, largely from the German speaking areas and Italy,

16th century+, largely 18th and 19th centuries; Rashi's commentary
on the prophets copied in 1271; Sermons of the Lubavich Chasidim,
partly copied from the autographs.   HS

366. Lloyd Library and Museum (1864)
      917 Plum Street, Cincinnati, Ohio 45202
      (513) 721-3707   (M-F 8:30-4:30)
      Mrs. C. M. Simons, Librarian

Eclectic Medical College of Cincinnati, archives, 1845-1939, 8 lf;
Curtis Gates Lloyd, correspondence and miscellaneous papers on
mycology, 25 boxes; John Uri Lloyd (pharmacist and college professor, correspondence and miscellaneous papers, 54 boxes; Corinne
Miller Simons, TSS of a biography of the Lloyd brothers and photographs, 2 lf; James Patison Walker (Surgeon-General of the British
Army), bound papers and MSS on eclectic methods, 529 vols.   LM

367. Public Library of Cincinnati and Hamilton County (1853)
      800 Vine Street, Cincinnati, Ohio 45202
      (513) 241-2636   (M-F 9-9; Sat 9-6)

Art and Music Dept.: (Catherine Kilcoyne, Head, Art and Music)
Paul Briol, buildings in Chillicothe, 1 vol of plates, boxed; Paul
Briol, Cincinnati Zoological Gardens, 1 vols of plates, boxed; Paul
Briol, Ohio River, 1 vol of plates, boxed; Paul Briol, photographs
of Cincinnati, 33 plates; Paul Briol, Union Terminal, 1 vol of plates,
boxed; Cincinnati composers, miscellaneous score collection, manuscripts, and autographed printed material, 12 boxes;

Dept. of Rare Books and Special Collections: (Yeatman Anderson, III,
Curator) Cincinnati House of Refuge, case records of children admit-
ted, covering cases 1-321, Oct 25, 1850 - July 17, 1852 and cases
4909-5300, Sept 19, 1883 - Sept 7, 1885; John Hough James (lawyer,
state senator, banker, and businessman of Urbana, Ohio), papers,
1815-81, 4 lf; Miscellaneous manuscript material (includes Daniel
Bailey, 17 folders; Oberlin M. Carter, 7 boxes; John Piatt, 2 boxes;
and Samuel W. Williams, 29 folders); For a complete listing of inland rivers materials, see Clyde N. Bowden (comp.), Catalog of the
Inland Rivers Library, Cincinnati, 1968;

Films and Recordings Center: (Jayne Craven, Head of Films and Recordings) Cincinnati radio station WCKY, "The Fountain Speaks," a
recorded history of Cincinnati sponsored by the J. & F. Schroth Packing Company, 26 albums, 78 discs; Slides, 1810+, 2,350 lf.   HS

368. University of Cincinnati Library
      Main Library, Room 610, Cincinnati, Ohio 45211
      (513) 475-6459   (M-F 9-5; Sat 9-12)
      William D. Aeschbacher, University Archivist
      Helen W. Slotkin, Head of Special Collections Division

Archives of Medical History: (Henry D. Shapiro, Curator) George
H. Acheson (professor and head of the Department of Pharmacology
at the University of Cincinnati), papers relating to his editorship of
the Pharmacological Review, 1959-70, 4 lf; Karl Wolfgang Ascher
(ophthalmologist),papers (publications, correspondence, and notes
relating to his professional work, especially the discovery of aqueous
veins; chief correspondents are George Hawkins Acheson, Harry
David Gideonse, Clifford Grosselle, Walter Consuelo Langsan, Albert Bruce Sabin, Potter Stewart, Derrick Tilton Vail, Raymond
Walters, Stephen Marvin Young), 18 lf;

Bibliography on Insanity from the Boston Medical and Surgical
Journal, 1828-1851, 42 pp TS; Children's Clinic of the Ohio-Miami
Medical College, annual report, 1913-14, 1 item; Dr. Christian R.
Holmes, scrapbooks, 1900-1920, 2 lf, photographs of Cincinnati
City Hospital, 20 lf, publications, 1 lf, records, 1861-1950 of Cin-
cinnati General Hospital and Cincinnati City Hospital, 33 lf;

University of Cincinnati, College of Medicine, records (includes
material from the Clinical and Pathological School of the Cincinnati
Hospital, Ohio-Miami Medical College, Medical College of Ohio,
Cincinnati College of Medicine and Surgery, UC College of Medicine,
CGH, Eclectic Medical College of Cincinnati, Academy of Medicine
of Cincinnati, Women's State Hospital and Medical College, and
University of Cincinnati, 15 lf; Eclectic Medical Institute Items (ma-
triculation ticket and correspondence with Louis C. Wattring),1896-
98, 3 items;

Frederick Hecht (specialist in genetics and pediatrics), papers;
Estelle Bode Juettner Collection (scrapbooks, correspondence, and
personal papers of Estelle Bode Juettner and of her husband, Otto
Juettner, M.D., including copies of his publications and her travel
diaries in Europe during the 1930s), 1885-1950, 9 lf; William Howard
Lewis, M.D., TSS of A Century of Medical Practice (recollections of
medical education and medical practice, 1903-65, in Cincinnati and
northern Ohio; Rome, Georgia; and at the Mayo Clinic, 1911-15), 125
pp;

Mussey collection (memorabilia, pamphlets, and printed materials),

6 in.; Ohio procedures at time of death (pamphlets relating to procedures to be followed by physicians, undertakers, and registrars at time of death), 1908, 26 items; Pennsylvania Medical College items (cards of admission and notice of examination of Andrew J. Atkinson), 1842-44, 10 items; John J. Phair (former professor and head of the Department of Preventive Medicine at the University of Cincinnati) collection (relating to his research, teaching, administrative duties, and public activities in epidemiology, public health, and industrial medicine), 1936-70, 144 lf;

Pharmacological materials (primarily old prescriptions, from as far back as 1896), 1 lf; Albert Sabin (discoverer of the attenuated live-poliovirus vaccine), papers (relating to his research and to his public activities), 1936-73, 240 lf; Edward A. Wagner (prominent Cincinnati pediatrician, former director of the Department of Pediatrics at Good Samaritan Hospital and of the Premature Department at Cincinnati General Hospital), papers (relating to the development of pediatric research and premature care, primarily in Cincinnati), 1914-70, 10 in.

College Conservatory of Music: (Robert O. Johnson, Librarian) Anatole Chujoy Memorial Dance Collection (tape recordings of radio program "Cincinnati Dance"), 3 lf; Leigh Harline collection (books and musical scores), 3 lf; Harline's personal collection of records, manuscripts, and scores related to radio, television and film, 18 lf); Frederick W. Ziv (founder and president of the Frederick W. Ziv Co. and Ziv Television Programs, Inc., leaders in the field of syndicated programming in radio and television. These companies produced more than 80 series, for a national, as well as an international market), archives (production, promotional, and business materials relevant to the production of the series, including contracts, scripts, ratings correspondence, cue sheets, sales brochures, newspaper clippings, music sheets. Among the radio programs represented are Arch Oboler, Barry Wood, Bold Venture, Cisco Kid, Dearest Mother, Dorothy and Dick, Eddie Cantor Show, Eye Witness News, Fred Waring, Guy Lombardo, I Was a Communist for the F.B.I., Red Skelton Show. Television programs include Aquanauts, Bat Masterson, Cisco Kid, Highway Patrol, I Led Three Lives, MacKenzie's Raiders, Miami Undercover, Perry Mason, Science Fiction Theatre, Sea Hunt, This Man Dawson. Master transcriptions of radio programs from the 1930s and 1940s, include the Cisco Kid, the Wayne King Show, The World's Greatest Mysteries, and Korn Kobblers), 2,105 lf.

Ohio Network Collection and Special Collections: (June Alexander, Archivist and Zane Miller, Curator) Ada Hart Arlitt (national chairwoman of Parent Education and associate editor of Child Welfare Magazine), correspondence with Ralph P. Bridgman, Isa Compton, and Martha Sprague Mason, TSS carbon and galley proofs of Psychology of Adolescence, published in 1933 as Adolescent Psychology; Roderick D. Barney, scrapbook, 1893-1911, 2 in.; Alfred Bettman (prominent Cincinnati attorney, member of Cincinnati City Planning Commission), papers, 1910-45, 32 lf; Gilbert Bettman (prominent Cincinnati attorney, state attorney general), papers, 32 lf; Ambrose Bierce, letters to Myles Walsh, 1895-1911, 62 items; Dorothy Brett, letters from John Middleton Murray, Virginia Woolf, Siegfried Sassoon, J. M. Keynes, and others, ca. 90 items;

Census tract data center collection (raw census tract material and published reports pertaining to the tri-state area, with special emphasis on Cincinnati), 1930s-1960s, 9 lf; Cincinnati Division of Police, annual reports, 1934-61, 2 lf; University of Cincinnati pamphlets, 1 in.; Cist advertisers (old Cincinnati advertisement sheets), 1845, 1847-48, 1851, 3 lf; Clinton County collection (legal documents dealing with a variety of cases, primarily in the Court of Common Pleas and involving questions of land tenure and inheritance), 1850-70, 3 lf;

Addison T. Culter (professor of economics at the University of Cincinnati, formerly research analyst at Federal Reserve Bank of Cleveland), papers, including materials relating to economic theory and economic planning, 1936-70, 1 lf; College of Education papers, 1903-32, 35 lf; Pierre Teilhard de Chardin, facsimile MSS, 19 vols; Elliston poetry lecture series (tapes of lectures by Allen Curnow, Donald Davie, Denis Donoghue, Richard Eberhart, Robert Frost, Donald Hall, Daniel Hoffman, Donald Justice, John Press, George Thompson, and David Wagoner), 1955+; Earle Edward Eubank (former professor of sociology at University of Cincinnati), papers, 3 lf; John C. Fuhr, papers relating to the operation of his hardware business and stove company in Williamsburg, Ohio, 1891-1917, 5 in. ;

Robert P. Goldman (Cincinnati attorney) collection (correspondence, newspaper clippings, and assorted printed matter dealing with the activities of Robert P. Goldman for proportional representation on behalf of the Cincinnati Charter Committee; also general information concerning Cincinnati politics from 1920s to 1960s), 4 lf; Arthur T. Hamlin, letters and postcards to, ca. 10 items; "The Isoline," newsletter of the Department of Geography, University of Cincinnati, 1966+, 5 in.; Anne Jackson MSS, autobiography, ca. 1630-83; D. H. Lawrence collection (four autobiographical sketches and letters), ca. 160 items; William T.

Lawrence collection (history of Dublin stage), 1909-34, 99 vols; James A. Maxwell, TS of "The First Hundred Years" (a history of the Pogue Department Store in Cincinnati), 26 pp; National Municipal League, materials relating to the history of "proportional representation" as advocated by the National Municipal League, especially during the 1930s, 3 lf; Newspaper clippings from the Boston Journal concerning the Spanish-American War, 1 folder; Sir Isaac Newton, correspondence of Newton and Prof. Cotes (corrections and additions to letters in the Edlestone collection, hand copied from the Portsmouth collection at Cambridge), 1710-11, 1 vol; Police-community relations in Cincinnati (various materials relating to a proposed NSF interdisciplinary study of police-community relations in Cincinnati), 1875-1971, 2 in.;

Queensgate II Development Program (historical and sociological data), 1968-70, 6 in.; James Alfred Quinn (former professor of sociology at University of Cincinnati), papers, 5 in.; Martha Ransohoff (prominent Cincinnati educator), papers relating to her activities on behalf of the development of child care facilities and early childhood education programs, including children's television, in Cincinnati, 35 lf; Jacob G. Schmidlapp, papers, 1895-1919, 2 lf; Department of Sociology collection (article abstracts and various studies pertaining to Cincinnati), 5 in.; Stephen Spender, notebook of essays, verse rhyme and other experiments, 1925-28, 1 vol; Gerald Springer, papers relating to his activities in state and local politics, 1969, 2 in.; Raymond Walters (president of University of Cincinnati), diaries, 1925-28, 1930-60 (closed until 1977); Daniel Webster, clippings from newspapers concerning his life and public services, published at the time of his death in 1851, 1 in.; Laurence G. Wolf, "Stalag '68 and the Hippy Haymarket," a mimeographed report on the Democratic National Convention of 1968 at Chicago by an alternate delegate from the Second Congressional District of Ohio, 9 pp. HS

369. Xavier University Library (1831)
    Dana and Victory Parkway, Cincinnati, Ohio 45207
    (513) 745-3681 (M-F 8-4:30)
    John Vigle, Director

Moses Dawson (editor and proprietor of The Advertiser, a Jacksonian Democratic newspaper), letters, 1811-45 (letters from William Henry Harrison, Andrew Jackson, Martin Van Buren, and Levi Woodbury), 184 items; Father Finn collection (miscellaneous cards, notes, photographs, and memoirs), 3 lf; Literary manuscripts of Francis J. Finn, Jr., and Henry S. Spalding. FH

INSTITUTIONAL RECORDS

370. Academy of Medicine, Cincinnati
      320 Broadway, Cincinnati, Ohio 45202
      (513) 421-7010   (M-F 8:30-5; Sat 9-12)
      Edward F. Willenborg, Executive Secretary

Professional organization.

Minutes, 1857+, 25 lf. LM

371. AFL-CIO Community Services, Cincinnati (1942)
      2400 Reading Road, Cincinnati, Ohio 45202
      (513) 621-5000   (M-F 9-5)
      Robert Lamb, Executive Director

Administrative records; Agreements, 1942+; Case problems, 2-year
retention; Financial statements, 7-year retention; Newsletter, 1971+;
20 lf total. BM

372. AFL-CIO Labor Council, Cincinnati (1960)
      1015 Vine Street, Cincinnati, Ohio 45202
      (513) 421-1846   (M-F 8:30-4:30)
      William Sheehan, Secretary-Treasurer

Administrative records, 1960-69; AFL Central Labor Council, news-
paper, 1893-1959; Correspondence, 1960+; Financial records, 1960+;
History prior to 1960 (bound minutes), 1889-1959; Inventories, 1960+;
Labor history library of monographs and pamphlets; Minutes, 1960+;
Publications (newspaper to 1964, newsletter 1964+); Receipts, 1960+;
Scrapbooks, pre-1960. BM

373. American Federation of Radio and TV Artists (1964)
      Terrace Hilton Building, Cincinnati, Ohio 45202
      (513) 241-7332   (M-F 9-5)
      H. Thomas Brown, Executive Secretary

Administrative records, 1964; Agreements, 1971+; Cashbooks, 1971+;
Contracts, 1971+; Correspondence, 2-year retention; Financial statements; Minutes, 1971+; Receipts; 3 lf total. HG

374. American Federation of State, County, and Municipal Employees
      Union No. 51
      2607 Vine Street, Cincinnati, Ohio 45219
      (513) 221-3169   (M-F 9-4:30)
      Al Van Hagen, Staff Director

Administrative records, 1942+; Agreements, 10-year retention; Annual
reports, 6-year retention; Bulletins; Correspondence, 1963+; Financial
statements, 7-year retention; Membership lists; Minutes, 1942+; Scrapbooks; Tax records, 7-year retention; 65 lf total.   BM

375. Appalachian Hardwood Manufacturers (1933)
      607 Mercantile Library Building, Cincinnati, Ohio 45202
      (513) 621-5068   (M-F 8:30-5)
      H. D. Bennett, Executive Vice-President

Administrative records, 1933+; Agreements, 1933+; Annual reports,
1933+; Bulletins; Contracts, 1933+; Correspondence; Financial statements, 1933+; Membership directory, annual; Minutes, 1933+; Newsletter, 1933+; Proceedings, 1933+; Receipts, 1933+; Scrapbooks, 1933+;
Tax records, 1933+; 80 lf total.   BM

376. Archdiocesan Department for Social Action (1969)
      The Fenwick Club, 426 East Fifth Street, Cincinnati, Ohio 45202
      (513) 621-7633   (M-F 9-5)
      Bill Schumaker, Director

Agency to design and develop programs to serve community and educational needs; main liaison between church and community.

Administrative records, 1971; Agreements; Daybooks; Financial statements; Journals; Ledgers; Minutes; Quarterly newsletter, 1972.   HG

377. Brewery Workers International Union (1886)
      2347 Vine Street, Cincinnati, Ohio 45219
      (513) 421-9700   (M-F 8:45-4:30)
      Karl F. Feller, President

Administrative records, 1886+; Agreements, 1886-1955; Annual reports, 1886+; Contract statistics, 1911-42; Contracts, 1886-1955;
Correspondence, microfilmed; Deeds, 1910; Financial records, 1886+;
Journals, 1886+; Membership records, 1886+; Minutes, 1886+; Photographs, 1886+; Plats, 1910; Proceedings, 1886+; Publications, 1886+;

Scrapbooks; Tax records, 7-year retention; 150 lf total.   BM

378. Burger Brewing Company (1874)
        Central Parkway at Liberty, Cincinnati, Ohio 45214
        (M-F 8:30-5)
        Florence Mayer, Assistant Secretary

Annual reports, 1932+; Minutes, 1932+; Monthly publication, "World
of Burger."   FH

379. Chamber of Commerce, Cincinnati (1839)
        309 Vine Street, Cincinnati, Ohio 45202
        (513) 721-3300
        Sue Hart, Researcher

Agreements, 1971+; Annual reports, 1850+, 4 lf; Contracts, 1972+;
Correspondence, 1-year retention; Ledgers, business conditions in
Cincinnati, 1926-35, 1 lf; Membership files, 1935+, 8 lf; Minutes,
1925+, 3 lf; Publications, 1919+, 6 lf.   BM

380. Charter Committee of Cincinnati and Hamilton County (1924)
        441 Vine Street, Cincinnati, Ohio 45202
        (513) 241-0303   (M-F 9-5)
        Forest Frank, Executive Director

Administrative records, 1924+; Annual reports; Campaign material,
2-year retention; Correspondence; Minutes; Publications; 4 lf total.
HG

381. Christ Episcopal Church (1817)
        318 East Fourth Street, Cincinnati, Ohio 45202
        (513) 621-1960
        J. Wesley Morris, Parish Historiographer

Annual reports, 1870-1942; Parish register, 1817+; Scrapbooks of
parish societies, 1905+, 6 lf; Vestry minutes, 1817+, 3 lf.   JH

382. Cincinnati Art Museum (1881)
        Eden Park, Cincinnati, Ohio 45202
        (513) 721-5204   (M-F 10-4:30)
        Alice Hook, Librarian

Annual reports, 1881-1926, 1930+, 5 lf; Board of trustees, minutes,
1881+, 8 lf; Business and treasurers' records, 1881+; Index to annual
exhibitions and Cincinnati artists, on index cards, 12 lf; Miscellaneous
archival material relating to the museum, 10 lf; Publications, 1882+,
2 lf; Published materials on national and international art museums, 23
lf; Scrapbooks, 1901+, 8 lf; Vertical file on Cincinnati and area artists,
1900+, 16 lf; Vertical file material on accessions, 12 lf.   FH

383. Cincinnati Association for the Blind (1910)
         2045 Gilbert Avenue, Cincinnati, Ohio 45202
         (513) 221-8558   (M-F 8:30-4:30)
         Milton A. Jahoda, Executive Director

Administrative records, 1910+; Agreements, 1918; Annual reports,
1910+; Correspondence, 7-year retention; Daybooks, 1910+; Deeds,
1967; Minutes, 1910+; Newsletters, 1958+; Pamphlets, 1910+; Payroll
records, 1910; Publications, 1969; Scrapbooks, 1910+; Tax records
(tax-free); 40 lf total.   BM

384. Cincinnati Better Business Bureau, Inc. (1923)
         26 East Sixth Street, Cincinnati, Ohio 45202
         (513) 421-3015   (M-F 8:30-5)
         George C. Young, President

Administrative records, 1923+; Annual reports, 1946+; Case files
(includes information on companies, complaints, and follow-ups),
1923+, 400+ lf; Membership records, 1923+, 2 lf; Minutes, 1923+,
4 in.; Publications, 1946+; Scrapbooks, 1946+, 2 lf.   FH

385. Cincinnati Law Library Association
         601 Court House, Cincinnati, Ohio 45202
         (513) 632-6500   (M-F 8-4)
         Carol M. Bratton, Librarian

Private organization which supports the law library with its member-
ships.

Board of trustees, minutes, 1847+, 5 vols.   LM

386. The Cincinnati Masonic Temple Company (1917)
         East Fifth Street, Cincinnati, Ohio 45202
         (513) 621-4829   (M-F 9-3)
         Tony Caito, Building Manager

Administrative records, 1917; Agreements; Contracts; Correspondence; Deeds; Minutes; Scrapbooks, 1919-29; 16 lf total.   HG

387. The Cincinnati Reds (1869)
        Riverfront Stadium, Cincinnati, Ohio 45202
        (513) 421-4510   (M-F 8:30-5)
        Richard Wagner, Assistant to the Executive Vice-President

Administrative records, 1967; Annual reports, 1967; Cashbooks, 1967; Correspondence; Financial records, 1967; Inventories, 1967; Minutes, 1967; Publications; Scrapbooks, 1960s+; 200 lf total.   HG

388. Cincinnati School Foundation
        35 East Seventh Street, Cincinnati, Ohio   45202
        (513) 241-1177   (M-F 8-3)
        Mrs. Robert Grayman, Executive Secretary

A privately funded group formed to disseminate information about public schools, to foster research on education, and to stimulate interest in education.

Annual reports, 1952+; Correspondence, 1952+, 4 lf; Minutes, 1952+. LM

389. Cincinnati Symphony Orchestra (1895)
        Central Trust Tower, Cincinnati, Ohio 45202
        (513) 241-8121   (M-F 9-5)
        Paul Ebert, Controller

Administrative records, 1895+; Agreements, 1895+; Annual reports, 1895+; Cashbooks, 1895+; Contracts, 1895+; Correspondence, 1895+; Daybooks, 1895+; Financial statements, 1895+; Ledgers, 1895+; Minutes, 1895+; Proceedings, 1895+; Publications (bound annual programs); Scrapbooks, 1895+.   HG

390. Cincinnati Teachers' Association
        310 Oak Street, Suite 601, Cincinnati, Ohio 45246
        (513) 281-9936   (M-F 8:30-5; Sat by appt.)
        Joseph Landeau, Executive Director

Professional organization of teachers and administrators in Cincinnati public schools.

Board of trustees, minutes, 1921+; Correspondence, 1921+, 16 lf;
Newsletter, 1921+. LM

391. Cincinnati Typographical Union No. 3 (1846)
       1015 Vine Street, Cincinnati, Ohio 45202
       (513) 721-1253   (M-F 8:30-4:30)
       William A. Foxx, President

Administrative records, 1846+; Contracts, 1893, 1896; Correspondence,1853+; Financial statements, 1846+; Minutes, 1846+; Mortuary
benefits, 1891+; Publications (bound newspaper), 1846+; Receipts, 7-
year retention; Tax records, 7-year retention; Union Printers Home,
operated for the aged and disabled; 76 lf total.   BM

392. Communications Workers No. 4400 (1937)
       414 Walnut Street, Cincinnati, Ohio 45202
       (513) 621-3422   (M-F 8:30-4:30)
       Richard Nagle, President

Administrative records, 1937+; Agreements, 1937+; Annual reports,
1937+; Contracts, 1937+; Correspondence, 1937+; Daybooks, 9-year
retention; Financial statements, 7-year retention; Grievance records,
1937+; Membership records, 1937+; Minutes, 1937+; Monthly publications, 1956+; Negotiation records, 1937+; Receipts, 7-year retention;
Scrapbooks; Tax records, 7-year retention; 70 lf total.   BM

393. Community Chest (1915)
       2400 Reading Road, Cincinnati, Ohio 45202
       (513) 721-3160   (M-F 9-5)
       Paul Mecklenburg, Comptroller

Administrative records, 1915-55, 3 in.; Correspondence, 1-year retention; Deeds, 7 boxes; Financial records, 10-year retention, 15 lf;
Membership records, 5-year retention; Minutes, 1915+, 20 lf; Plats,
1 drawer; Scrapbooks, 2-year retention; Tax records, 3-4 back years.
BM

394. Contemporary Arts Center (1940)
       115 East Fifth Street, Cincinnati, Ohio 45202
       (513) 721-0390
       William A. Leonard, Director

Correspondence (contemporary artists), 1964+, 1 folder.   LM

395. Democratic Party, Hamilton County (1954)
        615 Main, Cincinnati, Ohio 45202
        (513) 421-0495   (M-F 9-5)
        Mildred Atkinson, Assistant Director

Clippings, 3 lf; Financial records, 5 lf; Policy committee and long-
range planning committee, minutes, 1968+, 1 lf.   HG

396. Distillers Feed Research Council (1946)
        1435 Enquirer Building, Cincinnati, Ohio 45202
        (513) 621-5985   (M-F 9-5)
        Lawrence Carpenter, Executive Director

Administrative records; Annual reports, 1946+; Board of directors,
minutes, 1946+; Cashbooks, 1946+; Correspondence; Financial statements, 1946+; Ledgers, 1946+; Project files, 1946+; Publications,
1947; Research review of bibliographic sources; Scrapbooks, 1945+.
BM

397. Drackett Company (1910)
        5020 Spring Grove Avenue, Cincinnati, Ohio 45232
        (513) 632-1240   (M-F 9:30-4)
        Jack Hilborn, Public Relations

This company became a subsidiary of Bristol-Meyers Corporation in
1965 and records after that date are maintained in New York.

Administrative records, 1910+; Agreements, 1910+; Annual reports,
1910+; Contracts, 1910+; Correspondence, 2-4 year retention; Deeds,
1910; Financial statements, 7-year retention; Ledgers, 7-year retention; Minutes, 1910+; Publications, bi-monthly, mid-1930s; Scrapbooks, 1930s; Subsidiaries, 1965+; Tax records, 7-year retention.
BM

398. Episcopal Diocese of Southern Ohio (1875)
        412 Sycamore, Cincinnati, Ohio 45202
        (513) 421-0311   (Hours by appointment)
        William Paddock, Registrar

Administrative records, 1875+; Annual reports, 1875+; Correspondence; Financial records, 7-year retention; History of every congregation in diocese; Journals, 1875+; Minutes, 1875+; Proceedings, 1875+; Publications, monthly, 1875+; Scrapbooks; Tax records, 7-year retention; 50 lf total.   HG

399. Family Planning Association of the Ohio River Valley (1971)
        3333 Vine Street, Cincinnati, Ohio 45202
        (M-F 9-5)
        Ron C. Leach, Project Director

Administrative records, 1971+, 4 lf; Annual reports, 1971+; Correspondence, 1971+; Financial statements, 1969-71; Parent records; Receipts, 1969-71; Statistical records, 1970+, 24 lf; Tax records, 1969-71.   BM

400. First United Church on Walnut Hills (1958)
        Gilbert Avenue and William Howard Taft Road, Cincinnati, Ohio 45206
        (513) 751-6677   (M-F 9-5)
        Mrs. Howard Perin, Church Secretary

This church is the result of numerous mergers and has accumulated quantities of records from each merger: (1) First Presbyterian Church on Walnut Hills, founded 1918; (2) Lane Seminary Presbyterian Church, 1831, merged into one,1878; (3) Avondale Presbyterian Church merged with Walnut Hills Congregational Church in 1941 and became the First United Church of Cincinnati; (4) The First United Church of Cincinnati merged with the First Presbyterian Church on Walnut Hills and in 1958 became the First United Church on Walnut Hills.

Avondale Presbyterian Church; First Presbyterian Church on Walnut Hills, records, 1918+; Lane Seminary Presbyterian Church records, 1831-78.   LM

401. Greater Cincinnati Safety Council (1936)
        309 Vine Street, Cincinnati, Ohio 45202
        (513) 421-6163   (M-F 9-4)
        Alice Taylor, Assistant to Director

Administrative records, 1951+; Agreements, 1951+; Annual reports, 1951+; Contracts, 1951+; Correspondence, 1951+; Daybooks, 1951+; Education; Financial statements, 1951+; Industrial campaign; Inventories, 1951+; Journals,

1951+; Ledgers, 1951+; Minutes of board meetings, 1951+; Proceedings, 1951+; Publications, 1951-71; Receipts, 1951+; Scrapbooks; Tax records, 1951+; 13 lf total.   HG

402. Institute for Governmental Research (1968)
        3333 Vine Street, Cincinnati, Ohio 45202
        (M-F 8-5)
        Iola O. Hessler, Senior Research Associate

The institute is affiliated with the University of Cincinnati and conducts studies on housing, labor relations, municipal government, and constitutional revision.

Administrative records, 1968+; Correspondence; Publications, 1968+; Unpublished studies; 30 lf total.   BM

403. Institute for Metropolitan Studies (1967)
        3333 Vine Street, Cincinnati, Ohio 45202
        (M-F 9-5)

The institute is associated with the University of Cincinnati and conducts studies of metropolitan Cincinnati.

Administrative records, 1967+; Applied research; Contracts, 1967+; Financial records; Publications, 1967+; Receipts; Scrapbooks; Statistical studies; Tax records.   BM

404. International Molders and Allied Workers Union (1870)
        1225 East McMillan Street, Cincinnati, Ohio 45221
        (513) 221-1525   (M-F 9-5)
        James E. Wolfe, Education Director

Administrative records, 1859+; Contracts, 1870+; Correspondence, 1859+, mf; Deeds, 1949; Financial records, quarterly, 6 lf; Minutes, 1859+, 12 lf; Mortuary benefits, mf; Pamphlets, 1971; Proceedings, 1859+, 10 lf; Publications (monthly magazine), 1863+, 10 lf; Scrapbooks, 1967+, 6 in.; Tax records.   BM

405. Junior League of Cincinnati
        Cincinnati Art Museum, Eden Park, Cincinnati, Ohio 45202
        (513) 621-8359   (M-F 9-3)
        Mrs. William Nowland, Placement Secretary

Branch of Junior League of America, a training organization for community service.

Annual reports, 1920+; Board minutes, 1920+, 2 lf; Correspondence, 1920+; Scrapbooks, 8 vols. LM

406. Legal Aid Society, Cincinnati (1907)
        2400 Reading Road, Cincinnati, Ohio 45202
        (513) 241-9400   (M-F 8:30-4:30)
        Robert E. L. Young, Chief Counsel, Project Director

The seventh oldest Legal Aid Society in the United States.

Annual reports; Civil and criminal cases; Contracts; Correspondence, 10 years/clients; Financial statements; Minutes, 1907+; Monthly reports; Personnel records; Scrapbooks from earlier period; Statistical records; Tax records, 1940-66. BM

407. Literary Club (1849)
        500 East Fourth Street, Cincinnati, Ohio 45202
        (513) 621-6589
        Carl Vitz, Librarian

The 100 members of the Literary Club meet once a week from September to June. Members present literary papers.

Biographical file on members, 1849+, 4 lf; Board minutes, 1849+, 5 lf; Literary Club, 1849+; Papers delivered at meetings (bound), 1885+, 20 lf. LM

408. Mercantile Library (1835)
        414 Walnut Street, 11th Floor, Cincinnati, Ohio 45202
        (513) 621-0717   (M-F 9-5:30)
        Jean Springer, Executive Director

Administrative records, 1835+; Agreements, 1840+, 10,000 year lease; Board of directors, annual reports, 1835+; Financial statements, 1835+; Ledgers, 1835+; Minutes, 1835+; Publications (pamphlets, photographs); Receipts; Scrapbooks, 1885+ (incomplete); Tax records, 20-year retention; 75 lf total. BM

409. Methodist Publishing Company (1820)
     Mercantile Library Building, Cincinnati, Ohio 45202
     (513) 381-1100   (M-F 9-5)
     Eleanor Bovard, Co-Manager

The Cincinnati office holds records on a six-month retention basis.
Earlier records are stored at the United Methodist Publishing House
Co., Nashville, Tennessee.

Administrative records, 1820+; Annual reports, 1820+; Contracts,
1971; Correspondence, 2-year retention; Financial statements, 1820+;
Minutes, 1820+; Proceedings, 1820+; Publications, 1820+; Tax records, 7-year retention.   BM

410. Metropolitan Area Religious Coalition (1968)
     Provident Bank Building, Cincinnati, Ohio 45202
     (513) 721-4843   (M-F 9-5)
     Joseph Sprague, Executive Director

This organization sees itself as an issue-oriented intermediary body.
Consequently, it both initiates action on its own and acts as an information dispensary. Its main activity is research and it has much material on local campaigns for "social action."

Administrative records, 1969+; Cashbooks, 1969+; Financial statements, 1969+; Minutes, 1969+; Publications, 1969+; Receipts, 1969+;
6 lf total.   HG

411. Mt. St. Mary's Seminary of the West Library
     5440 Moeller, Norwood, Ohio 45212
     (513) 731-2630   (Hours by appointment)
     Fr. Stricker, Librarian

Correspondence (letters written by early priests and lay people to
the Bishop and his replies; contain history of Catholic church in Cincinnati and surrounding region, including in early period Michigan
and Kentucky), 1821-55, 25 lf.   LM

412. Ninth Street Baptist Church (1830)
     25 West Ninth Street, Cincinnati, Ohio 45202
     (513) 241-4643
     Louise Heisel, Church Secretary

Clerk's record book (includes membership, trustees' meetings), 1845+, 9 lf; Publications, 1900+; Scrapbooks, 1880s and 1890s.   FH

413. Ohio Association of Nurses (1903)
        3333 Vine Street, Cincinnati, Ohio 45202
        (513) 961-2981   (M-F 9-5)
        Eliza Williams, Executive Secretary

Oldest assocation of nurses in Ohio.

Administrative records, 1903; Annual reports, 1897+, 8 lf; Correspondence; Financial records, 7-year retention; Membership lists, 1897+; Minutes, 1897+; Publications, 6 lf; Registry of nurses, 1898+; Tax records, 7-year retention.   BM

414. Ohio Thoroughbred Breeders and Owners (1956)
        812 Race Street, Cincinnati, Ohio 45202
        (513) 241-4589   (M-F 9-6)
        Edward A. Babst, Executive Secretary

Administrative records, 1956+; Annual reports, 1956+; Correspondence, 1956+; Financial records, 1956+; Inventories, 1956+; Minutes, 1956+; Photographs; Proceedings, 1956+; Quarterly magazine, 1970+; 8 lf total.   HG

415. Ohio Valley Carpenters' District Council
        1230 Walnut Street, Cincinnati, Ohio 45210
        (513) 721-2627   (M-F 7:30-4:30)
        Russell Austin, Secretary

Financial records, 1889+, 10 lf; Council minutes, 1889+, 10 lf.   LM

416. Phillippus Evangelical and Reformed Church (1890)
        106 West McMicken Avenue, Cincinnati, Ohio 45210
        (513) 241-5244
        Milford Bollinger, Lay Assistant

Minutes (includes 17 vols. of minutes of parent church, St. Matthews Evangelical and Reform Church, 1823-1919), 1842+, 6 lf.   FH

417. The Procter and Gamble Company (1837)
        Sixth and Sycamore Streets, Cincinnati, Ohio 45202
        (513) 562-2595   (M-F 8:30-4:30)
        Charles F. Darden, Supervisor of Press Relations and Infor-
        mation Services

Administrative records, 1837+; Annual reports, 1838+; Advertising
and display materials; Certificates; Contracts; Correspondence,1838+;
Financial records, 1838+; Minutes, 1837+; Plats; Proceedings, 1838+;
Publications; Receipts, 1837-early 1900s; Scrapbooks.   LM

418. Railway Clerks Building (1922)
        1015 Vine Street, Cincinnati, Ohio 45202
        (513) 721-7820   (M-F 8:30-4:30)
        Warren L. Gelter, Building Superintendent

This building has been the major headquarters of organized labor in
Cincinnati since 1922. Material is primarily on the Railway Clerks'
Union.

Administrative records, 1922+; Annual reports, 1922+; Contracts,
1922+; Deeds, 1922+; Financial records, 1922+; Inventories, 1922+;
Ledgers, 1922+; Tax records, 1922+; 100 lf total.   BM

419. Republican Party, Hamilton County
        700 Walnut Street, Cincinnati, Ohio 45202
        (513) 381-5454   (M-F 8:30-5)
        Mrs. MacFarland, Secretary

Administrative records; Agreements; Cashbooks; Contracts; Correspondence, 2-year retention; Deeds; Financial statements; Inventories; Minutes; Scrapbooks, 6 years; 10 lf total.   HG

420. Seventh Presbyterian Church (1850)
        Madison Road and Glenview Avenue, Cincinnati, Ohio 45206
        (M-F 9-5)
        Allen Ward Beach, Minister

Registers, financial books, and session records, 1850+, 6 vols and
loose unarranged material.   LM

421. Sisters of Charity of Cincinnati (1852)
        Mount Saint Joseph, Delhi Hills, Ohio 45051
        (513) 244-4624
        Sr. Marie Anne Austin, Archivist

Keep records of various institutions run by the Sisters of Charity
from several locations in the U.S. and around the world.

Administrative records; Agreements, 1952+; Annual reports, 1952+;
Cashbooks, 1952+; Community annals, 1852+; Contracts, 1952+; Correspondence, 1952+; Daybooks, 1952+; Deeds, 1952+; Financial statements, 1952+; Journals, 1952+; Ledgers, 1952+; Plats, 1952+; Publications, 1952+; Receipts, 1952+; Scrapbooks, 1952+; Mother Seton
(foundress of order), letters, ca. 1300 items.   HS

422. Taft Museum (1932)
        316 Pike Street, Cincinnati, Ohio 45202
        (513) 241-0343   (M-F 10-5)
        Katherine Hanna, Director

Privately endowed museum of period rooms (1850s) with painting mas-
terpieces from Europe and America, fine enamels, majolicas, porce-
lains, and crystals, all collected by Mr. and Mrs. Charles Phelps Taft
and opened to the public in 1932.

Board of trustees, minutes, 1945+, 1 vol; Correspondence, 1932+, 30
lf; Inventories (file folders on art objects in collections), 1931-32, 6 lf;
Scrapbooks, 1932+, 4 lf.   LM

423. Telecare-Easy Riders (1970)
        2400 Reading Road, Cincinnati, Ohio 45202
        (513) 651-2611   (M-F 9-5)
        Eva Cunningham, Executive Secretary & Assistant Treasurer

A privately funded organization involved in a three-year pilot project
to provide transportation for the infirm.

Administrative records, 1970+; Annual reports; Correspondence, 1971+;
Minutes, 1971+; Scrapbooks, 1971+; Statistical records, 1971+; 10 lf
total.   FH

424. United Steelworkers, Cincinnati District Office (1936)
        3333 Vine Street, Cincinnati, Ohio 45202
        (M-F 9-5)
        Rita Parker, Office Secretary

Administrative records, 1936+; Agreements, 6-year retention; Annual reports, 1936+; Contracts, 6-year retention; Correspondence,
6-year retention, 6 in.; Financial records, 7-year retention; Proceedings, 1936+, 7 lf; Publications, international, monthly; Receipts, 7-
year retention; Tax records, 7-year retention, 6 in.   BM

425. Urban League, Cincinnati (1948)
        2400 Reading Road, Cincinnati, Ohio 45202
        (513) 721-2237   (M-F 9-4)
        Joseph Hall, Executive Director

Annual reports, 1948+; Correspondence, 1948+; Daybooks, 1947+; Financial records, 1948+; Ledgers, 1948+; Minutes, 1948+; Scrapbooks
(newspaper clippings, programs); Special project publications; 40 lf
total.   FH

426. Xavier University Archives (McDonald Memorial Library) (1840)
        Xavier University, Victory Parkway, Cincinnati, Ohio 45207
        (513) 853-3681   (M-F 8-10; Sat 8-5; Sun 1-5)
        Fr. Manning, Archivist

Correspondence, 1850+, 64 lf; Financial statements, 1930+, 3 vols
and 4 lf; Minutes, 1847+, 40 vols; Scrapbooks, 1920+, 5 vols; Society
of Jesus, catalog, 1917+, 20 vols.   LM

427. YMCA, Cincinnati (1853)
        1105 Elm, Cincinnati, Ohio 45202
        (513) 241-5348   (M-Sat 9-5)
        Mr. Strothman, Executive Director Central Branch

Administrative records, 1853; Agreements, 1853+; Annual reports,
1853+; Bimonthly bulletin, 1930+; Cashbooks, 1853+; Contracts, 1853+;
Correspondence, 1853+; Daybooks; Financial statements, 1853+; Inventories, scattered; Journals; Ledgers; Minutes, 1853+; Proceedings,
1853+; Scrapbooks (pictures and newspaper clippings), 1900+; Tax records; 100 lf total.   HG

428. YWCA, Cincinnati (1868) .
      9th and Walnut, Cincinnati, Ohio 45202
      (513) 241-7090   (M-F 9-5)
      Mrs. Rautio, Metropolitan Executive Director

Administrative records, 1868+; Agreements; Annual reports, 1868+;
Cashbooks; Contracts; Daybooks, 1868+; Deeds; Financial statements;
Journals, 1868+; Ledgers, 1868+; Minutes, 1868+; Newsletter; Re-
ceipts; Scrapbooks; 75 lf total.   HG

                        HANCOCK COUNTY

INSTITUTIONAL RECORDS

429. La Raza Unida De Ohio
      P. O. Box 144, Findlay, Ohio 45840
      (419) 423-4022   (M-F 8-4)
      Angustina Davala, Director, Farm Workers Division

A non-violent, political pressure group for farm workers and Spanish-
speaking people, which is responsible for hearing grievances between
farm workers and growers.

Correspondence, 1969+, 8 lf; Minutes, 1969+, 2 lf; Monthly newsletter,
1969+.   PY

430. United Fund of Hancock County (1955)
      First National Bank Building, Findlay, Ohio 45840
      (419) 423-1432   (M-F 9-5)
      H. B. Schieber, Executive Director

Administrative records, 1955+; Annual reports, 1955+; Financial statements, 7-year retention; Minutes, 1955+; Publications (campaign literature), 1960+; Scrapbooks, 1955+; 18 lf total.   PY

431. United Rubber Workers, Local #207 (1941)
      131 North Main, Findlay, Ohio 45840
      (419) 422-4224   (M 1-5)
      Donald E. Gilbert, President

Administrative records, 1941+; Agreements, 1941+; Cancelled checks,
1941+, 5 lf; Contracts, 1941+; Financial statements, 1941+; Grievance

records, 1941+, 6 lf; Minutes, 1941+; "News & Views," monthly newsletter for members, ca. 1961; Newsclippings and photos.   PY

HARDIN COUNTY

MANUSCRIPTS

432.   Hardin County Historical Society (1967)
        121 North Detroit, Kenton, Ohio 43326
        (419) 673-6201   (F 7-9; Sun 2-4)
        Helen Soulisberry, Secretary

Account books and notebooks, miscellaneous; Deeds; Forest Review
(Forest, Ohio, newspaper), 5 lf; Hardin County Civil War soldiers'
discharges; Photographs; Scioto Sign Company, account books, ca.
1899 - ca. 1922; Edward Sorgen, correspondence, 1863-65.   SF

433.   Hardin County Library
        East Columbus, Kenton, Ohio 43326
        (419) 673-2278   (M, Tu, W 9:30-8; Th, F, Sat 9:30-5)
        Judy Wilson, Head Librarian

Newspaper, Kenton Times, 1972+; Periodicals, 5-year retention. SF

INSTITUTIONAL RECORDS

434.   Chamber of Commerce, Kenton
        8 North Main Street, Kenton, Ohio 43326
        (419) 675-2427   (M-F 8-5)
        Holmes Stein, President

Annual reports, 1969+; Board of directors, minutes, 1969+; Brochures,
1969+; Correspondence, 1969+; Financial records, 1969+; News releases,
1969+; Scrapbooks, 1969+; 16 lf total.   SF

435.   Hardin County Historical Society (1967)
        121 North Detroit, Kenton, Ohio 43326
        (419) 673-6201   (F 7-9; Sun 2-4)
        Helen Soulisberry, Secretary

Accessions records, 1967+; Annual reports, 1967+; Board of trustees,

minutes, 1967+; Bulletin, quarterly, 1974+; Financial records, 1967+;
Membership records, 1967+.   SF

436. Moose Lodge #428 (1913)
      214 West Franklin, Kenton, Ohio 43326
      (419) 673-6297   (M-F 10:30-12)
      George Hamilton, Secretary

Correspondence; Financial records; Lodge and club records, 1913+;
Membership records; Minutes; Photographs.   SF

HARRISON COUNTY

MANUSCRIPTS

437. Harrison County Historical Society
      Harrison County Courthouse, Cadiz, Ohio 43907
      (614) 942-3257   (Hours by appointment)
      John S. Campbell, Director

Commissioners journal, 1813-1900, 25 lf; Genealogical studies, 19th
century, 3 lf; Harrison County poll books, 1813-45, 5 lf; Harrison
County property maps, 1862, 1904, 1930s.   LS

INSTITUTIONAL RECORDS

438. Cadiz Public Library (1880)
      Harrison County Courthouse, Cadiz, Ohio 43907
      (614) 942-2623   (M, Tu, Th, F 9-8; W 9-12; Sat 9-6)
      Katherine McOllister, Library Manager

Journals, 1883+, 5 vols.   LS

HENRY COUNTY

INSTITUTIONAL RECORDS

439. The Bank of Henry County
      701 North Perry Street, Napoleon, Ohio 43545
      (419) 599-2010   (M, Tu, Th 9-3; W, Sat 9-12; F 9-5:30)
      W. J. Merz, President

Administrative records, 1935; Annual reports, 1935+; Correspondence, 1960-72, 10 lf; Minutes, 1935+. PY

440. Napoleon Publishing Company
      610 North Perry Street, Napoleon, Ohio 43545
      (419) 592-5055   (M-F 8-5)
      James K. Kuser, Publisher

Administrative records, 1966; Annual reports, 1966+; Minutes, 1966+; Northwest-Signal, 1962+, 50 vols. PY

HIGHLAND COUNTY

MANUSCRIPTS

441. Highland County District Library (1878)
      10 Willettsville Pike, Hillsboro, Ohio 45133
      (513) 393-3114   (M-Sat 9-5)
      Helen C. Satterfield, Head Librarian

Genealogy collection, 1 lf; Roster of veterans buried in Hillsboro and some outlying cemeteries, compiled May 1965, 25 pp. FH

442. Highland County Historical Society (1965)
      154 East Main Street, Hillsboro, Ohio 45311
      (513) 393-3392   (M-F 2-5)
      Joseph G. Rockhold, President

Bells Opera House, bookings and management records, 1920-22, 3 in.; Crusade material, 1873-1934, newspaper clippings, correspondence of Eliza Jane Thompson (Hillsboro, 1873, first town to go dry in U.S.), 2 lf; June Doorley, scrapbook on WWII, 1941-45, 2 in.; Elk B.P.O. #361, membership list, 1915, 1 in.; Hibben Dry Goods Store, ledgers of sales to customers (oldest family owned store west of Alleghenies until sold in 1958), 1927-58, 18 in.; Kramer House, register for 1886, 2 in.; Sparger Brothers Co., general merchants, ledger, 1869-78, 3 in.; Allen Trimble, 7th Governor of Ohio, 1815-30, 10 pieces; Miscellaneous vertical file material, Highland, Hillsboro and local material, 1815+, 6 lf. FH

INSTITUTIONAL RECORDS

443. Chamber of Commerce, Hillsboro (1948)
    126 South High Street, Hillsboro, Ohio 45133
    (513) 393-1111   (Hours by appointment)
    Walter Shannon, Executive Secretary

Annual reports, 1960+; Ledgers, 1962+; Minutes, 1960+; Publications,
1972+; Scrapbooks, 1960+; Tax records, 1960+; 5 in. total.   FH

444. First Presbyterian Church (1804)
    201 East Main Street, Hillsboro, Ohio 45133
    (513) 393-3171
    Dean R. Montgomery, Minister

Annual directory, 1963+, 1 in.; Annual reports, 1953+, 2 in.; Board
of Deacons, 1963+, 3 in.; Church bulletin, 1957+, 3 in.; Church register, 1910-17, 1937+, 6 in.; Correspondence, 7-year retention; History of the church, 1940, 1 in.; Session minutes, 1928+, 9 in.   FH

445. First United Methodist Church
    133 East Walnut Street, Hillsboro, Ohio 45133
    (513) 393-2981   (M-F 9-12, 1-4)
    Charles B. Reed, Minister

Annual reports, 1960, 1 in.; Church register, 1854+, 18 in.; Evangelical United Brethren Sunday School, 1957-68; Minutes, 1890-92, 1962+,
1 in.; Publication (bulletin), 1955+, 2 lf.   FH

446. Merchants National Bank of Hillsboro (1879)
    100 North High Street, Hillsboro, Ohio 45133
    (513) 393-1993   (M-F 9:30-2:30)
    Paul W. Pence, President

Annual reports, 1900+; Cashbooks; Certificates, ca. 1900+; Contracts;
Deeds; Journals,1890s+; Ledgers, 1890s+; Minutes, ca. 1890s+, 3 lf;
Scrapbooks, ca. 1900s+; Tax records, 10-year retention.   FH

447. The Union Stockyard Company (1939)
    West Main and Elm Street, Hillsboro, Ohio 45133
    (M-F 8-5)
    William Butler, Manager

Agreements, 1939+; Annual reports, 1939+; Certificates, 5-year retention; Correspondence, 5-year retention; Daybooks, 5-year retention;
Deeds, 1939+; Financial statements, 1939+; General expenses, 5-year
retention; Inventories, 5-year retention; Journals, 10-year retention;
Ledgers, 5-year retention; Minutes, 1939+; 60 lf total.   FH

                                HOCKING COUNTY

MANUSCRIPTS

448. Logan-Hocking County District Library (1897)
        120 East Main Street, Logan, Ohio 43138
        (614) 385-2348   (M, W, F 9-9; Tu, Sat 9-6)
        Mrs. William Miller, Assistant Librarian

The Butins in America, family genealogy; Local history collection
(pamphlets, notes, clippings), 1920+, 1 lf; The Wolfe Genealogy,
local family, 1961, 13 pp.   RR

INSTITUTIONAL RECORDS

449. Farmers & Merchants Bank (1909)
        11 West Main Street, Logan, Ohio 43138
        (614) 385-5644
        Ted McVey, Vice-President

Abstracts, local property; Annual reports, 1909+; Certificates of deposit, 6-year retention; Contracts, 6-year retention; Daybooks, 3-5-
year retention; Financial statements, 6-year retention; Inventories,
probate court, 1909+; Journals, 1909+; Ledgers, general, 1909+;
Legal correspondence, 6-year retention; Minutes, 1909+.   RR

450. Immanuel United Methodist Church (1849)
        66 East Hunter, Logan, Ohio 43138
        Conrad Diehm, Minister

Church register, 1856+, 18 in.; Correspondence, 2-year retention;
Financial statements, 7-year retention; Newsletter and bulletin,
1968+, 4 in.; Official board minutes, 1957+, 1 in.; Receipts, 7-year
retention; Tax records, 7-year retention.   FH

451. Logan Monument Company (1890)
      156 West Main Street, Logan, Ohio 43138
      (614) 385-5522
      George C. Shaw, President

Cashbooks, 1930s+, 2 lf; Contracts, includes information on location,
inscription, plot number, etc., 1930s+, 25 lf; Correspondence, 1955+,
8 lf; Ledgers, 1930s+, 3 lf; Receipts, 1930s+. FH

                        HOLMES COUNTY

MANUSCRIPTS

452. Holmes County District Public Library
      West Jackson Street, Millersburg, Ohio 44654
      (216) 674-5974   (M-Th, Sat 9-9; F 9-6)
      Caroline Mohr, Librarian

Miscellaneous MSS on local history and local church histories; Newspaper clippings; George F. Newton, "History of Holmes County, Ohio,"
1899; Scrapbooks on county history. SF

INSTITUTIONAL RECORDS

453. Chamber of Commerce, Millersburg
      Hotel Millersburg, Millersburg, Ohio 44654
      (216) 674-4866   (M-F 8-5)
      Mrs. Frank Reno, Corresponding Secretary

Annual reports, ca. 1955+; Board of directors, minutes, ca. 1955+;
Correspondence, ca. 1955+; Financial records, ca. 1955+; Publicity
material, ca. 1955+; Scrapbooks, ca. 1955+; 6 lf total. SF

454. Holmes County Regional Planning Commission
      Hotel Millersburg, Millersburg, Ohio 44654
      (216) 674-4866   (M-F 8-5)
      Mrs. Frank Reno, Corresponding Secretary

Aerial maps; Annual reports, 1967+; Correspondence, 1967+; Financial records, 1967+; Minutes, 1967+; Reports on zoning, land use,
transportation, businesses, and industries, 1967+; 16 lf total. SF

MANUSCRIPTS

455. Fire Lands Historical Society
       4 Case Street, Norwalk, Ohio 44857
       (419) 662-5011   (Tu-Sat 12-6 May, June, Sept, Oct; M-Sat 9-6
       July, Aug; Sat, Sun 1-6 Apr, Nov; closed Dec-Mar except by appt)
       Henry R. Timmons, President

Deeds; Diaries; "Fire-Lands," early history MSS; Fire Sufferers Land
Society, final record book; Genealogy collection; Indentures; Mexican War
and Civil War muster rolls and papers; Notes; Plank road company, records; Elisha Whittlesey, papers. SF

456. Norwalk Public Library (1861)
       46 West Main Street, Norwalk, Ohio 44857
       (419) 663-7151   (M-F 9:30-8:30; Sat 12-5)
       Enid Denham, Head Librarian

Newspaper clippings on local history, ca. 1965+; Photographs (general). SF

INSTITUTIONAL RECORDS

457. Chamber of Commerce, Norwalk (1938)
       2 East Seminary, Norwalk, Ohio 44857
       (419) 662-1011   (M-F 9-12, 1-5)
       Christine Keller, Executive Secretary

Annual reports, 1940+; Board of directors, minutes, 1940+; Committee
minutes, 1940+; Correspondence,1940+; Financial records, 1940+;News-
paper clippings, 1940+; Photographs, 1940+; Publicity material, 1940+;
16 lf total. SF

458. St. Paul's Episcopal Church (1821)
       85 West Main Street, Norwalk, Ohio 44857
       (419) 668-1937   (Hours by appointment)
       Elden Smith, Minister

Annual reports, ca. 1870+; Baptismal records; Bulletins; Church cemetery records; Correspondence; Death records; Marriage records; Photographs; Scrapbooks; Sermons; Sunday school records; Treasurer's reports, 1821+; Vestry minutes, 1821+. SF

MANUSCRIPTS

459. Sylvester Memorial Wellston Public Library (1928)
     135 East Second, Wellston, Ohio 45692
     (614) 384-6660   (M-W, F 1-8; Th, Sat 1-5)
     Frances L. Sellers, Librarian

Marjorie Evalyn Thomas, history of public library service in Jackson County, Ohio, 1 vol; Keystone Furnace Company Store, daybook,
showing names of customers and commodities purchased, 1856, 1 in.;
Pamphlets and newspaper clippings about Jackson County, 1960s, 6 in.;
Wellston City Building (built 1884), photographs and history of the
building, 1 folder.   RR

                        JEFFERSON COUNTY

MANUSCRIPTS

460. Mount Pleasant Historical Society (1948)
     Mount Pleasant, Ohio 43939
     (614) 769-2558   (Hours by appointment)
     Mrs. Horace Hussey, Committee Member

Crew's Store, cashbook, 1826-28, 1 vol; Diaries and miscellanea,
20 lf; Mt. Pleasant Free Produce Company, minutes, 1848-57;
Mt. Pleasant High School Alumni Association, minutes, 1908-57;
Mt. Pleasant-Martinsville Bank, correspondence, 1854-83; Photographs, 1844+, 50 items; Thomas General Store, ledger, 1818-19,
1844-80, 1 lf; Town Council, minutes, 1853-95; Women's Temperance League, minutes, 1874-78.   LS

461. Toronto Historical Society (1969)
     924 Biltmore Avenue, Toronto, Ohio 43964
     (614) 537-2315   (Hours by appointment)
     Walter Kestner, President

Improved Order of Red Men (benevolent society of a Toronto Indian
tribe), records of sick benefits, membership lists, dues record,
1910-24, 14 vols; Northeastern Ohio Volunteer Firemen's Association, proceedings and events pamphlets, 1898-1908, 7 pamphlets;
Thimble Bee Club (social organization), minutes, 1907+, 4 vols;

Toronto Cemetery Association, interment records, 1896+, 5 vols;
Toronto Volunteer Fire Department, motions to attend various con-
ventions, 1888-89, 16 pp.   JWG

INSTITUTIONAL RECORDS

462. American Red Cross, Steubenville (1917)
        623 North Fourth Street, Steubenville, Ohio 43952
        (614) 282-6251   (M-F 9-4)
        Lettia D. Louer, Director

Administrative records; Cashbooks, 1958+; Correspondence, 1966+;
Ledgers, 1966+; Minutes, 1970+.   LS

463. Calvary United Methodist Church (1943)
        301 North Fourth Street, P. O. Box 669, Steubenville, Ohio 43952
        (614) 282-6163   (M-F 8:30-12:30)
        William C. Creasy, Pastor

This church is the successor to the First M. E. Church (1810-1943)
and Hamline M. E. Church (1845-1943).

Calvary Church records and registers, 1810+.   LS

464. Chamber of Commerce, Steubenville (1908)
        162 North Fourth Street, Steubenville, Ohio 43952
        (614) 282-6226   (M-F 8:30-5)
        Joseph Kennedy, Executive Vice-President

Delinquent lists, 1944+, 6 in.; Minutes, 1949+, 2 lf; Publications,
1963+, 1 lf; Receipts and expenditures, 1949+, 18 in.; Retail Merchants Board, minutes, 1948+, 1 lf; Scrapbooks, 1949+, 3 lf.   LS

465. The College of Steubenville Library
        Franciscan Way, Steubenville, Ohio 43952
        (614) 283-3771   (M-F 8-5)
        Jeannine Kreyenbuhl, Librarian

Publications, The Assisian, 1965+, Baronette, 1947+; Scrapbooks,
1946+.   WM

466. Community Chest, Steubenville (1931)
        162 North Fourth Street, Steubenville, Ohio 43952
        (614) 282-6226   (M-F 8:30-5)
        Joseph Kennedy, Secretary

Financial statements, 1941+, 1 lf; Minutes, 1941+, 6 in.; Scrapbooks,
1931+, 2 lf.   LS

467. YWCA, Steubenville (1913)
        320 North Fourth Street, Steubenville, Ohio 43952
        (614) 282-1261   (M-F 9-4)
        Mary Barnes, Executive Director

Administrative records, 1913+; Annual reports, 1913+; Financial
statements, 1913+; Minutes, 1960+; Publications, 1955+; Scrapbooks, 1966+; 10 lf total.   WM

KNOX COUNTY

INSTITUTIONAL RECORDS

468. Chamber of Commerce, Mt. Vernon (1913)
        51 Public Square, Mt. Vernon, Ohio 43050
        (614) 393-1111   (M-F 9-5; Sat 9-12)
        Paul E. Slaughter, Executive Vice-President

Administrative records; Cashbooks, 1916+; Correspondence, 20-year
retention; Financial statements, 1916+; Minutes, 1916+; Monthly reports; Publications, 1971+; Scrapbooks, ca. 1956+; Tax records, 1957+;
50 lf total.   SF

469. Kenyon College Archives (1964)
        Chalmers Memorial Library, Kenyon College, Gambier, Ohio 43022
        (614) 427-2244   (M-F 9-12, while in session)
        Thomas B. Greenslade, Archivist

Alumni faculty files, 1875-1972, 50 lf; Archives correspondence, 1964+,
1 lf; Autograph collections, famous people and presidents, 18 in.; Gordon
K. Chalmers (president of college 1937-56), correspondence, clippings,
biographical information, 2 lf; Philander Chase (founder of college, first
bishop of Ohio), collection (correspondence, diaries, journals, pictures),

1792-1852, ca. 2,000 items; College catalogs, 1831+, 3 lf; Commencement pictures, 1924-67, 18 in.; Faculty minutes and grades, 1842+, 4 lf; Greenslade collection of photographs of all houses in Gambier, 1967+, 1 lf; Harcourt parish (local Episcopal Church), register, 1843-1920, 4 lf; Honors papers (bound), 1949+, 12 lf; Kenyon Alumni bulletin, 1942+, 1 lf; Kenyon College bulletin, 1906-69, 3 lf; Kenyon College Calendar, 1936+ (bound), 1 lf; Kenyon College treasurer's reports, 1905-36, 4 in.; Kenyon Military Academy, college bulletins, 1886-1905, 3 in.; Franz E. Lund (president of college, 1957-68), correspondence, clippings, miscellany, 3 in.; Bishop Charles P. McIlvaine (second bishop of Ohio, second president of college), correspondence, clippings, family register, accounts, 1799-1873, 2 lf; Nu Pi Kappa Literary Society, records, 1832-1960, 4 lf;

Philomathesian Literary Society, records, 1829-1960, 8 lf; Photographs, 32 lf; Presidential reports, 1905-37, 4 in.; Publicity department, news releases, correspondence, 1952-57, 18 in.; Ralston records of maintenance of college buildings, 1910-50, 3 in.; A. G. Scott (dry goods merchant and grocer), ledger, 1872-73, 6 in.; Scrapbooks, 1846+, 20 lf.
SF

470. Knox County Savings Bank (1873)
      West Side Public Square, Mt. Vernon, Ohio 43050
      (M-F 9-2:30)
      Rex C. Hostetler, President

Administrative records; Annual reports; Financial statements, daily, pre-1873 in ledger form, 1873+; Ledgers, 1873+; Minutes, 1873+; Publications (semi-annual financial reports), 1952+; Tax records, 1925+.
WM

471. Martin Memorial Hospital (1890)
      200 North Mulberry, Mt. Vernon, Ohio 43050
      (614) 397-5311   (M-F 9-5)
      Orville Weissman, Administrator

Administrative records, 1962+, 1 in.; Correspondence and departmental records, 1962+, 25 lf; Deeds, 1962+; Financial statements, 1962+, 3 lf; Inventories; Medical records, 1942+, 200 lf; Minutes, 1955+, 8 lf; Publications, 1971+, 1 in.; Scrapbooks, 1960+, 6 in.   SF

472. Mt. Vernon Area Development (1953)
        51 Public Square, Mt. Vernon, Ohio 43050
        (614) 393-1111   (M-F 9-5; Sat 9-12)

Administrative records, 1955+; Correspondence, 1955+; Financial
statements, 1955+; Minutes, 1955+; Scrapbooks, 1955+; 12 lf total.
FH

473. Mt. Vernon Nazarene College (1966?)
        Martinsburg Road, Mt. Vernon, Ohio 43050
        (614) 392-1244   (M-F 8-5)
        Richard L. Schuster, Librarian

Administrative records, ca. 1966+; Board of trustees, minutes,
1966+, 1 lf; Development office publications, 1967+; Financial
statements, 1967+, 6 in.; Lakeholm Viewer, 1967+, 3 in.; President's reports, 1966+, 3 in.; Publications, 1967+, 4 in.; Scrapbooks, 1967+, 2 lf; Student Council minutes, 1967+; Yearbooks,
1967+, 6 in.   FH

474. Retail Merchants Council (1957)
        51 Public Square, Mt. Vernon, Ohio 43050
        (614) 393-1111   (M-F 9-5; Sat 9-12)
        Paul E. Slaughter, Executive Vice-President

Administrative records, 1957+; Annual reports, 1957+; Correspondence, 1957+; Financial statements, 1957+; Minutes, 1957+;
6 lf total.   SF

475. United Community Fund, Inc. (1950)
        10 East High Street, Mt. Vernon, Ohio 43050
        (614) 392-5721   (M-F 9-3)
        Twila Culbertson, Secretary

Agency records (records of agencies receiving money), 1950+;
Annual reports, 1950+; Financial statements, 1950+.   WM

476. YMCA, Mt. Vernon (1876)
        103 North Main, Mt. Vernon, Ohio 43050
        (614) 397-4065   (M-Sat 8-10)
        Robert A. Senzer, Executive Director

Annual reports, 1936-67; Financial statements, 1908+; History
folder (photos, letters, speeches); Membership list, 1908+;

Minutes, 1908+; Receipts, current; Scrapbooks; 8 lf total.   WM

LAKE COUNTY

MANUSCRIPTS

477. The Fairport Harbor Historical Society (1945)
      The Fairport Marine Museum
      129 Second Street, P. O. Box 1042, Fairport Harbor, Ohio 44077
      (216) 354-4825   (Sat, Sun, Holidays 1-6, Memorial Day-Labor Day)
      Alice Van Jura, Secretary

Papers, 19th and 20th century, relating to Western Reserve, Mentor, Ohio,
and shipping, includes miscellaneous papers of Paine and Abraham Skinner
families, 3 lf.   DH

478. Lake County Historical Society
      8095 Mentor Avenue, Mentor, Ohio 44060
      (216) 255-8722   (M-F 9-5; Sat 9-5, May-Oct only)
      Mrs. William H. Slack, Administrative Secretary

James A. Garfield (U. S. Representative and president), papers, 1865-
ca. 1930, including papers of other members of the Garfield family, 2
lf; Edward Paine (soldier, founder of Painesville, Ohio), papers, 1796-
1850, including papers of other members of the family, 1 lf.   KP

479. Morley Public Library (1899)
      184 Phelps Street, Painesville, Ohio 44077
      (216) 352-3383   (M-F 10-9; Sat 10-6, winter only)
      Alice Wright, Head Librarian

Most of the collections have been microfilmed by the Church of Jesus
Christ of Latter-Day Saints.

DAR records, Connecticut chapter, 6 in.; DAR scrapbooks, 1890-1940,
4 vols; Geauga County marriage records, 1803-52, 261 pp; Index to
History of Geauga and Lake Counties, 1878, 100 pp; Lake County Probate Court marriage records, 1840-65, 131 pp; Lake County cemetery
inscriptions, 412 pp; Leroy Township journal, 1820-41, 268 pp; Leroy
Township miscellaneous poll records, 1830s and 1840s, 300 pp; Local
family genealogies, 1650-1960, 1 lf; Local history scrapbooks, 1904-
72, 14 vols; Morley Library scrapbooks, 1898-1972, 6 vols; Perry
Township School District records, 1831-95.   DH

480. Willoughy-Eastlake Public Library (1827)
        263 East 305th Street, Willowick, Ohio 44094
        (216) 943-4151   (M-Th 12-8:30; F 12-6; Sat 9-5)
        H. Rowland Macha, Director

"A History of Willoughy and its Schools," by F.N. Shankland, 1950,
3 vols; O.B. Gridley memorandum book, 1883-86, 1 vol; Mill record,
grist mill, 1839-45, 1 vol; Photograph file of Willoughby, 6 in.; Unidentified cashbook, 1868-69, 1 vol.   JG

INSTITUTIONAL RECORDS

481. American Red Cross, Painesville (1918)
        243 North State, Painesville, Ohio 44077
        (216) 352-3171   (M-F 9-5)
        Mrs. Emil C. Gabor, Executive Director

Disaster committee, 1958+; Financial records, 1960+; Minutes, 1918+;
Service to military families, 10-year retention; Volunteer records,
1945+.   WM

482. First Church, Congregational (1810)
        22 Liberty Street, Painesville, Ohio 44077
        (216) 357-7518   (M-F 8:30-4:30; Sat 9-12)
        John Mitchell, Chairman of Board

Beardslee Fellowship records, 1946-50,1967-68, 4 vols; "Best" scrapbook, 1922-40, 1 vol;Choir records, ca. 1900, 1 vol; Church record,
1810-1910, 4 vols;Church register,1810-89,1937-55, 4 vols;Congrega-
tional Christian social,1878-98, 1 vol; Home Missionary Society records,
1881-1906, 4 vols;Membership books, 1819-1954, 4 vols; Miscellaneous
financial, 1935-36, 1 vol; Missionary Society accounts,1888-95, 1898-1907,
2 vols;Photographs and typed histories, 6 in.; Prayer meeting records,1896-
97, 1 vol; Standing committee minutes, 1841-46, 1910-35, 1952-54, 4
vols; Sunday school attendance, 1864-66, 1 vol; Sunday school records,
1931-33, 1 vol; Treasurer's accounts, 1847-53, 1916-26, 1933-37,
1959-69, 5 vols; Treasurer's reports and receipts, 1908-27, 1 vol;
Trustees minutes, 1898-1931, 1950-66, 6 vols; Visitors' registers,
1874-87, 1953-62, 1966-68, 5 vols; Weekly offerings, 1919-22,1925-
26, 3 vols; Women's Fellowship Club, minutes, 1952-59, 2 vols; Women's Missionary Society, records, 1881-93, 1906-11, 2 vols; Young

Ladies Missionary Society, minutes, 1892-96, 1 vol; Y.P.S.C.E. records, 1890-98, 3 vols. JG

483. Good Shepherd Lutheran Church (1961)
        7643 Lake Shore Boulevard, Mentor, Ohio 44060
        (216) 257-7822   (Hours by appointment)
        David Wood, Pastor

Church register, 1961+, 1 vol; Council and congregational minutes, 1961+, 1 in.; Publications, 1961+, 3 lf; Yearly reports, 1961+, 1 in. JG

484. Holden Arboretum (1931)
        9500 Sperry Road, Mentor, Ohio 44060
        (216) 946-4400   (M-F 9-5)
        Elizabeth Norweb, Librarian

Accession records, 1957+, 10 vols; Annual reports, 1933-37, 1939-48, 3 in.; Bluebird records (records of bluebird nestings), ca. 1962+, 1 in.; Dead files, index to plants which died, 6 lf; Educational masters, 1960+, 6 in.; Inventory (list of plants at arboretum), 1 in.; Live files, index to living plants at arboretum, 6 lf; Map files, maps of arboretum grounds and plants, 18 in.; Membership records, ca. 1931+, 8 lf; Reports, histories and reports concerning the Holden and other arboretums, 1 in.; Slide file, 8,000 slides; Subject file A-Z, pamphlets, manuscripts and clippings regarding horticulture, 5 lf; Work reports, 1948-54, 6 in. JG

485. Lake County Republican Organization (1960)
        125 East Erie Street, Room 112, Painesville, Ohio 44077
        (216) 352-0796   (M-F 8:30-4)
        Loraine Creaven, Assistant Administrative Manager

Clipping files, ca. 1960, 2 lf; County chairman's manual, 1 vol; Current alphabetical files, 1968+, 2 lf; Ledgers, 1960, 1 vol; Minutes, 1959-60, 1 in. DH

486. Lake Erie College Archives (1847)
        Painesville, Ohio 44077
        (216) 352-3361   (M-F 9-5)
        Paul Weaver, President

Board of trustees, minutes, 1901+, 18 in.; Photographs, 1859-ca. 1920, 18 in.   DH

487. Mentor United Methodist Church (1822)
   8600 Mentor Avenue, Mentor, Ohio 44060
   (216) 255-3496   (M-F 8:30-4)

Board minutes, 1952-62, 1 vol; Church register, 1866-1930, 4 vols; Membership records, 6 vols; Methodist circuit rider, quarterly reports, 1883-96, 1 vol; Publications, 1947+, 5 lf.   JG

488. Painesville Telegraph (1822)
   84 North State Street, Painesville, Ohio 44077
   (216) 354-4333   (M-F 9-5)
   Howard Mobley, Editor

Clippings and photographs arranged under 17,000 topics, 70 lf.   JG

489. United Way of Lake County (1935)
   8 North State Street, Painesville, Ohio 44077
   (216) 352-3166   (M, Tu, Th 9-4:30; W, F 9-4)
   Stephan J. Hryshko, Executive Consultant

Minutes, 1935-45, 1957+, 3 lf; Miscellaneous files, 1958+, 23 lf.   WM

490. Wickliffe Public Library (1936)
   1713 Lincoln Road, Wickliffe, Ohio 44092
   (216) 944-6010   (M-Th 9-9; F, Sat 9-5; Sun 1-5)
   Frank Coryell, Director

Board of trustees, minutes, 1936+, 6 in.; Financial records, 7-year retention, 20 lf.   JG

491. YMCA, Painesville (1867)
   Mentor Avenue, Painesville, Ohio 44077
   (216) 352-3303   (M-F 9-5)
   Lynn Russell, Executive Director

Administrative records, 1910; Annual reports, 1955+, 3 in.; Correspondence, 5-year retention; Financial records, 7-year retention; Mechanical drawings of buildings, 1955+; Membership records, 2-year retention, 2 lf; Minutes, 1955+, 10 lf; Pictures, 1950+, 3 lf; Publications, 2-
year retention; Scrapbooks, 1960; Tax records, 7-year retention.   WM

                          LAWRENCE COUNTY

INSTITUTIONAL RECORDS

492. Ironton Tribune (1852)
        324-28 Railroad Street, Ironton, Ohio 45638
        (614) 532-1441   (M-Sat 11-2:30)
        C. L. Waller, Editor and Publisher

Administrative records, 1927+; Advertising contracts, 3-year retention; Annual financial reports to board of directors, 1960; Cashbooks,
daily record, 7-year retention; Correspondence, 2-year retention;
Daybooks, legal advertising and display, 1945+; Deeds; Inventories,
1960; Journals, income and disbursements, cash, 1945+; Ledgers, 1945+;
Morgue picture file; Plats, county, city and state, 10 years earliest;
Scrapbooks, clipping files, ca. 1960+; Service, syndication contracts,
1956+; Stockholders minutes, 1960; Tax records, ca. 1940+.   FH

                          LICKING COUNTY

MANUSCRIPTS

493. Granville Public Library (1804)
        217 East Broadway, Granville, Ohio 43023
        (614) 582-1631   (M-F 9-9; Sat 9-6)
        Tom Plaeg, Librarian

Fortnightly Club, programs, 1895-1915, 1 vol; "A History of Granville,
Ohio," M.A. thesis, by James H. Smith, 1 folder; Library records, ca.
1920+, 8 lf; Licking County cemetery records, 3 in.; Masonic Lodge of
Granville (Center Star Lodge #11), directories, 1914-64, 3 in.; Old
Burying Ground grave records, epitaphs (name index), 1 folder; "A
Pen Picture of Newark and Vicinity," by Wellington Stanbery, 1818,
typescript, 1 folder; Isaac Smuckers, scrapbook, clippings (subject in-
dex), 1808-82, 6 in.; Travelers Club, programs, 1896-1926.   SF

494. Licking County Historical Society (1947)
      P. O. Box 535, Newark, Ohio 43055
      (614) 345-4898   (M, W, F-Sun 9-5)
      Mrs. James Betts, Executive Director

Account books, 1818-1907, 4 vols; American Red Cross, scrapbook,
1941-45, 1 in.; Canal Society collection; Colonel Robert Davidson,
ledger, 1838-49; Davidson and Company account book, 1827-35; W.
F. Daviss tapes (memories of old Newark, recollections of Civil
War), 24 tapes; Family genealogies, 1961+, 1 lf; Huston and Meach
Transit Company, records, 1839-52; Mary Sherwood Wright Jones,
original drawings, 1 in.; Justice of the peace dockets, 1827-42;Fred-
erick Kochendorfer, papers, 1893-95, 1 folder; Ledgers, dry goods
stores, 1818-76, 1 in.; Licking County Agricultural Society, minutes,
1898-1917; Licking County Historical Society, records, 1952-69; Licking County Infirmary, ledger, 1842-1913; Licking County Treasurer's
Office, receipts, 1900-1913; Maryann Forge (blacksmith shop), accounts,
1819-27; Merchant's account book, 1849-52; Mound Builders Country
Club, roster, 1948-49; Captain Lew Moser, muster roll, 1822-24;Ports-
mouth and Newark Railroad, payroll book, 1863, 1 in.; Photographs,
Licking County events and people, 5 lf; W. Schenck (founder of Newark),
correspondence; Soldiers and Sailors Monument, cornerstone, contents,
1894, 6 in.; W. A. R. minutes (group that aided in war effort, bandages,
medicines), 1863-65, 1 in.; Clarence White photograph collection, 3 in.;
Winegarner, Robbins, and Wing and Co., banking firm, account books
(includes hardware store accounts), 1865-69; Woods family business
papers, 1864-85, 1 in. SF

495. Newark Public Library (1900)
      88 West Church Street, Newark, Ohio 43055
      (614) 345-1750   (M-F 9-9; Sat 9-6)
      Robert Simon, Adult Services

Licking County History materials, primarily clippings, 1900+, 4 lf;
Obituary material on Licking County families and related individuals,
primarily newspaper clippings, 1900+, 18 lf. FH

INSTITUTIONAL RECORDS

496. AFL-CIO Council, Newark
      68 West Main, Newark, Ohio 43055
      (M-F 8-5)
      Tom Mellars

AFL-CIO council, financial reports, minutes, 1961-69, 2 in.; AFL-CIO reports on Newark Labor Council, 1961-67, 2 in.; American Federation of Musicians, Local #122, minutes, finances, and undated roster, 1919-23, 1940-56, 4 in.; Employees' quarterly federal tax return, for the Newark Labor Club, 1956-67, 1 in.; Financial records, 1946-60, 2 in.; Labor daybook, minutes and finances, 12 pp; Ledger book, 1947-51, 1 in.; Membership roll (American Flint Glassworkers Union #30, Brewery Workers Union #47, Bus Drivers Local, Carpenters Union #136, Firefighters #109),1935, 2 in.;National convention, 1936, held in Newark, general arrangements committee, 1936, 25 pp; Newark Federation of Labor, records of proceedings and finances, 1938-60, 2 in.; Newark Trade and Labor Association minutes and finances, 1908-38, 6 in.; Union charters, framed, 45 charters.   WM

497.   Boy Scouts of Newark (1919)
          21 South First Street, Newark, Ohio 43055
          (614) 345-4540   (M-F 9-5)
          Harold Hayes, Scout Executive

Administrative records, 1919+; Contracts, 1955+, 1 in.; Correspondence, 1-year retention; Daybooks, 7-year retention; Deeds, 1930s+, 1 in.; Financial records, ca. 1950+, 25 lf; Inventories, 1-year retention; Minutes, 1919+, 3 lf; Newsletter, 1-year retention, 1 in.; Scrapbooks, ca. 1920+, 6 in.; Troop personnel records, 1912+, 16 lf.   FH

498.   Catholic Welfare Council of Licking County (ca. 1957)
          21 West First Street, Newark, Ohio 43055
          (614) 345-2565   (M-F 8:30-5)
          Kathy Shoppell, Caseworker

Case files are kept until cases are closed, then are sent to Columbus Catholic Welfare Services.

Appointment calendar, 1970+, 1 in.; Brief service form, case of person who gets one-shot service, 1969+, 1 folder; Case files, monthly log of casework load, 1969+, 1 vol; Correspondence, 1968+, 1 folder; Financial statements, 1970+, 1 folder; Minutes and agenda of board meetings, 1970+, 3 in.; Scrapbooks, 1968+, 1 in.   SF

499.   Chamber of Commerce, Newark Area (1915)
          36 West Church, Newark, Ohio 43055
          (614) 345-9757   (M-F 8:30-5)
          C. Allen Millikan, Executive Vice-President

Administrative records, 1915+; Annual reports, 1946+; Board of directors minutes, 1915+; Contracts, ca. 1915+; Correspondence, ca. 1920+; Deeds, ca. 1915+; Financial statements, 1913+; Miscellaneous records, photographs, publicity, promotional files, committee reports, reference materials, ca. 1954+; Publications, ca. 1964+; Receipts, 1965+; Scrapbooks, late 1920s+; 70 lf total.   FH

500. Dawes Arboretum (1931)
    Rt. 5, Newark, Ohio 43055
    (614) 345-2355   (M-F 8:30-4:30)
    Barbara Shelly, Secretary

Annual reports, 1931+, 2 lf; Bookkeeping records (annual reports from companies in which the arboretum holds stock), 2 lf; Financial statements, 1931+, 18 in.; Miscellaneous (includes organizations the arboretum belongs to, activities, correspondence), 1968+, 8 lf; Monthly newsletter, 1968+; Photographs of people who planted trees, 1931+, 3 lf; Visitors' registration, 1965+, 6 in.   WM

501. Denison University Archives (1831)
    Granville, Ohio 43023
    (614) 582-9189   (M-F 8-12; Sat 9-5; Sun 12-12)
    Josephine Moss, University Archivist

Administrative papers, 1932+; Administrative records, 1957-60; Biography files, Denisonians, faculty, presidents, trustees, 1904+; Paschal Carter, correspondence and diaries, 1836-ca. 1890; Calliopean Society, minutes, 1835-1918; Willis A. Chamberlain, papers, 1917-62; Denison Christian Emphasis Program, 1943-60; Commencement records, 1831+; Conservatory of Music, records, 1893+; Convocations, 1950-66; William Howard Doane Library, records, 1939-59; Faculty records, departmental reports, minutes, publications, 1920+; Faculty societies and associations, records, 1859+;

Financial records and campaigns, 1882-1952; Franklin Literary Society, 1842-1914; Fraternity publications; Ben Jones Pioneers of Licking County; Physical education, all sports programs, 1905-34; Presidential records, 1853+; T.D. Price family papers, 1849-1904; Student organizations, 1844-1967; Theater arts department, 1896-1965; Theses, honors and masters; Trustees records, 1832-1950; Welsh Hills Players, history.   FH

502. Edward H. Everett Company (1885)
     21 West First, Newark, Ohio 43055
     (M-F 8-5)
     K. M. Kew, President

Administrative records, 1885+; Agreements, pre-1915; Annual reports, 1912+; Contracts, pre-1915; Correspondence, 1912+; Deeds,
1885+; Financial statements, 1912+; Maps of oil fields, 1925+; Minutes, 1885+; Patents, 1897+. SF

503. Family Service Association of Licking County (1965)
     21 South First, Newark, Ohio 43055
     (614) 345-4920   (M-F 9-5)
     Eleanor Edwards, Office Manager

Board of trustees, minutes, 1965+, 7 lf; Case histories, 1965+, 4 lf;
Financial records, 1965+. WM

504. First Presbyterian Church (1805)
     Broadway and Main, Granville, Ohio 43023
     (614) 582-1411   (M-F 9-5)
     A. Gary Angleberger, Pastor

Annual reports, ca. 1948+; Church register, 1805, 1830+, 500 pp;
Minutes, 1830-1940, 400 pp, include financial information, 1940+,
300 pp; Women's Association, financial statements, ca. 1920+, 1
notebook. WM

505. Kaiser Aluminum and Chemical Corporation (1949)
     P.O. Box 671, Newark, Ohio 43055
     (614) 344-1151   (M-F 8-5)
     L. G. McDaniel, Works Manager

Annual reports, 1949+; Financial statements (a monthly report which
shows unit cost, over-production, under-production and other financial reports, confidential); Personnel records, 1949+, 275 lf; Production and sales records, 1949+, 1,000 lf; Publications, 1971+; Tax
records. WM

506. Licking County Cooperative Extension Service (ca. 1918)
     40 South Fourth, Newark, Ohio 43055
     (614) 345-6631   (M-F 8:30-4:30)
     Merle Scheety, County Extension Agent, Agriculture

Advisory committees, minutes, 1954+, 2 lf; Annual reports, 1918+,
2 lf; Correspondence, 1966+, 2 lf; Financial statements, 1966+, 2 lf;
4-H Club, membership records, 1946+, 2 lf; Published research
files, 1960+, 46 lf.   FH

507. Licking County Memorial Hospital (1898)
      1320 West Main, Newark, Ohio 43055
      (614) 344-0331   (M-F 8-5)
      Elizabeth Roberts, Director of Medical Records

Board of trustees, records, 1957+, 3 lf; Financial statements, 1939+,
3 lf and 151 mf rolls; Medical records, 1935+, 935 mf rolls; Minutes,
1909+, 3 lf; Miscellaneous reports, covers cardiology, donations, med-
icare, mental health, regional planning, etc., 11 lf; Nursing records,
personnel material, 12 lf; Physical therapy reports, 5-year retention,
40 lf; X-rays, 290 lf.   WM

508. Ohio Baptist Convention (1834)
      141 East Broadway, Granville, Ohio 43023
      (614) 582-9158   (M-F 8-4:30)
      Coretta Swanson, Administrative Assistant

Administrative records, ca. 1834, 1 in.; Correspondence, ca. 1950s+,
50 lf; Deeds to church properties, 19th century, 1 lf; Financial records,
ca. 1860+, 22 lf; Minutes and annual reports,1860+, 2 lf; Personnel files,
55 lf; Pictures, 2 in.; Publications, ca. 1900; Staff schedule records,
1965+; Tax records, ca. 1960+, 3 lf.   SF

509. Ohio State University-Newark Campus (1968)
      University Drive, Newark, Ohio 43055
      (M-Th 8-9; Sun 6-9)
      Elizabeth Jenkins, Head Librarian

Faculty bulletins, 1972+; Faculty Council, minutes, 1968+, 3 in.;
Oracle, Newark campus newspaper, 3 in.   SF

510. Planned Parenthood of Licking County (1967)
      17 North First, Newark, Ohio 43055
      (614) 345-7445   (M 8:30-8:30; Tu-F 8:30-5)
      Marilyn Conard, Executive Director

Administrative records, 1969, 1 folder; Board of directors, minutes,
1966+, 2 lf; Contracts, OEO, county, 1969+; Correspondence, 1966+,

8 lf; Financial records, 1966+, 8 lf; Patient records, 1967+, restricted,
24 lf; Proceedings, 1966+, 1 lf; Scrapbooks, 1968+, 3 in.; Statistical records, 1967+, 2 lf; Tax records, employee, 1969+.   SF

511.   Trinity Episcopal Church (1826)
            76 East Main, Newark, Ohio 43055
            (614) 345-9535   (M-F 9-4)
            John Baker, Rector

Church history, centennial issue, 1826-1926, 43 pp; Church register,
1826+, 18 in.; Contracts, 1960+, 3 in.; Correspondence, 5-year retention, 2 in.; Financial records, ca. 1830s+, incompl; Inventories, 1971+,
1 in.; Membership lists, active and inactive, 1 lf; Parish and diocesan
reports, 1940+, 3 in.; Vestry minutes, annual, 1834+; Weekly newsletter,
1968+, 1 lf.   FH

512.   United Appeal of Licking County (1932)
            21 South First, Room 205, Newark, Ohio 43055
            (614) 345-6685   (M-F 8:30-5)
            Herman Saltzman, Executive Director

Accounts received, 3 lf; Audit reports, 1933+, 6 in.; Award placques,
2 lf; Board books, includes distribution of funds information, 1952+, 1
lf; Budgets, 1942+, 30 in.; Campaign analysis sheets, list of corpor-
ations, amount of donations, 1960-68, 18 in.; Cash receipts, all income
records, 1957+, 6 in.; Correspondence and activities, includes campaign
literature and other miscellaneous material, 13 lf; Publications, brochures,
and pamphlets; Scrapbooks, 1935-38, 1954+, 7 in.   WM

513.   WHTH Radio (1970)
            1000 North 40th, Newark, Ohio 43055
            (614) 344-0361   (M-F 8-5)
            Kenneth L. Gray, News Director

Board of directors, minutes, 1970+; Correspondence, 2 lf; Financial
statements; News broadcast typescripts, 1970+, 3 lf; Tax records.
SF

MANUSCRIPTS

514. Logan County District Library (1902)
140 North Main Street, Bellefontaine, Ohio 43311
(513) 592-5986   (M-F 10-8:30; Sat 10-5:30)
Norma L. Shoots, Assistant Librarian

Family genealogies, 6 in.; Logan County marriage records, 1818-
46; Methodist Church history, 1816-1963.   RS

INSTITUTIONAL RECORDS

515. Chamber of Commerce, Bellefontaine (1941)
117 West Chillicothe, Bellefontaine, Ohio 43311
(513) 592-1736   (M-F 9-5)
David Kotterman, Executive Vice-President

Administrative records, 1962+; Annual reports, 1962+; Correspondence, 1940s+; Financial statements, 5-year retention; Minutes, 1970+;
Publications, 1970+; Scrapbooks, 1972+; 8 lf total.   RS

516. Logan Farm Co-op Association (1935)
912 South Detroit, Bellefontaine, Ohio 43311
(513) 592-6861   (M-F 8-5; Sat 8-12)
Jean Harman, Head Bookkeeper

Administrative records; Agreements, 1935+; Annual reports, ca.1935+;
Correspondence, 1969+; Financial statements, 1970-71; History, by
John W. Kemper, 1940s, 1 in.; Inventories, 1970-71; Ledgers, business
dealings, 1966+; Minutes, ca. 1935+; Scrapbooks, ca. 1940s; Stock certificates, ca. 1935+.   RS

LORAIN COUNTY

MANUSCRIPTS

517. Avon Lake Public Library (1931)
32649 Electric Boulevard, Avon Lake, Ohio 44012
(216) 933-8128   (M-Th 12-9; F, Sat 10-5)
Doris L. Sunderland, Director of Library

Avon Lake history file (clippings, TSS histories, and photographs relating to the history of Avon Lake and Lorain County), ca. 1950+, 3
lf; Library publicity (scrapbooks containing photos and clippings relating to the library), 1966+, 4 in.   JG

518. Elyria Public Library (1870)
      320 Washington Avenue, Elyria, Ohio 44035
      (216) 323-5747   (M-F 9-8:30; Sat 9-6)
      Mrs. Robert M. Shultz, Head of Reference Department

Heman Ely (founder of Elyria), papers, 1727-1893, 9 lf.   JG

519. Great Lakes Historical Society
      480 Main Street, Vermillion, Ohio 44089
      (216) 967-3467   (M-F 9-5)
      Barbara Ward, Office Secretary

Builder's ship blueprint tracings, 1800s, 300 items; S.S. Cliffs
Victory, picture story, 1951, 2 in.; S.S. Detroit, Detroit Ship-
building and Buffalo Drydock Company photo albums, ca. 1880-
1930, 2 lf; Greater Detroit and Greater Buffalo picture album, 4
in.; Groundings, collisions and losses on the Great Lakes, 1874-
84, 1 in.; Hermonic rescue account, 1925, 2 in.; Eugene Herna,
papers, photos, and printed material, 1 in.; "May-Bell," account
book, 1836-38, 1 in.;

Photographs, 9 lf; Rivers and Harbors Improvement Association,
1946+, 1 notebook, mostly photos; Col. S.C. Sabin (builder of nos.
3 and 4 locks on Soo Canal and president of the Lake Carriers Association), scrapbooks, 2 in.; Scrapbooks, 1896, 4 in.; Shipwreck
journal (record of wrecks near Waugoshance lighthouse), 1876-1906,
1 in.; Toledo Fire and Marine Insurance Company, annual reports,
1848-1905, minutes, 1905-21, 4 in.   FH

520. Lorain County Historical Society (1889)
      331 Fifth Street, Elyria, Ohio 44035
      (216) 322-3341   (Tu, Sat 2-5)
      Mildred Haines, Director

Ely papers (relating to the family and descendents of Heman Ely,
founder of Elyria), 1750-1900, 9 lf; Gates family, papers (diaries,

letters, and notebooks), ca. 1870-1900, 18 in.; Lorain County court
records, 1824-58, 12 vols; Membership books and dues payment records, 1889-1912, 2 lf; Rev. John Monteith (founder of the University
of Michigan), papers (including correspondence and current printed
material, ca. 1817, 18 in.; Reuben Mussey (Elyria justice of the peace),
letters and docket books, 1831-32, 1 lf; National Union Records, Elyria
Council 40, labor union active in Elyria area, 1883-1912, 10 vols; Penfield family papers, ca. 1810-60, 1 lf.   JG

521. Lorain County Public Library (1883)
        Lorain, Ohio 44035
        (216) 244-1192   (M-F 9-5)
        George Lafferty, Reference Librarian

The Andersons of Virginia and some of their descendents, 1908, 1 in.;
Auroraville, Wisconsin, history, 1957, 1 in.; Captains coursebook on
the Great Lakes, 1902, 1 in.; The Cleveland Southeastern and Columbus
Railway Story, 1 in.; Congregational Church of Lorain, history, 1897;
First Methodist Church, history, 1956, 1 in.; Interurbans and street
railways, photographs, 2 notebooks; Lorain County Public Library, history to 1926, 1 in.; Lorain, Ohio, history, 1924, 1 in.; Photographs of
Ohio, 1 in.; Puerto Ricans in Lorain, survey, 1954, 1 in.; Root family
reminiscences, 1873; Sheffield County, justice of the peace dockets, 1
in.; St. Peters church, history, 1966, 1 in.; Scrapbooks, Lorain area
and personalities, 1924 tornado, 4 in.; Sheffield, history, 1865-1915,
1965, 1 in.; Ship's log, 1902, 1 in.; Social service agencies of Lorain,
1958, 1 notebook; UFO scrapbook, 1953-54, 1 in.; The Women's view,
a consumer's report on downtown Lorain, 1966, 1 in.   FH

522. Oberlin College Library (1966)
        Oberlin, Ohio 44074
        (216) 774-1221, ext. 3170   (M-F 8-12, 1-5; Sat by appointment)
        W. E. Bigglestone, Archivist

Amherst Justice Court, records, 1854-74, 5 vols; George W. Andrews
(educator, musician), papers, 1870-1910, 5 in.; Elijah P. Barrows
(minister, educator), papers, 1832-81, 5 in.; Dan B. Bradley (missionary), papers, 1800-1873, 300-400 items; John W. Bradshaw (minister),
papers, 1900-1911?, 10 in.; Henry C. Burr (minister), papers, 1904-
40, 10 in.; Elam J. Comings (minister), papers, 1834-1907, 10 in.;
Paul L. Corbin (minister), papers, 1904-36, 10 in.; Henry Cowles (educator), papers, 1824-81, 3 lf; Jacob D. Cox (politician, army general,
historian, educator), papers, 1842-1927, 15 lf;

Joseph H. Crooker (minister), papers, 1873-1931, 18 in.; Edward Dickinson (educator, musician), papers, 1876-1934, 10 in.; James H. Fairchild (educator), papers, 1838-1903, 15 lf; Finitimi Society (women's literary and social group), records, 1902-23, 5 notebooks; Charles G. Finney (revivalist, educator), papers, 1817-75, 5 lf; Florence M. Fitch (educator), papers, 1807-1951, 7 lf; Robert S. Fletcher (educator), papers, 1818-1941, 9 lf; Foote & Locke (merchants), records, 1837-43, 2 vols; Free Will Baptist Church, records, 1835-69, 1 vol; Wesley Frost (foreign service officer), papers, 1891-1944, 3 lf; Kemper Fullerton (educator), papers, 1834-1946, 5 lf; Nathaniel Gerrish, financial records, 1837-55, 1 vol;

William Goodell (editor and reformer), papers, 1737-1882, 18 in.; E. L. Goodrich & Co., financial records, 1835-44, 1 vol; Elliott Grabill (Civil War officer), papers, 1859-1901, 18 in.; Lyman B. Hall (educator), papers, 1871-1917, 18 in.; William A. Hobbs (minister), papers, 1882-1902, 18 in.; Walter M. Horton (educator), papers, 1914-66, 6 lf; Frances J. Hosford (educator), papers, 1925-35, 18 in.; Henry C. King (educator), papers, 1873-1934, 63 lf; Fred E. Leonard (educator), papers, 1821-1950, 14 lf; Alice Little (Africa educator), letters from foreign missionaries, 1862-1948, 10 in.;

James C. McCullough (educator), papers, 1911-48, 18 in.; E.W. Metcalf, letters re the "Alabama Claims,", 1873-90, 90 items; Irving W. Metcalf (minister and businessman), papers, 1881-1948, 2 lf; M. Portia Mickey (missionary), papers, 1914-20, 10 in.; James Monroe (politician, educator, U.S. Consul), papers, 1841-98, 12 lf; John Morgan (educator), papers, 1830-83, 95 items; Henry E. Mussey Company (quarry), payroll records, 1872-74, 1 vol; Pittsfield Township School District, records, 1869-97, 5 vols; Chauncey N. Pond, letters from foreign missionaries, 1852-1919, 10 items;

Azariah S. Root (librarian), papers, 1887-1928, 4 lf; Abel H. Ross (minister), papers, 1861-93, 2 lf; Philo Safford (student and teacher), papers, 1867-88, 3 lf; Giles W. Shurtleff (Civil War officer and educator), papers, 1846-1902, 5 lf; Raymond H. Stetson (educator), papers, 1926-50, 3 lf; Ernest H. Wilkins (educator), papers, 1927-46, 87 lf; Mr. and Mrs. G. L. Williams (missionaries), papers, 1883-1952, 2 lf; George E. Woodberry (educator, poet, and critic), papers, 1903-27, 46 items; Albert A. Wright (educator), papers, 1858-1900, 2 lf; G. Frederick Wright (educator), papers, 1850-1921, 22 lf.   JG

INSTITUTIONAL RECORDS

523. American Red Cross, Lorain County
        2929 West River Road, Elyria, Ohio 44035
        (216) 324-2929   (M-F 8:30-5)
        Clyde McDonald, Jr., Executive Director

Board minutes, 1956+, 6 in.; Disaster file, ca. 1960+, contains written and printed materials concerning area disasters and instructions
for coping with them, 1 lf; Photographs, 1 lf; Scrapbooks, 1943,1946-
56, 1961, 8 vols. JG

524. Chamber of Commerce, Elyria Area (1899)
        356 Second Street, Elyria, Ohio 44035
        (216) 322-5438   (M-F 8-5)
        Richard J. Elliott, General Manager

Administrative records; Correspondence, 10-year retention; Minutes,
1916+; Publications, 118-page publication filled with pictures of Elyria,
1903; Scrapbooks, ca. 1950-60. WM

525. Chamber of Commerce, Greater Lorain (1883)
        204 West Fifth Street, Lorain, Ohio 44052
        (216) 244-2292   (M-F 9-5)

Administrative records, 1883; Minutes, 1883-1911, 1963-64, 5 vols;
Payroll book, 1937-64, 1 vol. DH

526. Farm Bureau Cooperative Association of Lorain County (1932)
        210 Huron Street, Elyria, Ohio 44035
        (216) 323-3270   (M-Sat 8-5)
        Frank Hermann, General Manager

Non-current records are transferred to state headquarters in Columbus.

Minutes, 1925-32, 1 vol; Miscellaneous membership and financial   records, ca. 1932+, 1 lf. JG

527. First Congregational Church (1879)
        320 Second Street, Elyria, Ohio 44035
        (216) 323-5454   (M-F 8:30-4:30)
        Mrs. Robert A. Happel, Church Secretary

The church was founded in 1824 as First Presbyterian.

Building committee records, 1960-64, 1 vol; Building fund campaign, 1961, 1 vol; "Book of Remembrance," 1824-1954, 1 vol; Church members, 1824-86, 1 vol; Church registers, 1824-1964, 7 vols; Junior Boys Mission Club minutes, 1894-96, 1 vol; Marriage licenses, 1939-66, 4 vols; Minutes, 1831-65, 1898-1916, 4 vols; Minutes of clerk, 1932-67, 18 in.; Pledge book, 1955-56, 1 vol; Publications, 1942-48; Records of First Presbyterian, 1824-80, 1 vol.   DH

528. First United Methodist Church, Elyria (1816)
        312 Third Street, Elyria, Ohio 44035
        (216) 322-6622   (M-F 9-5)
        Charles Hamilton, Pastor

Annual reports, 1884-1911; Church register, 1858-84; Guest register, 1948-58, 1 vol; Marriage licenses, 1930-38, 2 vols; Membership book, 1946-52, 2 vols; Proceedings, 1911-22, 1929-35, 6 vols; Quarterly conference records, 1898-1902, 1 vol; Scrapbooks, 1922-32, 1 vol.   JG

529. First United Methodist Church, Lorain (1856)
        559 Reid, Lorain, Ohio 44052
        (216) 245-5238   (M-F 1-5)
        Donald W. Walton, Pastor

Building committee minutes, 1924-27, 1 vol; Church register, 1896-1903, 1910-20, 2 vols; Church school attendance, 1919-21, 1923-33, 2 vols; Congregational minutes, 1896-1906, 1921-43, 2 vols; Corporation record, 1957-58, 1 vol; Current membership book, 2 vols; Donors letters, ca. 1927-30, 1 in.; Guest registers, 1927-28, 1943-45, 1968+, 3 vols; House department record, 1 vol; Membership register, 1959+, 2 vols; Pledge ledger, 1954, 1 vol; Total membership books, ca. 1872+, 2 vols.   JG

530. First United Methodist Church, Oberlin (1869)
        South Professor Street, Oberlin, Ohio 44074
        (216) 774-9321   (M-F 9-12)
        Forrest J. Waller, Pastor

Church register, 1875-1929, 1969-71, 6 vols; History, 28 pp; Membership books, 1940+, 2 vols; Trustees minutes, 1869-1908, 1 vol.   DH

531. Grace Evangelical Lutheran Church (1936)
        310 West Lorain Street, Oberlin, Ohio 44074
        (216) 775-3271   (M-Sat 9-12)
        Roger Janke, Pastor

Church register, 1936+, 1 vol; Constitution, 1970, 13 pp; Current files,
1 lf; History, 1971, 14 pp; Sunday bulletins, 1938+, 2 lf; Sunday school
records, 1960+, 1 lf; Voters and council minutes, 1936+, 1 lf.   DH

532. Grace Lutheran Church (1907)
        9685 East River, Elyria, Ohio 44035
        (216) 322-2694   (M-F 9-3)
        Peter Mealwitz, Pastor

Church register, 1907-69, 3 vols; Congregation minutes, 1906-37, 1
vol; Council minutes, 1908-49, 2 vols; Dedication book, 1968, 1 vol;
Fellowship Club records, 1956-71, 2 vols; Guest books, 1959+, 3 vols;
Ladies' Aid Society minutes, 1918-34, 1952-56, 2 vols; Members and
dues, 1905-16, 1 vol; Memorial offerings book, 1968, 1 vol; Publications, 1956+; Sunday school reports, 1908-18, 1925-51, 2 vols; Treasurer's reports, 1914-42, 1962-69, 7 vols; Voters attendance, 1921-
47, 1 vol; Young People's minutes, 1908-35, 2 vols; Young People's
treasury book, 1908-31, 1 vol.   JG

533. Grange No. 2487, Chatham (1929)
        8785 Chippawa Road, Chatham, Ohio 44254
        (216) 667-2403   (No set hours)
        Russel Fish, Deputy Master of Medina County

This grange is the successor to no. 1437, which was organized in the
early 1890s.

Annual reports, 1939-48; Correspondence, 1957-68; Daybooks, 1948-
50, 9 vols; Dues account books, 1929-40, 1952-63, 2 vols; Grange record book, 1929-38; Proceedings, 1948-57; Roll books, 1899-1910, 1929-
36, 1940-51, 4 vols.   DH

534. Jaycees, Elyria (1940)
        114 Harwood Avenue, Elyria, Ohio 44035
        (216) 323-3610   (M-F 9-5, phone contact only)
        Jack Parks, President

Board minutes, 1963+, 1 vol; Membership minutes, 1963+, 1 vol; Project reports, 9 lf; Scrapbooks, 1 lf.   JG

535. LaPorte United Methodist Church (1834)
  2071 Grafton Road, LaPorte, Ohio 44035
  (216) 458-5717 (M-Th 9-3)
  Otis Bell, Pastor

Board of trustees, minutes, 1951-62, 1 vol; Building committee minutes, ca. 1940, 1 vol; Church school meetings, 1949-50, 1 vol; Contribution books, 1951-58, 3 vols; Financial records, 1937-71, 8 vols; Ladies' Aid Society records, 1899-1920, 1 vol; Membership records, 1834-47, 1932-36, 2 vols; Miscellaneous file, 1959-65, 1 in.; Miscellaneous volume, 1956-61, 1 vol; Sunday school attendance records, 1869, 1892, 1959, 2 vols; Treasurer's reports, 1946-61, 2 vols. DH

536. Oberlin College Archives (1966)
  Oberlin, Ohio 44074
  (216) 774-1221, ext. 3170 (M-F 8-12, 1-5; Sat by appointment)
  W. E. Bigglestone, Archivist

Administrative records, 1833-1970, 504 lf; Alumni records, ca. 1840-1971, 144 lf; Class files, 1860-1970, 12 lf; Photographs and negatives, ca. 1840-1970, 45 lf; Printed matter, 1834-1970, 48 lf; Student life, ca. 1840-1971, 30 lf; Tape recordings, 1960-70, 11 lf. DH

537. Old Stone United Methodist Church (1837)
  553 South Main, Amherst, Ohio 44001
  (216) 988-4203 (Tu-Sat 9-12)
  Robert W. Sutherland, Pastor

Formerly First Evangelical Church.

Annual meeting records, 1917-46, 2 vols; Church administration council, minutes, 1946+, 4 vols; Church registers, 1891-1972, 2 vols; Conference records, 1895-1950, 5 vols; General minutes and financial records, 1895-1916, ca. 1920-45, 12 vols; Ledgers, 1964-70, 2 vols; New building records, 1962-68, 1 vol; Sunday school class records, ca. 1930-50, 2 lf; Sunday school records, 1924-66, scattered, 7 vols. DH

538. St. Andrews Episcopal Church (1837)
  300 Third Street, Elyria, Ohio 44035
  (216) 322-2126 (M, Tu, Th, F 9-4:30; W, Sat 9-12)
  G. Russel Hargate, Rector

Central guild records, 1941-53, 1 vol; Church service records, 1953+, 3 vols; Financial statements, 1944-68, 1 vol; Parish register, 1837-1922, 14 vols; Photographs, 3 in.; Vestry minutes, 1942+, 3 vols; Vestry minutes, annual meetings and treasurer's accounts, 1837-79, 1898, 1 vol. DH

539. St. Paul Evangelical Lutheran Church (1875)
    115 Central, Amherst, Ohio 44001
    (216) 988-4157   (No set hours)
    Wilhol Latvala, Pastor

Annual reports, 1925-30, 1 vol; Cashbooks, 1919-23, 1 vol; Church registers, 1875-1925, 1 vol; Communicant record, 1942+, 1 vol; Council minutes, 1933-40, 1 vol; Daybooks, 1915-39, 1 vol; Financial records, 1920-25, 1 vol; Ledgers, 1940+, 1 vol; Proceedings, 1940+, 1 vol; "Protocol Buch" (constitution and minutes of the congregation), 1875-1914, 1 vol. JG

540. YMCA, Elyria (1911)
    Third and Court Streets, Elyria, Ohio 44035
    (216) 322-4605   (M-F 9-5)
    Russell C. Gleason, Executive Director

Administrative records; Board minutes, 1960-70, 2 lf.   JG

541. YWCA, Lorain (1956)
    630 Reid Avenue, Lorain, Ohio 44052
    (216) 244-1919   (M-W 9-8; Th, F 9-5; Sat 9:30-3:30)
    Lila Burke, Executive Director

Board and executive committee minutes, 1956+, 8 in.; Financial records, 1956-72, 8 in.; Membership card file, 1956-72, 23 lf; Scrapbooks, 1956-72, 8 vols. JG

LUCAS COUNTY

MANUSCRIPTS

542. Toledo and Lucas County Public Library (1941)
    325 Michigan Avenue, Toledo, Ohio 43624
    (419) 242-7361   (M-F 9-5:30)
    Morgan Barclay, Local History Librarian

Historical Society of N. W. Ohio (The Maumee Valley Historical Society), facts file (index of historical facts about Toledo and area, includes photographs of Miami-Erie Canal Locks and boats), 1815+, 15,000 cards; Maps of N.W. Ohio, 100 maps; Obituary index of Toledo residents published in the Blade, 1837+, 250,000 cards; Organization file, officers of local clubs and organizations, current, 1,000 cards; Scrapbooks, clippings of important Toledo events, 1940+, 150 vols.   PY

543. Waterville Historical Society (1964)
        19-1/2 North Third Street, Waterville, Ohio 43566
        (2-4 first Sunday of every month, May-Oct)
        Mrs. John W. Amstutz, Curator

Photographs, 1900s, high school and Waterville; Scrapbooks, 5 lf. PY

INSTITUTIONAL RECORDS

544. Bar Association, Toledo
        218 Huron, Toledo, Ohio 43604
        (419) 255-1725   (M-F 9-5)
        Marion Hebenstreit, Executive Secretary

Awards of merit, 1949-50, 1953, 1955, 1957, 1959, 5 vols; Bail bond reform program, 1965, 1 vol; Correspondence, 1957+, 15 lf; Minutes, 1917-45, 1956+, 2 lf; Newsletter, 1955-64, 2 lf; Scrapbooks, 1935-52, 4 vols.   PY

545. Better Business Bureau, Toledo (1917)
        Board of Trade Building, Room 214, Toledo, Ohio 43604
        (419) 241-6276   (M-F 9-5)
        John Howard, Executive Vice-President

Administrative records, 1917+; Agreements, 1917+; Annual reports, 1917+; Contracts, 1917+; Correspondence, 1917+; Financial statements, 1917+; Journals, 1917+; Ledgers, 1917+; Publications, 1952+; Scrapbooks, 1917+; Tax records, 1917+; 120 lf total.   PY

546. Board of Realtors
          Colton Building, Madison and Erie, Toledo, Ohio 43604
          (419) 241-1294   (M-F 8:30-5)
          Roy A. Bryan, Ex Vice-President

Correspondence, 1950-72, 15 lf; Minutes, articles of incorporation,
names of members, resolutions, qualifications, qualification approv-
als, 1910+, 8 vols; Monthly bulletin, 1960+.   PY

547. Boy Scouts of America, Toledo Area Council (1912)
          1 Stranahan Square, Toledo, Ohio 43604
          (419) 241-7293   (M-F 8:30-5)
          Paul Reinbolt

Articles of incorporation, 1918; Audits, 1920s; Executive board, minutes, 1918+, 4 vols; Membership cards, early 1920-60; Scrapbooks,
1920s; Unit registration folders, 1920s.   PY

548. Bronze Raven (1947)
          920 Collingwood, Toledo, Ohio 43602
          (419) 243-5643   (M-F 9-6)
          Richard Belcher, Owner-Publisher

Correspondence, 1968; Daybooks, 1968; Newspaper, Bronze Raven
1947+; Scrapbooks, 1947+.   DR

549. Catholic Diocese of Toledo
          2544 Parkwood Avenue, Toledo, Ohio 43610
          (419) 255-1935   (M-F 9-4)
          Jim Richards, Communications Director

Bishop correspondence (letters to and from parishes, other priests
and bishops, and general daily correspondence), 1910+, 15 lf; Catholic Chronicle, newspaper, 1933+; Cemetery records, 1910+; Historical files (name of parish, agreements, church histories, photographs, annual reports, newspaper clippings), 1910+, 20 lf; Organizational files (correspondence, social organization files, inactive
minutes of social groups and service groups, and general office
files), 1910+; Yearbooks (financial reports, lists of parishes, list
of priests, social organizations, annual messages, and bishop's
report), 1910+, 3 lf.   PY

550. Chamber of Commerce, Toledo Area
        218 Huron Street, Toledo, Ohio 43604
        (419) 243-8191
        Kent J. Galvin, Manager, Public Relations

Board of directors, minutes, 1922-26; Correspondence, 1950s-60s,
8 lf; General files, 80 lf; Minutes of meetings, 1926-39, 13 vols; Miscellaneous files, 10 lf; Predecessors to the chamber (Businessmen's
Chamber of Commerce, 1899-1908, Meeting of Manufacturers, 1803-
96, 1 vol, Toledo Commerce Club, 1911-21), records; Scrapbooks,
1917-60, scattered, 33 vols; Toledo Convention Bureau, 1957-62, 2
lf. PY

551. Champion Spark Plug Company (1907)
        900 Upton, Toledo, Ohio 43607
        (419) 536-3711   (M-F 8-4:30)
        Mr. Mougey, Assistant Public Relations Manager

Administrative records, 1907+; Agreements, 1907+; Annual reports,
1907+; Cashbooks, 1907+; Contracts, 1907+; Correspondence, 1907+;
Daybooks, 1907+; Financial statements, 1907+; Journals, 1907+; Ledgers, 1907+; Minutes, 1907+; Proceedings, 1907+; Receipts, 1907+;
Scrapbooks, 1920+. DR

552. Community Chest, Greater Toledo (1918)
        Suite 114, Community Services Building, 1 Stranahan Square
        Toledo, Ohio 43604
        (M-F 8:30-4:30)
        Chris P. Regas, Executive Director

Audits (yearly audits of each organization in the chest and of the chest),
1920s+, 16 lf; Board of Directors and Budget Committee (the organizations making up the chest and the chest's proceedings), 1920+, 15 vols;
Campaign records, 1920s+, 12 lf; Correspondence, 1920+, 16 lf; Newsletter, 1936+, 2 vol; Scrapbooks, 1941+, 8 lf; Summarized report of the
organizations involved with the chest, 1918+, 1 vol.   PY

553. Community Planning Council (1945)
        441 North Huron, Toledo, Ohio 43604
        (419) 248-4231   (M-F 8:30-5)
        Charlotte Shafer, Executive Director

Administrative records; Agreements; Annual reports; Contracts; Correspondence; Financial statements; Ledgers; Minutes; Publications;
90 lf total.   EL

554. Dana Corporation (1946)
        4100 Bennett Road, Toledo, Ohio 43612
        (419) 531-7333   (M-F 9-5)
        Frank Voss, Director of Public Relations

Administrative records, 1905+; Annual reports, 1905+; Contracts,
1905+; Correspondence, 1970+; Daybooks, 1963+; Financial statements,
1963+; Minutes, 1905+; Publications, 1905+; Scrapbooks, 7 lf; Tax records,   1905+.   EL

555. Democratic Party, Lucas County
        619 Madison Avenue, Toledo, Ohio 43604
        (419) 246-9301   (M-F 9-5)
        William Boyle, Executive Director

Administrative records, 1966+; Correspondence, 1966+; Daybooks,
1966+; Minutes, 1966+; Publications, 1966+; 10 lf total.   EL

556. Downtown Toledo Association (1955)
        Spitzer Building, Toledo, Ohio 43604
        (419) 241-9757   (M-F 9-5)
        Bert Silverman, Director

Organization of retail merchants and downtown businessmen serving
"business community and local body politic."

Administrative records, 1955+; Bulletins, 1955+; Cashbooks, 1955+;
Correspondence, 1950s+; Daybooks, 1955+; Financial statements,
1955+; Journals, 1955+; Ledgers, 1955+; Minutes, 1955+; Receipts,
1955+; 40 lf total.   EL

557. First National Bank of Toledo
        606 Madison, Toledo, Ohio 43604
        (419) 244-1935   (M-F 9-5)
        John Yager, Trust Division

Administrative records, 1914+, 6 lf; Annual meeting files, 1955+, 2 lf; Annual reports, 1947+, 3 lf; Correspondence, 1960+, 25 lf; Ledgers, 1930+, 10 lf; Minutes, 1914+, 14 lf; Tax records, 1934+, 5 lf. PY

558. First Presbyterian Church
        Connant Avenue, Maumee, Ohio 43537
        (419) 893-0223   (M-F 9-3)
        Calvin H. Buchanan, Pastor

Administrative records, 1836-66, 1 vol; Correspondence, 1955+, 10 lf; Scrapbooks, 1950+, 3 lf; Session minutes, 1820+, 5 lf.   PY

559. Lions Club, Toledo
        218 North Huron, Toledo, Ohio 43604
        (419) 255-1725   (M-F 9-4:30)
        A. B. Snyder, President

Bulletins, 1921+; Correspondence, 1930+, 8 lf; Minutes, 1954+, 3 lf; Scrapbooks, 1956+, 2 vols.   PY

560. Lucas County State Bank (1916)
        515 Madison Avenue, Toledo, Ohio 43604
        (419) 248-1491   (M-F 9-4)
        Tom Trepinski, Assistant Treasurer

Administrative records, 1916+; Correspondence, 1916+, scattered; Daybooks, 1916+, scattered; Financial statements, 1916+, scattered; Minutes, 1916+.   EL

561. Marine Engineers Beneficial Association
        927 North Summit Street, Toledo, Ohio 43604
        (419) 248-2431   (M-F 8:30-5)
        Tom Conway, Vice-President

Correspondence, 1964+; Minutes of membership meetings and executive board, 1964+; Photographs, 1964+, picket lines, strikes.   PY

562. Mary Manse College Library
        2484 Parkwood, Toledo, Ohio 43620
        (419) 243-9241
        Genevieve A. Ludwig, Librarian

Scrapbooks, 1922+, 15 lf.   PY

563.   Northwest Ohio Restaurant Association
        218 North Huron, Toledo, Ohio 43604
        (419) 243-8191   (M-F 9-4:30)
        Wanda Mitchell, Executive Secretary

Administrative records, 1944+; Correspondence, general office files
and daily correspondence, 1938+, 10 lf; Minutes, 1944+, 3 vols; Photographs of meetings, workshops, 1956+, 1 lf; Scrapbooks, 1952+, 1 vol.
PY

564.   Owens/Corning Fiberglass (1938)
        Fiberglass Tower, Toledo, Ohio 43601
        (419) 259-3734   (M-F 8:30-4:45)
        James E. Murphy, Director of Merchandising

Administrative records, 1938+; Agreements, 1938+; Annual reports,
1938+; Bibliography of glass documents and books, 1947-51; Cashbooks, 1938+; Contracts, 1938+; Correspondence; Daybooks, 1938+;
Financial statements, 1938+; Journals, 1938+; Ledgers, 1938+; Minutes, 1938+; Proceedings, 1938+; Publications; Receipts, 1938+;
Scrapbooks, 1940s+.   DR

565.   Port of Toledo (1946)
        241 Superior Street, Toledo, Ohio 43604
        (419) 243-8251   (M-F 8-4:30)
        John A. McWilliam, General Manager

Administrative records, 1946, 1955; Annual reports, 1946+, 12 lf;
Contracts, 1959+; Correspondence, 1955+, 15 lf; Daybooks, 1956+,
10 lf; Financial statements, 1956+; Journals, 1956+; Ledgers, 1956+;
Minutes, 1946+; Publications, 1946+; Scrapbooks, 1965+, 10 lf.   DR

566.   Republican Executive Committee, Lucas County
        Gardner Building, Superior and Madison, Toledo, Ohio 43604
        (419) 248-4474   (M-F 8-4:30)
        Jane Kuebbeler, Executive Director

Correspondence (candidates, party supporters, national party chair-
men), 1952+; Duplicate election abstracts, 1966+; Executive committee,

minutes (date, names of members present, campaign proporate, issues, policies, endorsements), 1930+, 4 vols; Publications, brochures, campaign materials, 1952+; Scrapbooks, 1952+, 5 lf; Ward and precinct statistics, registered-nonregistered Republican, Democrat, and Independent, 1968+. PY

567. St. Anns Catholic Church
        1119 West Bancroft Avenue, Toledo, Ohio 43604
        (419) 241-4544   (M-F 9-4)
        Fr. Dale Wernert, Pastor

Baptismals, 1898+, 2 lf; Deaths, 1898+, 2 lf; First confirmations, 1898+, 1 lf; Marriages, 1898+, 2 lf. PY

568. Scottish Rite (1882)
        4645 Heathdowns Boulevard, Toledo, Ohio 43614
        (419) 893-8726   (M-F 9-5)
        Donald Kretzinger, AASR Secretary

Annual reports, 1882+, 5 lf; Membership photos, 1945+, 3 lf; Proceedings, 1882+, 15 lf; Semi-annual reunion programs, 1882+, 5 lf. EL

569. Small Business Association
        218 North Huron, Toledo, Ohio 43604
        (M-F 9-4:30)
        Frank R. Smith, Executive Director

Administrative records, 1942+; Annual reports, 1945+; Bulletins, 1956+; Correspondence, 1942+, 7 lf; Directories, member names, 1945+; Minutes, 1942+, 3 lf; Scrapbooks, 1956+, 1 vol newspaper clippings. PY

570. Toledo Area Governmental Research Association
        1 Stranahan Square, Toledo, Ohio 43604
        (419) 241-5229   (M 8:30-4:30)
        Patrick J. Kessler, Research Assistant

The Governmental Research Association is a non-profit, non-partisan organization engaged in research and education on and about local government.

Administrative records, 1935; Correspondence, 1935+, 20 lf; Minutes, 1935+, 10 vol; Publications on urban affairs, 1955+; Toledo
Municipal News, newspaper, 1945-68.   PY

571. Toledo Board of Trade (1876)
        Board of Trade Building, Toledo, Ohio 43604
        (419) 241-1131   (M-F 8-5)
        Alfred E. Schultz, Executive Manager

Administrative records, 1876+; Annual reports, 1876+; Cashbooks,
1876+; Correspondence, 1960+, 4 lf; Daybooks, 1876+; Financial
statements, 1876+; Journals, 1876+; Ledgers, 1876+; Minutes, 1876+;
Proceedings, 1876+; Publications, 1876+, 25 lf; Scrapbooks, 1940, 3
lf; Statistical research on grain prices and shipments.   DR

572. The Toledo Edison Company (1901)
        420 Madison Avenue, Toledo, Ohio 43604
        (419) 242-5731   (M-F 8:30-5)
        Chester J. Lipinski, Director, Administrative Systems

Administrative records, 1901+; Annual reports, 1950+; Cashbooks,
1950+; Contracts, 1901+; Correspondence, 1901+; Daybooks, 1950+;
Deeds, 1901+; Financial statements, 1950+; Journals, 1950+; Ledgers, 1950+; Minutes, 1950+; Oral history tapes, former executives;
Publications, 1920+; Receipts, 1950+; Scrapbooks, 1946+.   DR

573. Toledo-Lucas County Regional Area Plan for Action Commission (1912)
        Huron Building, North Huron and Jackson, Toledo, Ohio 43604
        (419) 255-1500   (M-F 8-4:45)
        Lawrence Murray, Director

Predecessors to the commission were the Toledo Planning Commission
and the Lucas County Planning Commission.

Administrative records, 1912+; Annual reports, 1959+; Correspondence,
1960s+; Daybooks, 1950s+; Ledgers, 1950s+; Minutes, 1912+; Publications,
1912+; Research reports, 1912+, scattered; 150 lf total.   EL

574. Toledo Metropolitan Area Council of Governments (1968)
        1040 National Bank Building, Madison and Huron, Toledo, Ohio 43604
        (419) 241-9155   (M-F 8:30-5)
        Michael D. Duermit, Director, Regional Planning

Contracts, 1968+, 2 lf; Correspondence, 1968+, 10 lf; Executive committee, 1968+; Financial records, 1968+, 5 lf; Reports from similar agencies all over the country, 1968+, 50 lf; Report on all federally funded projects in the area, 1968+, 7 lf.   PY

575. Toledo Museum of Art (1901)
      2445 Monroe, Toledo, Ohio 43620
      (419) 255-8000   (M, Sat 1-5; Tu-F 9-5)
      Rudolf McRiefstahl, Curator

Correspondence, 1969+; Exhibition catalogs, 1901+; Scrapbooks, 1901+; George W. Stevens collection, pre-Egyptian, 200 bound volumes and 500 documents.   DR

576. Toledo Symphony
      1 Stranahan Square, Toledo, Ohio 43604
      (419) 248-6447   (M-F 9-5)
      Helyn A. Frye, Secretary

Correspondence, 1955+, 7 lf; Minutes, 1919+, 2 lf; News releases, 1967-70, 2 vols; Photographs, 1951+, 3 lf; Programs, 1955+, 2 vols; Publication, Journal, 1955-60, 2 vols.   PY

577. Toledo Trust Company (1868)
      245 Summit Street, Toledo, Ohio 43604
      (419) 248-6771   (M-F 9-4:30)
      R. Johnston, Public Relations and Marketing Director

Administrative records, 1868+; Annual reports, 1960+; Correspondence, 7-year retention; Publications, 1965+; Receipts, 1868+; Research projects, 1960+; Tax records, 1960+.   EL

578. Toledo Urban Renewal Agency (1956)
      Toledo, Ohio
      (M-F 8:45-4:45)
      Arthur Lanier, Assistant to Director

Administrative records, 1956+; Annual reports, 1965+; Correspondence, 8-year retention; Daybooks, 1959+, scattered; Ledgers, 1962+; Minutes, 1956+; Project files, 1959+; Publications, 1967+; Research reports, 1962+; 100 lf total.   EL

579. United Cavalcade of Mercy (1918)
      443 Huron Street, Toledo, Ohio 43604
      (419) 248-2424   (M-Sat 8-4:30)
      Chris Regas, Executive Director

Administrative records, 1918+; Annual reports; Cashbooks, 1918+;
Correspondence, 1918+; Daybooks, 1918+; Financial statements,
1918+; Journals, 1918+; Ledgers, 1918+; Minutes, 1918+; Receipts,
1918+; 250 lf total.   EL

580. United Jewish Fund of Toledo (1907)
      2247 Collingwood, Toledo, Ohio 43620
      (419) 241-8111   (M-F 8:30-5)
      Mr. Levinson, Director

Administrative records, 1907+; Annual reports, 1943+; Campaign
pledges, 1938+; Contracts, 1943+; Daybooks, 1960+; Journals, 1960+;
Ledgers, 1960+; Minutes, 1907+; Proceedings, 1943+; Publications,
1960+; Scrapbooks, 1943+; 20 lf total.   DR

581. The University of Toledo Archives
      2801 West Bancroft Street, Toledo, Ohio 43606
      (419) 531-5711   (M-F 8:30-12, 1-5)
      Lucille B. Emch, Associate Director for Rare Books, Special
      Collections and Archives

The archives contain the major administrative record series of the
university along with many artifacts. Inventory available.

College of Arts and Sciences, annual reports, budgets, faculty lists;
College of Education, deans' papers, bulletins, faculty minutes; College of Engineering, annual reports, bulletins, deans' papers; College
of Pharmacy, bulletins, deans' papers; Faculty, committee reports,
minutes; Film-sound collection, color transparencies, films, tape
recordings; Office of the president, papers; Offices of vice-presidents,
papers and memoranda; Publications, administration, faculty, students.
PY

582. WCWA Radio (1930)
      604 Jackson Avenue, Toledo, Ohio 43604
      (419) 248-2627   (M-F 8:30-5)
      Garry Miller, Station Manager

Administrative records, 1930+; Correspondence, 1-year retention;
Minutes, 1930+; Publications, 1965+; Scrapbooks, 1965+; 35 lf total.
EL

583. WTOL-TV (Channel 11) (1958)
      604 Jackson Avenue, Toledo, Ohio 43604
      (419) 244-7411   (M-F 9-5)
      J. Scott, Assistant Public Relations Director

Administrative records, 1958+; Correspondence, 1958+; Market research, 1958+; Minutes, 1958+; Publications, 5-year retention; 50+
lf total.   EL

584. YMCA, Toledo
      1110 Jefferson Avenue, Toledo, Ohio 43624
      (419) 247-7177   (M-F 8-5)
      Leigh Kendrick, Vice-President

Achievement appraisal files, 1958-65, 1 box; Board of trustees, minutes, 1882-1972, 10 vols; Central YMCA board of managers, minutes,
1945+, 6 vols; Correspondence, 1920+, 20 lf; General and executive
committee, minutes, 1883-86, 1895-1914, 1929-60, date, names of
members present, policies, resolutions, financial reports, membership programs, 8 vols; Ledgers, 1920+, 10 lf; Membership program,
1930-34, 2 vols; Photographs, 1880-1970, 5 lf; Program development,
1961-62, 3 vols; YMCA yearbook, 1937-68, 32 vols; Scrapbooks, 1889-
1906, 1957+, 13 vols.   PY

                          MADISON COUNTY

MANUSCRIPTS

585. London Public Library (1902)
      20 East First Street, London, Ohio 43140
      (614) 852-9543   (M-W, F 9-5; Th 9-5, 7-9; Sat 9-12)

Local history collection, clipping file on events in London and Madison
County, 1904-40, 1 in.; Scrapbook, 1962+, 1 in.   FH

586. Madison County Historical Society (1965)
     P. O. Box 124, London, Ohio 43140
     Mrs. Edward Cox, President, R.R. #1, London, Ohio 43140
     (614) 852-9369

Auburn and Smith, prescription book, 3 lf; Mrs. L. R. Bostwick, postcards, 1913-15, 15 items; Children's Home of Madison County, record
book, 1896-98, 1 lf; Houston and Burnham, journal, 1880-83, 1 lf; Ledgers, 1871-1918, 1923-25, 2 in.; J. M. Morse (doctor) account books
and record of narcotics, 1915-20, 1948-60, 18 in.; J. Tuttle (doctor),
financial records, 1857-60, 1 vol.   SF

INSTITUTIONAL RECORDS

587. Chamber of Commerce, London (ca. 1950)
     1 East High Street, London, Ohio 43140
     (614) 852-2250   (M-F 9-5; Sat 9-12)
     James L. Minshall, Secretary

Administrative records, ca. 1950+, 1 in.; Agreements, 1969+, 2 in.;
Annual reports, ca. 1965+, 3 in.; Bi-monthly bulletin, ca. 1969+; Correspondence, 1969+, 1 lf; Financial statements, 1964+, 3 in.; Minutes,
ca. 1960+, 6 in.; Receipts, 1964+, 2 in.; Scrapbooks, 1965+, 3 in.;Tax
records, personnel, 1969+, 2 in.   FH

588. Creamer Sheet Metal Products
     77 South Madison Road, London, Ohio 43140
     (614) 852-1752
     Donna Creamer, Vice-President and Secretary

Administrative records, 1962+, 1 in.; Correspondence, 5-year retention, 2 lf; Financial statements, ca. 1955; Inventories, 10-year retention, 6 in.; Journals, 1946+, 18 in.; Ledgers, 1946+, 2 lf; Minutes,
1962+, 1 in.; Payroll, 1945+, 2 lf; Publications, new catalog with price
changes, ca. 1960+; Tax records, 1946+, 1 lf.   FH

589. Farm Bureau Co-Op, London (1946)
     254 West High Street, London, Ohio 43140
     (614) 852-2062   (M-F 7:30-5:30)
     Charles Wyscarver, General Manager

Administrative records, 1946+, 1 in.; Annual reports, 1946+, 1 lf;
Audit reports, 1946+, 18 in.; Financial statements, 1946+, 2 lf; Min-
utes, 1946+, 1 lf; Receipts, 7-year retention; Tax records, 1946+.
WM

590. First Presbyterian Church (ca. 1829)
        55 South Walnut, London, Ohio 43140
        (614) 852-1215   (Tu-F 9-12)
        Pastor

Administrative records, ca. 1830, 5-10 pp; Board of trustees, minutes, 1953+, 2 in.; Bulletin, 1958+, 1 in.; Church register, 1837-77,
1964+, 2 lf; Deacons minutes, 1962-66, 1 in.; Membership rolls, 1829+,
27 in.; Miscellaneous files, 1961+, 3 lf; Pledge records, 1964+, 7 file
boxes; Receipts, 1963+, 2 lf; Session minutes, 1898+, 9 in.   FH

591. First United Methodist Church (1813)
        North Main and Fourth Street, London, Ohio 43140
        (614) 852-0462   (M-F 1-5)
        Virgil Hamilton, Minister

Church register, 1861+, 2 lf; Financial statements, 1913, 1951, 1 in.;
Minutes, 1913-27, 2 in.; Miscellaneous files, ca. 1960+, 1 lf; Sunday
bulletin and newsletter, 1957+, 9 in.; Women's Society, minutes, 1941-
46, 2 in.   FH

592. Madison County Hospital (1962)
        210 North Main, London, Ohio 43140
        (614) 852-1372   (M-F 8-4:30)
        Richard Harley, Administrator

Cancer registry; Death registry; Financial records section, reveal a
daily cost account broken into separate divisions of the hospital, 1962+;
Medical records section: history and physicals, discharge summary,
laboratory work, X-rays taken, surgery, specialty work, doctor's progress notes, nursing notes, physician order sheets, consultation with
specialists, 1962+, 170 lf and mf; Monthly hospital statistics; Scrapbooks of newspaper clippings and photographs, 1962+, 3 lf.   WM

593. Trinity Episcopal Church (1875)
      10 East Fourth Street, London, Ohio 43140
      (614) 852-2861
      Fr. Thomas Timmons, Pastor

Annual reports, ca. 1955+, 1 in.; Church register, 1876+, 4 in.;
Sallie Doon's history of Trinity Church, ca. 1918-20, 40 pp; Financial statements, ca. 1955+, 1 in.; Minutes, ca. 1910+, 3 in.; Parish
letter, 1955+, 1 in.; Vestry minutes, ca. 1910+, 2 in. FH

594. United Industrial Workers of North America (1969)
      249 West High Street, London, Ohio 43140
      (614) 852-2495
      William Dobbins, Regional Director

Active grievance file, 1972+, 3 in.; Settled grievances, 1969+, 1 lf;
Minutes, 1970+, 2 in.; Personnel, health and welfare, 1969+, 8 lf.
FH

595. Paul M. Yauger Company (1918)
      126 South Main Street, London, Ohio 43140
      (614) 852-1553   (M-Sat 8-5; Sun 1-5)
      Donald Rife, Sr., Manager

Cemetery monument company.

Monument records (what was sold, who made the purchase, where
the monument was placed, inscriptions, amount of purchase, cemetery placed in, names, birthdates, death dates), 1918+, 110 lf. WM

MAHONING COUNTY

MANUSCRIPTS

596. Industrial Information Institute (1947)
      6219 Market Street, Youngstown, Ohio 44501
      (216) 758-2339   (M-F 8:30-5)
      Robert B. Collins, Director

Tape recorded accounts of area history for Columbiana, Mahoning,
and Trumbull counties, 1947+, 210 7-1/2 inch tape reels. JWG

597. Mahoning Valley Historical Society (1875)
        648 Wick Avenue, Youngstown, Ohio 44502
        (216) 743-2589
        Mrs. Walter Schaff, Jr., Director

Giles Harber (Navy admiral), letters, diaries, newspaper clippings, official naval records, 1895-1910, 1 MS box; Miscellaneous papers of prominent Mahoning individuals, letters, diaries, bills of sale, photographs, 1840-1930, 3 lf; O'Connor Brothers, business records, 1898-1917, 3 vols; Pennsylvania and Ohio Canal toll collectors' records, 1866-72, 2 vols; William Rayen, business records, 1796-1840, 11 vols; Stambaugh papers, family business papers, diaries, 1820-1900, 3 MS boxes; David Tod, papers (letters, diaries), 1835-80, 4 MS boxes; B.F. Wirt collection, diaries, 1910-30, 2 lf; Youngstown Industrial Exchange, business records, 1887-95, 2 vols; Youngstown Printing Company, business records, 1875-82, 6 vols. CB

598. Public Library of Youngstown and Mahoning County (1880)
        305 Wick Avenue, Youngstown, Ohio 44503
        (216) 744-8636   (M-F 9-9; Sat 9-5:30)
        Hazel Ohl, Head, General Reference

Henry R. Baldwin, cemetery inscriptions, 5 lf; Butler Institute of Art, various programs and booklets, 1953+, 1 box; Kenneth Lloyd, correspondence, reports, plans, documents pertaining to a Lake Erie-Ohio River Canal, 1930-67, 138 bound vols; Periodicals of local organizations, 1969+, 4 lf; Service organizations of Mahoning County, annual reports and financial statements, 1929+, 8 lf; Tales of the Mahoning and Shenango valleys, radio scripts of 19th century history of Mahoning Valley, 1951-57, 2 lf; WPA newspaper indexes: Mahoning County Register, 1865-Feb 1875, Ohio Republican, June 6, 1851-July 23, 1852, Olive Branch and Literary Messenger, Aug 25, 1843-Aug 2, 1844, Trumbull County Democrat, Dec 1838-Jan 1840, June-Sept 1841, Western Reserve Transcript, Nov 25, 1852-June 2, 1853; Youngstown annual reports, bound, 1902-20, 1 lf; Youngstown Playhouse, programs, 1951+, 6 in.; Youngstown Symphony Society, programs, 1953+, 1 lf.

Library records: Administrative records, 1880+; Annual reports, 1888+, 18 in.; Board of trustees, minutes, 1880+, 3 lf; Circulation statistics, 1952+, 1 folder; Correspondence, 1929-50, 3 lf; Financial statements, 1880+, 3 lf; Manuals of instruction for library staff, ca. 1920, 6 in.; Scrapbooks, 1890-1900, 1 folder. CB

INSTITUTIONAL RECORDS

599. Butler Institute of American Art (1919)
        524 Wick Avenue, Youngstown, Ohio 44502
        (216) 743-1711   (Tu-Sat 10-4:30)
        Alice B. Goldcamp, Educational Director

Board of directors, minutes, 1919+; Catalogs, 1919+; Correspondence
of American artists, 1750-1969, 3500 items; Inventories of institute
holdings, 1919+.   CB

600. Catholic Diocese of Youngstown
        140 Wood Street, Youngstown, Ohio
        (216) 744-5341
        Msgr. J. Paul O'Connor, Chancellor

Parish records of all parishes in the diocese, mf.   CB

601. Chamber of Commerce, Youngstown Area (1905)
        200 Wick Building, Youngstown, Ohio 44503
        (216) 744-2131
        W. O. Johnstone, Executive Vice-President

Administrative records, 1905+; Annual reports, 1905+; Committee
minutes, 1905+; Monthly reports of chamber activities, 1959+; Publications; Scrapbooks, 1905+.   CB

602. First Presbyterian Church (1799)
        201 Wick Avenue, Youngstown, Ohio 44503
        (216) 744-4307
        William F. Miller, Pastor Emeritus

Annual reports, 1949+; Membership records, 1799+, 4 vols; Minutes, 1800+; Publication (weekly paper), 1938+; Scrapbooks, 1938+;
Service records, 1900+, 3 lf; Session records, 1799+, 4 vols.   CB

603. Mahoning Valley Association of Churches (1914)
        631 Wick Avenue, Youngstown, Ohio 44502
        (216) 744-8946
        Norman M. Parr, Executive Director

Administrative records, 1914+; Annual reports, 1914+; Correspondence, 1914+; Executive committee, minutes, 1914+; Filmstrips, church stories and special holidays, 200 strips; Financial statements, 1914+; Inventories, 1914+; Publications, 1951+; Scrapbooks.   C B

604. Penn-Ohio Junior College (1941)
      3517 Market Street, Youngstown, Ohio 44507
      (216) 788-5084
      William Clark, President

Annual reports, 1964+, 6 in.; Cashbooks, 1941+; Catalogs, 1941+; Correspondence, 1941+; Deeds; Financial statements, 1941+; Journals, 1941+; Ledgers, 1941+; Minutes, 1941+, 1 lf; Student newspapers; Tax records, 1941+.   C B

605. Republican Party, Mahoning County (ca. 1900)
      901 Realty Building, Youngstown, Ohio 44503
      (216) 747-9064   (M-F 9-4)
      Mrs. Panis, Secretary

Correspondence, 1963+, 3 lf; Ledgers, 1967+; Lists of candidates, 1972+, 3 in.; Minutes; Publications, pamphlets and leaflets; Receipts, ca. 1967+; Voting lists, 1971+, 1 lf.   C B

606. Trinity United Methodist Church (1803)
      30 West Front Street, Youngstown, Ohio 44511
      (216) 744-5032   (M-F 9-4)
      Homer Elford, Senior Pastor

Administrative records, 1856+; Annual reports, 1952+; Chimes, monthly publication, 1945+, 1 lf; Church register, 1856-1901, 1910+, 1 lf; Ladies' Society records, 1892-1938, 3 lf.   C B

607. United Steelworkers, District 26 Headquarters (1942)
      400 Realty Building, Youngstown, Ohio 44503
      (216) 747-1961
      Frank D. Anness, Staff Representative

Administrative records, 1942+; Agreements, 1942+; Annual reports, 1942+; Contracts, 1942+; Correspondence, 1942+; Financial statements, 1942+; Minutes, 1942+; Publications (bulletins of the international), 1942+; Tax records, 1942+.   C B

608. United Way-United Appeals (1917)
         Realty Building, Youngstown, Ohio 44503
         (216) 746-8494   (M-F 8:30-4:45)
         William J. Brennan, Director

Administrative records; Annual reports, 1917+; Directories of organizations, 1917+; Financial statements, 1917+; Minutes, 1917+; Scrapbooks, 1917+; Studies of community problems, 1917+, 24 lf; Tax records, 1917+. CB

609. Youngstown Sheet and Tube Company (1900)
         P.O. Box 900, 7655 Market Street, Youngstown, Ohio 44501
         (216) 758-6411   (M-F 9-4)
         Edward Beardmore, Public Relations Director

Minutes, 1900-1908, 2 vols; Miscellaneous reports, land contracts
and tax reports, 1920-22, 1 vol; Photographs, 275 items; Scrapbooks,
1942-60, 3 vols.   JWG

610. Youngstown State University Archives (1931)
         410 Wick Avenue, Youngstown, Ohio 44503
         (216) 744-4851   (M-Sat 7:30-10; Sun 1-5)
         George Jones, Librarian

College catalogs, 1931+; General university announcements, 1968+;
Jambar, student paper, 1931+; Proceedings of all university committees, 1965+. CB

611. Youngstown Vindicator (1868)
         Vindicator Square, Youngstown, Ohio 44501
         (216) 747-1471   (M-F 9-4)
         Irving L. Mansell, Managing Editor

Newspaper index, according to biography or subject, early 1920s+,
100 cf. JWG

INSTITUTIONAL RECORDS

612. Chamber of Commerce, Marion County Area (1915)
      215 South Main Street, Marion, Ohio 43302
      (614) 382-2181   (M-F 8-5)
      Jack Lautenslager, Manager

Administrative records, 1915+; Annual reports, 1949+; Board of directors, minutes, 1914+; Correspondence, ca. 1969+; Financial records, ca. 1949+; Monthly newsletter, "Activities," ca. 1945+; Scrapbooks, ca. 1920s+; Tax records, primarily on staff and property; 134 lf total. SF

613. Family Service Society of Marion County (1952)
      186 West Church Street, Marion, Ohio 43302
      (614) 383-3127   (M-F 8:30-5)
      Roy S. Merwin, Director

Administrative records, 1952, 1 in.; Agreements, 1968, 2 in.; Annual reports, 1962+, 1 in.; Board minutes, 1952+, 1 lf; Correspondence, 5-year retention, 6 in.; Financial statements, 1952+, 6 in.; Newsletter, 1972+, 1 in.; Scrapbooks, 1952+, 6 in.; Tax records, 1952+, 1 in.   FH

614. First Presbyterian Church (1828)
      Church and Prospect, Marion, Ohio 43302
      (614) 382-9545   (M-F 9-4)
      James N. Urquhart, Pastor

Administrative records, 1828+; Board of deacons, 1934-39, 1 in.; Church rolls, 1828+, 6 in.; Congregational meeting minutes, 1846-1958, 2 in.; Financial statements, 1846-92, 3 in.; Ledgers, 3 in.; Minutes, 1828+, 1 lf; Minutes book, maternal organization, 1853-59, 1 in.; Publications, 1969+, 6 in.; Trustees records, 1892-1929, 1 in. FH

615. Goodwill Industries of Central Ohio, Marion Division (1959)
      235 East Center, Marion, Ohio 43302
      (614) 382-1129   (M-F 8-4:30)
      Elwyn Pilley, Director

Contracts, 1959+, 3 in.; Correspondence, 3-year retention, 6 in.;

Financial records, 1959+, 3 in.; Inventories, equipment records,
1959+, 2 lf; Minutes, 1959+, 1 lf; Personnel records, 1959+, 2 lf;
Scrapbooks, 1959, 3 in.   FH

616. Harding Memorial Association (1923)
        116 South Main Street, Marion, Ohio 43302
        (614) 383-6396   (M-F 9-5)
        Paul D. Michel, Secretary and Assistant Treasurer

Administrative records; Correspondence, including accession records, 1923+, 10 lf; Deeds to Harding property, July 1924, 1 file
folder; Executive committee and trustees, minutes, 1923+, 18 in.;
Financial records, 1964+, 2 lf; Legal records, 1923+, 2 lf.   SF

617. Marion Business College (1895)
        131 East Center, Marion, Ohio 43302
        (614) 382-0454   (M-F 8-1:15)
        Mrs. Milbourne Donaugh, Secretary-Treasurer

Correspondence, ca. 1955+, 12 lf; Financial records, 1955+, 1 lf;
Minutes, ca. 1920+, 1 lf; Publications, college brochure and catalog.
FH

618. Marion County Bank (1839)
        P. O. Box 503, Marion, Ohio 43302
        (614) 383-4051
        Robert Hensel, Cashier

Administrative records, 1839+, 1 in.; Annual reports, ca. 1900+,
3 in.; Correspondence, 7-year retention, 7 lf; Minutes, ca. 1900+,
2 lf; Receipts, 3-year retention; Scrapbooks, ca. 1940+, 4 in.; Tax
records, 7-year retention.   FH

619. Marion County Regional Planning Commission (1960)
        169-1/2 East Center, Marion, Ohio 43302
        (614) 382-6182   (M-F 8-12, 1-5)
        J. Lee Brown, Director

Land use files, data sheets on IBM cards, 24 lf; Maps, 10 file drawers;
Minutes, 1963+; Scrapbooks, 1963+, 8 in.; Township maps, 31 items.
WM

620. Marion General Hospital (1955)
         McKinley Park Drive, Marion, Ohio 43302
         (614) 383-6731   (M-F 7-5:30)
         Miles L. Waggoner, Administrator

Medical records, 1938+ (1938-62 on mf; 1962-67 on microcards; 1967+
in file folders), 405 rolls microfilm, 86 microcards, 395 lf folders;
X-rays, 145 lf. WM

621. Marion Public Library (1886)
         244 South Main Street, Marion, Ohio 43302
         (614) 383-3191   (M-F 9-9; Sat 9-5:30)
         Janet Berg, Librarian

Library records (minutes of meetings, vouchers, cancelled checks,
cash journals, payroll, and balance sheets), 1950+, 36 lf; Scrapbook,
Harding clippings, ca. 1914-20, 2 in. SF

622. Masonic Lodge, Marion (1840)
         119 West Church Street, Marion, Ohio 43302
         (614) 382-4017   (M-Sat 9-5)
         Harold W. Hall, Secretary

Administrative records, 1902; Annual reports, 1840+, 1 lf; Contracts,
1902; Correspondence, 1955+, 20 lf; Deeds, 1902; Ledgers on membership, 1840+, 3 lf; Minutes, 1840+, 15 lf; Newsletter, 1941+, 6 in.;
Photographs, lodge members, 1841+, 4 lf. SF

623. Ohio Jersey Breeders Association (1883)
         Prospect, Ohio 43342
         (614) 494-2312   (M-F 9-4)
         Kenneth Miller, Secretary and Fieldman

Administrative records, ca. 1948+; Annual reports, ca. 1936+; Correspondence, ca. 1950+; Financial records, ca. 1930s+; Ledgers,
treasurer's, ca. 1936+; Minutes, ca. 1936+; Publication, "Ohio Jersey
News," ca. 1936+; 80 lf total. SF

624. Ohio Junior Chamber of Commerce State Office (1932)
         241 Executive Drive, Marion, Ohio 43302
         (614) 383-6389   (M-F 8:30-5)
         James Frederick, Executive Vice-President

Administrative records, 1932, 1 file folder; Annual reports, 1972,
6 lf; Contracts from building commission, equipment, etc., 1961+,
1 lf; Correspondence, 1967+, 40 lf; Financial statements, 1956+, 4
in.; Minutes, 1965+, 4 in.; Publication, "Ohio Tomorrow," ca. 1947+;
Scrapbooks, 810 lf.   SF

625. Prospect United Methodist Church (ca. 1835)
        203 North Elm, Prospect, Ohio 43342
        (614) 494-2611
        Donald Shaver, Minister

Administrative records, 1949; Annual reports, ca. 1950+, 6 in.; Correspondence, 1964+, 2 lf; Financial records, 1964+; Minutes, ca.1950+,
18 in.; Publications, 1964+, 1 lf; Scrapbooks, ca. 1900+, 6 in.   SF

626. Rotary Club, Marion (1922)
        119 West Church Street, Marion, Ohio 43302
        (614) 382-4017   (M-Sat 9-5)
        Harold W. Hall, Secretary-Treasurer

Correspondence, 1947+, 4 lf; Financial statements, 1947+, included
in minutes books, also a yearly report, 1947+, 6 in.; Minutes, 1922+,
3 in.; Rotary Foundation, Inc., records, 1960+, 1 lf; "Rotary News
of the Week," 1922+, 2 lf.   SF

627. United Church of Christ (1846)
        207 East Water, Prospect, Ohio 43342
        (614) 494-2583   (M-F 8:30-12)
        John Kim, Minister

Annual reports, 1946+; Church register, 1940+; Correspondence,
1967+; Minutes, 1930+; Scrapbooks, 1890+; 26 lf total.   SF

628. YMCA, Marion (1892)
        193 East Church Street, Marion, Ohio 43302
        (614) 382-0144   (M-F 8-5)
        D. Allen Shaffer, Director

Administrative records, 1892+, 1 in.; Financial statements, 1951+,
1 in.; Minutes, 1951+, 3 in.   FH

MANUSCRIPTS

629. Medina County Historical Society (1922)
      P. O. Box 306, Medina, Ohio 44256
      (216) 725-4353   (First Sat of each month, 1-5)
      Mrs. J. J. Cochran, Curator

Historical files, materials include photographs, ledgers, correspondence, typed and handwritten histories, clippings and newspapers, ca.
1810+, 8 lf. JG

630. Seville Chronicle (1946)
      17 East Main Street, Seville, Ohio 44273
      (216) 769-3497   (M, Tu, Th, F 9-5; W, Sat 9-12)
      Lee Cavin, Editor

A. B. Kulp, ditching records, 1890-1902, 3 vols; Miscellaneous clippings and old correspondence relating to Seville, 1825+, 6 in.; Photographs and negative files, 1 lf; Seville town records (Board of education, minutes, 1854-1914, 1 vol; Council records, town council meetings, 1869-1902, 1913-21, 3 vols; Court dockets, 1878, 1927-49, 2
vols); Unidentified household record, record of sale of household products, 1875-84, 1 vol. JG

INSTITUTIONAL RECORDS

631. American Red Cross, Medina County (1917)
      234-1/2 South Court, Medina, Ohio 44256
      (216) 723-4565   (M-F 8:30-4:30)
      Mrs. Carl Becks, Executive Director

Blood program files, 1956+, 5 lf; Current files, ca. 1940+, 15 lf;
Disaster records, 1969+; Finanical records, ca. 1917+, 5 lf; Minutes, 1917+, 1 lf; Water safety instruction, 1961+, 2 lf. DH

632. Chamber of Commerce, Hinckley (1949)
      958 Ridge Road, Hinckley, Ohio 44233
      (216) 278-7111   (No set hours)
      Dave Milhalko, Secretary

Administrative files, 1952-69, 18 in.; Executive committee, minutes, 1959+, 1 vol; Publication, The Hinckley Reporter, 1958+. JG

633. Chamber of Commerce, Medina (1938)
      120 North Elmwood Avenue, Medina, Ohio 44256
      (216) 723-8773   (M-F 9-5)
      M. Larry Schmith, Executive Manager

Administrative records, 1938; Annual reports, 1938+; Financial statements, 1938+; Minutes, 1938+; 1 lf total. DH

634. Chamber of Commerce, Seville (1948)
      Jaffe Industrial Park, Seville, Ohio 44273
      (216) 769-2051   (M-F 9-5)
      Stan Jaffe, President

Administrative records, 1948, 3 pp; Minutes, 1948-49, 1962+, 2 vols.
JG

635. Chamber of Commerce, Valley City (1967)
      6815 School Street, Valley City, Ohio 44280
      (216) 483-3368   (No set hours)
      Peter Berger, Secretary

Administrative records, 1967; Minutes, 1969+, 1 vol; Scrapbooks,
1967+, 1 vol. DH

636. Chamber of Commerce, Wadsworth (1954)
      125 High Street, Wadsworth, Ohio 44281
      (216) 334-2530   (M-F 9-5; Sat 9-12)
      William Hoerger, Executive Vice-President

Administrative records, 1954+, 13 pp; Agreements, 1954+, 10 pp;
Annual reports, 1954+, 20 pp; Contracts, 1954+, 20 pp; Correspondence, 1954+, 900 pp; Financial statements, 1954+, 216 pp; Ledgers,
1954+, 200 pp; Minutes, 1954+, 440 pp; Publications, 1955+; Scrapbooks, 1956-71; Tax records, 1954+. JG

637. Grange No. 2449, Gilford (1928)
      9875 Gilford Road, Seville, Ohio 44273
      (216) 769-2760   (No set hours)
      Mrs. Ernest Shook, Grange Secretary

Dues account books, 1934-68, 6 vols; Inspection sheets, ca. 1943-70,

1 in.; Membership applications, 1943+, 4 in.; Quarterly reports, 1928-70, 4 in.; Roll call book, 1934-50, 1 vol; Secretary's books, 1934-70, 8 vols.   JG

638. Grange No. 1347, Hinckley (1890)
        1746 Maple Hill Drive, Hinckley, Ohio 44233
        (216) 278-3902   (No set hours)
        Wilma Damon, Master

Roll book, 1890-1919, 1 vol; Secretary's books, 1890-1965, 16 vols. DH

639. Grange No. 2446, Lafayette (1928)
        5078 Airhart Road, Medina, Ohio 44256
        (216) 722-2258   (No set hours)
        Jill Heath, Secretary

Secretary's books, 1928+, 6 vols.   JG

640. Grange No. 1453, Mallet Creek (1898)
        6200 Wolf Road, Medina, Ohio 44256
        (216) 722-4288   (No set hours)
        Mrs. Walter Wolff, Secretary

Dues books, 1928+, 4 vols; Membership book, contains names of all members, past and present, 1 vol; Secretary's books, 1921-30, 1937+, 4 vols.   JG

641. Medina County Publications, Inc. (1832)
        885 West Liberty, Medina, Ohio 44256
        (216) 725-4166   (M-F 8-5; Sat 9-12)
        Stuart Borden, General Manager

Financial statements, 7-year retention, 33 lf; Ledgers, ca. 1945-65, 4 vols; Publication, The Medina County Gazette.   JG

642. York Methodist Church (1841)
        R. D. 3, Box 51, Medina, Ohio 44256
        (216) 725-5591   (Hours vary)
        David Freeman, Pastor

Board minutes, 1958-60, 1 in.; Church registers, 1881-89, 1 vol; Financial statements, 1 lf; Membership roll, A-Z, 1 vol; Proceedings, 1927-36, 1 vol; Quarterly conference records, 1895-1926, 1 vol; Treasurer's records, 1945-55, 4 vols.   JG

643. YMCA, Medina (1923)
        739 Weymouth Road, Medina, Ohio 44256
        (216) 725-6627   (M-F 9-5)
        Jack Stands, Director

Administrative records, 1923, 6 sheets; Board minutes, 1956+, 6 in.; Scrapbooks, 5 vols.   DH

644. YWCA, Medina
        739 Weymouth Road, Medina, Ohio 44256
        (216) 725-6627   (M-F 9-9; Sat 9-4)
        Alice Kramer, Executive Director

Administrative records, 1945; Agreements, for new building of YMCA and YWCA; Annual reports, 1950+, 4 folders; Correspondence, 1960+, 2 folders; Financial statements, 1945+, 6 folders; Journals, 1950+, 1 vol; Ledgers, 1950+, 1 vol; Minutes, 1945+, 4 folders; Scrapbooks, 1944-64, 5 books; Tax records, 1967+, 1 folder.   JG

MEIGS COUNTY

INSTITUTIONAL RECORDS

645. Citizens National Bank (1906)
        97 North Second Street, Middleport, Ohio 45760
        (614) 992-2657
        Harold E. Hubbard, President

Administrative records, 1906; Annual reports, 1906, 1 lf; Certificates,   stock book, 1906+; Contracts for loans, etc., 1920s; Correspondence, 10-year retention; Deeds, mortgage, etc., 15-year retention; Financial statements, 1906+; Journals, 1920s; Ledgers, 1906+; Minutes, 1920s+; Scrapbooks, 1930s; Tax records, 7-year retention.   RR

INSTITUTIONAL RECORDS

646. Dwyer-Mercer District Library (1907)
      Main Street, Celina, Ohio 45822
      (419) 586-2314   (M-F 10-9; Sat 10-6)
      Wilma G. Deitsch, Acting Librarian

Index to the servicemen of the War of 1812, compiled by Ohio Society U.S. Daughters of 1812, 1969, 1 in.; Scrapbooks, WW II, 1942,
1943, 1943 (war), 1944, 6 in.   RS

                        MIAMI COUNTY

MANUSCRIPTS

647. Flesh Public Library (1931)
      124 West Greene, Piqua, Ohio 45356
      (513) 773-6753   (M-F 9-8:30; Sat 9-6)
      Patricia J. Best, Adult Services Librarian

The Booker genealogy, 1 in.; Federation of women's clubs, 1899-
ca. 1910, 6 in.; Genealogy: the American descendents of Christian
DuBois of Wicres, France, 6 in.; G.A.R., Alexander Mitchell Post,
records (burial records, background sketches, administrative records, rosters), 18 in.; History of the First Regiment, Ohio Volunteer Infantry, in the Civil War, 1 in.;

History Club records, 1897, 1906-33, 6 in.; Johnston Cemetery, inscription records, 1819+, 1 in.; Christopher F. Kunz, photograph
collection, 1913 flood; Capt. A.R. Johnston (Indian agent for the area,
forefather of Pattersons of Dayton), journal, 1846-47, 1 in.; Round Table
Club records, ca. 1930-42, 6 in.; Scrapbook of Piqua, 1948-64, 1 in. FH

648. Troy Miami County Public Library (1896)
      301 West Main Street, Troy, Ohio 45373
      (513) 335-0502   (M-Th 9-9; F 9-6; Sat 9-5)
      Shirley Mott, Librarian Assistant

Almanacs (one German almanac printed in 1786), 1786-1800s, 2 in.;
Eusebia Bloggett, scrapbook, 1 in.; Cemetery records, 1 in.; Darke
County Common Pleas Court records, 1817-60, 1 in.; John Shannon
Fergus (early settler), account books, 1860-75, 1 in.; Samuel Raper
Fergus (orchard and nursery operator), account books, 1890-1901,

1 in.; Vretta Garnsey poetry album, 1925, 1 in.; Genealogy records,
1 in.; Thomas C. Harbaugh, clippings of three stories written by Harbaugh for Miami Union, 1830, 1 in.; Isaac Hite (surveyor at the falls
of the Ohio, 1773), journal, repr. 1954, 2 in.;

Manual of rules and regulations and course of study of Troy Public
School, 1895, 1 in.; Minutes of Miami Union correspondence, 1907-
24, 1 in.; Photograph album, late 1800s, 2 in.; Sketches of the Civil
War, personal recollections, 1865, 1 vol; Scrapbook collections, 1
in.; Teachers daily and general register, school district #3, Monroe
Township, 1839-51, 1 in.; The Trojan, yearbook of Troy High School,
1928-70, 1 lf; Troy Historical Society materials (maps, newspapers,
photos, society records), 6 lf; Troy industries, catalogs and pamphlets,
Hobart Company, 6 in.; Troy Sunshade Company (furniture company),
1913-70, 18 in.   RS

INSTITUTIONAL RECORDS

649. American Red Cross, Miami County (1917)
        16 East Franklin, Troy, Ohio 45373
        (513) 335-3810   (M-F 9-12, 1-4:30)
        Mrs. Howard G. Cherrington, Executive Secretary

Annual reports, 1950+, 1 lf; Contracts, 1958, 1 in.; Correspondence,
5-year retention, 5 lf; Financial statements, 1941+, 3 lf; Membership,
1941+, 18 in.; Minutes, ca. 1946+, 2 lf; Scrapbooks, 1941+, 6 in.;Tax
records, 1941+, 6 in.   RS

MONROE COUNTY

MANUSCRIPTS

650. Monroe County District Library
        101 North Main Street, Woodsfield, Ohio 43793
        (614) 472-1954   (M, W, Th 12-5, Sept-June; M, Sat 12-5,
        Tu-F 12-8, June-Aug)
        Eva Moffat, Librarian

Genealogy and local history collections, 1880+, 2 lf.   SF

MANUSCRIPTS

651. Air Force Museum (1924)
        Wright-Patterson AFB, Fairborn, Ohio 45433
        (513) 255-3284   (M-F 9-4)
        Air Force Museum Research Division

The museum's research collection contains more than 75,000 documents relating to the history of military aviation and most specif-
ically to the history of the USAF. Holdings include photos, text
reports, aircraft operation and maintenance manuals, magazine
articles, newspaper clippings, aircraft drawings, and other materials related to USAF history--its personnel, aircraft and related
subsystems, and operations. Collection involves an estimated total
of 2,000 lf of documents.

Capt. John Harding (participated in 1924 first around-the-world
flight), 3 lf; Gen. Curtis LeMay (former USAF Chief of Staff), 3 lf;
Capt. E. V. Rickenbacker (WWI aviator), 3 lf; MGen. Ralph Royce,
5 lf; Capt. Albert W. Stevens (high altitude research and photography), 4 lf; Col. Jesse Vincent (developer of famous WWI "Liberty" engine), 3 lf; Gen. Thomas D. White (former USAF Chief of
Staff), 15 lf.   FH

652. Dayton and Montgomery County Public Library (1847)
        215 East Third Street, Dayton, Ohio 45402
        (513) 224-1651   (M-F 9-9; Sat 9-6)
        Stanley Clarke Wyllie, Jr., Dayton Collection Librarian

W.D. Bickham (editor, Dayton Journal), collection, mid-nineteenth
century, 3 lf; Bowen collection, 1 lf; Brown-Patterson collection,
forage papers, 1812-14, 3 lf; Davis collection, diary and weather
notes, 4 lf; Doren collection, correspondence, 48 lf; Forrer-Pierce-
Wood collection (Ziegler papers, deeds, land warrants, correspondence, 1792-1821; Forrer-Wood-Pierce papers, correspondence,
diaries, business papers, 1802-96), 34 lf; Lowe collection, correspondence from the Mexican War front, 1847-48, 5 lf; Van Cleve-
Dover collection (John Van Cleve, correspondence, business papers,
scrapbooks, journals, drawings and sketches, scientific notes; Thomas Dover, pharmacist, papers), mid-nineteenth century, 3 lf.   RS

653. Montgomery County Historical Society (1897)
        Old Court House, Dayton, Ohio 45402
        (513) 228-6271   (M-F 8:30-4:30)
        John Kerwood, Executive Director

Dayton Manufacturing Company, business records, 1883-1930, 25 lf;
Moraine Park School, miscellaneous photos, pamphlets, papers, 1917-
56, 1 lf; Young Women's League (service organization, provided lodge
in Dayton for single working girls), records (lodge book, board of directors notebook, miscellaneous materials), 1898-1943, 2 lf.   RS

654. St. Leonard College Library (1960)
        8100 Clyo Road, Centerville, Ohio 45459
        (513) 885-7676   (M-F 9-4)
        Fr. George Hellmann, Librarian

Miscellaneous correspondence, deals with construction of St. Leonard,
1956, and other miscellaneous topics, 1913-62, 18 in.; John Berchman
Wuest, OFM, correspondence, 1942-45, 1 lf; Rev. Ralph Ohlman, OFM,
correspondence, 1951, relating to the definition of the Assumption of the
Blessed Virgin Mary, 1 lf.   RS

655. Wright State University Archives and Special Collections
        Colonel Glenn Highway, Dayton, Ohio 45431
        (513) 426-6650, ext. 1424   (M-F 9-5)
        Patrick Nolan, Head

James M. Cox, papers, 1923-60, 24 lf; Dayton Urban League, records,
1947-67, 50 lf; O.S. Kelly Company, records, 1840s-1940s, 200 lf; Logan County Welfare Department, case files, 1940s-50s; Miami Conser-
vancy District, records, 1913-69, 50 lf; Montgomery County Engineer,
records, 1850s-1900s, 19 lf; Montgomery County Welfare Department,
case files, 1930-60; Jane Newberry League of Women Voters, publications, 1940s-71, 3 lf; Springfield Police Department, arrest records,
1921-40s, 24 lf; Springfield Urban League, records, 1963-71, 25 lf;
University archives material, 1964+, 110 lf; Wright brothers collection
(photographs, correspondence, annotated journals, newspapers, genealogical papers, diaries of their father Milton Wright, financial records), 1820-
1948, 40 lf.   RS

INSTITUTIONAL RECORDS

656. Amateur Trapshooting Association of America (1923)
        601 West National Road, Vandalia, Ohio 45377
        (513) 898-4638   (M-F 8-4:30)
        Hugh L. McKenley, Manager

Administrative records, 1923+; Agreements, 1923+; Annual reports,

1923+; Board of directors, minutes, 1923+; Contracts, 1923+; Correspondence, 1923+; Deeds, 1923+; Executive minutes, 1923+; Financial statements, 1923+; Inventories, 1923+; Journals, 1923+; Ledgers, 1923+;Membership files, 1923+; Photographs, past winners and presidents, on display in lobby, 1923+; Plats, 1923+; Publication, 1900+, Trap and Field; 75 lf total. RS

657. American Cancer Society, Dayton (1946)
        44 South Ludlow, Dayton, Ohio 45402
        (513) 223-8521   (M-F 8-4:30)
        Don Sweeney, Director

Board and executive council, minutes, 1946+, 1 lf; Membership list, 1946+, 4 lf; Publications, 1946-49, 4 lf.   RS

658. American Red Cross, Dayton (ca. 1910)
        370 West First Street, Dayton, Ohio 45402
        (513) 222-6711   (M-F 8-4)
        Mr. Johnson, Director

Annual reports, 1939-68, 1 lf; Board minutes, 1917-57, 2 lf; Correspondence, 1955, 1 lf; Scrapbooks (photos, clippings, programs, etc.), 1943, 1 lf. RS

659. Bar Association, Dayton (ca. 1930)
        4 South Main Street, Dayton, Ohio 45402
        (513) 222-7902   (M-F 8-4:30)
        Peggy Young, Director

Correspondence, 1950, 1 folder; Minutes of monthly meetings, n.d.; Miscellaneous records, list of attorneys, biographical sketches, committee reports, photos, 1943-45, 5 lf. RS

660. Barney Childrens Medical Center (1906)
        1723 Chapel Street, Dayton, Ohio 45404
        (513) 461-4790   (M-F 8-4:30)
        William F. Lohrer, Director

Annual reports, 1936+, 1 lf; Board of trustees, minutes, 1918-50, 1 lf; Publications, ca. 1960s, 1 lf; Scrapbooks, 1906-66, 1 lf. RS

661. Bookbinders Local No. 199, Dayton (1933)
        2621 East Third Street, Dayton, Ohio 45403
        (513) 256-2491
        Doyle Lainhart, Secretary

Annual reports, 1965+; Contracts, 1947+; Correspondence, 3-year
retention; Deeds, 1947+; Financial statements, 7-year retention;
Ledgers, 1947+; Membership records; Minutes, 1963+; Receipts,
1953; Tax records, 7-year retention; 39 lf total.   RS

662. Campfire Girls, Dayton (1930s)
        184 Salem Avenue, Dayton, Ohio 45406
        (513) 222-6327   (M-F 8-4)
        Florence Shutly, Secretary

Annual reports, 1966+, 1 lf; Board minutes, 1945+, 1 lf; Commemorative account of Golden Jubilee History, 1960, 1 lf; Miscellaneous
clippings, photos, slides, history, deeds, 1939+, 1 lf.   RS

663. Central Christian Church, Disciples of Christ (1829)
        1200 Forrer Boulevard, Dayton, Ohio 45420
        (513) 252-2649   (M-F 8-4)
        Ted G. Faulconer, Minister

Administrative records, 1939-44, 1 lf; Annual reports, 1945-50 (pastors report, treasurer's report), 1 lf; Correspondence, n.d., 1 lf; Executive board, minutes, 1947-53, 1 lf; Financial statements, 1894-99
(some later), 1 lf; Membership, n.d., 1 lf; Publications, 1930, 1940+,
1 lf.   JD

664. Child Guidance Center (ca. 1935)
        141 Firwood Drive, Dayton, Ohio 45419
        (513) 298-7301   (M-F 8-4)
        James Cunningham

Annual reports, 1932-33, 1939-40, 1944-47, 1 lf; Board minutes,
1947+, 1 lf; Financial statements, 1935-50, 1 lf; Scrapbooks, 1944,
1 lf.   RS

665. Christ Lutheran Church (1896)
        511 Hart Street, Dayton, Ohio 45404
        (513) 228-0893   (M-F 8-4)
        Victor Rothenberger, Pastor

Agreements, n.d., 1 lf; Building committee scrapbook, 1916-17, 1 lf;
Financial statements, 1908-59, 1 lf; Ladies Aid Society, records, 1929-
47, 1 lf; Membership (officers, baptisms, deaths, marriages), 1900-
1953, 1 lf; Photographs of church and pastors, 1896-1946, 1 lf; Vestry
minutes, 1900-1950, 1 lf.   JD

666. Church of the Holy Angels (1901)
         218 K. Street, Dayton, Ohio 45409
         (513) 222-7807   (Tu-F 9:30-2:30)
         Msgr. Joseph D. McFarland, Pastor

Publications (Sunday Bulletin, 1952 history of church), 1949+, 1 lf;
Sacramental: baptisms, 1902+, marriages, 1902+, confirmations,
1904+, deaths, 1902+, 5 lf.   JD

667. Concordia Lutheran Church (1926)
         250 Peach Orchard Avenue, Dayton, Ohio 45419
         (513) 299-1912   (M-F 9-4)
         Pastor Kohn

Anniversary historical sketch, 1967, 1 lf; Church register, 1927-67,
1 lf; Financial statements, 1925-50, 1 lf; Ledgers, 1928-53, 1 lf; Vestry minutes, 1928-60, 1 lf; Voters assembly minutes, 1945-60, 1 lf.
JD

668. Corpus Christi Church (1911)
         208 Squirrel, Dayton, Ohio 45405
         (513) 228-6672   (M 9-5)
         Fr. Robert Maher, Pastor

Publication, the first 50 years, historical sketch and photos, 1 lf;
Sacramental: marriages, 1911+, baptisms, 1911+, deaths, 1940-
41, 1954+, 1 lf.   JD

669. Dayton Area Board of Realtors (1909)
         45 Riverview Drive, Dayton, Ohio 45405
         (513) 224-9901   (M-F 8-4)
         William Strong, Executive Secretary

Board of directors, minutes, 1910+, 1 lf; 50th anniversary historical sketch, 1959, 75 pp.   RS

670. Dayton Art Institute (1919)
      405 West Riverview Avenue, Dayton, Ohio 45405
      (513) 223-5277   (M-F 8-5)
      Thomas C. Colt, Director

Annual reports, 1927-53, 1 lf; Board minutes, 1919+, 2 lf; "Catalog"
institute collection listed and programs and catalogs of visiting exhibitions included, 1929+, 6 in.; Exhibition, 1929+, 1 lf; Financial records, 1930+, 2 lf; General information, miscellaneous, 1930, 6 in.;
History, 1959-65, 6 in.; Institute school brochures (courses and programs), 1929-64, 6 in.; Lectures, 1930+, 6 in.; Ledgers, 1931-43;
Membership, 1940+, 6 in.; Newsletter, 1928+; Publicity releases,
1931-54, 6 in.; Scrapbooks, 1912+, 6 in.   RS

671. Dayton Boys' Club (ca. 1930s)
      127 Bradford Street, Dayton, Ohio 45410
      (513) 222-1111   (M-Sat 8-4)
      Bill Kirchener, Director

Commemorative account, n.d., 6 in.; Minutes, 1930-64, 1 lf; Miscellaneous records (personnel, policies, practices, annual reports),
1937-41, 1 lf.   RS

672. Dayton Christian Center (1920s)
      1352 West Riverview Avenue, Dayton, Ohio 45407
      (513) 275-7174   (M-F 8-5)
      Mark A. Kinnaman, Director

Board minutes, 1946-52, 6 in.; Commemorative history of center,
1932, 1 lf; Financial statements, 1929-50, 6 in.; Miscellaneous clippings, reports, record attendance, 1944-50s, 1 lf; Publication, "Lamp-
lighter," 1947+, 6 in.   RS

673. Dayton Classroom Teachers Association (ca. 1924)
      323 Salem Avenue, Dayton, Ohio 45406
      (513) 224-7236   (M-F 8-4)
      Robert Niles, President

Ledgers, 1924-41, 1 vol; Official records (minutes, correspondence,
membership records), 1924-49, 4 vols.   RS

674. Dayton Council on World Affairs (ca. 1947)
        205 East First Street, Dayton, Ohio 45402
        (513) 223-6203   (M-F 8-5)
        Betty Click, Director

Annual reports, 1952+, 8 in.; Board minutes, 1947+, 6 in.; Scrapbooks, 1949, 6 in. RS

675. Dayton Metropolitan Housing Authority (ca. 1934)
        340 West Fourth Street, Dayton, Ohio 45402
        (513) 222-6982   (M-F 8-4:30)
        Harry Schmitz, Director

Annual reports, 1969+, 6 in.; Board minutes, 1934-50, 6 in.   JD

676. Dayton Museum of Natural History (1880s)
        2629 Ridge Avenue, Dayton, Ohio 45414
        (513) 275-7432   (M-F 8-5)
        E. J. Koestner, Director

Annual reports, 1893+, 1 lf; Commemorative, "The Living Museum,"
n.d., 6 in.; Minutes, 1952+, 4 in.; Publication, "Museum Notes,"
1954+, 6 in.; Scrapbooks, 1919+, 1 lf; Summer lectures, accession
records, 1930s, 6 in. RS

677. East Dayton Church of the Brethren (1903)
        3520 East Third Street, Dayton, Ohio 45403
        (513) 252-0021   (M-F 8-4)
        J. Calvin Bright, Pastor

Church, council, and meetings, minutes, 1903-65, 1 lf; Newsletter,
May-Sept 1931, 2 in. JD

678. Elder Beerman Stores Corp. (1960)
        3155 Elbee Road, Dayton, Ohio 45439
        (513) 294-3111   (M-F 8-4)
        Mrs. Collier, Executive Secretary

Agreements, 1937; Annual reports, 1967+; Cashbooks, 1966+; Contracts, 1937; Correspondence, 1970+; Financial statements, 1966+;
Inventories, 1970+; Minutes, ca. 1960; Newsletter, 1968+; Receipts,
1966+; Tax records, ca. 1960+; 250 lf total. RS

679. Emmanuel Church (1837)
    149 Franklin Street, Dayton, Ohio 45402
    (513) 228-2013
    Fr. Wagner, Pastor

Sacramental (baptisms, 1840+, marriages, 1853+, deaths, 1853+, confirmations, 1882-1955), 1 lf. JD

680. Engineers Club (1914)
    112 East Monument Avenue, Dayton, Ohio 45401
    (513) 228-2148   (M-F 8-4)
    Mr. Malchisloan, Facilities Manager

Board of directors, minutes, 1914+, 16 vols; Bulletin, "The Engineer," 1946+, 1 lf; Membership list, n.d., 8 lf; Photos, building construction, 1916-17; Proceedings, 1914-16, 3 vols; Scrapbooks, programs, bulletins, yearbook, by-laws, 1917-45, 7 vols. RS

681. Faith Lutheran Church (1930)
    3315 Martel, Dayton, Ohio 45420
    (513) 253-2156   (M-W 8:30-5)
    Willard O. Drefke, Pastor

Bulletins, 1934+, 1 lf; Church register, 1930-70, 6 in.; Correspondence, 1931, 6 in.; Deacon's report on Sunday collections, 1949, 1950, 6 in.; Financial statements, 1945-53, 1 lf; Minutes of congregation, 1944-50, minutes of council meetings, 1938-45, 1 lf; Parochial report (membership, resources, services), 1929-38, 1940-50, 1 lf. JD

682. First Baptist Church (1820s)
    117 West Monument Avenue, Dayton, Ohio 45402
    (513) 222-4691   (M-F 8-4)
    Mrs. Wann, Membership Chairman

Annual reports, 1940-48, 6 in.; Deacons minutes, 1866-1917, 6 in.; Financial statements, 1844-56, 1946-47, 1 lf; First Regular Baptist Church, records (minutes, membership, annual reports), 1848-1925, 6 in.; Histories, n.d., 6 in.; Membership, new members, dismissions, 1870+, 6 in.; Minutes, 1829-47, 6 in.; Publications, historical account, 1931, 6 in. JD

683. First Lutheran Church (1839)
138 West First Street, Dayton, Ohio 45401
(513) 222-7848   (Tu-Th 8:30-4:30)
Walter Saupe, Pastor

Church register, 1841-1933; Council minutes, 1880-1911; McCauley
Missionary Society, minutes, 1935-55; Miscellaneous records (church
school materials, some minutes), 1934-52; Missionary Society, minutes, 1914-24; Woman's Society, records, 1877-1945; 5 lf total. JD

684. First United Methodist Church (1848)
1516 Salem Avenue, Dayton, Ohio 45406
(513) 278-7341   (M-F 8-5)
C. Willard Fetter, Minister

Cowden Memorial United Brethren Church, minutes, 1913-29; Financial statements, 1920-30, 6 in.; First Church of the Brethren, records,
1888-1930, 1 lf; First United Methodist Church, attendance records,
1891-1900, 1938-42, 1 lf; Home Avenue Brethren Church: records,1896-
1900, 6 in., baptismal record, 1927-47, 1 lf; Minutes, 1901-52, 2 lf;
Riverdale United Brethren Church, minutes, 1899-1913; Summit Street
United Brethren Church, minutes, 1874-81. RS

685. Health and Welfare Planning Council (ca. 1915)
184 Salem Avenue, Dayton, Ohio 45406
(513) 461-5603   (M-F 8-5)
Bernard Hyman, Executive Director

Board of trustees, minutes, ca. 1920+, 6 vols; Dayton Community
Chest board and budget minutes, 1915-50, 1 lf; Miscellaneous infor-
mation, 1920, 2 lf; "Shop Talk," published by the Council of Social
Agencies, 6 in. RS

686. Holy Cross Church (1914)
1922 Leo Street, Dayton, Ohio 45404
(513) 228-8902
Fr. Titas Narbutas, Pastor

Financial statements, 1917+, 1 lf; Lithuanian daily paper, n.d.,
6 in.; Sacramental, 1914+, 1 lf; School donations, 1940, 6 in.; Scrapbooks, 1963+, 1 lf. JD

687. Holy Family Church (1905)
        140 South Findlay Street, Dayton, Ohio 45403
        (513) 253-1109
        Fr. Evers, Pastor

Historical records (dates, pastors, building improvements), 1905+,
1 lf; Parish monthly, 1905-61, 4 lf; Sacramental (church record),
1905+, 1 lf.   JD

688. Holy Name Church (1906)
        408 North Conover Street, Dayton, Ohio 45407
        (513) 228-4033   (M 9-5)
        Fr. Alfred Drapp, Pastor

Fiftieth anniversary album, history of church and school, n.d., 1 lf;
Parish history, 1956+, 1 lf; Sacramental, 1906+, 1 lf.   JD

689. Holy Trinity Church (1859)
        272 Bainbridge Street, Dayton, Ohio 45402
        (513) 228-1223
        Rev. Lewis Funk, Pastor

Baptism records, 1861+; Confirmation records, 1900+; Death records,
1861+; Marriage records, 1861+; 3 lf total.   JD

690. Hope Lutheran Church (1886)
        500 Hickory Street, Dayton, Ohio 45410
        (513) 228-5191   (M-F 8-4)
        Mr. Kayser, Head Trustee

Church register, 1889-1946, 1 lf; Congregational record, 1894-1935,
1 lf; Constitution and by-laws adopted at 1905 meeting, 6 in.; History
(clippings, photos, pamphlets, history, anniversaries), n.d., 1 lf;
Minutes: Council meetings, Young Peoples Society, Women's Missionary Society, and Ladies Aid Society, 1896-1902, 1931-51, 1 lf; Publications, "Lutheran Messenger," 1946-53, 6 in.   JD

691. Immaculate Conception Church (1938)
        2300 South Smithville Road, Dayton, Ohio 45420
        (513) 252-9919
        Fr. Sherman, Pastor

Annual reports, 1938+, 3 lf; Bulletin, 1956+, 1 lf; Sacramental, 1938+,
2 lf.   JD

692.   Junior League of Dayton (ca. 1919)
       3120 Far Hills, Dayton, Ohio 45429
       (513) 298-7387   (M-F 8-4)
       Mrs. Richard Zeigler, Director

Annual reports, 1920+, 1 lf; Board minutes, 1920-56, 1 lf; Membership list, n.d., 6 in.; Newsheet, publication, 1943+, 6 in.; Scrapbooks, 1919+, 6 in.   RS

693.   League of Women Voters, Dayton (1920)
       44 South Ludlow Street, Dayton, Ohio 45402
       (513) 228-4041   (M-F 8-4)
       Mrs. H. V. Powell, Director

Annual reports, 1932-52, 6 in.; History, 1921-50s, 6 in.; Membership list, 1935+, 6 in.; Minutes, 1920+, 6 in.; Miscellaneous records,
1930s-40s, 6 in.; Publications, 1924+, 1 lf.   RS

694.   Linden Avenue Baptist Church (1872)
       101 Linden Avenue, Dayton, Ohio 45403
       (513) 254-1724   (M-F 8-5)
       B. Lawrence Sweeney, Pastor

Anniversary photographs, n.d., 6 in.; Church record, 1938-49, 6 in.;
Correspondence, 1944, 6 in.; Dayton Baptist Union, minutes, 1866-72,
6 in.; Financial statements, 1910-55, 6 in.; Membership, 1872-1944,
6 in.; Records, 1917-21, 6 in.; Weekly newspaper, 1930-49, 6 in.   JD

695.   Lower Miami Church of the Brethren (1805)
       5353 Germantown Pike, Dayton, Ohio 45418
       (513) 263-5111   (Morning hours only)
       Robert E. Martin, Reverend

Council minutes, 1896-1950, 1 lf; Photos, newsclippings, brief historical sketch, 1878+, 1 lf.   JD

696. Lutheran Church of Our Savior (1941)
        155 East Thruston Boulevard, Dayton, Ohio 45419
        (513) 293-1147   (M-F 8-4)
        J. A. Updegraff, Pastor

Church council and congregational minutes, 1940-52, 1 lf; Men's Club,
minutes and programs, treasurer's reports, 1948-58, 6 in.; Parish
register, 1940-70, 1 lf; Sunday bulletins, 1940-50, 1 lf; Scrapbooks,
mostly after 1950, 6 in.; Woman's Guild, minutes, 1943-48, 6 in. JD

697. Lutheran Social Service (1922)
        563 Superior Avenue, Dayton, Ohio 45407
        (513) 278-4896   (M-F 8-4)
        Nelson Trout, Executive Director

Annual reports, 1935-50, 1 lf; Board of trustees, minutes, 1934-51,
6 in.; Publication, "The Voice," 1927-52, 6 in.; Scrapbooks, 1941-
59, 6 in. RS

698. Mack Memorial Church of the Brethren (1889)
        1717 Mack Memorial, Dayton, Ohio 45406
        (513) 277-9336   (M-F 8-4)
        John Kreitzer, Chairman of the Board

Anniversary historical sketch, 1889-1939, 1 lf; Membership lists,
past and present, 1922, 1927, 1 lf; Miscellaneous financial data and
minutes of men's club, various financial reports to church, n.d.,
1 lf; Quarterly council and affirmation board, minutes, 1911-39, 1 lf.
JD

699. Memorial United Presbyterian Church (1867)
        1541 South Smithville Road, Dayton, Ohio 45410
        (513) 256-4473   (M-F 8-4:30)
        Paul C. Nicholson, Pastor

Building committee, minutes, 1871, 6 in.; Church register, 1868-
1951, 1 lf; Financial statements, 1898-1923, 6 in.; Session minutes,
1866-1951, 2 lf; Women's Missionary Society, minutes, 1920-32, 6
in. JD

700. Miami Valley Hospital
      1 Wyoming Avenue, Dayton, Ohio 45409
      (513) 223-6192   (M-F 8-4:30)
      Frank C. Sutton, Director

Annual reports, 1891-1939; Minutes, n.d. , 6 in. ; Patient records,
1890s+, 1 lf; Scrapbooks, 1890+, 6 in. RS

701. Montgomery-Greene Tuberculosis Association (ca. 1913)
      226 Bellmonte Park East, Dayton, Ohio 45405
      (513) 222-8391   (M-F 8-4)
      Fred Nathanson, Director

Board minutes, 1913-40s, 6 in. ; Commemorative historical accounts,
1920s-1940s, 6 in.; List of officers, 1930+, 6 in. ; Scrapbooks, 1924+,
6 in. RS

702. Montgomery Society for Crippled Children and Adults (1936)
      210 North Main Street, Dayton, Ohio 45402
      (513) 222-9872   (M-F 8-5)
      Lilian C. Wright, Director

Commemorative history, 1936-49, 6 in. ; Financial statements, 1940s,
6 in.; Scrapbooks, 1940s, 6 in. RS

703. North Riverdale Lutheran Church (1911)
      45 Kurtz Avenue, Dayton, Ohio 45405
      (513) 275-5750   (M-F 8-4)
      John W. Zimmian, Minister

Church register, 1911-56, 1 lf; Correspondence, 1925-66, 1 lf; Council and congregation, minutes, 1911-69, 3 lf; Financial statements,
1912-20, 1 lf; Ladies Aid Society, minutes, 1919-34, 1 lf; Luther League,
minutes, 1923-45, 1 lf; Sunday bulletins, 1932+, 4 lf.   JD

704. Ohio Nurses Association (ca. 1900)
      123 North Main Street, Dayton, Ohio 45402
      (513) 228-5105   (M-F 8:30-5)
      Teresa Olivas, Director

Board minutes, 1911+, 4 envelopes; Historical materials, 1906-57, 6
in. ; History of offices, 1904+, 1 notebook; Newsletter, 1949+, 6 in. RS

705. Our Lady of Mercy Church (1928)
    545 Odlin Drive, Dayton, Ohio 45405
    (513) 274-9431 (No set hours)

Church register, 1928-58, 1 lf; Publications, 1953, 8 pp. JD

706. Our Lady of the Rosary Church (1887)
    22 Notre Dame Avenue, Dayton, Ohio 45404
    (513) 228-8802 (M-F 8:15-9:15)
    Fr. Cornelius Berning, Pastor

Booklet on history of parish, 1888-1963, 1 lf; Sacramental, 1888+,
1 lf. JD

707. Resurrection Church (1920)
    130 Gramont Avenue, Dayton, Ohio 45417
    (513) 268-6697 (M-F 8-4)
    Fr. Conlan, Pastor

Financial statements, 1920, 6 in.; Sacramental, 1920+, 1 lf. JD

708. Riverdale Congregational Christian Church (1924)
    2560 North Main Street, Dayton, Ohio 45405
    (513) 275-8381 (M-F 8-4)
    Rev. Snyder, Pastor

Church register, 1923-42, 1 lf; Martha Mary Circle, minutes, 1944-
56, 6 in.; Scrapbooks, 1947-50s, 6 in. JD

709. St. Adalbert Church (1903)
    1511 Valley Street, Dayton, Ohio 45404
    (513) 228-8782 (After 2 M-F)
    Richard Danielak, Pastor

Daybooks, 1932-55, 1 lf; Financial statements, 1926+, 1 lf; Photographs, n.d., 6 in.; Publications, 6 in.; Sacramental, 1902+, 1 lf;
Scrapbooks, 1960s, 6 in. JD

710. St. Agnes Catholic Church (1915)
    811 North Summit Street, Dayton, Ohio 45407
    (513) 274-2212
    Fr. Dorenbusch, Pastor

Sacramental, 1914-63, 1 lf; Scrapbooks, 1915+, 6 in.   JD

711. St. Elizabeth Medical Center (1878)
        601 Miami Boulevard West, Dayton, Ohio 45408
        (513) 223-3141   (M-F 8-4:30)
        E. C. Kuhbander, Executive Director

Annual reports, 1897+, 1 lf; Commemorative history, n.d., 6 in.;
Correspondence, 1880-1935, 1 lf; Minutes of state meetings, 1916-
32, 6 in.; Scrapbooks, 1882+, 6 in.   RS

712. St. John's Lutheran Church (1863)
        141 South Ludlow Street, Dayton, Ohio 45402
        (513) 223-4444   (Morning hours only, M-F)
        Pastor Borchers

Anniversary historical sketches, 1940-64; Financial statements, 1870-
75, 6 in.; Minutes, 1939+, 1 lf; Parish register, 1933-34, 1 lf; Publication, "St. John's Messenger," 1938-44, 1 lf; Records of officers'
meetings, congregational meetings, some correspondence, 1900-1936,
1 lf.   JD

713. St. Joseph Church (1847)
        411 East Second Street, Dayton, Ohio 45402
        (513) 228-9272
        Fr. Robert Lux, Pastor

Photographs, n.d., 1 lf; Publications, 1892-1923, 2 lf; Sacramental,
1854-1968.   JD

714. St. Mary Church (1859)
        310 Allen Street, Dayton, Ohio 45403
        (513) 256-5633   (M-F 8-4)
        Fr. Sterwerf, Pastor

Building Committee, minutes, 1904-6, 1 lf; Financial statements, 1860-
1956, 5 lf; Ledgers, 1905+, 1 lf; Sacramental, 1860+, 2 lf; Scrapbooks,
1928-38, 1 lf.   JD

715. St. Paul's Lutheran Church (1852)
     239 Wayne Avenue, Dayton, Ohio 45402
     (513) 224-0589   (M-F 8-5)
     John Theiss, Treasurer

Church register, 1859+, 1 lf; Constitution, 1892, 6 in.; History, 1852-
1952, 6 in.; Pastoral diaries, 1884-1925, 5 lf.   JD

716. St. Rita Church (1922)
     5401 North Main Street, Dayton, Ohio 45415
     (513) 275-1771   (M-F 8-4)
     Fr. Francis B. Pilliod, Pastor

Annual reports, 1922+, 1 lf; Financial statements, 1922-37, 6 in.;
Photographs, 1922+, 6 in.; Publications (clergy bulletins, pamphlet
on new building), 1943-51, 1967, 1 lf; Sacramental, 1922+, 1 lf.   JD

717. St. Stephens Church (1906)
     1114 Troy Street, Dayton, Ohio 45404
     (513) 222-3634   (M-F 8-4)
     Fr. Sauter, Pastor

Building of new church, 1945-53, 1 lf; Clergy bulletin, 1944+; Fiftieth anniversary album, n.d., 1 lf; Financial statements, 1927+, 2
lf; Sacramental, 1937+, 1 lf.   JD

718. Santa Clara Christian Church (Disciples of Christ) (1914)
     60 Santa Clara Avenue, Dayton, Ohio 45405
     (513) 274-5126   (M-F 8-4)
     Stephen J. Brack, Minister

Church bulletins, 1946+, 1 lf; Church records (budgets, pastor's reports, board meetings, attendance), 1936-50, 1 lf; Financial statements, 1928-38, 6 in.; History, 1914-54, 1 lf; Publications (program
of Christian education, Santa Clarion), 1944, 1945+, 8 in.; Yearbook,
1947, 1948, 1 lf.   JD

719. Second Church of Christ, Scientist (1920)
     720 Bellemonte Park North, Dayton, Ohio 45405
     (513) 228-6582   (Hours after 5 daily, Sat 8-4)
     Mrs. Baughman, Clerk

Minutes, trustees meetings, membership meetings, 1919-50, 4 lf.
JD

720. Shiloh Congregational Church (1853)
      5300 Philadelphia, Dayton, Ohio 45415
      (513) 277-8953   (M-F 8-4)
      James E. Shapland, Pastor

Church register, 1937+, 1 lf; Minutes (trustees meetings), 1926-
56, 1 lf; Miscellaneous bills, receipts, correspondence, building
items, 1930-48, 6 in.; Publications, Christian Missionary, 1902-4,
Herald of Gospel Liberty, 1920-28, 6 in.   JD

721. South Park United Methodist Church (1932)
      140 Stonemill Road, Dayton, Ohio
      (513) 224-1731   (M-F 8-4)
      Donald W. Cryer, Pastor

Administrative board, minutes, 1936+, 1 lf; Church record, 1930s-
50s, 1 lf; Ledgers (minutes of quarterly conference), 1888-91, 6 in.;
Official board minutes, 1857-1905, 1 lf; Publications, 1849-63, 1 lf;
Scrapbooks, n.d., 6 in.   RS

722. Sugarcreek United Presbyterian Church (1811)
      4419 Bigger Road, Dayton, Ohio 45440
      (513) 298-3743   (M-F 8-4:30)
      Warren G. McCready, Pastor

Church register, 1831-1952, 1 lf; Congregational meetings, constitutional resolves, joint meetings, records, 1814-47, 1 lf; Session
minutes, 1811-1950, 1 lf; Sunday School records, 1916-25, 6 in. RS

723. Summit Christian Church (Disciples of Christ) (1912)
      238 Mercer Avenue, Dayton, Ohio 45407
      (513) 228-1024   (M-F 8-4)
      William K. Fox, Pastor

Church history, photos, history of four Christian Disciples churches,
1912-65, 1829-1947, 1 lf.   JD

724. Temple Israel (1850)
    1821 Emerson Avenue, Dayton, Ohio 45406
    (513) 278-9621   (M-F 8-4)
    S. Liebermann, Executive Director

Board of trustees, minutes, 1921-50, 1 lf; Confirmation, 1901+, 6
in.; Weddings, 1947-66, 5 in.   JD

725. Trinity Evangelical Lutheran Church (1926)
    6540 North Main Street, Dayton, Ohio 45415
    (513) 275-7461   (AM only, M-F)
    Paul E. Becher, Pastor

Administrative records, 1924; Church register, 1893-1960, 1 lf;
Council and congregational meetings, minutes, 1901-48, 1 lf; History, 1904, 1 lf; Miscellaneous records, 1893+.   JD

726. United Theological Seminary (1860s)
    1810 Harvard Boulevard, Dayton, Ohio 45406
    (513) 278-5817   (M-F 8-5)
    John Knecht, President

Annual reports, 1847-1933, 1 lf; Board of trustees, minutes, 1869-
1950, 2 lf; Bonebrake Theological Seminary faculty, minutes, 1871-
1939, 1 lf; Building Committee, fund notes and minutes, 1895-1924,
1 lf; Class pictures, 1874-1954, 1 lf; Executive committee, minutes,
1880-1954, 2 lf.   RS

727. Victory United Methodist Church (1817)
    4800 North Dixie Drive, Dayton, Ohio 45414
    (513) 275-7993   (M-F 8-4:30)
    Richard T. Brison, Pastor

Board minutes, 1905-55, 1 lf; Church register, 1895-1924, 1 lf; Financial statements, 1884-94, 1915-24, 2 lf; Historical record of baptisms,
marriages, deaths, members, pastors, 1924+, 1 lf; Miscellaneous records, 1915-18, 5 in.; Scrapbooks, 1817-1967, 6 in.   JD

728. Widow's Home (1872)
    50 South Findlay Street, Dayton, Ohio 45403
    (513) 252-1661   (M-F 8-4)
    Olive Mahoney, Director

MONTGOMERY COUNTY

Board minutes, 1891+, 1 lf; History, 1960, 4 in.   RS

729. The Winters National Bank and Trust Company of Dayton (1814)
      Winters Bank Tower, Dayton, Ohio 45401
      (513) 449-8600   (M-Th 9:30-3; F 9:30-6)
      K. B. Graham, Senior Vice-President

Annual shareholders' meeting, minutes, 1881-1949; Board of directors, minutes, 1881+; Executive committee, minutes, ca. 1960+;
Scrapbooks, 1918-54, 10 vols.   FH

730. YMCA, Dayton (1858)
      117 West Monument Avenue, Dayton, Ohio 45402
      (513) 223-5201   (M-F 8-4)
      Mr. Swormztedt, Director

Correspondence, 1939-59, 4 in.; Departmental reports, 1907-50s,
8 in.; Minutes, 1875+, 1 lf; Newsletters, 1887-1953, 2 lf; Scrapbooks,
n.d., 1 lf.   RS

731. YWCA, Dayton (1870)
      141 West Third Street, Dayton, Ohio 45402
      (513) 461-5550   (M-F 8-4:30)
      Mary Ellen Hubbard, Director

Annual reports, 1872-1966, 5 bound vols and 4 folders; Historical
files, 1946-66, 1 lf; Minutes, 1895-1951, 8 vols;Miscellaneous material,ca. 1890s-1960s, 4 lf; Program and events, 1871+, 2 lf.   RS

MORGAN COUNTY

MANUSCRIPTS

732. Kate Love Simpson Morgan County Library
      358 East Main Street, McConnelsville, Ohio 43756
      (614) 962-2533   (M, W, Th, Sat 10-5; Tu, F 10-8)
      Joy Mazza, Assistant Librarian

James Ball Naylor; Mrs. Morris; Township booklets, local material,
newspaper clippings.   RR

INSTITUTIONAL RECORDS

733. Morgan County Agricultural Society (1853)
      104 South Kennebec, McConnelsville, Ohio 43756
      (614) 962-4652
      Ray G. Smith, Secretary

Administrative records, 1853+; Minutes, 1853+; Proceedings, 1853+;
ca. 1 lf total.   RR

                          MORROW COUNTY

MANUSCRIPTS

734. Morrow County Historical Society (1971)
      Mt. Gilead, Ohio 43338
      (419) 946-2821
      Barton E. Silver, President

Buckeye Mills counter charge list, 1880-1940; Cox and Trowbridge,
daybook and accounts of a Chesterville store, 1872-76, 5 in.; Diary,
1880, 1 in.; Dog tax duplicates, 1878; Ebenezer Baptist Church, register, 1833-75, 1 in.; Franklin Township records, 1824-73, 1 in.;
Mrs. Lodema Gottshall, photographs of a Cardington family, ca. 1909;

Indentures of apprenticeship (record of 25 indentures, includes record
of stray cattle, 1835-67, and of cattle earmarks, 1824-53), 1 in.; Liberty Community Club, records, 1927-41; North Canaan Sunday school,
attendance record, 1902-3, 1 in.; Peck family, 25 photographs, ca.
1907; Postcard collection (postcard photos and picture postcards of central Ohio), 1909-12, 2 in.; Toquet Club (social group organized by afflu-
ent   townspeople), guest register, 1919-20.   WM

INSTITUTIONAL RECORDS

735. Morrow County Hospital (1952)
      Marion Road, Mt. Gilead, Ohio 43338
      (419) 946-5015   (M-F 7-5)
      Helen Frayer, Medical Records Librarian

Administrative records, 1952+; Board of trustees and doctors staff,
minutes, 1952+, 2 lf; Deeds, 1952; Medical records, 1952+, 100 rolls
mf and 300 lf; Patient records, 1952+, 50 lf; Scrapbooks, 1952+, 1 lf.
FH

736. Trinity United Methodist Church (1829)
         East High at Vine, Mt. Gilead, Ohio 43338
         (419) 946-4606   (M-F 9-12)
         Harold T. Milford, Pastor

Annual reports, ca. 1950+, 18 in.; Church register, 1855+, 1 lf; Correspondence, 1967+, 2 lf; Financial statements, 1960+, 2 lf; Minutes,
1850+, 4 lf; Monthly newsletter and church bulletin, ca. 1950+.   SF

MUSKINGUM COUNTY

MANUSCRIPTS

737. John McIntire Public Library (1901)
         North Fifth Street, Zanesville, Ohio 43701
         (614) 453-0391   (M-F 9-8)
         Leonard Hammer, Director

Herron and Leedon genealogy, 1972, 87 pp; Library scrapbooks, 1920-
38, 1942-47, 4 in.; Muskingum County Courthouse, dedication, 1877,
90 pp; Muskingum Presbyterian Church, records, 1819-86, 37 pp; Photo
album, 1913 flood in Zanesville, 1 in.; Putnam Female Seminary, minutes and secretary's record, 1839, 1 in.; Putnam Presbyterian Church,
history, 1835-1910, 82 pp; Putnam Seminary for Girls, catalog, 1846-
76 (incompl.), 4 in.; Isaac Banning Turner, genealogy, 56 pp; Ephraim
Tutt, biography, by Arthur Train, 1920s, 4 in.; Zanesville Atheneum,
book catalog, 1855, 105 pp; Zanesville High School yearbook, 1900-1903,
1914-28, 1 lf.   FH

INSTITUTIONAL RECORDS

738. Community Improvement Corporation (1963)
         47 North Fourth Street, Zanesville, Ohio 43701
         (614) 453-0666   (M-F 9-5)
         Gene MacDonald, Executive Director

Administrative records, 1963; Annual reports, 1966+, 1 in.; Contracts, 1965+, 2 in.; Correspondence, 1963+; Daybooks, 1966+, 2 lf; Deeds, 1970+, 2 items; Financial statements, 1963+; Minutes, 1963+, 1 lf; Publications, 1963+, 1 in.; Reports sent to Department of Economic and Community Development, Columbus, 1963+. FH

739. Muskingum College Archives (1837)
        New Concord, Ohio 43762
        (614) 826-8153   (Hours vary with academic schedule)
        Lorle A. Porter, College Archivist

Muskingum College archives (records, papers, correspondence, etc., pertaining to the college), ca. 1837+, 100 lf.   RR

740. St. James Episcopal Church (1816)
        155 North Sixth Street, Zanesville, Ohio 43701
        (614) 453-9459   (M-F 7:30-4)
        Fr. Jack C. Bennett, Rector

Annual reports, 1820+; Church register, 1852+; Minutes, 1816+, 18 in.; Publication (bi-monthly parish letter), 1957+; Scrapbooks, 1966+. FH

NOBLE COUNTY

INSTITUTIONAL RECORDS

741. Caldwell United Methodist Church (1839)
        537 Main Street, Caldwell, Ohio 43724
        (614) 732-4033
        Marshall Peterson, Minister

Bulletins and newsletters, 1970+, 3 in.; Church board, minutes, 1941+, 2 lf; Financial records, ca. 1930+, 1 lf.   RR

MANUSCRIPTS

742. Ida Rupp Public Library
        310 Madison Street, Port Clinton, Ohio 43452
        (419) 732-3212   (M- Th 10-8:30; F, Sat 10-5:30)
        Jeanne Deems, Librarian

Local history and genealogy file on Port Clinton and Ottawa County; includes printed materials, 2 folders. SF

                    PAULDING COUNTY

INSTITUTIONAL RECORDS

743. Chamber of Commerce, Paulding
        112 West Jackson, Paulding, Ohio 45879
        (419) 399-2816   (M-Sat 8-5)
        Carl Ankney, Executive Secretary

Annual reports, 1969+; Board minutes, 1969+; Committee reports
and miscellaneous records, 1969+; Correspondence, 1969+; Financial
records, 1969+; Membership records, 1969+; Photographs, 1969+; 12
lf total.   SF

744. Farm Bureau Federation, Paulding
        122 West Jackson, Paulding, Ohio 45879
        (419) 399-2949   (W, F 8-5)
        Burl Barnes, Secretary

Annual reports, ca. 1960+; Board minutes, ca. 1960+; Correspondence, ca. 1960+; Financial records, ca. 1960+; Membership records, ca. 1960+; Monthly newsletter, 1970+; Newspaper clippings,
ca. 1960+; Photographs, ca. 1960+; 28 lf total.   SF

745. Masonic Temple
        Perry and Main, Paulding, Ohio 45879
        (419) 399-2746   (Hours by appointment)
        Leonard Shields, Secretary

Annual reports, 1894+; Correspondence, 1894+; Dues records, 1894+;
Financial records, 1894+; Membership records, 1894+; Minutes, 1894+;
Newspaper clippings, 1894+; 4 lf total.   SF

MANUSCRIPTS

746. Perry County District Library, New Lexington (1920s)
      113 South Main Street, New Lexington, Ohio 43764
      (614) 342-1077   (M-Th, Sat 9-5; F 9-8)
      Mildred Flora, Library Manager

New Straitsville Centennial, 1870-1970, scrapbook of information
about New Straitsville, 1 in. RR

747. Perry County District Library, Somerset Branch
      North Columbus Street, Somerset, Ohio 43783
      (M, W, F 12:30-5; Sat 10-12, 12:30-4:30)
      Rhea Scallan, Librarian

Pamphlets about Somerset and Perry County, ca. 1960, 1 in.; St.
Paul's United Church of Christ, Glenford, Ohio, history, 1964,
24 pp. RR

748. Perry County District Library, Thornville
      Box 292, Thornville, Ohio 43076
      (614) 246-5133   (M, F 10:30-4:30; W 10:30-4:30, 6-8)
      Helen Koehler, Librarian

Scrapbooks, 1941-68, 2 in.; Thornville News, newspapers, 1890
(vol 9), 1 in. RR

INSTITUTIONAL RECORDS

749. First United Methodist Church (1828)
      South High at Park Avenue, New Lexington, Ohio 43764
      (614) 342-1063
      J. Brooks Gregory, Minister

Administrative records; Annual reports, ca. 1950+; Cemetery records of the church cemetery, 19th century; Correspondence, 4-5
year retention; Financial records, ca. 1950+; Journals, ca. 1950+;
Minutes, ca. 1950+; Newsletters and bulletins, ca. 1950+; Proceedings, ca. 1950+; 6 lf total. RR

MANUSCRIPTS

750. Pickaway County District Public Library (ca. 1872)
        165 East Main Street, Circleville, Ohio 43113
        (614) 474-2318   (M-Th 9-9 Sept 1-June 1; M-Th 9-6 June 1-
        Sept 1; F, Sat 9-5 year round)
        Maxine Dowler, Assistant Librarian

J. B. F. Morgan (doctor), typescript of diary with personal reminiscences of Deercreek Settlement, Clarksburg, Ohio, 1837-1923, 3 in.;
Scrapbooks on pumpkin show, 1905+, 15 in.   SF

751. Pickaway County Historical Society (1959)
        Scioto and Union, Circleville, Ohio 43113
        (614) 474-2659   (Hours by appointment)
        Mrs. Ray W. Davis, Editor, Pickaway Quarterly

Charles Davenport, journal of journey to West Coast, Feb 24, 1831-
June 30, 1831, 1 vol; Land patents, ca. 1803-20; Michael Sweetman,
Civil War diary, ca. 1862-65; Scrapbook collection, organized by
subjects, 1917-56.   FH

INSTITUTIONAL RECORDS

752. Advocate Publishing Company (1909)
        459 East Ohio, Circleville, Ohio 43113
        (M-F 8-4:30)
        P. Lewis Brevard, Editor

Annual reports, 1909+; Financial statements, 1948+; Minutes, 1909+;
Proceedings, 1909+; Publications, The Advocate, 1949+, Missionary
Tidings, 1949+.   WM

753. Chamber of Commerce, Circleville (1916)
        113-1/2 South Court, Circleville, Ohio 43113
        (614) 474-4923   (M-F 9-5)
        Jean Ankrom, Manager

Cashbooks, 1916, 1938, 1950, 9 in.; Certificates, 1931; Correspondence, 1946+, 10 lf; Financial statements, 1956+, 2 lf; Inventories,
1935-41, 1 lf; Minutes, 1926-45, 1955-59, 1963+, 2 lf; Receipts,1955+,
1 lf; Scrapbooks, 1940-42, 1968-69, 6 in.   SF

754. Farm Bureau, Pickaway County (1928)
      Box 485, Circleville, Ohio 43113
      (614) 474-6284   (M-F 8-5)
      Tom Ellifritz, Organization Director

Administrative records, 1928; Corn Growers Association, records,
1907-11, 1 in.; Correspondence, 6 in.; Financial statements, 1945+;
Insurance files, 3 lf; Minutes, 1928+, 1 lf; Newsletter, quarterly;
Scrapbooks; Tax records, 1928-53, 3 in.   WM

755. First Methodist Church (1815)
      Pickaway Street, Circleville, Ohio 43113
      (614) 474-4796   (M-F 9-5)
      Chairman of Trustees

Administrative records, 1955+, 2 lf; Church register, 1816+, 1 lf;
Education office records, 7 lf; Financial statements, 1957+, 1 lf;
Membership records, 1884+, 6 in.; Minutes, 1844+; Newsletter, 1956,
9 in.; Receipts, 1955+, 2 lf; Women's Society of Christian Service,
1944+, 18 in.   FH

756. First National Bank of Circleville (1863)
      100 East Main Street, Circleville, Ohio 43113
      (614) 474-8811   (M, Tu, Th, F 9-2:30; W, Sat 9-12)
      Frank A. Gans, President

Administrative records, 1863+; Correspondence, 10-year retention;
Financial records; Minutes, 1863+; Tax records, 10-year retention;
15 cf total.   FH

757. Pickaway County Community Action Organization (1965)
      165 East Main Street, Circleville, Ohio 43113
      (614) 474-7452   (M-F 8-4:30)
      James Stanford, Executive Director

All records deal with the activities of PICCA and its programs, which
include health, housing, and education. All records are strictly confidential.

Annual reports, 1965+; Correspondence, 1965+; Financial statements,
1965+; Minutes, 1965+; Proceedings, 1965+; Receipts, 1965+; 60 lf
total.   SF

758. The Savings Bank (1912)
         118-120 North Court, Circleville, Ohio 43113
         (614) 474-3191   (M, Tu, Th 9-2:30; F 9-2:30, 6-8; Sat 9-12)
         Velma M. Burtner, Assistant Cashier

Agreements, 1960+; Annual reports, 1960+; Cashbooks, 1912+; Con-
tracts, 1960+; Correspondence, 1960+; Daybooks, 1960+; Deeds, 1960+;
Financial statements, 1960+; Inventories, 1960+; Receipts, 1960+;
Journals, 1960+; Ledgers, 1960+; Minutes, 1912+; Proceedings, 1960+.
WM

759. WNRE-FM (1965)
         119-1/2 South Court, Circleville, Ohio 43113
         (614) 473-3344   (M-F 9-5)
         Nelson Embrey, President and General Manager

Financial records, 1965+; L.B.J. Labor Day speech, 1956, tape; Ted
Lewis, 2-hour taped interview on his life, Oct. 1966; News reports,
1956+, 25 lf; Program logs, 1956+, 5 lf.   WM

                          PIKE COUNTY

INSTITUTIONAL RECORDS

760. Chamber of Commerce, Waverly
         111 East Second, Waverly, Ohio 45690
         (614) 947-5613   (Hours by appointment)
         William Foster, Secretary

Financial records, ca. 1964+; Maps of Pike County; Membership records, ca. 1964+; Minutes, ca. 1964+; National Research Bureau, newsletter; Publicity materials, ca. 1964+; 2 lf total.   SF

761. First Presbyterian Church
         122 East North, Waverly, Ohio 45690
         (614) 947-2905   (M-F 9-3:30)
         Jack L. Pursell, Minister

Bulletins; Board of deacons, minutes, 1842+; Board of trustees, minutes, 1842+; Church register, 1842+; Correspondence, 1842+; Financial records, 1842+; Membership records, 1842+; Sermons; Session

minutes, 1842+; Women's Association, minutes, 1842+; ca. 30 lf
total.   SF

762. Pike County Free Public Library
      East Second, Waverly, Ohio 45690
      (614) 947-4921   (M, Tu, Th 8:30-8; W, F 8:30-4:30; Sat 9-5)
      John Redman, Director

Annual reports; Board minutes, 1931+; Financial records; Genealogy and local history material.   SF

                        PORTAGE COUNTY

MANUSCRIPTS

763. Aurora Historical Society (1968)
      115 Aurora Road, Aurora, Ohio 44202
      (216) 562-8203   (M, Th 1-8:30; Tu, W, F 1-5:30)
      Arthur Moebius, Curator

Aurora School District, school board minutes, 1827-84, 1 vol; Can-
field School District, attendance book, 1870, 1 vol; Ben S. Harmon,
account book, 1827, 1 vol; Root Harmon, general store account books,
1846-47, 1849-52, 1854-55, 1857-62, 9 vols; School District No. 5,
attendance book, 1861, 1 vol.   DH

764. Hiram Township Historical Society (1951)
      6910 Wakefield Road, Hiram, Ohio 44234
      (216) 569-7581   (No set hours)
      Mildred Bennett, Secretary

Hiram homes and owners, file, 1940+, 1 lf; Hiram Township Historical Society, minutes, 1951+, 1 lf; Miscellaneous genealogies of Hiram
families, early 19th century, 1 lf; Miscellaneous maps of home sites
and Indian trails, 1 lf; Scrapbooks of Hiram area and people, early 19th
century, 3 lf.   LS

765. Kent State University Archives (1912)
      Library, Kent State University, Kent, Ohio 44240
      (216) 672-2411   (M-F 8-4)
      Les Stegh, Archivist

Annual reports of 13 university divisions, 1963-72, 7 lf; Dwight L. Arnold (professor of guidance and counseling, peace activist), papers, 1927-73, 6 in.; Board of trustees, minutes, 1911+, 19 rolls mf; Contracts and inventories, 1971, 6 in.; Directors council, minutes, 1972, 6 in.; Arthur DuBois (English professor), papers, 1935-65, 13 lf; Faculty senate, minutes, 1970+, 6 in.; Mona Fletcher (political science professor), papers, 1930-60, 10 lf; W. Leslie Garnett (advisor of Kent internationals), papers, 1960s, 3 lf; Graduate council, minutes, 1948-71, 9 in.; Graduate student council, minutes, 1939-62, 2 mf rolls; Edward T. Heald (YMCA represenative in Russia), papers, 1917-19, 8 lf; Helen W. Machan (professor of classics and romance languages), papers, 1926-65, 6 in.; Ohio Board of Regents, minutes, 1963+, 4 lf; Publications, 1912+, 140 lf and 260 mf rolls; Phillip R. Shriver (history professor and active in AAUP), papers, 1912-64, 8 lf;

Special Collections Division (Dean H. Keller, Curator): American historical MSS, 1765-1969, 14 in.; American literatary MSS, 1836-1971, 3 lf; Carol Bergé (poet), papers, 1961-62, 4 lf; Georges Bidault (former prime minister of France), papers, 2 lf; Hector Bolitho (author), papers, 1927-68, 7 in.; Jean Bothwell (author of juvenile literature), papers, 1955-70, 4 in.; M.J. Bruccoli (literature professor), papers, 3 lf; Canadian literary MSS, 1925, 3 items; Joseph Chaikin (actor-director, papers, late 1950s-1972, 16 in.; Hart Crane (poet), papers, 1923-26, 4 lf;

August Derleth (author), papers, 1966, 7 in.; Robert Duncan (poet), papers, 1947-57, 3 in.; English historical MSS, 1782-1926, 3 in.; English literary MSS, 1819-1963, 4 in.; Dorothy Fuldheim, (news commentator), papers, 8 in.; Mister Hoit (traveler), papers, 1834-78, 2 in.; Constance Holme (novelist), papers, 1918-37, 3 in.; Joseph Katz (literature professor), papers, 1 lf; Lithuanian MSS, 1953-70, 14 in.;

Robert Lowry (novelist), papers, 1960s-1970s, 17 in.; Mariana collection, 1907-60, 3 in.; John Alfred Means (Civil War captain), papers, 1860s, 2 in.; Medieval MSS, 15th century, 6 in.; Miscellaneous MSS, 1725-1954, 3 lf; Charles A. Mosher (congressman), 1960s-1970s; Ohio history MSS, 1839-1940, 10 in.; Open theater archives, 1960s-1970s, 3 lf; Origin III archives, 1960s, 5 lf; Harriet Packard (verse writer), papers, 1930s-1940s, 1 in.; Austin Pendleton (actor-playwright), papers, 1972, 1 in.; John Perreault (poet-critic), papers, 1960s-1970s, 1 lf; Atlee Pomerene (U.S. senator), papers, 1911-35, 17 lf; Leo Rosten (novelist), papers, 1962, 2 lf;

George Bernard Shaw (playwright), papers, 1879-1927 (copies), 3 lf; Logan P. Smith (author), papers, 1883-1943, 1 lf; Gary Snyder (poet),

papers, 1959-68, 7 in.; James Stephens (poet), papers, 1915-28, 1 lf;
George Jason Streator (naturalist), papers, 1880-1924, 1 lf; Albion W.
Tourgee (novelist-judge), papers, 1882-96, 1 in.; Jean-Claude van
Itallie (playwright), papers,1954-72, 5 lf; Anthony Wayne (military officer),papers, 1793-95 (copies), 1 lf; West family, papers,1809-1911, 19
in.; Thornton Wilder (playwright), papers, 1926-67, 4 in.; Loring Williams (editor-poet),papers, 1963-67, 2 in.; William Carlos Williams
(poet), papers, 1940-65, 7 in.; Lois Wilson (actress), papers, 1920s-
1970s, 3 lf; Richard Wright (novelist), papers, 1938-45, 1 in.; Louis
Zukofsky (poet), papers, 1961-64, 3 in.   LS

766. Portage County Historical Society (1951)
        6549-51 North Chestnut Street, Ravenna, Ohio 44266
        (216) 296-3523   (Tu, Th 2-4; Sun 2-5)
        Cyrus Plough, Director

William Alford family (Garrettsville family), papers, 1890-1960, 3 lf;
William Alford photograph collection (photos and negatives of U.S., Lat-
in America, and Japan), 1870-1900, 3,000 items; King family (Newton
Falls family), papers, 1880-1910, 2 lf; Portage County Probate Court,
records, 1808-1910, 150 lf; Scrapbooks, 1890-1950, 5 lf; Scott family
(Garrettsville family), papers, 1890-1960, 10 lf; Theiss family (Theiss
was auto battery and ignition pioneer at Ravenna), papers, early 20th
century, 10 lf.   LS

767. Reed Memorial Library (1915)
        167 East Main Street, Ravenna, Ohio 44266
        (216) 296-6526   (M-F 12-9; Sat 10-6)
        Estella Daniels, Librarian

Ravenna Temperance Society, constitution, articles and resolutions,
membership list, and proceedings, 1830-38, 1 vol.   JWG

INSTITUTIONAL RECORDS

768. First United Methodist Church (1831)
        South Prospect and Riddle Avenue, Ravenna, Ohio 44266
        (216) 297-7196   (M-F 9-4)
        J. Wilbur Koch, Chairman, History Committee

Church board, minutes, 1841-57, 1865-74, 2 vols; Church register,
1830-1919, 2 vols; East Ohio Conference, minutes, 1859-91, 1 vol;

Ladies Aid Society, minutes, 1900-1912, 1 vol; Quarterly conference, records, 1881-90, 2 vols; Receipts and expenditures, 1833-51, 59 pp; Scrapbooks, 1881-1931, 1 vol; Women's Foreign Missionary Society, minutes, 1901-5, 2 vols; Women's Home Missionary Society, minutes, 1920-28, 1 vol.   JWG

769. Hiram College Archives (1850)
        Hiram, Ohio 44234
        (216) 569-3211   (M-Th 8-4:30)
        Carolyne Weasner, Archivist

College Archives: George H. Colton (alumnus and faculty treasurer), papers, 1895-1926, 27 items; Marcia Henry (alumna, faculty and trustee), papers, 1870-1944, 84 items; Hiram College, catalogues, 1851+, 8 lf; Photograph album, 1860s-90s, 2 items; Adelaide Rudolph (alumna), papers, 1883-1940, 16 items; Scrapbooks, 1900-1913, 1 item; E. B. Wakefield (alumnus, faculty, acting president, and trustee), papers, 1860-1919; Western Reserve Eclectic Institute, records, 1849-67, 40 lf;

Manuscripts Collections: Eugene Adams (musician), correspondence relating to work and salary at college, 1945-47, 8 items; Gaylord S. Bates (doctor and missionary), correspondence relating to veterans' hospital, Wayne University, mission, and church work, 1938-46, 16 items; George Bellamy (founder of Hiram House), correspondence relating to college curriculum and Hiram House, 1942-60, 13 items; Harold Burton (Cleveland mayor, U.S. senator, Hiram College trustee), correspondence, 1941-51, 50 items; Lucretia Garfield Comer (author, granddaughter of James A. Garfield), correspondence relating to book; Paul H. Fall (college president and chemistry professor), MS of "Dismantling of German Chemical Plants After WWII" and correspondence, 1940-57, 3 lf;

James A. Garfield (U.S. president, U.S. congressman, and Ohio legislator), and Lucretia Rudolph Garfield, correspondence, speeches, family papers, legal documents, scrapbooks, pictures, diary, 1850-81, 3 lf; Jacob H. Goldner (Disciples of Christ minister), correspondence with James Garfield Warren and David D. Kimmel, 1944-49, 30 items; Elizabeth S. Hayden (wife of alumnus and trustee), correspondence relating to college development and to Smith College, 1938-58, 1 in.; Henry family of Geauga (Simon, Charles, Frederick; attorney, friend of Garfield, U.S. Postal Department advisor, college trustee), correspondence, family papers, documents, diaries, ledgers, memorabilia, 1850-1960, 16 lf;

Burke Aaron Hinsdale (educator, president of Hiram College, superintendent of Cleveland schools, professor of education at Michigan),
MSS of works printed, correspondence, 1860-1900, 8 lf; Charles Edward Hubbell (insurance agent, Hiram College trustee), correspondence, MSS of college play, 1949-50, 5 items; John Samuel Kenyon
(etymologist, contributor to dictionary, professor of English), correspondence, 1940-50, 15 items; Nicholas Vachel Lindsay (artist,
poet, Hiram student), MSS, drawings, correspondence, scrapbooks,
photos, 1901-31, 3 lf. JWG

770. Immaculate Conception Church (1857)
        409 West Main Street, Ravenna, Ohio 44266
        (216) 296-6434   (W 1-4)
        Fr. Francis J. Haidet, Pastor

Church registers, 1858+, 24 vols. JWG

771. United Fund of Portage County (1968)
        120 East Main Street, Ravenna, Ohio 44266
        (216) 297-1424   (M-F 9-4)
        Arthur Glover, Executive Director

Administrative records, 1967, 9 pp; Board of trustees, minutes,
1966-70, 5 reports; Campaign posters and literature, 1968-71, 2 lf;
Master book for budgeting funds and statistical reports, 1967+, 1 vol.
JWG

                          PREBLE COUNTY

MANUSCRIPTS

772. Preble County District Library (ca. 1900)
        301 North Barron Street, Eaton, Ohio 45320
        (513) 456-4331   (M, W, F 2-8; Tu 10-8; Sat 12-5)
        Inez Stack, Librarian

Buriff family genealogy, 1836-1963, 30 pp; Cemetery inscriptions of
Preble County, by Mrs. Don R. Short, 100 pp; Diefenbaugh family
genealogy, 1743-1941, 50 pp; Descendents of Andrew J. Wikle and
Mary Wikle, by H. F. Zigler, 1808-1968, 90 pp; History and genealogy of the Ozias family, by Albert Rohrer, 1840-1943, 255 pp; Index to grave records of servicemen of the War of 1812, by the Ohio

Society, U.S. Daughters of 1812, 1969, 77 pp; Krekler and related
families, genealogy, 1800-1963, 35 pp; Plat book, Preble County,
Ohio, 1912, 50 pp; Preble County marriage records, by Mrs. Don
R. Short and Mrs. Dale Bowers, 1808-40, 100 pp; Preble County
pioneers, by Grace Carroll Runyon, 1939, 54 pp; Preble, Pribble,
Prible genealogy, 30 pp; Scrapbook of Preble County history, by
Grace Carrol Runyon, 1840-1947, 430 pp; The Smelser family in
America, 1779-1961, 277 pp; Vance genealogy, 1916-60, 74 pp;
Vance family scrapbook, 1750+, 227 pp.   FH

INSTITUTIONAL RECORDS

773. Chamber of Commerce, Eaton (1932)
        402 East Main Street, Eaton, Ohio 45320
        (513) 494-4949
        Fred Brown, Secretary

Annual reports, 1952+; Correspondence, 1969+; Financial statements, 1952+; Journals, 1952+; Ledgers, 1952+; Minutes, 1932+,
incompl. for first 20 yrs; Newsletter, 1952+; Proceedings, minutes of monthly meetings, 1952+; Receipts, 1952+.   RS

774. Farm Bureau Federation, Eaton (1919)
        515 North Barron Street, Eaton, Ohio 45320
        (513) 456-5515
        William J. Murphy, President

Administrative records, 1949+; Contracts, 1950+; Correspondence,
4-year retention; Financial statements, 1957+; Ledgers, 15-year retention; Membership lists, 1919+; Minutes, including annual reports,
1919+, 2 lf; Monthly publication, 1-year retention; Scrapbooks, 1972+;
Tax records, 10-year retention.   FH

775. Farm Co-op Association, Eaton (1935)
        515 North Barron Street, Eaton, Ohio 45320
        (513) 456-5515
        Dick Muenchenbach, General Manager

Agreements, 1927+; Annual reports, 1935+; Cashbooks, 1949+; Certificates, 1935+; Contracts, 1970+; Correspondence, 1964+; Deeds,

1935+; Financial statements, 1935+; Inventories, 1965+; Journals, 1965+; Ledgers, 1965+; Minutes, 1935+; Plats, 1935+; Tax records, 1965+; 152 lf total.   RS

776. Henny Penny Corporation (1955)
         217 North Barron Street, Eaton, Ohio 45320
         (513) 456-4171
         William Cressell, Assistant Treasurer

Administrative records, 1956+; Agreements, 1956+; Annual reports, 1956+; Cashbooks, 1956+; Contracts, 1956+; Correspondence, 1962+; Daybooks, 1956+; Deeds, 1956+; Financial statements, 1956+; Inventories, 1956+; Journals, 1956+; Ledgers, 1956+; Minutes, 1956+; Receipts, 1956+; 700 lf total.   FH

PUTNAM COUNTY

MANUSCRIPTS

777. Putnam County District Library
         364 East Main Street, Ottawa, Ohio 45875
         (419) 523-3747   (M-Th, Sat 10-8; F 10-6)
         Hildred Safford, Librarian

Family histories; Library records (annual reports, board minutes, 1924-74, financial records); Newspaper clippings on local history. SF

INSTITUTIONAL RECORDS

778. Chamber of Commerce, Ottawa
         956 North Locust, Ottawa, Ohio 45875
         (419) 523-3141   (M-Sat 9-4:30)
         Frank Sunderhouse, Secretary

Annual reports, ca. 1964+; Board of directors, minutes, ca. 1964+; Committee reports, ca. 1964+; Correspondence, ca. 1964+; Financial records, ca. 1964+; Membership records, ca. 1964+; Newspaper clippings, ca. 1964+; Photographs, ca. 1964+; Publicity materials, ca. 1964+; 10 lf total.   SF

MANUSCRIPTS

779. Mansfield Public Library (1893)
        43 West Third Street, Mansfield, Ohio 44902
        (419) 522-3631   (M-F 9-9; Sat 9-5)
        A. T. Dickinson, Director

Circuit court records, 1820-33, 4 in.; Greystone Night Club, corporate records, 1947-50; Security Savings and Loan Company, minutes,
1921-38, 1 vol; John Sherman, correspondence, 20 items.   WM

780. Richland County Historical Society
        403 Richland Trust Building, Mansfield, Ohio 44902
        (419) 522-9299
        Marshall C. Moore, President

Photographs of early Mansfield and Richland County, 500 items. WM

INSTITUTIONAL RECORDS

781. American Red Cross, Mansfield (1917)
        39 North Park Street, Mansfield, Ohio 44902
        (419) 524-0311   (M-F 8:30-4:30)
        Everett W. Miller, Executive Director

Correspondence, 1960+; Financial records, 1955+; Minutes, 1916+;
Photographs, 1955+, 30 items; Scrapbooks, 1950-55+; Servicemen
cases, 1941+.   WM

782. Belleville Star (1921)
        88 Main Street, Belleville, Ohio 44813
        (419) 886-2291   (Th, F 9-5)
        Mrs. David Richardson, Assistant to the Publisher

Deeds, 1952, agreements to development project; Financial statements, 1930-40; Journals, 1929; Publications, 1897-98, 1906,1913,
1915, 1942+.   KS

783. Family Service of North Central Ohio (1961)
        35 North Park, Mansfield, Ohio 44902
        (419) 522-0167   (M-F 8:30-4:30)
        James Kulig, Director

Administrative records, 1961+; Board of directors, minutes, 1961+; Case files, organized by family name; Correspondence, 1961+; Financial records, 1961+; Scrapbooks, 1961+.   WM

784. First Congregational Church (1835)
        640 Millsboro Road, Mansfield, Ohio 44903
        (419) 756-3046
        R. Hutchison, Historian

Administrative records, 1835+, 6 in.; Annual reports, 1926-50; Correspondence, William Scott, 1851; Minutes, 1890-96; Plats, 1871-73, 1950; Publications, 1898-99, 1910-69.   KS

785. First Lutheran Church (1853)
        53 Park Avenue West, Mansfield, Ohio 44901
        (419) 522-0662   (M-F 8-5)
        Jerry Schmalenberger, Sr. Pastor

Annual reports; Church register, 1862+, 7 vols; Deeds; Minutes; Publications, 1967+; Scrapbooks, 1972+.   WM

786. First United Methodist Church (1814)
        Mansfield, Ohio 44902
        (M-F 9-4:30)
        Robert A. Baker, Sr. Minister

Church register, 1868-74, 1880-95, 1905-20, 4 vols; Minutes, 1828-65, 1 vol; Photographs, 100 items; Scrapbooks, 1905-11.   WM

787. League of Women Voters of Mansfield (1950)
        Mansfield, Ohio 44901
        (419) 756-7177

Annual reports and minutes; Correspondence, 1950+; Financial statements, 1950+; Local studies, 1950+; Membership lists, 1950+; Minutes, 1950+; Scrapbooks, 1950+; 8 lf total.   WM

788. Mansfield Art Guild (1945)
        700 Marion, Mansfield, Ohio
        (419) 756-1700   (Tu-Sun 12-5)
        H. Daniel Butts, III, Director

Annual reports, 1966-69; Artist shows, 1945+; Building blueprints;
Deeds; Financial statements, 1963+; Ledgers, 1968+; May show,
card catalog of local artists competing, 1968+; Minutes, 1963+;Scrap-
books, 1945+; Tours, 1968+.   WM

789. Mansfield Public Library (1893)
        43 West Third Street, Mansfield, Ohio 44902
        (419) 522-3631   (M-F 9-9; Sat 9-5)
        A. T. Dickinson, Director

Annual reports, 1888-1908, 1 in.; Minutes, 1887-1944, 6 in.   KS

790. Mission of the Sacred Hearts Center (1934)
        Route 1, Box 168, Shelby, Ohio 44975
        (419) 747-4772
        Fr. Marcel DuPont, Librarian

The mission is no longer a school, but has served as a retreat house
since 1970.

Administrative records, 1934-70, grades and transcripts of all those
enrolled in the school, 4 in.; Agreements; Certificates, 1934+, ordina-
tions and classes, 6 in.; Deeds, 1934, original deeds; Publication, 1946-
58, 6 in.   KS

791. News Journal (1930)
        70 West Fourth Street, Mansfield, Ohio 44902
        (419) 522-3311   (M-F 8-5)
        R. J. Blake, General Manager

Publication, the News Journal, 1881+, mf; Scrapbooks, cross-refer-
enced   file on prominent people and subjects of the area, 1930+, 300
lf.   KS

792. Richland County Foundation (1945)
        24 North Mulberry, Mansfield, Ohio 44902
        (419) 525-3020   (M-F 9-12, 1-5)
        Betty Crawford, Executive Assistant

Administrative records, 1945; Annual reports, 1945+; Correspondence,
1945+; Deeds; Financial statements, 1945+; Minutes, 1945+; Publications,
1945+; Scrapbooks, 1945+; 25 lf total.   WM

793. United Community Services (1920)
        35 North Park Street, Mansfield, Ohio 44902
        (419) 524-3423   525-2816   (M-F 8:30-5)
        John Bradley Rhind, Executive Director

United Appeal is the drive of United Community Services.

Agency records, agencies which request allocations, 1959+; Annual
reports, 1920+; Bequest records, 1959+; Financial statements; Minutes, 1920+; Publications, campaign materials; Scrapbooks, 1920+.
WM

794. WMAN Radio (1939)
        144-1/2 Park Avenue West, Mansfield, Ohio 44901
        (419) 524-2211   (M-F 8:30-5; Sat 9-12)
        Robert James, Program Director

Annual reports, 1968+; Financial statements, 1968+; Minutes, 1968+;
Radio logs, 5-year retention.   WM

795. YMCA, Mansfield (1867)
        455 Park Avenue West, Mansfield, Ohio 44906
        (419) 524-1787   (M-F 8-5)
        Franklin Erck, Associate General Secretary

Correspondence, 1963+; Deeds; Financial statements, includes records of gifts and membership, 1900-1925, 1963+, 2 lf; Membership rolls, part of financial records; Minutes, 1867-74, 1891-1916,
1924+; Photographs, 1910-50, 150 items; Scrapbooks, 1921-35, 18
in.   WM

ROSS COUNTY

MANUSCRIPTS

796. Chillicothe-Ross County Public Library (1906)
        140-146 South Paint Street, Chillicothe, Ohio 45601
        (614) 774-1114   (M-F 9-9; Sat 9-5:30)
        Marie-Louise Sheehan, Librarian

Local history, cemetery records, pamphlets, about Chillicothe and
Ross County, 1940+, 1 lf; E.S. Weris (newspaper columnist), scrap-

book of his columns, "Quaint Tales of Old Chillicothe," 1935-36, 2 in.
RR

INSTITUTIONAL RECORDS

797. Chamber of Commerce, Chillicothe (1912)
        85 West Main Street, Chillicothe, Ohio 45601
        (614) 772-4530   (M-F 8:30-5)
        Gerald Long, Executive Vice-President

Administrative records, 1912+; Agreements, ca. 1952+; Annual reports, 5-year retention; Committee and board minutes, ca. 1953+;
Contracts, ca. 1952+; Correspondence, 1-year retention; Deeds, ca.
1952+; Financial records, ca. 1952+; Plats, ca. 1952+; Publications,
ca. 1963+; Scrapbooks, ca. 1963+; Tax records, ca. 1957+; 24 lf
total.   RR

798. Trinity United Methodist Church (1803)
        24 South Mulberry, Chillicothe, Ohio 45601
        (614) 772-4065
        Floyd Fought, Minister

Administrative records, 1962+; Agreements, 1950-71; Annual reports of conferences, 1965+; Cashbooks, 1951+; Certificates, 1951+;
Contracts, 1950-71; Correspondence, 1960+; Deeds, 1842-1964; Financial statements, 1943+; Inventories, 1962-71; Journals, 1951+; Ledgers, 1951+; Membership records, 1842+; Minutes, 1943+; Publications,
1954+; Scrapbooks, 1945+; Tax records, 1951+.   RR

SANDUSKY COUNTY

MANUSCRIPTS

799. Birchard Public Library of Sandusky County
        423 Croghan, Fremont, Ohio 43420
        (419) 332-1121   (M-F 9:30-8:30; Sat 9:30-6)
        Richard Gooch, Director

Lucy Keeler, scrapbook (mostly newspaper and magazine articles);
Library records (board of trustees, minutes, 1874+; annual reports,

scattered); Newspaper clippings on local history; 15 lf total.   SF

800. Rutherford B. Hayes Library
        1337 Hayes Avenue, Fremont, Ohio 43420
        (419) 332-2081
        Watt Marchman, Director

See Andrea Lentz, A Guide to Manuscripts at the Ohio Historical
Society, 1972.

INSTITUTIONAL RECORDS

801. Opportunity Center
        109 South Front Street, Fremont, Ohio 43420
        (419) 332-2603   (M-F 8-5)
        Randy Neff, Director

A community action group which is part of WSOS Community Action
Commission, Inc. The group provides general services to low income people, primarily Spanish speaking.

Case files (services rendered to, or needed by, each client), 1964+;
Correspondence, 1964+; Financial records, 1964+; Staff activities
records, daily, 1964+; Statistical records (breakdown of services
rendered by type), 1964+.   SF

802. St. John's Lutheran Church
        200 North Clover, Fremont, Ohio 43420
        (419) 332-4521   (M-F 8-4; Sat 8-12)
        A. J. Klopfer, Minister

Anniversary publications; Annual reports; Bills and receipts; Bulletins; Church council, minutes; Church register; Correspondence;
Financial records; Membership records; Newspaper clippings; Photographs; Sermons; Sunday school records; Women's circles and men
of the church records; 1841+, 36 lf total.   SF

MANUSCRIPTS

803.	Portsmouth Public Library (1903)
	1220 Gallia, Portsmouth, Ohio 45662
	(614) 354-7506
	Henrietta Montavon, Reference Librarian

Circulation records and register of borrowers of the library, 1931+,
30 in.; N.W. Evans, MS of History of Scioto County, sketches of
people, places, events, and institutions, indexed, transcribed in
1900, 2 lf; H.A. Lorberg, scrapbook, writing, pictures, 1875-1935,
4 lf; Sons of Temperance, minutes, 1846-61, 1 in.; Presbytery in
Portsmouth, records, 1882-95, 2 in.; Portsmouth High School
Alumni Association, 1890-1900, 1 in.; Scrapbooks, history of Scioto
County, 1829-1900, 8 lf; Scioto County Regional Planning Commission, report, 1964, 6 in.; Women's Literary Club, 1925-61, 2 in.
FH

INSTITUTIONAL RECORDS

804.	Bigelow United Methodist Church (1803)
	415 Washington, Portsmouth, Ohio 45662
	(614) 353-3019	(M-F 9-4)
	James Wolfe, Minister

Board minutes, 1947-49, 1955+, 3 in.; Church register, ca. 1880-
1911, 1 lf; Clippings, notes, correspondence, re sesquicentennial
celebration, 1953, 2 in.; Collection receipts, 1960+, 2 in.; Financial reports, 1952+, 4 in.; Official quarterly records, 1902-14,
1941+, 6 in.; Publications, ca. 1955, 6 in.; Record of pew rents,
1884-93, 1 in.; Sunday school records, 1895-1904, 1937-45, 3 in.;
Women's Federation, minutes, 1949-52; Women's Foreign Mission-
ary Society, minutes, 1907-18.	FH

805.	Catholic Social Services (1957)
	534 Sixth, Portsmouth, Ohio 45662
	(614) 353-3185	(M-F 9:30-4)
	William Streisel, Director, Branch Offices

Administrative records, 1957; Annual reports, ca. 1960+; Board
minutes, 1957+; Case records, 1957; Financial statements, 1957+;
Scrapbooks, 1957+, 6 lf.	RR

806. Chamber of Commerce, Portsmouth (1920)
     740 Second, Portsmouth, Ohio 45662
     (614) 353-1116   (M-F 9-5)
     James Secrest, Executive Manager

Administrative records, 1920; Correspondence, 3-year retention;
Financial statements, ca. 1940+; Minutes, ca. 1928+; 10 lf total.
FH

807. First Presbyterian Church (1817)
     221 Court Street, Portsmouth, Ohio 45662
     (614) 353-4259   (M-F 10-5)
     Louise Moore, Church Secretary

Church register, ca. 1959+, 1 vol; Correspondence, some from
about 20 years back; Financial records, ca. 1950+; Publications,
ca. 1949+; Scrapbooks, ca. 1940s, 3 in.; Session minutes, 1817+,
2 lf. RR

808. Scioto County Cooperative Milk Producers Association (1924)
     2301 Vinton, Portsmouth, Ohio 45662
     (614) 353-3430   (M-F 8-4; Sat 8-12)
     E. C. Herdman, Secretary-Treasurer

Annual reports, 1930+, 1 lf; Contracts, membership, ca. 1930+,
10 lf; Membership records; Milk records, volume and price; Minutes, 1930+, 1 lf. RR

809. United Way, Scioto County (1942)
     74 National Bank Building, Portsmouth, Ohio 45662
     (614) 353-5121   (M-F 8:30-4:30)
     H. H. Stoops, Executive Secretary

Administrative records, 1961; Annual reports, 1961+; Campaign records, 1961+; Correspondence, 2-year retention; Federal reports
and tax records, 7-year retention; Financial statements, 1961+; Individual agency reports and requests for money, 1961+; Ledgers,
1947+; Minutes, ca. 1940+; Scrapbooks, 1961+; 20 lf total.   FH

810. YMCA, Portsmouth (1882)
     1236 Gallia, Portsmouth, Ohio 45662
     (614) 354-3211   (M-Sat 9-5)
     Paul Hickman, Executive Director

Administrative records, 1882+; Agreements, ca. 1940+; Annual reports, ca. 1930+; Contracts, ca. 1960+; Correspondence, 5-year retention; Deeds, 1941+; Ledgers, 10-year retention; Minutes, 1940+;
Membership records, 3-10 year retention; Monthly reports; Newsletters; Pictures, building photos, programs, blueprints, etc., ca.
1945+; Scrapbooks, ca. 1945+; Tax records, 5-10 year retention.
FH

SENECA COUNTY

INSTITUTIONAL RECORDS

811. American Red Cross, Seneca County (1917)
      30 East Perry Street, Tiffin, Ohio 44883
      (419) 447-1424   (M-F 9-12, 1-4:30)
      Mary Tillotson, Executive Director

Board of directors, minutes, 1917-30, 1951+, 4 vols; Scrapbooks,
newspaper clippings, 1942+, 9 vols.   PY

812. Chamber of Commerce, Tiffin Area (1914)
      70 East Perry Street, Tiffin, Ohio 44883
      (419) 447-4141   (M-F 9-5)
      Tom Cahill, Executive Manager

Board of directors, minutes, 1960+; Community information, 1950,
1 folder; General files, 1955+, 4 lf; List of past residents, 1962+;
Monthly bulletins, 1962+, 4 vols; Postcards of the community, 1
folder; Tiffin business files, 1940+, 2 lf.   PY

813. Community Health Services, Inc.
      89 East Perry Street, Tiffin, Ohio 44883
      (419) 448-9723   (M-F 8-5)
      Dorothy J. Seeberger, Administrative Director

An organization to provide primary health care for migrant workers.

Board of directors, minutes, 1970+, 1 folder; Correspondence, 1968+,
2 lf.   PY

814. Daughters of America
        North Sandusky Road, Tiffin, Ohio 44883
        (419) 447-4742   (M-F 8-5)

Annual session of the Daughters of America, proceedings, 1912+,
2 lf; Board of directors, minutes, 1927+, 3 lf; Correspondence,
1927+, 10 lf; Resident register, 1931+, 1 vol.   PY

815. Farm Bureau Co-op, Tiffin
        Leitner Avenue, Tiffin, Ohio 44883
        (419) 447-2616   (M-F 8-5:30; Sat 8-12:30)
        Alice Kenner, Secretary

Administrative records, 1918, 2 lf; Correspondence, 1960+, 10 lf;
Ledgers, 1965+; Minutes, 1918+, 5 lf; Stock certificates, 1934+, 4
lf. PY

816. Tiffin University Library
        155 Miami, Tiffin, Ohio 44883
        (419) 447-6442   (M-F 8-5:30; Sat 8-12:30)
        Kathryn Kay, Librarian

Minutes, held by the president, 1918+.   PY

817. United Community Fund, Tiffin (1944)
        70 East Perry Street, Tiffin, Ohio 44883
        (419) 447-4141   (M-F 9-5)
        Tom Cahill, Director

Board of directors, minutes, finances, campaigns and membership,
1945+, 15 vols; Scrapbooks, 1960+, 6 vols; Tiffin community and
national war funds, 1944, 1 vol.   PY

818. Ursuline Convent (Ursuline Academy, 1863)
        Jefferson, Tiffin, Ohio 44883
        (419) 447-0265
        Sr. Mary Charles

"Echoes from Ursuline," concerns the first 50 years of Ursuline
Academy from 1863 to 1913, 1913, 1 vol; Photographs, 1895-1927,
75 items; Scrapbook, 1900-1915, 1 vol.   PY

819. WTTF Radio, Inc. (1959)
      185 South Washington, Tiffin, Ohio 44883
      (419) 447-2212   (M-F 9-5)
      Robert G. Wright, President

Administrative records; Annual reports, 1959+; Board of directors,
minutes, 1959+; Logs, 3-year retention.   PY

                          SHELBY COUNTY

MANUSCRIPTS

820. Amos Memorial Library (1869)
      230 East North Street, Sidney, Ohio 45365
      (513) 492-8354   (M-F 9-8:30; Sat 9-6)
      Linda Short, Librarian

The Anna School, alumni records, ca. 1939; Cemetery records, 3 in.;
Family genealogies, 6 in.; Finding list of Virginia marriage records
before 1853, 1 in.; Korn brothers, MS material, fliers, ca. 1910, mostly
photographs, 2 in.; Plum Creek Church records, 1967, 1 in.; St. Jacobs
Evangelical Lutheran Church, church register, 1832-1966, 1 in.; Veterans of War of 1812, Revolutionary War and Mexican War, 1 in.   RS

INSTITUTIONAL RECORDS

821. Chamber of Commerce, Sidney (1945)
      133 South Ohio, Sidney, Ohio 45365
      (513) 492-9122   (M-F 8:30-11:30, 12:30-5)
      George Sponseller, Executive Vice-President

Contracts, 1971+; Financial statements, 1967+; Journals, 1967+; Ledgers, 1967+; Minutes, 1945+; Publications, 1970+.   RS

MANUSCRIPTS

822. Malone College Library (1889)
          515 Twenty-Fifth Street NW, Canton, Ohio 44709
          (216) 454-3517   (M-F 7:30-10; Sat 9-5; Sun 2-5)
          Martha Cox, Director of Library Services

Esther E. Baird (missionary to India), 5 diaries and correspondence
with Nora Darnell, 8 in.; Everett L. Cattell (immediate past president
of Malone College), papers, 1960-72, 4 lf; Minutes of Friends meetings,
1813+, 18 lf; Helen Monnette, poetry covering 10-year period, 4 in.;
Byron L. Osborne (past president of Malone College), papers, 6 lf;
Shacketon-Edmund Burke correspondence, 1744-90, 1 lf.   KS

823. The Massillon Museum
          212 Lincoln Way East, Massillon, Ohio 44646
          (216) 833-4061   (M-Sat 10-5; Sun 2-5)
          Mary Merwin, Director

Atwater papers, papers and ledgers of early shipping business, 1836-
70; Frank L. Baldwin (Massillon lawyer), papers, including business
activities, 1849-1917; Brown and Harter families (letters and papers,
mostly letters sent by James Brown to Mary, his wife), 1828-1922, 500
items; Corns papers (business papers of prominent man), 1880-1922,
149 items; Coxey papers (concern 1894 and 1914 marches to Washington, 1932 presidential campaign, 1936 presidential campaign, and
1900-1910 business papers), 10 items, 120 documents and other   material;Caroline M. Everhard (leader in state and national suffrage
movement), papers, 1886-1902, 15 items; Hess, Snyder and Co.
(Massillon metal working and forging company), records, ca. 200
items; Russell & Co. (the largest and most important business in Massillon during its existence), records, 1879-1921, 31 items; Charles K.
Skinner & Co., business records and family papers, 100 items; Wellman & Co. (produce and wheat shipping business in 1830s), records,
1833-51, 2,651 items.   WM

824. Massillon Public Library
          208 Lincoln Way East, Massillon, Ohio 44646
          (216) 832-9831   (M-F 9:30-9)
          Ethel Conrad, Librarian

Kendall Society, minutes, 1828-29, 6 in.; Rotch-Wales correspondence, 1790-1870, 3,000 items.   KS

825. <u>Stark County Historical Society (1945)</u>
      P. O. Box 483, Canton, Ohio 44701
      (216) 455-7043   (Tu-Th 9-4)
      Gervis Brady, Director

Diebold Brick Company, stock certificates, 1893, 1 in.; E. T. Herald, "History of William McKinley," unpub., 4 lf; McKinley correspondence, 1847-1901, 4 lf; McKinley National Memorial Association, proceedings of board of trustees, 1901-38, 1 lf; Maps of Canton, 1916-24; Photographs, 18 lf; Scrapbooks, clippings of Canton industries, 1940+, 4 lf. KS

INSTITUTIONAL RECORDS

826. <u>Alfred Nickle's Bakery, Inc. (1909)</u>
      26 Main Street, Navarre, Ohio 44662
      (216) 879-5835   (M-F 8-4:30; Sat 8-12)
      David E. Gardner, Sr. Vice-President of Administration

Administrative records, 1927, 1934, 1956; Board of trustees, minutes, 1927+, 2 lf; Deeds, 1909; Inventories, 1960-70; Photographs, 1920s+, 1 lf; Publications, 1939, 1959 (30th and 50th anniversary publications); Scrapbooks, 1950-60, 6 in. KS

827. <u>American Manufacturers Export Association (1950)</u>
      618 Tenth Street NW, Canton, Ohio 44703
      (216) 453-8187   (M-F 8-5)
      M. K. Morse, Proprietor

Correspondence, 1950+; Financial statements, 1950+; Tax records, 1950+; 20 lf total. WM

828. <u>American Red Cross, Canton (1917)</u>
      618 Second Street NW, Canton, Ohio 44703
      (216) 453-0146   (M-F 8:30-4:30)
      Mr. Thomas, Director

Administrative records, 1950+; Annual reports, 1950+; Minutes, 1950+; Publication, "The Red Cross Review," 1961+; Scrapbooks, 1917+. WM

829. Aultman Hospital (1891)
     2600 Sixth Street SW, Canton, Ohio 44710
     (216) 452-9911
     H. R. Taylor, Executive Vice-President

Administrative records: Hospital, 1891+, School of nursing, 1894-
1970, 17 lf; Annual reports, 1892-1970; Minutes, 1916+, 27 lf; Publications, 1949+, 6 in.; Scrapbooks, school of nursing, 1925-70, 18
in. KS

830. Bar Association, Stark County (1900)
     Room 321, Peoples Merchants Trust Building, Canton, Ohio 44702
     (M-F 8:30-4:30)
     Mary L. Holland, Executive Secretary

Administrative records, 8 lf; Minutes, 1900+; Publications, 1952+;
Scrapbooks, 1954-58. WM

831. Better Business Bureau of Stark County (1961)
     203 Market, Canton, Ohio 44702
     (216) 454-9401
     Edward Katz, President

Administrative records, 1961+, 4 lf; Advertising files, current, 8 lf;
Annual reports, 1961+, 4 lf; Business files, 1961+, 50 lf; Financial
statements, 1961; Membership files, 1961+; Minutes, 1961+, 4 lf;
Publications, 1961+; Scrapbooks, 1961+, 3 in. WM

832. Canal Fulton Public Library (1948)
     Canal Fulton, Ohio 44614
     (216) 854-3977
     Joetta Brownfield, Reference Librarian

Ledgers, 1874, 1881, 2 lf; Minutes, 1948+; Plats, 1923; Proceedings, 1890-early 1900s, 18 in.; Scrapbooks, 1969+. KS

833. Canton Public Library (1884)
     236 Third Street, Canton, Ohio 44702
     (216) 452-0665   (M-Th 9-9; F, Sat 9-5)
     Merlin Wolcott, Librarian

Annual reports, 1939+; Circulation statistics; Contracts, 1880; Correspondence, 1950+; Financial statements, 1884; Minutes, 1884; Publications, 1960+; Scrapbooks, 1955+; Genealogies of Canton residents, includes the Buchtel, Duryee, Mock, and Sumner families, 1700-1944. WM

834. Chamber of Commerce, Canton (1914)
        Wells and Third Street NW, Canton, Ohio 44703
        (M-F 8:30-5)
        Harlan D. Dabry, Executive Vice-President

Administrative records, 1914+; Annual reports, 1969+; Financial statements, 1969+; Minutes, 1969+; Publications, 1969+. WM

835. Chamber of Commerce, Massillon (1914)
        33 City Hall Street SE, Massillon, Ohio 44646
        (216) 833-3146   (M-F 8:30-5)
        Harold F. Bostic, Executive Director

Administrative records, 1914+; Annual reports, 1914+; Financial statements, 1914+; Journals, 1914+; Ledgers, 1914+; Minutes, 1914+; Publications; Scrapbooks, 1948+; 250 lf total. WM

836. Church of the Saviour, United Methodist (1864)
        120 Cleveland Avenue SW, Canton, Ohio 44702
        (216) 445-0153   (M-F 8:30-4:30)
        Howard J. Wiant, Senior Minister

Administrative records, 1958-60+; Annual reports; Church register; Minutes. WM

837. The First Baptist Church (ca. 1845)
        906 Tuscarawas Street W, Canton, Ohio 44702
        (216) 452-9744   (M-F 8:30-4)
        Marvin E. Hall, Pastor

Administrative records, 1971+; Church register, 1856+, 2 lf; Contracts for building and land; Minutes, 1958+; Photographs, 6 in.; Publications, 1968+; Scrapbooks, 2 lf. WM

838. First Christian Church (1898)
       430 Cleveland Avenue SW, Canton, Ohio 44702
       (216) 456-4717   (M-F 8-5)
       Alice Wiener, Senior Secretary

Annual reports, 1901+; Church register, 1898+, 45 lf; Deeds, 1898;
Publication, "The Canton Christian," 1907+, 6 lf.   KS

839. Hoover Company (1880s)
       101 East Maple, Canton, Ohio 44720
       (216) 499-9200   (M-F 8-4)
       C. V. Batton, Vice-President of Administration

Annual reports, 1943+, 4 in.; Proceedings, home institute school,
1937+, 1 in.; Publications, "The Fabulous Dustpan," by F. Hoover,
1955, "Hoover News," 1917+, 3 lf, Ibaisaic, sales publication, 1921+,
3 lf; Scrapbooks, 1880s+, 6 vols.   KS

840. Massillon Industrial Development Foundation (1950)
       33 City Hall Street SE, Massillon, Ohio 44646
       (216) 833-3146   (M-F 8:30-5)
       Harold F. Bostic, Executive Director

Administrative records, 1950+; Annual reports, 1950+; Correspondence, 1950+; Financial statements, 1950+; Minutes, 1950+; 13 lf
total.   WM

841. Merchants Association (1952)
       33 City Hall Street SE, Massillon, Ohio 44646
       (216) 833-3146   (M-F 8:30-5)
       Harold F. Bostic, Executive Director

Administrative records, 1952+; Annual reports, 1952+; Financial
statements, 1952+; Minutes, 1952+; Programs, sidewalk sales,
parades, 1952+; 5 lf total.   WM

842. Mount Union College Archives (1846)
       Alliance, Ohio 44601
       (216) 821-5322   (M-Th 8-5, 6:30-11; F 8-5; Sat 8:30-5;
       Sun 2-5, 6:30-11)
       Yost Osborne, Librarian

Mount Union College historical collection, 1846+, 2 lf; Scio College historical collection, 1857-1911, 2 lf.   GK

843. SCIA (1968)
        1247 Market Street South, Canton, Ohio 44707
        (216) 452-7221   (M-Sat 8-10)
        Aleem Mshindi, Chairman

SCIA is the Society for Cooperative Improvement of Afro-Americans.

Administrative records, 1968+; Contracts, 1968+; Financial statements, 1968+; Minutes; Publication, "Freedom's Journal," 1968+; Scrapbooks, 1968+; Tax records, 1968+.   WM

844. The Stark County Foundation (1963)
        618 Second Street NW, Canton, Ohio 44703
        (216) 454-3426   (M-F 8:30-4)
        W. D. Hunter, Executive Secretary

Administrative records, 1964+; Annual reports, 1965+; Correspondence, 1965+; Financial statements, 1965+; Minutes, 1964+; Scrapbooks, 1965+.   WM

845. Sugardale Company (1919)
        1600 Harmont, Canton, Ohio 44705
        (216) 455-5253   (M-F 8:30-5)
        Mrs. P. Blattert, Secretary to the President

Agreements, 1960-71; Annual reports, 1968-71; Financial statements, 1930+; Ledgers, 1960-71; Minutes, 1968-71; Photographs and engineering drawings, 1919+, 6 lf.   KS

846. Teledyne Monarch Rubber (1926)
        10 Lincoln Park, Hartville, Ohio 44632
        (216) 877-9311   (M-Sun 9-5)
        Robert J. Himmelright, President

Administrative records, 1926-68, 2 lf; Agreements, 1926-68, 3 in.; Annual reports, 1945-68; Contracts, 1926-68, 3 in.; Correspondence, 1926-68; Deeds, 1926-68, 3 in.; Financial statements, 1945-68, 3 in.; Minutes, 1926-68; Photographs, 1926-71, 3 in.; Plats, 1926-68, 3 in.; Scrapbooks, 1926-71, 6 in.   GK

847. Timken Company (1898)
       1835 Deuber Avenue SW, Canton, Ohio 44706
       (216) 453-4511   (M-F 8-5)
       R. A. Wagner, Public Relations Manager

Journals, 1921-61, 6 in.; Ledgers, 1908-10, 6 in.; Publications,
1919-69; Scrapbooks, WWII period, 1 lf.   KS

848. United Fund of Central Stark County (1922)
       618 Second Street NW, Canton, Ohio 44703
       (216) 455-0378   (M-F 8:30-5)
       Douglas H. Worth, Executive Secretary

Administrative records, 1922+; Annual reports, 1922+; Audits,1949+;
Budget books, 1922+; Financial statements, 1922+; Minutes, 1922+;
Publications; Scrapbooks, 1920s+; 24 lf total.   WM

849. United Fund of Western Stark County, Inc. (1927)
       305 Massillon Building, Massillon, Ohio 44646
       (216) 833-4129   (M-F 9-5)
       Richard Swanson, Executive Director

Administrative records, 1927+; Annual reports, 1927+; Correspondence, 1927+; Financial statements, 1927+; Minutes, 1927+; Publications, 1927+; Scrapbooks, 1927+; 75 lf total.   WM

850. Urban League, Canton (1921)
       415 13th Street SE, Canton, Ohio 44707
       (216) 456-3479   (M-F 9-5)
       C. A. Thomas, Executive Director

Administrative records, 1930+; Annual reports, 1953+; Correspondence, 1953+; Deeds, 1927+; Financial statements, 1953+; Minutes,
1953+; Publications, 1953+; Scrapbooks, 1953+; 24 lf total.   WM

851. Urban League, Massillon (1936)
       318 Massillon Building, Massillon, Ohio 44646
       (216) 833-4149   (M-F 9:30-5)
       Wilfred Reynolds, Executive Director

Administrative records, 1936+; Annual reports, 1936+; Correspondence, 1930s+; Deeds, 1935+; Financial statements, 1935+; Minutes,
1936+; Scrapbooks, 1936+; 9 lf total.   WM

MANUSCRIPTS

852. Akron Public Library (1877)
        55 South Main Street, Akron, Ohio 44308
        (216) 762-7621   (M-Th 9-9; F 9-6; Sat 9-5)
        John H. Rebenack, Chief Librarian

Frederick B. Barton (freelance writer and war correspondent), letters and papers; Hazel Fetzer, The Story of Jake, TS biography of
Herman Fetzer ("Jake Falstaff"); First Congregational Church, Hudson, Ohio, minutes, 1802-37, 45 pp; Samuel A. Lane, photographs
of Akron; Sr. Mary Loretta Petit, unpublished biography of U. S.
Senator Charles Dick, 1948, 52 pp; Summit County Civil Defense
Council, clippings on the agency's activities, 1939-45, 3 vols; Tall-
madge, Ohio, Historical Society, miscellaneous papers and records,
3 mf rolls; Women's Art League, account book of the Akron Rubber
Ball, 1939;

Library records: Annual reports, 1915+, 2 lf; Correspondence, 5
lf; Deeds, 1 lf; Financial statements, 1874+, 2 lf; Minutes, 1874+,
12 lf; Scrapbooks, 1938+, 3 lf.   KS

853. Barberton Public Library (1903)
        602 West Park Avenue, Barberton, Ohio 44203
        (216) 745-1194   (M-Sat 10-8:30)
        Mr. Brownfield, Reference Librarian

Blueprints of Barber Mansion, 1915; William A. Johnston (civil
engineer who laid out Barberton), papers, early 20th century, 1 lf;
Pamphlet file, Barberton history, 1891+, 4 lf; Photographs, 1930s,
1 lf; Plats, local maps of Barberton, early 20th century.   KS

854. Hudson Library and Historical Society (1910)
        22 Aurora Street, Hudson, Ohio 44236
        (216) 653-6658   (M, Tu, Th-Sat 10-5)
        Thomas L. Vince, Librarian

Jeremiah Brown (John Brown's half brother), collection (concerning
activities with U. S. Sanitary Commission during the Civil War and
family life), 4 lf; John Brown collection (photostat letters, papers,
holographs, genealogy, books, records, pictures), 24 lf.   KS

855. The University of Akron Library
      Akron, Ohio 44325
      (216) 375-7670   (M-F 8-5)
      John Miller, Director of Archival Services

American History Research Center (Bierce Library; David Kyvig,
Director): Akron Better Business Bureau, records (minutes, correspondence, case files, reports, publications and scrapbooks),
1921-70, 10 cf; Charles Blair (member, governing board, the Summit County-Greater Akron Community Action Council), papers,
(minutes, correspondence, reports, publications, and clippings),
1965-71, 3 cf; Mary Gladwin (Red Cross nurse who served in the
Spanish-American War, the Russo-Japanese War, and WWI), papers (photographs, memoirs, and a WWI diary), ca. 1895-1920,
1 cf; Sandy and Beaver Canal, papers of four mid-19th century
canal shippers, Richard K. Gray, Joseph Ranne, Frederick Mackaman, and James Morledge, 100 items; J. Blaine Wise (Waynes-
burg businessman active in the early 20th century development of
the Stark County gas and oil industry), papers, 24 cf; W. Richard
Wright (chairman, Ohio Youth Services Advisory Board), papers
(board minutes, inspection reports, the chairman's correspondence
and reference information files, clippings, photographs, and printed
materials), 1963-66, 2 lf.

Archives of the History of American Psychology (Marian McPherson
Popplestone, Director): Ward Campbell Halstead (professor, Univ.
of Chicago), papers, ?-1969, 10 lf; Harry Levi Hollingworth (professor, Barnard College), papers, 1905-56, 4 lf; Leta A. Stettor
Hollingworth (professor, Teachers College, Columbia), papers, 1913-
39, 5 lf; John Anthony Morris Kimber (clinician, marriage counselor),
papers, 6 in.; Miscellaneous materials (tests, card file, 2 lf; 1100
photographs, 50 films, 22 anatomical models, 100 slides, 25 large
teaching diagrams; apparatus, 1890-1945, 532 pieces); Miscellaneous
psychologists' papers, 88 living persons; Denis Carl Ober (clinician,
Univ. of Missouri at St. Louis), papers, 5 lf; Oral history transcripts,
1962-69, 13 subjects; Organizational ephemera, national, 26 lf; Everett
F. Patten (professor, Miami Univ.), correspondence with Clark Hull,
4 in.; Professional associations (American Psychological Association-
Division 6 and Division 16, International Council of Psychologists, International Society for Clinical and Experimental Hypnosis, Inter-University Council for School Psychology, Midwestern Psychological Association, New Jersey Psychological Association), records, 1936-69, 18 lf;
Professional publications (Animal Behavior, Journal of the Experimental
Analysis of Behavior, Journal of Marriage and Family, Southern Universities Press - reports, perceptual and motor skills), MSS material, correspondence, editorial evaluations, mostly 1960s, 150 lf; Dorothy Reth-

lingshafer (professor, Univ. of Florida), papers, 4 lf; Martin Scheerer (professor, Univ. of Kansas), papers, 1939-61, 12 lf; Secondary materials related to MSS collections, 192 lf; Walter Cleveland Shipley (professor, Wheaton College), papers, 1941-66, 2 lf; Edward Chace Tolman (professor, Univ. of California; president, American Psychological Association, 1937), papers, 1914-54, 3 lf.

University Archives (John Miller, Director of Archival Services): Administrative records, 1870+; Faculty records, 1872+; Capt. William McCollam, correspondence, May-Sept 1864; Lt. Col. John J. Polsley, correspondence, 1831-66; Student records, 1872+; 584 lf total.   GK

INSTITUTIONAL RECORDS

856.   Akron Art Institute (1922)
         69 East Market, Akron, Ohio 44308
         (216) 376-9185   (M-F 9-5)
         David Trowbridge, Director

Administrative records, 1922, 1937; Annual reports, 1937+; Correspondence, 1937+, 40 lf; Daybooks, 1968+; Financial statements, 1937+, 2 lf; Minutes, 1937+, 35 books; Receipts, 1937+; Scrapbooks, 1958+. KC

857.   Akron-Canton Airport (1945)
         North Canton, Akron-Canton, Ohio 44720
         (216) 896-2355   (M-F 8-4:30)
         Mr. Doyle, Manager

Contracts with airlines and freight companies, 1945+; Ledgers, 1955+, 3 lf; Minutes, 1945+, 3 lf; Plats, original blueprints and 11 additional projects, 1944; Scrapbooks, newspaper clippings, 1962.   KS

858.   Akron Education Association (1946)
         647 North Main Street, Akron, Ohio 44310
         (216) 434-2181   (M-F 8-4)
         Wade Underwood, President

Correspondence, 1970+, 8 lf; Financial statements, 1946+; Minutes, 1946+; Newsletter, 1946+.   KC

859. Akron General Medical Center (1914)
      400 Wabash Avenue, Akron, Ohio 44307
      Mr. Sauvageot, Public Relations

Annual reports, 1914+, 3 lf; Minutes, 1914+; Publication, monthly
"Voice," 1946+, 2 lf; Scrapbooks, 1946+, 12 lf.   GK

860. Akron Lodge No. 83, F & AM (1841)
      103 South High Street, Akron, Ohio 44308
      (216) 535-8154   (M-F 9-4)
      Charles Carter, Past Master

Administrative records, 1841; Membership list, 1841+, 1 vol; Minutes, 1841+, 2 lf.   GK

861. Akron Selle Company (1885)
      451 South High Street, Akron, Ohio 44311
      (216) 376-6161   (Hours by appointment only)
      Otis Hower, General Manager

Correspondence, 1885+, 180 lf; Financial records, 1885-1960, 8 lf;
Ledgers, 1885+, 10 lf.   GK

862. American Austrian Society (1895)
      133 East South, Akron, Ohio 44311
      (216) 253-0308   (M-Sat 9-5)
      Mike Gaudlme, Manager

Administrative records, 1895+, 5 lf; Annual reports, 1950+, 10 lf;
Financial statements; Minutes, 1950+, 5 lf; Newsletter, 1945-72,
10 lf; Proceedings, 1950+, 5 lf.   DK

863. AFL-CIO in conjunction with Human Resources Development (1969)
      5 East Buchtel, Room 314, Akron, Ohio 44308
      (216) 376-4908   (M-F 9-5)
      Mr. Anderson, Area Representative

Administrative records, 1969+; Annual reports, 1969+; Contracts,
1969+; Correspondence, 1969+; Financial statements, 1969+; Inventories, 1969+; Minutes, 1969+.   DK

864. AFL-CIO Laborers International Union of North America,
      Akron Regional Office
      Akron Savings and Loan Building, Room 1102, Akron, Ohio 44304
      (216) 253-6124   (M-F 8-4:45)
      Wanda Hall, Secretary

Administrative records, 1954+; Agreements, 1954+; Annual reports,
1954+; Contracts, 1954+; Financial statements, 1954+; Minutes, 1954+;
Proceedings; Publications, 1954+.   DK

865. Area Progress Board (1954)
      First National Tower, Akron, Ohio 44308
      (216) 253-5164   (M-F 8:30-5)
      Mrs. Bluhn, Secretary to Director

Administrative records, 1954+; Annual reports, 1954+; Financial records; Minutes, 1954+; Photograph file, 1954+; Scrapbooks, 1954+;
Tax records, 1965+; 100 lf total.   DK

866. B. F. Goodrich Company (1870)
      500 South Main Street, Akron, Ohio 44310
      (216) 379-2291   (M-F 8-5)
      Ruth Miller, Librarian

Annual reports, 1912+, 3 lf; Descriptive literature, sales campaigns,
advertisements, 1900+, 18 lf; Executive speeches, late 19th cen+, 6 lf;
Financial records, 1880+, 50 lf; Legal documents, 1900+, 6 lf; Photographs, 1870+, 6 lf; Promotional films, 1945, 5 lf; Publications, business and technical, late 19th cen+, 5 lf; Technical papers, 20th cen, 3
lf.   GK

867. Bar Association, Akron (1875)
      Ohio Building, Akron, Ohio 44308
      (216) 762-7453   (M-F 8:30-4:30)
      Elizabeth Glymph, Executive Director

Administrative records, 1875+; Annual reports, ca. 1875+, 10 lf;
Casework files, 1948+; Correspondence, 1965+, 12 lf; Financial statements, 1930+; Minutes, 1875+; Newsletter, 1954+.   KC

868. Better Business Bureau of Akron, Inc. (1920)
    225 West Exchange, Box 1314, Akron, Ohio 44309
    (216) 535-6158   (M-F 9-4:30)
    Rowland Jaspers, President and General Manager

Administrative records; Community service files, 1947, 1 notebook;
Correspondence, 10-year retention; Minutes; Publications, 1920+;
Radio talks, 1933-34, 1 notebook; Scrapbooks, 1947-57, 8 notebooks;
160 lf total. WM

869. Builders Exchange of Akron (1901)
    495 Wolf's Ledges, Akron, Ohio 44304
    (216) 434-5165   (M-F 8:30-5)
    George Mathers, Executive Secretary

Administrative records; Agreements; Annual reports; Contracts; Correspondence; Financial statements; Inventories; Minutes; Proceedings;
Receipts; Tax records; 7-year retention of all records; 200 lf total. DK

870. Catholic Service League (1920)
    640 North Main Street, Akron, Ohio 44310
    (216) 762-7481   (M-F 9-5)
    Rita Silvestro, Executive Director

Administrative records, 1920, 2 lf; Adoption records, 1936+, 12 lf;
Annual reports, 1936+, 2 lf; Case work records, 1960+, 40 lf; Correspondence, 1965+, 21 lf; Financial statements, 1950+, 2 lf; Ledgers, 1920+; Minutes, 1940+, 2 lf; Proceedings, 1940+; Publications,
Foster Newsletter Quarterly, Women's Auxiliary Monthly, 1950+; Receipts, 1967+; Tax records, 1972. KC

871. Chamber of Commerce, Akron (1907)
    137 South Main Street, Akron, Ohio 44308
    (216) 253-9181   (M-Sat 9-5)
    Paul Livick, Executive Assistant

Administrative records, 1907; Cashbooks, 1955+; Correspondence,
1957+, 228 lf; Financial statements, 1943+; Inventories, 1955+;
Journals, 1955+; Ledgers, ca. 1910, 1955+; Minutes, 1958+, 14 vols;
Newsletter, 1964+; Scrapbooks, 1909-30, 1947-68. KC

872. Croatian American Club (1941)
        798 Grant Street, Akron, Ohio 44311
        (216) 253-0477   (M-F 10-5)
        Kaddie Phillips, Business Manager

Administrative records, 1945-50, 1965+, 5 lf; Annual reports, 1945+,
5 lf; Correspondence, 1950s+, 3 lf; Financial statements, 5 lf; Minutes, 1945+, 5 lf; Tax records, 1965+. DK

873. Employers Association of Akron
        First National Tower, Room 611, Akron, Ohio 44308
        (216) 253-9175   (M-F 8-5)
        A. L. Fleckinger, General Manager

Annual reports, 2 lf; Correspondence, 3 lf; Data on wages of rubber
company employees, 1914+, 10 lf; Minutes, 3 lf; Proceedings, 2 lf;
Scrapbooks, 1940+. DK

874. Firestone Tire and Rubber Company (1900)
        1200 Firestone Parkway, Akron, Ohio 44317
        (M-F 9-5)
        Historian, Firestone Tire and Rubber Company

Camping trips, 1915, 1916, 1918, 1919, 1920, 1921, 1923, 1924,
includes photographs, clippings, diaries, and two publications, In
Nature's Laboratory (1916) and Our Vacation Days (1918), covering
the eight trips taken by Harvey Firestone, Henry Ford, Thomas
Edison, John Burroughs, and others, 5 lf; Development department
files, 1906-40, selected folders pertaining to product development,
particularly passenger, truck-bus, tractor and implement tires, 4
lf; Firestone Company files: advertising mailings and samples, 1900+,
clipping files, 1912+, magazine advertising, 1901+, advertising
proofs and tear sheets classified by subject or name of items featured,
photograph file, 1903+, publication files, 1916+, 52 lf; Harvey S. Firestone, business files, 1900-1921, 10 lf; Harvey S. Firestone, Jr., far
eastern trip files, Jan-May 1926, pertaining to rubber estates and
various rubber growing activities and conditions throughout the coun-
tries visited, 1 lf. GK

875. First Congregational Church, Akron (1832)
        292 East Market, Akron, Ohio 44304
        (216) 253-5109   (M-F 9-5; Sat 9-12)
        Harold H. Hibbard, Church Administrator

Administrative records, 1895+, 2 lf; Financial statements, 1903-18, 1926, 3 in.; Minutes, 1876-1902, 1921-35, 6 in.; Photographs, 1843+, 1 lf; Publications, 1870+, 2 in.; Scrapbooks, 1930-34, clippings concerning church and members, 1 lf.   KS

876. First Congregational Church, Hudson (1802)
        47 Aurora Street, Hudson, Ohio 44236
        (216) 653-6641   (M-F 8-5)
        G. F. Lane, Historian

Administrative records, 1802, 1817; Annual reports, 1945-50, 2 in.; Cashbooks, 1931-45; Church registers, 1802+, 1 lf; Correspondence, 1949-63; Deeds to present property, 1863; Journals, 1941-45; Minutes, 1840+, 1 lf; Photographs, late 19th century, 6 in.; Publications, 100th, 125th, and 150th anniversary texts; Society records, 1863-1958, 2 in. KS

877. First Presbyterian Church, Akron (1831)
        647 East Market Street, Akron, Ohio 44304
        (216) 434-5183   (M-F 8:30-4:30)
        Dorothy Campbell, Administrative Assistant

Church register, 1841+, 14 in.; Financial statements, 1940-60s; Session minutes, 1888-1957, 1963+; Trustees correspondence, 1901-47. KS

878. German American Club (1910)
        834 Grant Street, Akron, Ohio 44304
        (216) 762-4114   (M-Sat 9-5)
        R. A. Schwinald, Manager

Administrative records, 1965+, 5 lf; Financial statements, 1950+; Inventories, 1950+; Minutes, 1965+, 5 lf; Monthly meeting records, 1968+, 10 lf; Receipts, 1950+; Tax records, 1965+, 5 lf.   DK

879. Goodyear Tire and Rubber Company (1898)
        1144 East Market Street, Akron, Ohio 44316
        (216) 794-3675   (M-F 8:15-5)
        Mrs. Cecil R. Norman, Archives Librarian

Annual reports, 1910+; Correspondence, 20th century, 100 lf; News releases, published and unpublished histories, 5 lf; Photographs, 1918, 15 lf; Publications, "Aerospace Clan," 1947, "Goodyear News," 1923+, "Overseas Newsletter," 1919, "Triangle," 1919+, "Wingfast Clan," 1912+, 10 lf; Scrapbooks, 1918+.   GK

880. High Street Christian Church (1839)
    131 South High Street, Akron, Ohio 44308
    (216) 434-1039
    Harry E. Smith, Pastor

Ledgers, 1892+, 3 lf; Minutes (official board, trustees, elders, deacons), 1881+, 5 lf; Publications,"Akron Disciple," 1900+, 6 lf, "Denominational Yearbooks," 1918, 1926+, 6 lf.   KS

881. International Institute (1946)
    207 East Tallmadge Avenue, Akron, Ohio 44310
    (216) 376-5106   (M-F 9-5)
    Maxine Floreani, Education Supervisor

Administrative records, 1946, 1 lf; Annual reports, 1946+, 1 lf; Board of trustees, minutes, 1946+, 1 lf; Casework files, 1946+, 40 lf; Education files, 1946+, 10 lf; Financial records, 1946+, 26 journals and 2 lf; Ledgers, 1946+, 26 journals; Newsletter, 1946+, 3 lf; Students' records, 1946+, 18 lf.   KC

882. International Union of Operators (1907)
    First National Tower, Akron, Ohio 44308
    (216) 762-1886   (M-F 9-5)
    Josephine Windows, Secretary

Administrative records, 1917+; Agreements, 1955+; Annual reports, 1917+; Cashbooks, 1960+; Contracts, 1955+; Correspondence, 1950+; Daybooks, 1950+; Financial statements, 1960+; Inventories, 1955+; Journals, 1940+; Ledgers, 1950+; Minutes, 1917+; Proceedings; Receipts, 1955+; 160 lf total.   DK

883. Italian American Citizens Club (1930s)
    1521 Ninth, Akron, Ohio 44306
    (216) 928-0904   (M-F 9-5, Sat 8-12)
    Carmen Pirzo, Manager-Secretary

Administrative records, 1950+, 5 lf; Agreements, 1960-70; Annual
reports, 1950+, 5 lf; Contracts, 1960-70; Financial statements;
Membership list, 1940+, 5 lf; Minutes, 1950+, 5 lf; Newsletter, 5
lf; Receipts; Tax records, 1964+. DK

884. Italian Center (1935)
        134 East Tallmadge Avenue, Akron, Ohio 44310
        (216) 535-3919   (M-F 8-12)
        Nick Rinaldi, Manager

Administrative records, 20 lf; Agreements, 1965+, 5 lf; Annual reports, 1965+; Contracts, 1965+, 5 lf; Inventories, 1965+, 5 lf;
Journals, 1950+, 10 lf; Minutes, 1965+, 10 lf. DK

885. Jaycees, Akron (1932)
        201 Delaware Building, Akron, Ohio 44308
        (216) 253-7086   (M-F 8-4:30)
        Mrs. Andrews, Secretary

Annual reports, 1932+; Correspondence, 1932+, 10 lf; Financial
statements, 1932+, 4 lf; Minutes, 1932+, 35 looseleaf binders;
Newsletter, "The Pub," 1932+; Scrapbooks, 1932+. KC

886. Poor People's Office (1966)
        502 Wooster Avenue, Akron, Ohio 44307
        (216) 253-3610   (M-F 9-4; Sat 8-1)
        Marian Hall, Manager

Administrative records, 1970+; Agreements, 1966+; Annual reports, 1970+; Caseworkers files, 1970+; Cashbooks; Contracts,
1966+; Financial statements; Inventories, 1966+; Minutes, 1970+;
20 lf total. DK

887. Republican Party, Summit County (1930)
        First National Tower, Akron, Ohio 44308
        (216) 434-9151   (M-F 9-5)
        Mrs. Francis Rex, County Chairwoman

Annual reports, 1950+, campaign and expense accounts; Financial
statements; Minutes, 1930+; Scrapbooks, 1930+; Voter returns and
precinct profiles, 1960+; 70 lf total. DK

888. Rotary Club of Akron (1914)
        Second National Building, Akron, Ohio 44308
        (M-F 9-5)
        Elmer A. Stevens, Assistant Secretary-Treasurer

Administrative records, 1914+; Correspondence, 1968+, 2 lf; Deeds,
1943+; Financial statements, 1932+, 10 lf; Minutes, 1914+, 8 lf; Publication, "Akrotarian," 1931+; Scrapbooks, 1915+; Tax records, 1915+.
KC

889. St. Mary's Church (1897)
        715 Coburn, Akron, Ohio 44310
        (216) 762-9247
        John Hilkert, Pastor

Annual reports, 1915+, 1 in.; Church register, 1895+, 3 lf; Contracts,
1915, 3 in.; Correspondence, 1913; Minutes, 1955+, 6 in.; Publications:
Church bulletins, 1965+, Church guide, 1911.   KS

890. St. Vincent Church (1837)
        164 West Market Street, Akron, Ohio 44308
        (216) 535-3135   (M 8-5)
        T. H. Corrigan, Pastor

Agreements, description of premises and original plans, 1837, 3 in.;
Church register, 1837+, 5 lf; Photographs, late 19th century+; Publication, church history, 1837-1937, 1 in.   KS

891. Sheet Metal Workers, Local Union No. 70 (1945)
        720 Wolf's Ledges, Room 203, Akron, Ohio 44304
        (216) 253-8151   (M-F 7:30-5; Sat 8-4)
        Robert Kidney, Business Manager

Administrative records, 1955+; Agreements, 1945+; Annual reports,
1945+; Cashbooks, 1945+; Contracts, 1945+; Daybooks, 1960+; Financial statements, 1960+; Journals, 1960+; Minutes, 1955+; Receipts,
1960+; Tax records, 7-year retention; 100 lf total.   DK

892. Stan Hywet Hall Foundation (1911-15)
        714 North Portage Path, Akron, Ohio 44303
        (216) 836-5533   (Tu-Sat 10-4:30; Sun 1-5)
        Robert Dimit, Executive Director

Joseph Nash color plates, 1906, 704 prints; Tudor architecture,
photos and measure drawings, 1911, 3 vols.   KS

893. Sumner Home for the Aged (1910)
      First National Tower, Akron, Ohio 44308
      (216) 535-6710   (M-F 9-5)
      Evan Rogers, Assistant Treasurer and Secretary

Administrative records, 1945+; Agreements, 1945+; Annual reports,
1945+; Contracts, 1945+; Correspondence, 1945+; Inventories; Minutes, 1945+; Proceedings, 1945+; Receipts, 1945+; 100 lf total.   DK

894. Trinity Lutheran Church (1868)
      50 North Prospect Street, Akron, Ohio 44304
      (216) 376-5154   (M 9-5; Sat 9-12)
      Ruth Simon, Archivist

Administrative records (includes church register, early constitution,
and organizational papers), 1879+, 10 lf; Annual reports, 1845+, 1 lf;
Building blueprints, 1914; Correspondence, 1942-60, 6 in.; Financial
statements, 1885-92, 6 in.; Minutes, church council and woman's missionary, 1870+, 4 lf; Publications, bulletins and church papers, 1920+,
5 lf; Scrapbooks, 20th century, 2 lf.   KS

895. United Methodist Church (1837)
      263 East Mill Street, Akron, Ohio 44308
      (216) 376-8143   (M, W, F 9-3)
      Audrey Marriot, Children's Director

Correspondence, 1935; Financial statements, 1845-1912, 1 in.; Minutes, 1920-34, 3 in.; Publications, scattered, 6 in.   KS

896. United Rubber, Cork, Linoleum, and Plastic Workers of America,
      International Headquarters (1935)
      87 South High Street, Akron, Ohio 44308
      (216) 376-6181   (M-Sat 8:30-5)
      Robert Strauber, Director of Education

Administrative records, 1935+; Agreements, 1935+; Contracts, 1935+;
Correspondence, 1935+; Miscellaneous, 1935+ (contracts, international
constitutions and proceedings, manuscripts including letters, broadsides,

legal documents, notes on speeches, etc., local union bylaws, photographs), 50 lf; Proceedings, 1935+.   GK

897. United Steel Workers of America, District Office (1959)
        320 East South Street, Akron, Ohio 44311
        (216) 376-9181   (M-F 9-4:30)
        Bill Tagart, Staff Representative

Administrative records, 1959+, 5 lf; Annual reports, 1959+; Contracts for local unions, 1959+, 10 lf; Correspondence, 1959+, 5 lf;
Inventories, 1959+, 5 lf; Minutes, 1959+, 5 lf; Receipts, 1959+, 5
lf. DK

898. WAKR Radio (1940)
        853 Copley Road, Akron, Ohio 44320
        (216) 535-7837   (M-F 9-5)
        Phyllis Jimns, Administrative Manager

Administrative records, 1940+; Annual reports, 1940+; Cashbooks,
1940+; Contracts, 1940+; Correspondence, 1969+; Deeds; Financial
statements; Inventories, 1940+; Journals, 1940+; Ledgers, 1940+;
Minutes, 1940+; Receipts, 1969+; Scrapbooks, 1940+; 200 lf total.
DK

899. YMCA, Akron (1870)
        80 West Center Street, Akron, Ohio 44308
        (216) 376-7711
        William Markell, Executive Director

Administrative records, 1950+, 4 lf; Annual reports, 1888-89,
1920+, 3 in.; Board of trustees, minutes, 1910-39, 1 lf; Correspondence, 1929, 1931; William H. Hunt collection, 1887-1943. KS

900. Zion Lutheran Church (1854)
        139 South High Street, Akron, Ohio 44308
        (216) 253-3136   (Hours by appointment)
        James Regallis, Historian

Bulletin, 1928-38, 1947+, 6 in.; Daybooks (early ones in German),
1892-1937, 6 in.; Photographs (confirmation classes with names),
1908-38, 6 in. KS

MANUSCRIPTS

901. Girard Free Library (1920)
        105 East Prospect, Girard, Ohio 44420
        (216) 545-6214   (M-F 11-9)
        John W. Creager, Librarian

Local history file, clippings from various area newspapers, principally 1928-32, filed by subject, 1928-73, 3 lf.   CB

902. Hubbard Public Library (1937)
        436 West Liberty, Hubbard, Ohio 44425
        (216) 534-3512   (M-Th 11-8:30; F 11-5:30; Sat 11-5)
        Mrs. Malin, Librarian

Local history file, Hubbard history scrapbooks and MSS studies of
Hubbard history by local residents.   CB

903. McKinley Memorial Library (1917)
        40 North Main Street, Niles, Ohio 44446
        (216) 652-3414   (M-F 9-5)
        Chester B. Stout, Librarian

Chinese memorial scroll, presented to President McKinley, 1901;
Responses to solicitations for the library building, 1901-17, 50 lf.
JWG

904. Trumbull County Historical Society
        309 South Street, Warren, Ohio 44483
        (216) 394-4653
        Aubrey Sparks, Director

Ledger book, local business, 1840-50, 1 item.   CB

905. Warren Public Library (1888)
        444 Mahoning Avenue, Warren, Ohio 44483
        (216) 339-8807   (M-F 9-9; Sat 9-5)
        Mrs. Stephens, Reference Librarian

Annual reports, 1966+, 6 in.; Board of education, minutes, 1968+:
City Federation of Women's Clubs, minutes, 1930-40, 6 in.;Garden

Club programs, 1904-63, 2 lf; Perkins Realty Co. ledgers, 1845-1955, 2 lf; Trumbull County Probate Court records, 1803-1921, 85 mf rolls. LS

INSTITUTIONAL RECORDS

906. First Baptist Church, Girard (1880)
        East Kline and North State Streets, Girard, Ohio 44420
        (216) 545-9178
        Rev. Allen, Pastor

Annual reports, 1949-50, 2 items; Bulletins, 1964+, 2 lf; Church register, 1890+, 2 vols; Correspondence (letters of dismission), 1941-56, 1 folder; Ledgers (collections and expenses), 1890-1910, 1 vol; Minutes (annual meetings, business meetings, board meetings), 1941+, 6 in.; Sunday school, minutes, 1931-42, 1 vol. CB

907. First Baptist Church, Hubbard (1819)
        59 Orchard Street, Hubbard, Ohio 44425
        (216) 534-3727
        Alfred Mott, Church Historian

William E. Coleman, tape recording of ordination, 1971; Photographs, 1860-1963; Register of pastors, 1819+. CB

908. First Presbyterian Church (1804)
        22 Westview Avenue, Hubbard, Ohio 44425
        Mrs. Merwin, Secretary

Bulletin, scattered issues; Church register, 1878-1956, 3 vols; Session minutes, 1871-1956, 6 in. CB

909. First United Methodist Church of Hubbard (1803)
        48 Church Street, Hubbard, Ohio 44425
        (216) 534-3383   (M-F 8:30-1)
        John Hinerman, Pastor

Administrative records, 1956+; Bible class roll books, 1931-38; Building committee, minutes, 1922-41, 1965-67; Bulletin, 1949-51;

Church Board of Christian Education, minutes, 1941-64; Church register, 1874-1955, 2 vols; Church school records, 1916-62, 18 in.; Death notices (clippings of newspaper obituaries of church members), 1963-69, 6 in.; Laboratory school records, 1959; Scrapbooks, history of Methodism in Hubbard, 1803-1950; Victory Bible Class, minutes, 1932-53; Women's Foreign Missionary Society, minutes, 1922-36; Women's Society, minutes, 1940-55.   CB

910. Liberty United Presbyterian Church (1805)
      1451 Girard-Hubbard Road, Youngstown, Ohio 44505
      (216) 759-1556
      Paul R. Graham, Pastor

Church register, 1870+, 3 vols; Minutes, 1805+, 1 lf; Publications, 1953+.   CB

911. Trumbull Baptist Association (1850)
      c/o Alfred Mott, R. D. 1, Masury, Ohio 44438

Administrative records, 1850-1954; MS history of the association, 1850-1914, by Bruce Rogers; Minutes, 1850-1955, 4 lf.   CB

TUSCARAWAS COUNTY

MANUSCRIPTS

912. Dover Historical Society (1958)
      P. O. Box 485, Dover, Ohio 44622
      (216) 343-8258   (F 1-3; Summer Tu-F 1-3)
      Mrs. George Wills, Secretary

Deardorff family papers, 1832-1914; Minutes of military meetings to raise funds by bounty, 1860-64; Publications (atlas, maps, reminiscences), 1807-78; River Dam agreement, 1852; Rush Township leases, 1877; Tax receipts for land, 1835-64.   KS

INSTITUTIONAL RECORDS

913. Claymont Public Library (1899)
      219-1/2 North Main, Urichsville, Ohio 44683
      (614) 922-3626   (M-Sat 10-8:30)
      G. Dunn, Head Librarian

Board of trustees, minutes, 1934+, 2 lf; Circulation books, 1934+, 1 lf; Ledgers, 1934+, 6 in.   KS

914. Ohio Apple Institute (1937)
        224 Park Avenue, New Philadelphia, Ohio 44663
        (216) 343-8412   (M, W, F, 9-1)
        N. Witherspoon, Director

Administrative records, 1937, 1 in.; Annual reports, 1937+, 1 in.; Financial statements, 1937+, 2 lf; Membership file, 1937+, 2 lf; Minutes, 1937-57, 6 in.; Publication, "Apple Grower Bulletin," 1937+, 1 lf; Publicity and apple production cost file, 1967+, 4 lf; Receipts,1952+, 3 lf. KS

915. Tuscarawas County District Library (1901)
        121 Fair Avenue NW, New Philadelphia, Ohio 44663
        (216) 364-4474   (M 9-8:30; F 9-6; Sat 9-5; Sat summer 9-1)
        Ruth Gibson, Children's Librarian

Building blueprints; Contracts, 1935-36, for building construction; Correspondence, building construction with WPA funds, 1935-36; Donahey cartoons; Ledgers, 1938-70, 1 lf; List of library subscribers, 1905-8; Minutes, 1901-70, 3 lf; Scrapbooks, 1952-70. KS

                          UNION COUNTY

MANUSCRIPTS

916. Marysville Public Library
        231 South Court, Marysville, Ohio 43040
        (513) 642-1876   (M, W, Th 11:30-8; Tu, F, Sat 11:30-5)
        Pauline McLaughlin, Librarian

Genealogical index of Delaware and Union Counties, by Margaret Main Bouic, 1970, 1 vol; Historical notes on Union and Delaware County families, by Margaret Main Bouic, 1 vol; A history of Scioto Township, Delaware County, by Margaret Main Bouic, 1 vol.   FH

917. Union County Historical Society (1949)
        246 West Sixth, Marysville, Ohio 43040
        (513) 642-2631   (Th 1:30-4:30, other hours by appointment)
        Mrs. W. S. Kennedy, Curator

Calliopean Society, treasurer and secretary's records, 1869-85, 5
vols; Chatauqua Ladies Study Club, secretary's book, 1890, 1 vol; Genealogies (Scott, Pangle and Violett families), 2 vols; Harriet Hazen, TS
MSS of short stories, 6 in.; Ella Dolbear Lee (illustrator), mementoes,
original proof paintings for book covers and magazines and illustrations
for Mother Goose stories and ads, 1867-1954, 1 vol; Marysville Choral
Union, records, 1894, 1 vol; Marysville High School photo album, 1 vol;
Photograph collection, n.d., 5 lf; Union County Agricultural Society, records of races, 1904, 1 vol; Union County Farmer's Institute, secretary's
book, 1893-1906, 1 vol; Union County Pioneer Association, minutes, 1875-
95, 1 vol; Woman's Foreign Missionary Society of the Presbyterian
Church, Milford Center, Ohio, secretary's book, 1898-99, 1 vol; York
Church, session minutes, 1839-70, 1 vol.   SF

INSTITUTIONAL RECORDS

918. Chamber of Commerce, Marysville Area (1959)
       109 South Main, Marysville, Ohio 43040
       (513) 642-3922   (M, Tu 9-5; W-Sat 9-12)
       Edward Hardin, Executive Secretary and Treasurer

Annual reports, 1959+; Financial statements, 1959+; Minutes, 1959+;
Monthly newsletter, "Chamber Report," 1964+; Receipts, 1959+; Tax
records, 1959+; 52 lf total.   SF

919. Congregational United Church of Christ (1864)
       126 West Sixth Street, Marysville, Ohio 43040
       (513) 642-1611   (M-F 9-12)
       Ronald Botts, Pastor

Administrative records, 1864, 1 vol; Annual reports, 1911+; Blues
Creek Church, records, 1889-1929; Church bulletin, 1907+; Church
register, ca. 1920+; Church school record, 1864+; Correspondence,
1940+; Financial statements, 1940s+; Minutes, 1864+; Missionary
Society records, ca. 1880+; Sermons, Rev. Botts, 1970+; 6 lf total.
SF

920. Conrad Monument Works (1865)
       132 North Main Street, Marysville, Ohio 43040
       (513) 642-4801   (M-Sat 9-4)
       Lawrence Donal, Owner

Contracts for memorial stones, includes inscriptions on stones, 1865,
5 lf; Correspondence, 1890s+; Publications, some old advertisements
of memorial stones.   FH

VAN WERT COUNTY

INSTITUTIONAL RECORDS

921.   Chamber of Commerce, Delphos
         Commercial Building, Room 1, Delphos, Ohio 45833
         (419) 695-1771   (M-F 9-4:30)
         Stan Wiechart, Executive Manager

Annual reports; Committee and board of trustees minutes; Correspondence; Financial records; Photographs; Project files; Publicity material;   all ca. 1950+; 48 lf total.   SF

922.   Trinity United Methodist Church
         211 East Third, Delphos, Ohio 45833
         (419) 692-0651   (M-F 9-12)
         H. Eugene Risch, Minister

Annual reports, 1841+; Attendance records; Board of trustees, minutes; Bulletins; Church register, 1841+; Correspondence, 10-year retention; Dedication programs (building); Financial records, 1954+ (some
earlier); Historical sketch of church, 1974, 20 pp; Membership records,
1841+; Pastors list; Sunday school records; Women's and men's organizations,records; ca. 8 lf total.   SF

VINTON COUNTY

MANUSCRIPTS

923.   Herbert Wescott Memorial Library (1934)
         122 West Main Street, McArthur, Ohio 45651
         (614) 596-5691   (M, Tu 1-8; W 4-5; F, Sat 9-5)
         Jeanette Grim, Librarian

Vinton County scrapbook collection, compiled by Roselle Hunter, ca.
1960+, 4 lf; Vertical file material on Vinton County, 1 lf.   RR

924. <u>Vinton County Historical Society (1950)</u>
    McArthur, Ohio 45651
    (614) 596-5400
    George L. Knox, Secretary, c/o McArthur Savings & Loan

McArthur Civic Club, minutes and membership rolls, 1915-64, 6 in.;
McArthur Hook and Ladder Company, McArthur, Ohio, by-laws, minutes, lists of officers, 1875-79, 1 in.   RR

WARREN COUNTY

MANUSCRIPTS

925. <u>Warren County Historical Society</u>
    105 South Broadway, Lebanon, Ohio 45036
    (513) 932-1817   (Tu-Sat 9-4; Sun 12-4)
    Elva Adams, Director

Church records of Lebanon churches, 20 mf reels; Manuscript material on Warren County and prominent families (including Thomas
Corwin family and Jeremiah Morrow family), diaries, letters, newspaper clippings, photographs, genealogical and biographical material.
SF

INSTITUTIONAL RECORDS

926. <u>Lebanon United Methodist Church</u>
    122-128 East Silver, Lebanon, Ohio 45036
    (513) 932-4834   (M-Sat 8-3)

Administrative board, minutes; Annual and monthly meetings, records;
Annual reports; Bulletins; Church history, booklet; Church register;
Correspondence; Financial records; Membership records; Programs;
Sermons; Sunday school records; Women's and men's organizations,rec-
ords; 1798+; 20 lf.   SF

MANUSCRIPTS

927. Marietta College Library
        Marietta, Ohio 45750
        (614) 373-4643   (M, Tu, W, F 9-12,1-5;Th 1-5, 7-10;Sat by appt.)
        Mrs. Robert L. Jones, Special Collections Assistant

Ephraim Cutler and William Parker Cutler, papers, 1795-1885, 4 lf;
C. G. Dawes, autographed letters and documents of international figures, last 400 years, 132 items, correspondence, 1791-1934, 6 in.;
Harry Philip Fischer, photographic plates and negatives of local interest, collection of photos of Ohio River steamboats, 1901-49, 35 lf;
Oscar C. Hayward, letters, documents, diaries of Washington County
family of Waterford, 1804-65, 1 lf; Hildreth collection, natural history,
science, geology, medical and meteorological observations, 1815-63, 9
vols; Stephen Durward Hoag, photographs of people and scenes of Marietta area, mid-1900s, 7 lf; Dr. John McBurney, educational history of
Southeast Ohio in 19th century, 18 in., sets of periodicals on gems and
minerals, 1892-1961, 10 lf; Miscellaneous manuscript collection, documents, letters, etc., mostly of local interest, 1583-1785, 1816+, 12 lf;
Ohio Company of Associates, documents, records, minute books, deeds,
letters, 1786-1815, 8lf; Rufus Putnam, MSS, letters, surveys, field notes,
1 lf; Charles Goddard Slack collection (autographed single-page letters
and documents by leading Americans, 1500 framed, 200 unframed);Sloan
Collection, local genealogical records, colonial times-1963, 18 in.;
Strong-Dawes collection (correspondence of Wilbur D. Matson, editor
of Morgan County Herald, McConnelsville, Ohio, and Herbert Hoover),
1915-65, 6 in.; Charles Van Pelt philately collection, international
postage stamps, mounted in albums, 1 lf.   RR

928. Washington County Public Library
        615 Fifth Street, Marietta, Ohio 45750
        (614) 373-1057   (M-F 9-8:30; Sat 9:30-5)
        R. Mark Neyman, Director

Nye family collection, letters, account books, memorabilia, 1840-1939.
FH

INSTITUTIONAL RECORDS

929. Community Action Organization (1965)
        243 Front, Marietta, Ohio 45750
        (614) 373-3745   (M-F 8:30-5)
        Anthony Mele, Director

Administrative records, 1965; Agreements, 1966+; Annual reports, 1966+; Contracts, 1966+; Correspondence, 1966+; Financial records, 1966+; Inventories, 1966+; Publication, 1969, 3 in.; Scrapbooks, ca. 1966; Tax records, 1966; 90 lf total.   FH

930. Marietta Daily Times (1864)
        700 Channel Lane, Marietta, Ohio 45750
        (614) 373-2121   (M-F 8:30-4)
        William McKinney, General Manager

Annual reports, 1954+; Correspondence, 2-year retention; Financial records, 1921+, 5 vols; Minutes, 1907+; Newspaper morgue, 1969+; Personnel records, ca. 1925+; Publication, Times, 1864-91, 1900+, mf; Tax records, ca. 1920+; Stock book, 1908-54.   RR

931. United Appeal, Marietta (1928)
        319 Scammel, Marietta, Ohio 45750
        (614) 373-3333   (M-F 9-5)
        Julia Waggoner, Executive Secretary

Administrative records, 1 in., Contracts with sponsored service agencies, 1 in.; Correspondence, 2-3 year retention; Ledgers, 1966+; Minutes, 1939+, 2 lf; Pledge cards, 5-year retention; Scrapbooks, 1949+, 3 lf. RR

WAYNE COUNTY

MANUSCRIPTS

932. Wayne County Historical Society (1904)
        546 East Bowman, Wooster, Ohio 44691
        (216) 264-8856   (Tu-Sun 2-4:30)
        Mrs. Martin Baughan, 1029 Berger Dr., Wooster, Ohio 44691

Deeds, 1808, 100 lf; Journals from various early businesses, ca. 1850, 4 lf; Minutes, women's club and board of education, 1850-1900, 3 lf; Plats, first town maps, 1811; Proceedings, early town records, 1808; Publications, 1864 scattered, county atlases, 1853, 1897, old Bibles, 98 lf. KS

INSTITUTIONAL RECORDS

933. Ohio Agricultural Experiment Station (1882)
        Wooster, Ohio 44691
        (216) 264-1021   (M-F 8-5)
        William Krauss, Associate Director

Annual reports, 1882+, 3 lf; Correspondence of Dr. C. Thorne, first
director, 1887-1921; Inventories, 1966; Ledgers, 1892+; Minutes,
1905+, 8 lf; Publications, monographs and circular, 1882+, 39 lf; Receipts, 1948-66.   KS

934. Wayne County Library (1895)
        304 Market Street, Wooster, Ohio 44691
        (216) 262-0416   (M-F 9-9; Sat 9-6)
        Margaret Hauenstein, Head Librarian

Minutes, 1895, 3 lf; Proceedings, Penn.-German Society, 1890-1935,
7 lf; Publications, 1895+, 14 lf.   KS

                          WILLIAMS COUNTY

INSTITUTIONAL RECORDS

935. Bryan Library
        107 East High Street, Bryan, Ohio 43506
        (419) 352-5292   (M-F 2-8:30; Sat 10-5)
        William M. Potts, Librarian

Annual reports, 1958+; Correspondence, 1960+, 3 lf; Minutes, 1958+,
3 lf.   PY

936. The Bryan Times - The Bryan Press
        127 South Walnut, Bryan, Ohio 43506
        (419) 636-1111   (M-F 8-5)
        Ford Cullis, Publisher

Annual reports, 1950+; Board of directors, minutes, 1950+, 1 vol;
Employees files, 1955+, 1 lf; Negatives, 1959-63, 1 lf; Photo files,
1965+, 4 lf.   PY

937. Bryce Publications, Inc. (1968)
      325 North Jonesville Street, Montpelier, Ohio 43543
      (419) 485-3113   (M-F 8-5)
      Hugh Fullerton, Editor

Administrative records, 1968; Annual reports, 1968+; Minutes, 1968+;
Payroll records, 1951+.   TS

                          WOOD COUNTY

MANUSCRIPTS

938. Northwest Ohio-Great Lakes Research Center
      214-A Graduate Building, Bowling Green State University
      Bowling Green, Ohio 43403
      (419) 372-2474   (M-F 8-5)
      Richard Wright, Director, and Paul Yon, Archivist

American Red Cross, Ottawa County, records, 1917-19, 4 vols; Anchor
Oil and Gas Company, records, 1916, 1 vol; Auto Hospital Car Repair
Co., ledgers, 1921-24, 3 vols; Bay City Building and Loan Association,
records, 1868-77, 1 vol; The B.D. and W. Equipment Co., records,
1923, 1 vol; Beecher P. Brown Construction Co., ledger, 1905-6, 1 vol;
Blatz-Daugherty Co., records, 1912-15, 2 vols; The Builders of Memo-
rials Co., stock records, 1917-18, 2 vols; C. W. Campbell (Hardin
County farmer), diaries and business records, 1876-1932, 9 folders;

Canaan E.U.B. Church, Kansas, Ohio, records, 1854-1917, 3 vols and
2 folders; The Central Ohio Traction Co., records, 1901-3, 1 vol and 1
folder; The Cleveland, Cincinnati, Chicago, and St. Louis Railroad Co.,
car and seal record, 1917, 1 vol; The Co-operative Foundry and Machine
Co., stock records, 1893-97, 1 vol; The Curtice State Bank, minutes,
1919-31, 1 vol; The R. J. Dann Flavoring Co., records, 1916-18, 1 vol;
Delphos Woolen Mills, financial records, 1873-79, 2 vols; C. F. Denzer
Co., account books, 1930-35, 2 vols; E.I.B. and Co. (grocers and hardware), financial records, 1860-62, 2 vols;

Erie County Agricultural Society, records, 1921-31, 3 vols and 1 folder;
The Eureka Manufacturing Co., records, 1922-23, 1 vol and 1 folder;
Farmers' and Citizens' Banking Co., 1910-54, 8 boxes and 24 vols; The
Farmers Livestock Co., records, 1920-24, 1 vol; Farrell-Cheek Steel
Foundry Co., records, 1917, 1 folder; The Findlay Tooth-Pick Co., rec-
ords, 1893-94, 1 vol; First Presbyterian Church of Maumee, records,

1820-1969, 1 box; The Fostoria Foundry and Machine Co., records, 1904-5, 1 vol; Arthur C. Frederickson Collection, clippings, journals, logs, 1872-1965, 7 lf and 88 vols;

Golden Rule Aid Co., stock records, 1880-95; Great Lakes Ship photographs and port scenes, 1800+, 40,000 items; The Goosman Transfer and Storage Co., records, 1907-12, 1 vol; Grand Army of the Republic, Bowling Green, minutes, 1907-31, 1 vol; Green and Heilman Co., cashbook, 1890-92, 1 vol; A. C. Hershberger (Sycamore merchant), cash journal, 1902-5, 1 vol; George E. Hirsch Lumber Co., financial records, 1882-1927, 23 vols; Hotel Morcher, register, 1895, 1 vol; Henry Hubach Brewery, ledger, 1888-1912, 1 vol; The Jeffery Pickle & Kraut Co., account book, 1930-31, 3 folders;

Kelley Ice Cream Co., records, Jan 1925; The Klay Manufacturing Co., minutes, 1909-10, 1 vol; M. E. Kriss Co., financial records, 1899-1906, 3 vols; Lake View Summer Resort Hotel, Catawba Island, registers, 1891-1914, 2 vols; Lima Dime Savings Bank, minutes, 1924-27, 2 vols; J. R. McCord (railway excursion manager), scrapbook, 1908, 1 vol and 1 folder; Marine Historical Society of Detroit Archives, logs, scrapbooks, ship histories, 1679+, 7 boxes, 50,000 3x5 cards, and 12 lf; Maudelton Hotel Co., records, 1906, 1 vol and 1 folder; Miami Military Institute roll book, 1921-22, 1 vol;

Miscellaneous Great Lakes industries, corporate records, 1816+, 112 lf, 105 vols, 69 mf rolls, and 4 movie film rolls; The Mount Victory Bank, minutes, 1904-18, 1 vol; The National Railway Signal Co., records, 1910, 1 vol and 1 folder; Naval architectural drawings, 1888-1920, 300 items; New Galt House, register, 1895-96, 1 vol; New York Central & Hudson River Railroad, blueprints, 1915, 3 vols; New York Central Railroad Company, subway blueprints, 1918, 1 folder; The Oil Well Salvage Co., records, 1902-8, 1 vol and 1 folder; Perrysburg, Findlay, and Kenton Turnpike Road Co., records, 1844, 1 vol; Phillips House Hotel, register, 1875, 1 vol; Port Clinton Canning Co., records, 1900-1903, 5 vols;

The Republic Banking Co., cashbook, 1917-19, 1 vol; The Rising Sun Investment Co., cashbook, 1904, 1920-21, 1 vol; W. D. Robbins Co. (monument company), grave identification record, 1890-94, 1 vol; RockRiver Water-Power Silver Mining Co., stock books, 1869, 1 vol; J. K. Rohn Co., ledger, 1882-1901, 1 vol; The Sandusky Improvement and Investment Co., correspondence, 1894-96, 1 vol; Sandusky Seat Co., financial records, 1875-81, 2 vols; Sandusky Street Railway Co., records, 1881-93, 1 vol; Caspar Schraid (wine dealer), records, 1865-1924, 1 box; The Scioto Land Co., financial records, 1927-36, 2 vols;

Second National Bank, Sandusky, cashbook, 1930-31, 1 vol; The Seneca Driving Park Co., financial records, 1892-95, 1 vol; S. L. and C. Co., freight ledger and shipping record, 1890-98, 1 vol; Sloane Hotel, financial records, 1927-34, 2 vols; S. M. and Co., financial records, 1852-54, 1 vol; Sorgel Dorn and Raibel Co., cashbook, 1866-68, 1 vol; Spencerville Star Woolen Manufacturing Co., 1875-76, 1 vol; Sweet Valley Products Co., correspondence, 1920-22, 1 folder; Sweet Valley Wine Co., correspondence, 1901-2, 1 folder;

Tiffin Nail Co., cash ledger, 1888-90, 1 vol; Union Grange, records, 1898-1957, 3 boxes; The Wagner Lake Ice & Coal Co., stock records, 1899-1910, 2 vols; F. W. Wakefield Brass Co., records, 1910-62, 14 boxes; War Fund Committee, Port Clinton, cashbook, 1918-19, 1 vol; The West Huron Sporting Club Co., records, 1888-1908, 1 vol; Richard J. Wright Great Lakes Marine Collection, corporate records, logs, research notes, scrapbooks, 1679+, 45,000 3x5 index cards, 257 vols, and 8 mf reels. PY

INSTITUTIONAL RECORDS

939. American Cancer Society, Wood County Unit (1949)
      115 West Oak Street, Bowling Green, Ohio 43402
      (419) 354-2553   (M-F 1-4)
      Mrs. Harry Wagner, Executive Director

Annual reports, 1961+; Board of directors, minutes, 1949+; Correspondence; Pictures, 1960s; Publications, current; Receipts; Scrapbooks, 1950s, 1 vol. TS

940. Bank of Wood County Company (1931)
      130 South Main Street, Bowling Green, Ohio 43402
      (419) 352-5292   (M, Tu, Th, F 8:30-3; W 8:30-12)
      Don L. King, Secretary and Treasurer

Administrative records, 1931; Annual reports, 1931+; Board of directors, executive committee, minutes, 1931+; Correspondence, 1931+; Employees newspaper, 1969+; Scrapbooks, 1931+, 2 filing envelopes. TS

941. Bar Association, Wood County (1901)
      Wood County Courthouse, Law Library, Bowling Green, Ohio 43402
      (M, W 9-4)
      Evelyn Bachman, Secretary

Annual reports (includes financial records of the bar association as well
as records of the law library such as books purchased), 1933+, 5 lf; Correspondence, 1953+, 2 lf; Wood County Law Library Association, minutes, 1901-35, 1941+, 3 vols and 2 lf.   PY

942.   Bowling Green State University Archives (1967)
          University Library, Room 311, Bowling Green, Ohio 43403
          (419) 372-2973   (M-F 8-5)
          Steve Morton, University Archivist and Rare Books Librarian

Twenty-four record series in archives, 1910+; Administration, miscellaneous; Harold Anderson, scrapbooks, 1942-63, 26 vols; Board of regents;
Carroll County manuscript collection, ca. 1902, 1 vol; College of Arts and
Sciences; Councils and committees; Faculty Senate; Graduate school, miscellaneous; Graduate study programs; Improving university climate; Johnson's Island collection, 1862-64, 7 vols; Journalism department, photographs; Clayton C. Kohl, papers; Edwin Lincoln Moseley, papers; News
releases from university news service, 1946+, 17 lf; Office of the president; Office of the vice-president of student affairs; Ohio Theatre history,
compiled by Clyde Franklin, 1920s-50s, 18 lf; Religious activities committee;
Search and screening committee; University library; University relations
and alumni affairs; Vice-president for research and financial affairs;
Homer B. Williams, papers; Writings of faculty members (incompl); 400
lf total.   TS

943.   Chamber of Commerce, Bowling Green (1936)
          143 East Wooster Street, Bowling Green, Ohio 43402
          (419) 353-7945   (M-F 9-12, 1-5)
          Robert E. Hoagland, Executive Manager

Annual reports, 1948+; Correspondence, 1948+; Events promoted by the
Chamber of Commerce, 1960-62; Minutes, 1948+; Publications, current,
25 titles; Scrapbooks, 1948+, 8 vols; 15 lf total.   TS

944.   First Methodist Church
          200 West Second Street, Perrysburg, Ohio 43551
          (419) 874-4445   (M-F 8-12)
          Wheaton Webb, Pastor

Building committee, minutes, 1928-31, 1 vol; Epworth League, minutes,
1902-15, 1 vol; Expense books, 1877-1905, 1873-1907, 1920-25, 3 vols;
Ladies Aid Society, ledger, 1923-40, 1 vol, record book, 1933-42, 1 vol;

Leaders meetings, record of proceedings, 1849-62, 1 vol; Official board book, 1915-25, 1 vol; Quarterly conference record, 1835-1913, 1916+, 10 vols; Subscription record, 1872-90, 1916, 2 vols; Sunday school records, 1875-1931, 41 vols; Mary W. Taneyhill Class record, 1909-42, 1 vol; Treasurer's account book, 1909-42, 2 vols; Trustees books, 1854-84, 1 vol; Win-a-Couple Class records, 1928-35, 1 vol; Womans Society of Christian Service, minutes, 1942-52, 1 vol. T S

945. First National Bank (1952)
     222 South Main Street, Bowling Green, Ohio 43402
     (419) 352-5271   (M-F 8:30-3)
     Lois A. Morlock, Executive Vice-President

Administrative records, 1952, 1964; Annual reports, 1952+; Board of directors and shareholders, minutes, 1952+, 3 lf; Employee newspaper, 1962+; Scrapbooks, 1952+, 5 vols; Tax records, 1952+.   TS

946. First Presbyterian Church
     126 South Church Street, Bowling Green, Ohio 43402
     (419) 352-5176   (M-F 9-12, 1-4)
     Greer S. Imbrie, Minister

Baptismal record, 1916-33, 1 vol; Certificates of dismission and reception, 1950-67, 1 vol; Church registers, 1855+, 5 vols; Financial secretaries' cashbooks, 1930-64, 1 vol; Guest register, 1950-67, 1 vol; Presbyweds meetings minutes, 1953-65, 1 vol; Session minutes, 1896+, 7 vols; Trustees' records, 1909-65, 2 vols.   TS

947. North Baltimore Public Library
     North Main, North Baltimore, Ohio 45872
     (419) 257-6601   (M-F 10-6)
     Mrs. Thompson, Head Librarian

Correspondence, 1969+; Minutes, 1920+; Personal interviews with local residents concerning oil boom and oil history, 3 lf; Photographs of North Baltimore.   PY

948. Way Public Library
     Perrysburg, Ohio 43551
     (M-F 10-5:30, 6:30-8:30; Sat 9:30-5)
     Martha Hoffman, Librarian

Accession catalogue, 1881-1922, 1 vol; Annual reports; Membership register, 1881-1925, 1 vol; Minutes, 1881+, 3 vols.   PY

949. Weston Public Library
        Main Street, Weston, Ohio 43569
        (419) 669-3415
        Mary Gault, Librarian

Annual reports, 1965+, 4 lf; Photographs of Weston, 1890-1950, 3 lf. PY

950. WMGS Radio
        138 North Main Street, Bowling Green, Ohio 43402
        (419) 354-6612   (M 8:30-5)
        Carl A. Cook, Ex Vice-President

Annual reports, 1954+, 3 lf; Correspondence, 1968+, 7 lf; Minutes, 1954+, 2 lf; News releases, 1969+, 5 lf; Radio logs, 1969+, 10 lf. PY

951. Wood County District Public Library (1929)
        304 North Church Street, Bowling Green, Ohio 43402
        (419) 353-0504   (M-W, F 10-8:30; Th, Sat 10-5)
        Marion Parker, Head Librarian

Bowling Green Library Association, constitution, list of subscribers, account books, 1875-87, 2 vols; Subscription lists, circulation record, 1914-28, 6 vols; Town & Gown Club, minutes and papers submitted, 1927+, 5 lf.   TS

952. Wood County Monumental Works
        121 East Court, Bowling Green, Ohio 43402
        (419) 354-3463   (M-F 8-5; Sat 9-12)
        Art Carr, Office Manager

Contracts (name, date, type of monument, inscription, date of birth and death, name of cemetery), 1910+, 15 lf; Correspondence, 1939-41, 2 boxes; Minutes, 1931+, 3 vols.   PY

MANUSCRIPTS

953. Wyandot County Historical Society (1929)
        130 South Seventh Street, Upper Sandusky, Ohio 43351
        (419) 294-3857   (Tu 10-12, 1-5; W-Sun 1-5)
        Nina Myers, Curator

Diaries, local residents, 1 lf; Newspaper clippings, unpublished histories, 16 lf.   PY

INDEX

This index contains four types of entries: titles of institutions whose
holdings were inventoried (capital letters); cities included in the survey, cross referenced to the counties in which they are located; titles
of collections held by the repositories surveyed (lower case letters);
and a subject listing. The numbers in the entries refer to collection
entry numbers in this guide.

Subjects have been grouped in broad categories, which selectively
list topics of general interest. The subject index includes only institutional and organizational entries for the following categories:

>
> Agriculture
> Black organizations and institutions
> Business
>   Finance
>   Manufacturing and industry
>   Retail
>   Service
> Civic organizations
> Community services and welfare organizations
> Communications
> Cultural organizations and institutions
> Fraternal and social organizations
> Hospitals
> Labor unions
> Professional organizations
> Religion
> Transportation
> Women

INDEX

AMERICAN FEDERATION OF
STATE, COUNTY, AND
MUNICIPAL EMPLOYEES
(CINCINNATI), 374
American Flint Glassworkers
Union No. 30, 496
American Institute of Architects,
Cincinnati Chapter, 364
AMERICAN JEWISH ARCHIVES,
362
AMERICAN LUTHERAN
CHURCH--OHIO DISTRICT,
270
AMERICAN MANUFACTURERS
EXPORT ASSOCIATION, 827
American Psychological
Association, Divisions 6 and
16, 855
AMERICAN RED CROSS:
ASHTABULA, 19; CANTON,
828; CLEVELAND, 118;
DAYTON, 658; FAIRFIELD
COUNTY CHAPTER, 245;
HAMILTON AREA CHAPTER,
38; LORAIN COUNTY, 523;
MANSFIELD, 781; MEDINA
COUNTY, 631; MIAMI
COUNTY, 649; Newark, 494;
Ottawa County, 938; PAINES-
VILLE, 481; SENECA
COUNTY, 811; STEUBEN-
VILLE, 464
Amherst, see Lorain County
AMOS MEMORIAL LIBRARY
(SIDNEY), 820
ANCHOR-HOCKING GLASS
COMPANY (LANCASTER),
246
Anchor Oil and Gas Company,
938
Anderson, Harold, 942
Andrews, George W., 522
Angell, Thomas G., 22
Angus, Donald J., 100
The Anna School, 820
Anthroposophical Society of
America, 364

APPALACHIAN HARDWOOD
MANUFACTURERS, 375
ARCHDIOCESAN DEPARTMENT
FOR SOCIAL ACTION
(CINCINNATI), 376
ARCHIVES OF THE HISTORY OF
AMERICAN PSYCHOLOGY, 855
Archives of Medical History, 368
ARCHIVES OF THE OHIO SYNOD
OF THE LUTHERAN CHURCH
IN AMERICA, 61
Archives of Science and Tech-
nology, 100
AREA PROGRESS BOARD
(AKRON), 865
Arlitt, Ada Hart, 368
ARMCO STEEL CORPORATION,
39
Arnett, Benjamin, 357
Arnold, Dwight L., 765
Arnot family, 347
Ascher, Karl Wolfgang, 368
Ashland, see Ashland County
Ashtabula, see Ashtabula County
ASHTABULA COUNTY DISTRICT
LIBRARY, 14
THE ASPHALT INSTITUTE, 271
Association of Fenn College
Women, 155
Athens, see Athens County
Athens County Historical Society,
22
Atkins, Frank Pearce, 364
Atkinson, Andrew J., 368
AUGLAIZE COUNTY PUBLIC
LIBRARY, 24
AULTMAN HOSPITAL
(CANTON), 829
Aurora, see Portage County
AURORA HISTORICAL SOCIETY,
763
Auto Hospital Repair Company,
938
Avon Lake, see Lorain County
AVON LAKE PUBLIC LIBRARY,
517

282.

Babies and Children's Hospital
(Cleveland), 202
Bailey, Daniel, 367
Bailey, Parker, 105
Baird, Esther E., 822
Baldwin, Frank L., 823
Baldwin, Henry R., 598
Baldwin Piano Company, 364
BALDWIN-WALLACE
COLLEGE ARCHIVES, 119
Ball, Archie, 16
Ballard, Addison, 22
Balough, Louis, 105
THE BANK OF HENRY COUNTY,
439
BANK OF WOOD COUNTY
COMPANY, 940
BAR ASSOCIATIONS:
AKRON, 867; COLUMBUS,
288; DAYTON, 659; OHIO
STATE, 324; STARK COUNTY,
830; TOLEDO, 544; WOOD
COUNTY, 941
Barberton, see Summit County
BARBERTON PUBLIC
LIBRARY, 853
Barnes, George, 127
Barnes, James, 27
Barnesville, see Belmont
County
BARNEY CHILDREN'S
MEDICAL CENTER
(DAYTON), 660
Barney, Roderick D., 368
Barnhorn, Clement, 363
Barnum, George, 98
Barnum, John, 106
Barrows, Elijah P., 522
Barton, Frederick B., 852
Batavia, see Clermont County
Bateman, Warner M., 364
Bates family, 364
Bates, Gaylord S., 769
Bay City Building and Loan
Association, 938
Bay Village, see Cuyahoga
County

Bay Village Women's Club, 111
The B.D. and W. Equipment
Company, 938
Bebb, Even and William, 35
Beck, Claude S., 202
Beck, G. W., 76
Beck, Johann, 105
Bedford, see Cuyahoga County
Bedford Baptist Church, 98
BEDFORD HISTORICAL
SOCIETY, 98
Bedford Methodist Church, 98
Bedford Municipal Hospital, 98
BEDFORD TIMES REGISTER,
120
Beech, Maude, 351
Beer, Aaron, 365
Belhobek, Jeanie, 106
Bellaire, see Belmont County
Bellamy, George, 769
Bellefontaine, see Logan County
Belleville, see Richland County
BELLEVILLE STAR, 782
Bells Opera House, 442
Benesch, Alfred, 108
Bentley, Henry, 364
Bentleyville Village, see
Cuyahoga County
Berea, see Cuyahoga County
BEREA NEWS SUN, 121
Berge, Carol, 765
Bergsland, Theodora, 202
BETTER BUSINESS BUREAU:
Akron, 855; AKRON, 868;
CINCINNATI, 384; CLEVE-
LAND, 122; COLUMBUS, 272;
LIMA, 9; STARK COUNTY,
831; TOLEDO, 545
Bettman, Alfred and Gilbert,
368
Bexley, see Franklin County
B.F. GOODRICH COMPANY,
866
Bickham, W.D., 652
Bidault, Georges, 765
Bierce, Ambrose, 368
BIG BEAR STORES, 273

Bigelow, Herbert Seeley, 364
BIGELOW UNITED METHODIST
  CHURCH (PORTSMOUTH),
  804
Binkley, Robert C., 127
BIRCHARD PUBLIC LIBRARY
  OF SANDUSKY COUNTY, 799
Bishop, Robert Hamilton, 35
Black organizations, 116, 126,
  253, 290, 425, 655, 843, 850
Black, Robert Lounsbury, 364
Blair, Charles, 855
Blatz-Daugherty Company, 938
Bluffton, see Allen County
BLUFFTON COLLEGE
  ARCHIVES, 10
BLUFFTON COLLEGE
  LIBRARY, 8
Blum, Robert, 363
BOARD OF REALTORS:
  CLEVELAND AREA, 141;
  DAYTON AREA, 669;
  LANCASTER, 251; TOLEDO,
  546
Bobko, John, 106
Bolitho, Hector, 765
Bonebrake Theological Seminary
  (Dayton), 724
Bonham, Lewellyn, 35
BOOKBINDERS LOCAL NO. 199
  (DAYTON), 661
Booker family, 647
BORDEN, INC., 274
Bostwick, Mrs. L.R., 586
Bothwell, Jean, 765
Boutelle, Louise M., 105
Bowling Green, see Wood County
BOWLING GREEN STATE
  UNIVERSITY ARCHIVES, 942
BOY SCOUTS OF AMERICA:
  FIRELANDS COUNCIL, 234;
  TOLEDO AREA COUNCIL,
  547; NEWARK, 497
BOY'S CLUBS: CLEVELAND,
  123; DAYTON, 671
Brackney family, 24
Bradley, Dan B., 522

Bradshaw, John W., 522
Brecksville, see Cuyahoga
  County
BRECKSVILLE BRANCH,
  CUYAHOGA COUNTY
  PUBLIC LIBRARY, 106
BRECKSVILLE HISTORICAL
  ASSOCIATION, 99
Brett, Dorothy, 368
Brett, William Howard, 153
BREWERY WORKERS INTER-
  NATIONAL UNION
  (CINCINNATI), 377
Brewery Workers Union No. 47,
  496
Bricker, John W., Sr., 219
Bridgman, Ralph P., 368
Briol, Paul, 367
BROADWAY UNITED
  METHODIST CHURCH
  (CLEVELAND), 125
BRONZE RAVEN (TOLEDO),
  548
Brooklyn, see Cuyahoga County
Brookpark, see Cuyahoga County
BROOKPARK BRANCH,
  CUYAHOGA COUNTY PUBLIC
  LIBRARY, 106
Brotherhood of St. Andrew, 159
Brough, John, 364
Beecher P. Brown Construction
  Company, 938
Brown family, 823
Brown, Jeremiah and John, 854
Brown, Capt. Luther, 62
Brown, Rudston, 63
Bruccoli, M. J., 765
Brush, Charles F., 100
Bryan, see Williams County
BRYAN LIBRARY, 935
THE BRYAN TIMES, 936
Bryant, Billy, 105
BRYCE PUBLICATIONS, INC.,
  937
Buckingham, William D., 100
Bucyrus, see Crawford County
Buffalo Mission, 174

Harter family, 823
Hartupee, G. H., 220
Hartville, see Stark County
Hatch, Homer B., 105
Hatch, William Stanley, 364
Hawey, Alta, 34
Hayden, Elizabeth S., 769
RUTHERFORD B. HAYES
 LIBRARY, 800
Hayward, Oscar C., 927
Hazen, Harriet, 917
Heald, Edward T., 765
HEALTH AND WELFARE PLAN-
 NING COUNCIL (DAYTON),
 685
HEBREW UNION COLLEGE-
 JEWISH INSTITUTE OF
 RELIGION, 365
Hecht, Frederick, 368
Hecker, John, 112
Heckman, Katherine and Warren,
 24
Heinle, Robert W., 202
C. & A. Henking General Store,
 347
HENDERSON MEMORIAL
 LIBRARY (JEFFERSON), 17
HENNY PENNY CORPORATION,
 776
Henry, Charles, Frederick,
 Marcia, and Simon, 769
Herald, E. T., 825
Herna, Eugene, 519
Herrick, Francis H., 127
Herron family, 737
Herschberger, A. C., 938
Hess, Snyder and Company, 823
Heydler, Charles, 105
Hibben Dry Goods Store, 442
Hickenlooper, Andrew, 364
HIGH STREET CHRISTIAN
 CHURCH (AKRON), 880
HIGHLAND COUNTY DISTRICT
 LIBRARY, 441
HIGHLAND COUNTY HISTOR-
 ICAL SOCIETY, 442
Hilliard, see Franklin County
HILLIARD UNITED PRESBY-
 TERIAN CHURCH, 303

Hillsboro, see Highland County
Hinckley, see Medina County
HINCKLEY GRANGE NO. 1347,
 638
Hind, Arthur M., 103
Hinsdale, Burke Aaron, 769
Hiram, see Portage County
HIRAM COLLEGE ARCHIVES,
 769
HIRAM TOWNSHIP HISTOR-
 ICAL SOCIETY, 764
George E. Hirsch Lumber
 Company, 938
Historical Society of Northwest
 Ohio, 542
Hite, Isaac, 648
Hitt, Daniel, 220
Hoag, Stephen Durward, 927
Hoban, Edward F., 128
Hobbs, William A., 522
Hoffman, Charles W., 364
Hoffman, Daniel, 368
Hoffman, William, family, 212
HOLDEN ARBORETUM, 484
Holland, Clifford M., 100
Hollingworth, Harry and Leta,
 855
Holloway, E. S., 76
Holme, Constance, 765
Holmes, Dr. Christian R., 368
HOLMES COUNTY DISTRICT
 PUBLIC LIBRARY, 452
HOLMES COUNTY REGIONAL
 PLANNING COMMISSION,
 454
HOLY CROSS CHURCH (DAYTON),
 686
HOLY FAMILY CHURCH
 (DAYTON), 687
HOLY NAME CHURCH (DAYTON),
 688
HOLY TRINITY CHURCH
 (DAYTON), 689
Holzworth, Walter, 106
Home Avenue Brethren Church
 (Dayton), 684
Homeopathic Free Dispensary,
 364
HOOVER COMPANY, 839

Hoover, Herbert, 927
HOPE LUTHERAN CHURCH
(DAYTON), 690
HOPE UNITED METHODIST
CHURCH (CLEVELAND),
169
Horstmann, John F.I., 128
Horton, Walter M., 522
Hosford, Francis J., 522
HOSPITAL ASSOCIATION OF
GREATER CLEVELAND, 170
Hospitals, 98, 170, 202, 252,
364, 368, 471, 494, 507, 592,
620, 660, 700, 711, 735, 829,
859
Hotel Morcher, 938
Howard, John G., 330
Howe, John Ruskin, 330
Henry Hubach Brewery, 938
Hubbard, see Trumbull County
HUBBARD PUBLIC LIBRARY,
902
Hubbell, Charles Edward, 769
Hudson, see Summit County
HUDSON LIBRARY AND HIS-
TORICAL SOCIETY, 854
Hull, Clark, 855
Hunt, Minnie, 83
Hunter, Louise, 36
HUNTINGTON NATIONAL
BANK (COLUMBUS), 304
Hurley, Edward Timothy, 364
Huston and Meach Transit
Company, 494
HUTTON MEMORIAL PUBLIC
LIBRARY (BARNESVILLE), 27

IMMACULATE CONCEPTION
CHURCH: DAYTON, 691;
RAVENNA, 770
IMMANUEL UNITED METHODIST
CHURCH (LOGAN), 450
IMPERIAL GLASS CORPORATION,
31
Improved Order of Red Men
(Toronto), 461
Independence, see Cuyahoga
County

INDEPENDENCE PRESBYTER-
IAN CHURCH, 171
INDUSTRIAL INFORMATION
INSTITUTE (YOUNGSTOWN),
596
INSTITUTE FOR GOVERN-
MENTAL RESEARCH
(CINCINNATI), 402
INSTITUTE FOR METROPOLI-
TAN STUDIES (CINCINNATI),
403
International Council of Psychol-
ogists, 855
INTERNATIONAL INSTITUTE
(AKRON), 881
INTERNATIONAL MOLDERS
AND ALLIED WORKERS
UNION (CINCINNATI), 404
International Molders and Allied
Workers Union, Local 4, 364
International Society for Clinical
and Experimental Hypnosis,
855
INTERNATIONAL UNION OF
OPERATORS, 882
Inter-University Council for
School Psychology, 855
Ironton, see Lawrence County
IRONTON TRIBUNE, 492
ITALIAN AMERICAN CITIZENS
CLUB (AKRON), 883
ITALIAN CENTER (AKRON),
884

JAYCEES: AKRON, 885;
ELYRIA, 534
J. & F. Schroth Packing
Company, 367
Jackson, Andrew, 369
Jackson, Anne, 368
Jackson, Dr. Curtis, 101
Jackson, Isaac H., 364
James, John Hough, 35, 60,
367
Jefferson, see Ashtabula County
JEFFREY GALION AMERICA'S
CORPORATION, 305
The Jeffery Pickle and Kraut
Company, 938

LOGAN COUNTY DISTRICT
LIBRARY, 514
LOGAN-HOCKING COUNTY
DISTRICT LIBRARY, 448
LOGAN MONUMENT COMPANY,
451
Logan, William Harris, 220
London, see Madison County
LONDON PUBLIC LIBRARY, 585
Lone Rock Mining Company, 98
Long, Alexander, 364
Longworth, Nicholas, 364
Lorain, see Lorain County
LORAIN COUNTY HISTORICAL
SOCIETY, 520
LORAIN COUNTY PUBLIC
LIBRARY, 521
Lorberg, H. A., 803
LOWER MIAMI CHURCH OF THE
BRETHREN (DAYTON), 695
Lowry, Robert, 765
LUCAS COUNTY STATE BANK,
560
Lund, Franz E., 469
LUTHERAN CHURCH OF OUR
SAVIOR (DAYTON), 696
LUTHERAN COMMUNITY
SERVICES (SPRINGFIELD), 64
LUTHERAN SOCIAL SERVICE
(DAYTON), 697
Lyford, George Henry Anderson,
364
Lytle, Robert Todd, 364
Lytle, William, 364
Lytle, William Haynes, 364

MacDonald House, 202
McArthur, see Vinton County
McArthur Civic Club, 924
McArthur Hook and Ladder
Company, 924
McBride, James, 364
McBurney, John, 927
McConnelsville, see Morgan
County
McCord, J. R., 938
McCullough, James C., 522

McDonald, Dr. Gerald Doan, 74
McGuffey, William Holmes, 35
McIlvaine, Charles P., 469
JOHN MCINTIRE PUBLIC
LIBRARY (ZANESVILLE), 737
McIntyre, O. D., 347
MCKINLEY MEMORIAL LIBRARY
(CANTON), 903
McKinley National Memorial
Association, 825
McMyler Interstate Company, 98

Machan, Helen W., 765
MACK MEMORIAL CHURCH OF
THE BRETHREN (DAYTON),
698
Mackaman, Frederick, 855
Maclean, Catherine M., 63
MADISON COUNTY HISTORICAL
SOCIETY, 586
MADISON COUNTY HOSPITAL,
592
Magruder, James L., 56
MAHONING VALLEY ASSOCIA-
TION OF CHURCHES, 603
MAHONING VALLEY HISTOR-
ICAL SOCIETY, 597
Maley, George W., 220
MALLET CREEK GRANGE NO.
1453 (MEDINA), 640
MALONE COLLEGE LIBRARY,
822
Manchester, see Adams County
Mangles, James Henry, 22
Mansfield, see Richland County
MANSFIELD ART GUILD, 788
MANSFIELD NEWS JOURNAL,
791
MANSFIELD PUBLIC LIBRARY,
779, 789
Maple Heights, see Cuyahoga
County
Maple Knoll Hospital and Home
(Glendale), 364
Marietta, see Washington County
MARIETTA COLLEGE LIBRARY,
927

MIAMI UNIVERSITY LIBRARY, 35
MIAMI VALLEY HOSPITAL
(DAYTON), 700
Mickey, M. Portia, 522
MID-OHIO REGIONAL PLANNING
COMMISSION (COLUMBUS), 309
Middleport, see Meigs County
Middletown, see Butler County
MIDDLETOWN AREA SAFETY
COUNCIL, 46
MIDDLETOWN CIVIC ASSOCIA-
TION, INC., 47
MIDDLETOWN PUBLIC LIBRARY,
36
Midwestern Psychological Associa-
tion, 855
MILES AVENUE CHURCH OF
CHRIST (CLEVELAND), 179
MILES PARK PRESBYTERIAN
CHURCH (CLEVELAND), 180
MILES PARK UNITED METHOD-
IST CHURCH (CLEVELAND), 181
Miller, Dayton C., 100, 127
Millersburg, see Holmes County
Millis, John S., 127
Ministerial Association of Green-
ville, 209
MISSION OF THE SACRED
HEARTS CENTER (SHELBY), 790
Monnette, Helen, 822
MONROE COUNTY DISTRICT
LIBRARY, 650
Monroe, James, 522
Monson, Sir Edmund John, 22
Monteith, Rev. John, 520
MONTGOMERY COUNTY HISTOR-
ICAL SOCIETY, 653
MONTGOMERY-GREENE
TUBERCULOSIS ASSOCIATION,
701
MONTGOMERY SOCIETY FOR
CRIPPLED CHILDREN AND
ADULTS, 702
Montpelier, see Williams County
MOOSE LODGE NO. 428
(KENTON), 436
MORGAN COUNTY AGRICUL-
TURAL SOCIETY, 733

Morgan, J. B. F., 750
Morgan, John, 522
Morgenstern, Adolph Friedrich,
364
Moritz, Alan R., 202
MORLEY PUBLIC LIBRARY
(PAINESVILLE), 479
MORROW COUNTY HISTOR-
ICAL SOCIETY, 734
MORROW COUNTY HOSPITAL,
735
Morrow, Jeremiah, 925
Morrow, Josiah, 364
Morse, J. M., 586
Morse, Richard, 105
Moseley, Edwin Lincoln, 942
Moser, Capt. Lew, 494
Mosher, Charles A., 765
MOTHERS' CIRCLE (WASHING-
TON COURT HOUSE), 262
Mound Builders Country Club,
494
Mount Gilead, see Morrow
County
Mount Pleasant, see Jefferson
County
Mount Pleasant College, 268
Mount Pleasant Free Produce
Company, 460
MOUNT PLEASANT HISTOR-
ICAL SOCIETY, 460
Mount Pleasant-Martinsville
Bank, 460
MOUNT ST. MARY'S SEMINARY
OF THE WEST LIBRARY, 411
MOUNT UNION COLLEGE
ARCHIVES, 842
Mount Vernon, see Knox County
MOUNT VERNON AREA
DEVELOPMENT, 472
MOUNT VERNON NAZARENE
COLLEGE, 473
The Mount Victory Bank, 938
MOUNT ZION CONGREGA-
TIONAL CHURCH AND SO-
CIETY (CLEVELAND), 182
MULLINS MANUFACTURING
CORPORATION, 92

Northern Ohio Traction and Light
Company, 98
NORTHWEST OHIO-GREAT LAKES
RESEARCH CENTER, 938
NORTHWEST OHIO RESTAURANT
ASSOCIATION, 563
Norwalk, see Huron County
NORWALK PUBLIC LIBRARY, 456
Norwood, see Hamilton County
Null family, 347
Nu Pi Kappa Literary Society, 469
Nye family, 928

Oakley, Annie, 208
Ober, Denis Carl, 855
Oberlin, see Lorain County
OBERLIN COLLEGE ARCHIVES,
536
OBERLIN COLLEGE LIBRARY,
522
O'Connor brothers, 597
Odenbach, Frederick, 174
Oen, Henry, 24, 233
OHIO AGRICULTURAL EXPERI-
MENT STATION, 933
OHIO APPLE INSTITUTE, 914
OHIO ASSOCIATION OF NURSES,
413
OHIO BAKERS ASSOCIATION, 312
OHIO BANKERS ASSOCIATION, 313
OHIO BAPTIST CONVENTION, 508
OHIO CAVALRY BUFFS ASSOCI-
ATION (LEETONIA), 93
Ohio College Association, 268
Ohio Company of Associates, 927
OHIO FUNERAL DIRECTORS
ASSOCIATION, 315
OHIO HISTORICAL SOCIETY, 267
OHIO HOSPITAL ASSOCIATION,
316
OHIO JERSEY BREEDERS
ASSOCIATION, 623
OHIO JEWISH CHRONICLE, 317
OHIO JUNIOR CHAMBER OF
COMMERCE STATE OFFICE, 624
OHIO MANUFACTURERS' ASSOCI-
ATION, 318

Ohio-Miami Medical College,
368
OHIO MUNICIPAL LEAGUE,
319
THE OHIO NATIONAL BANK
(COLUMBUS), 320
OHIO NURSES ASSOCIATION,
704
OHIO PSYCHIATRIC ASSOCI-
ATION, 321
OHIO SAVINGS AND LOAN
LEAGUE, 322
OHIO STATE AUTOMOBILE
ASSOCIATION, 323
OHIO STATE UNIVERSITY
ARCHIVES, 325
OHIO STATE UNIVERSITY,
NEWARK CAMPUS, 509
OHIO SYNOD-LUTHERAN
CHURCH IN AMERICA, 326
OHIO THOROUGHBRED
BREEDERS AND OWNERS,
414
OHIO UNIVERSITY ARCHIVES,
23
OHIO UNIVERSITY LIBRARY,
22
OHIO VALLEY CARPENTERS'
DISTRICT COUNCIL, 415
OHIO VETERINARY MEDICINE
ASSOCIATION, 327
Ohio Volunteer Infantry, First
Regiment, 647
OHIO WELFARE CONFERENCE,
328
OHIO WESLEYAN UNIVERSITY
ARCHIVES, 229
OHIO WESLEYAN UNIVERSITY
LIBRARY, 221
OHIO WEST AREA UNITED
METHODIST CHURCH
(COLUMBUS), 329
Ohlman, Rev. Ralph, 654
The Oil Well Salvage Company,
938
OLD STONE HOUSE (LISBON),
81

OLD STONE UNITED METH-
ODIST CHURCH (AMHERST), 537
Olla Podrida Club (Urbana), 56
Olmstead Falls, see Cuyahoga
County
OLMSTEAD FALLS BRANCH,
CUYAHOGA COUNTY PUBLIC
LIBRARY, 106
OPPORTUNITY CENTER
(FREMONT), 801
Osborne, Byron L., 822
Ottawa, see Putnam County
OTTERBEIN COLLEGE
ARCHIVES, 330
OTTERBEIN COLLEGE LIBRARY,
268
OUR LADY OF MERCY CHURCH
(DAYTON), 705
OUR LADY OF THE ROSARY
CHURCH (DAYTON), 706
OWENS/CORNING FIBERGLASS,
564
Oxford, see Butler County
Ozias family, 772

Pacific Fire Engine and Hose
Company, 7
Packard, Harriet, 765
Paine, Edward, 478
Paine family, 477
Painesville, see Lake County
PAINESVILLE TELEGRAPH, 488
Palm Brothers Decalcomania
Company, 364
Pangle family, 917
Parent Teachers Association
(Chardon), 353
PARK SYNAGOGUE (CLEVELAND
HEIGHTS), 185
Parma, see Cuyahoga County
Parma Heights, see Cuyahoga
County
PARMA REGIONAL BRANCH,
CUYAHOGA COUNTY PUBLIC
LIBRARY, 106
Parmadale, 106
Parrott, Edwin, 220

Patten, Everett F., 855
Patterson, Thomas P., 356
Paulding, see Paulding County
Payne, Daniel Alexander, 357
Pearne, Denny, 105
Peck family, 734
Peebles, see Adams County
PEEBLES MONUMENT
COMPANY, 5
Pendleton, Austin, 765
Penfield family, 520
PENN-OHIO JUNIOR COLLEGE,
604
Pennsylvania Medical College,
368
Pennsylvania and Ohio Canal,
597
People's Church of Cincinnati,
364
Perkins Realty Company, 905
Perreault, John, 765
Perrin, William, 62
Perrysburg, see Wood County
Perrysburg, Findlay, and Kenton
Turnpike Road Company, 938
Peters, William E., 22
Phair, John J., 368
Phillips House Hotel, 938
PHILLIPUS EVANGELICAL
AND REFORMED CHURCH
(CINCINNATI), 416
Philomathesian Literary Society,
469
Piatt, John, 367
PICKAWAY COUNTY COMMUNI-
TY ACTION ORGANIZATION,
757
PICKAWAY COUNTY DISTRICT
PUBLIC LIBRARY, 750
PICKAWAY COUNTY HISTOR-
ICAL SOCIETY, 751
PIKE COUNTY FREE PUBLIC
LIBRARY, 762
PILGRIM BAPTIST CHURCH
(CLEVELAND), 186
Pioneer Associations: Cincin-
nati, 364; Darke County, 208;
Union County, 917

Piqua, see Miami County
Pitcairn, Joseph, 364
Pitman, Benn and Agnes, 364
PLAIN DEALER LIBRARY
(CLEVELAND), 187
PLANNED PARENTHOOD OF
LICKING COUNTY, 510
Plum Creek Church, 820
Pogue Department Store, 368
POLICE ATHLETIC LEAGUE
(CLEVELAND), 188
Pomerene, Atlee, 765
Pond, Chauncey N., 522
POOR PEOPLE'S OFFICE
(AKRON), 886
Port Clinton, see Ottawa County
Port Clinton Canning Company,
938
PORT OF TOLEDO, 565
PORTAGE COUNTY HISTOR-
ICAL SOCIETY, 766
PORTER PUBLIC LIBRARY
(WESTLAKE), 189
Portsmouth, see Scioto County
Portsmouth and Newark Railroad,
494
PORTSMOUTH PUBLIC LIBRARY,
803
Portsmouth Sand and Gravel Co., 22
PREBLE COUNTY DISTRICT
LIBRARY, 772
Preble, Pribble, Prible family, 772
Press, John, 368
Price, T. D., family, 501
Prince, Grace, 63
Prince, William, 364
Prior, Matthew, 35
THE PROCTER AND GAMBLE
COMPANY, 417
Professional organizations, 40,
44, 66, 141, 151, 184, 209, 251,
268, 271, 287, 288, 293, 310,
312, 313, 315, 316, 318, 321,
324, 327, 364, 368, 370, 375,
385, 390, 413, 414, 472, 544,
546, 562, 570, 595, 623, 659,
669, 673, 680, 704, 808, 827,

830, 840, 841, 855, 867, 869,
873, 927, 941
Progress-Research Club of
Chardon, 353
Prospect, see Marion County
PUBLIC LIBRARY OF CINCIN-
NATI AND HAMILTON COUNTY,
367
PUBLIC LIBRARY OF YOUNGS-
TOWN AND MAHONING COUNTY,
598
Puckett, Newbell Niles, 105
Pulte Medical College, 364
PUTNAM COUNTY DISTRICT
LIBRARY, 777
Putnam Female Seminary, 737
Putnam Presbyterian Church, 737
Putnam, Rufus, 927
Putnam Seminary for Girls, 737

Quaker Societies, 74
Queensgate II Development Pro-
gram, 368
Quinn, James Alfred, 368

RAILWAY CLERKS BUILDING
(CINCINNATI), 418
Rainbow Hospital (Cleveland),
202
Rances, Manuel, 22
Rankin, John Thomas, 32
Ranne, Joseph, 855
Ransohoff, Martha, 368
Ransom, Reverdy Cassius, 357
Rappe, Louis A., 128
Ravenna, see Portage County
Ravenna Temperance Society,
767
Rayen, William, 597
Reardon, Leslie J., 127
REED MEMORIAL LIBRARY
(RAVENNA), 767
Reemelin, Charles Gustav, 364
Rehfuss, Louis, 364
Reichart, Roland, 106
Religion:
Baptist, 98, 129, 142, 186,

Skinner family, 477
Sloane Hotel Company, 938
SMALL BUSINESS ASSOCIATION
(TOLEDO), 569
Smelser family, 772
Smith and Barlett Sash and Blind
Company, 938
Smith, Caleb Blood, James, and
John, 364
Smith, George, 105
Smith, Logan P., 765
Smuckers, Isaac, 493
Snyder, Gary, 765
SOCIETY FOR COOPERATIVE
IMPROVEMENT OF AFRO-
AMERICANS (SCIA), CANTON,
843
Soldiers Aid Society (Chagrin
Falls), 101
Soldiers and Sailors Monument,
494
Somerset, see Perry County
SOMERSET BRANCH, PERRY
COUNTY DISTRICT LIBRARY,
747
Sons of Temperance: Gallia County,
347; Portsmouth, 803
THE SORG PAPER COMPANY, 49
Sorgel, Dorn and Raibel Company,
938
Sorgen, Edward, 432
SOUTH PARK UNITED METHODIST
CHURCH (DAYTON), 721
Sovereign Hotel, 173
Spalding, Henry S., 369
Sparger Brothers Company, 442
Speer, Albert, 22
Spencerville Star Woolen Manufac-
turing Company, 938
Spender, Stephen, 368
Spenzer, Dr. John G., 102
Springer, Gerald, 368
Springfield, see Clark County
SPRINGFIELD ART ASSOCIATION,
65
SPRINGFIELD BAR AND LAW
LIBRARY, 66

Squire, Andrew, 127
Squire, Frank A., 101
Stambaugh family, 597
STAN HYWET HALL FOUN-
DATION (AKRON), 892
Stanleybrass, Edwin, 220
THE STARK COUNTY FOUN-
DATION, 844
STARK COUNTY HISTORICAL
SOCIETY, 825
Steoves, Sam, 56
Stephens, James, 765
Stetson, Raymond H., 522
Steubenville, see Jefferson
County
Stevens, Capt. Albert W., 651
Stevenson, Thomas B., 364
Stewart, Potter, 368
Streator, George Jason, 765
Strobridge Lithographing
Company, 364
Strohm, Isaac, 364
Strongsville, see Cuyahoga
County
Sturges, G. B., 159
SUGARCREEK UNITED PRES-
BYTERIAN CHURCH (DAYTON),
722
SUGARDALE COMPANY, 845
SUMMIT CHRISTIAN CHURCH,
DISCIPLES OF CHRIST
(DAYTON), 723
Summit County Civil Defense
Council, 852
Summit Street United Brethren
Church (Dayton), 684
SUMNER HOME FOR THE AGED
(AKRON), 893
Swanson, Howard, 105
Swanton, see Fulton County
SWANTON PUBLIC LIBRARY,
344
Sweet Valley Products Company,
938
Sweet Valley Wine Company, 938
Sweetman, Michael, 751
SYLVESTER MEMORIAL WELLS-
TON PUBLIC LIBRARY, 459

UNITED WAY: LAKE COUNTY,
489; SCIOTO COUNTY, 809;
YOUNGSTOWN, 608
University Heights, see Cuyahoga
County
THE UNIVERSITY OF AKRON-
AMERICAN HISTORY RESEARCH
CENTER, 855
University of Cincinnati College of
Medicine, 368
UNIVERSITY OF CINCINNATI
LIBRARY, 368
UNIVERSITY HOSPITALS OF
CLEVELAND (LAKESIDE HOS-
PITAL), 202
THE UNIVERSITY OF TOLEDO
ARCHIVES, 581
Upper Sandusky, see Wyandot
County
URBAN LEAGUE: CANTON, 850;
CINCINNATI, 425; Dayton, 655;
MASSILLON, 851; Springfield,
655
Urbana, see Champaign County
Urbana Banking Company, 364
URBANA COLLEGE LIBRARY, 60
Urichsville, see Tuscarawas
County
URSULINE CONVENT, 818

Vail, Derrick Tilton, 368
Vallette, Henry, 364
Valley City, see Medina County
VALLEY LUTHERAN CHURCH
(CHAGRIN FALLS), 203
Van Buren, Martin, 369
Van Cleve, John, 652
Vance family, 772
Vandalia, see Montgomery County
Van Helmont, Francis Mercury,
100
van Itallie, Jean-Claude, 765
Van Sweringen, Mantis J. and Otis
P., 112
Van Vorhes, Nelson Holmes, 22
Vermillion, see Lorain County
Veterans of Foreign Wars Post
2832, Chagrin Falls, 101

VETERANS OF WORLD WAR I,
U.S.A., INC., 337
VICTORY UNITED METHODIST
CHURCH (DAYTON), 727
Vincent, Col. Jesse, 651
VINTON COUNTY HISTORICAL
SOCIETY, 924
Violett family, 917
VOLUNTEER SERVICES AND
INFORMATION BUREAU
(HAMILTON), 50

Wade, James, 17
Wadsworth, see Medina County
Wagner, Edward A., 368
The Wagner Lake Ice & Coal
Company, 938
Wagoner, David, 368
Waite, Dr. Frederick C., 102
Wakefield, E. B., 769
F. W. Wakefield Brass Company,
938
WAKR RADIO (AKRON), 898
Walker, James Patison, 366
Stuart Walker Company, 364
Walker, Timothy, 364
Walker, William C., 98
Wallace, E., 100
STUART E. WALLACE &
COMPANY, 197
Walsh, Myles, 368
Walters, Raymond, 368
Walters, Reuben R. and Dr.
R. W., 101
Walton Hills, see Cuyahoga
County
Wapakoneta, see Auglaize
County
W.A.R. records, 494
War Fund Committee, Port
Clinton, 938
Ward, James, 98
Warner and Swasey, 100
Warren, see Trumbull County
WARREN COUNTY HISTORICAL
SOCIETY, 925
Warren, James Garfield, 769
WARREN PUBLIC LIBRARY, 905